# ECDL Advanced

# Spreadsheets

**Frank Kirk**

Blackrock Education Centre
2003

© Blackrock Education Centre

ISBN 0-9540287-2-4

*Published by*
Blackrock Education Centre
Kill Avenue, Dún Laoghaire
Co. Dublin, Ireland.

Tel. (+353 1) 2 302 709   Fax. (+353 1) 2 365 044
E-mail. ecdlsales@blackrock-edu.ie   Web. www.ecdlmanual.org   *and*   www.blackrock-edu.ie

First published          2003

All rights reserved. No part of this publication may be reproduced, stored in a retrieval system or transmitted, in any form or by any means without the prior written permission of the publisher, nor be otherwise circulated in any form of binding or cover other than that in which it is published and without a similar condition being imposed on any subsequent purchaser or user.

"European Computer Driving Licence" and ECDL and Stars device are registered trade marks of The European Computer Driving Licence Foundation Limited in Ireland and other countries. Blackrock Education Centre is an independent entity from The European Computer Driving Licence Foundation Limited, and not affiliated with The European Computer Driving Licence Foundation Limited in any manner. ECDL Advanced Spreadsheets may be used in assisting students to prepare for the European Computer Driving Licence, Module AM4, Spreadsheets – Advanced Level examination. Neither The European Computer Driving Licence Foundation Limited nor Blackrock Education Centre warrants that the use of this ECDL Advanced Spreadsheets manual will ensure passing the European Computer Driving Licence, Module AM4, Spreadsheets – Advanced Level examination. Use of the ECDL-F Approved Courseware Logo on this product signifies that it has been independently reviewed and approved by ECDL-F as complying with the following standards:

Acceptable coverage of all courseware content related to the European Computer Driving Licence, Module AM4, Spreadsheets – Advanced Level syllabus.

This courseware material has not been reviewed for technical accuracy and does not guarantee that the end user will pass the European Computer Driving Licence, Module AM4, Spreadsheets – Advanced Level examination. Any and all assessment items and/or performance-based exercises contained in this ECDL Advanced Spreadsheets manual relate solely to this ECDL Advanced Spreadsheets manual and do not constitute or imply certification by The European Driving Licence Foundation in respect of any ECDL examination. For details on sitting ECDL examinations in your country please contact your country's National ECDL/ICDL designated Licensee or visit The European Computer Driving Licence Foundation Limited web site at http://www.ecdl.com.

Candidates using this courseware material should have a valid ECDL/ICDL Skills Card. Without such a Skills Card, no ECDL/ICDL examinations can be taken and no ECDL/ICDL certificate, nor any other form of recognition, can be given to the candidate.

ECDL/ICDL Skills Cards may be obtained from any Approved ECDL/ICDL Test Centre or from your country's National ECDL/ICDL designated Licensee.

References to the European Computer Driving Licence (ECDL) include the International Computer Driving Licence (ICDL). European Computer Driving Licence, Module AM4, Spreadsheets – Advanced Level syllabus is published as the official syllabus for use within the European Computer Driving Licence (ECDL) and International Computer Driving Licence (ICDL) certification programme."

Microsoft® Windows®, Microsoft® Office, Microsoft® Word®, Microsoft® Access®, Microsoft® Excel®, Microsoft® PowerPoint®, Microsoft® Internet Explorer® and Microsoft® Outlook® are either registered trademarks or trademarks of the Microsoft Corporation.

Other products mentioned in this manual may be registered trademarks or trademarks of their respective companies or corporations.

The companies, organisations, products, the related people, their positions, names, addresses and other details used for instructional purposes in this manual and its related support materials on the manual's support website **www.ecdlmanual.org** are fictitious. No association with any real company, organisations, products or people are intended nor should any be inferred.

# Blackrock Education Centre

**Director/Stiurthóir**: Séamus Cannon / Séamus Ó Canainn
Walter Cullinane (Chairperson), Deirdre Keyes (Vice Chairperson), Betty Behan, Valerie Burke, Mary Crosbie, Phil Caulfield, Dóirín Creamer, Patrick Fox, Kieran Griffin, Joseph Keane, Jean Hughes, James Malseed, Thérèse McPhillips, Matt Reville, Donal Ryan, Cora Uí Chuinn.

## Blackrock Learning

This manual is produced by the Blackrock Learning division of Blackrock Education Centre. Executive Director: Siobhán Cluskey. Project Manager for this production was John Brennan. Technical editing: Denise O' Connor.

## Credits

*Design and Layout*
Frank Kirk

*Cover Design*
Vermillion

## Acknowledgements

The assistance of the following staff members is also acknowledged:
Aileen Benson, Geraldine Byrne, Emer Bradley, Val Collins, Monica Dowdall, Mark Fennell, Adela Fernandez, Phil Halpin, Evelyn Logan, Lil Lynch, Jenny Masterson, Helen McGoey, Chris Murphy, Tomás Ó Briain, Róisín Phillips, Mary Sorohan, Heather Friel.

**Blackrock Education Centre is an accredited ECDL Test Centre**

## Important

No part of this publication may be photocopied or reproduced in any form without the prior written permission of the publisher, in accordance with copyright law.

# Contents

| | | |
|---|---|---|
| **About This Book** | | vi |
| **Foreword** | | vii |
| **ECDL** | | viii |
| **Chapter 1** | Editing | 1 |
| **Chapter 2** | Data Handling | 63 |
| **Chapter 3** | Functions | 123 |
| **Chapter 4** | Analysis | 189 |
| **Chapter 5** | Special Tools | 239 |
| | Solutions – Self Check Exercises | 267 |
| | Index | 275 |

# About This Book

## The Manual

'ECDL Advanced Spreadsheets' offers a practical, step-by-step guide for any person who wishes to increase their knowledge and competence in using Microsoft Excel. It has been designed as a study aid for the advanced spreadsheets module of the European Computer Driving Licence (the International Computer Driving Licence – ICDL – outside Europe). However, as is characteristic of Blackrock Education Centre training materials, the content of this manual offers far more by way of support information through explanations, demonstrations and practical exercises as well as a support website, **www.ecdlmanual.org**. Particular attention has been given to providing students with additional information on syllabus items to assist their understanding.

## Design

Every use has been made of the expertise we have gained from working closely with ECDL over the last several years. Additionally, the knowledge and skills of our substantial pool of trainers hugely influenced the content and layout of the material.

We use plain English, not computer jargon. We take you point by point through detailed explanations and action sequences. We pay particular attention to relating what you see on the pages of the manual to what you see on the computer screen.

You will also find that the A4 size of the manual, the side-by-side layout of graphics and text, and the spiral binding all combine to make it an ideal *desk-top-friendly* training manual.

## Exercises

At the end of each section, there are two kinds of exercises. There are self-check questions designed to jog your memory of important details. There are also practical exercises that have been designed to revise some of the more important skills associated with using Microsoft Excel.

In successfully completing a set of exercises, you can be confident of your progress in learning the skills associated with each section of the syllabus.

## Web Support

Support material is available on the Internet at **www.ecdlmanual.org** – a sister site of Blackrock Education Centre (**www.blackrock-edu.ie**). Should there be any minor amendments to the ECDL syllabus in the future, updates and/or additional material will be posted there.

*This manual was produced – text, design and layout – using only the Microsoft Office suite of programs. The screen shots were captured using a small utility program and most were inserted directly onto the page.*

# Foreword

Blackrock Education Centre provides support services to teachers and to partners in education under the auspices of the Department of Education and Science in Ireland. It is one of a network of thirty Centres dispersed throughout the country. For many years the Education Centre has provided training for teachers in the use of Information and Communications Technology. While introductory courses were always popular, we frequently experienced difficulties in progressing beyond the basics. There was a large gap between the introductory course and what was being offered at university, with little in between that was both comprehensive and practical. There was a need for a training programme that measured progressive development of competency across a range of skills.

The European Computer Driving Licence – ECDL (ICDL outside Europe) – provides a very good framework for such a training programme. Blackrock Education Centre put a programme in place on a pilot basis in 1997 and subsequently opened it up to larger numbers. The initial response was very encouraging and demand has grown dramatically over the years. More recently, a clear need emerged for advanced manuals which would expand and develop teacher knowledge in particular modules. This advanced manual is the first in what we hope will be a series.

The key attractions of ECDL/ICDL are the focus on practical competency and the flexible syllabus, independent of platform or software. These enabled us to tailor our training while maintaining standards that are recognised internationally. It is the experience of Blackrock Education Centre that completing the ECDL/ICDL programme gives the user confidence in using the computer, a significant level of practical skill and an excellent preparation for further study.

In the Information Age, all of us are required to engage in continuous lifelong learning. We have been aware that many of the schools we work with want to offer a programme to parents and to other members of the community. Increased access to learning opportunities, through libraries and other community institutions, is more and more the norm. Our training programme has encouraged this development and many schools have themselves become accredited ECDL/ICDL test centres offering local training. In addition, *Training for ECDL*, our first manual, has come to be used extensively in the commercial and corporate training sectors, both in Ireland and abroad.

We are pleased to note how many users of our training manuals comment on their continued usefulness as reference materials after they have completed their courses. We believe this reflects well on all who work on our development projects who deserve great credit in maintaining high standards. Particular thanks are due to Director Séamus Ó Canainn, to John Brennan, Project Manager, to Frank Kirk the author and to Siobhán Cluskey, the Executive Director of Blackrock Learning. These training materials are a testament to the thoroughness with which they have addressed the requirements of lifelong learning in the Information Age.

Walter Cullinane
*Chairperson*

Blackrock Education Centre
June 2003

# ECDL

## The European Computer Driving Licence
## (ICDL outside Europe)

The European Computer Driving Licence is a means of indicating that you have acquired the basic skills to use a computer in a wide variety of applications, just as your standard Driving Licence indicates that you have acquired the skills necessary to drive a car on public roads.

As with learning to drive a car, a variety of skills has to be learnt before the licence is issued. Also, it is important that these skills be acquired by actually using the computer: one does not expect to have a vehicle Driving Licence issued just by reading all about it and answering questions in a written examination.

The ECDL concept originated in Finland in 1988 and has spread all over Europe since then, with headquarters now established in Dublin. In each country, ECDL operates under the auspices of and in association with the national computer society. In Ireland, this is the Computer Society of Ireland.

The success of ECDL throughout Europe has been due to the well thought out and structured modular approach which allows training establishments to provide flexible training in basic computer skills with varying degrees of emphasis according to the candidates' needs, while at the same time maintaining uniformly high standards.

ECDL has now spread beyond European borders and attracted the attention of trainers and training establishments in many parts of the world. It is now known internationally as ICDL – the International Computer Driving Licence.

On enrolling for an Advanced ECDL/ICDL course, candidates are issued with an Automated Test Unit number (ATU) which is used to register their successful completion of the course examination. The test for Module AM4, Spreadsheets – Advanced Level, is of one hour's duration. It is a practical hands-on test at the computer. On successful completion of the test, the result is returned to the national ECDL/ICDL office which then issues the appropriate Advanced ECDL certificate.

The issue of the Advanced certificate is administered in Ireland by ECDL Ireland, which controls accreditation and provides tester training on a national level. It also monitors very closely the standards under which ECDL/ICDL training and testing are carried out at the hundreds of accredited training centres throughout the country.

Training and training materials for the ECDL/ICDL are the responsibility of the individual training establishment. Blackrock Education Centre has over twenty years' experience in Information Technology training and has been closely associated with ECDL Ireland from the beginning, organising and administering one of the first ECDL/ICDL pilot projects in this country.

# Chapter 1

## Editing

## Chapter One: AM 4.1 – Editing

### AM 4.1.1 Data

| | | Page |
|---|---|---|
| AM4.1.1.1 | Name cell range(s) in a worksheet | 5 |
| AM4.1.1.2 | Apply automatic formatting to a cell range | 12 |
| AM4.1.1.3 | Create custom number formats | 15 |
| AM4.1.1.4 | Use conditional formatting options | 18 |
| AM4.1.1.5 | Use paste special options | 22 |
| AM4.1.1.6 | Import a text file and delimit by comma, space or tab | 25 |

### AM 4.1.2 Display

| | | |
|---|---|---|
| AM4.1.2.1 | Freeze row and /or column titles | 31 |
| AM4.1.2.2 | Hide / unhide rows or columns | 36 |
| AM4.1.2.3 | Hide / unhide worksheets | 39 |
| AM4.1.2.4 | Use sub-totalling features | 41 |
| AM4.1.2.5 | Use one-input or two-input Data tables / What-if tables | 46, 49 |

### AM 4.1.3 Protection

| | | |
|---|---|---|
| AM4.1.3.1 | Protect / unprotect a worksheet with a password | 51 |
| AM4.1.3.2 | Protect / unprotect designated cells in a worksheet with a password | 53, 54 |

### AM 4.1.4 Security

| | | |
|---|---|---|
| AM4.1.4.1 | Add password protection to a spreadsheet | 56 |
| AM4.1.4.2 | Remove password protection from a spreadsheet | 58 |

# Section 1    Data

## 1.1  Cell ranges

Cells are located and referred to by their cell reference. The letter(s) indicate the column and the number(s), the row. E.g. **A25**. The cell is in the first column A, and the twenty-fifth row.

Single cells such as **A1** (first cell) or **IV65536** (last cell) in a spreadsheet.

A range of contiguous (adjacent or adjoining) cells such as **A1:A10, C5:D9, H12:M18, AA4:AD18**.
**A1:A65536** (or **A:A**) is the range of all cells in column A.
**A1:IV1** (or **1:1**) is the range of all cells in row 1.

Non-contiguous cells such as **A1, B6, C10** or **A2, C7:D10, E15**

It is useful to name cells and ranges as it makes an explanation of the spreadsheet much more meaningful. Spreadsheets tend to be more accurate when ranges are named.

E.g. Naming a range **Expenses** rather than **B12:B16** or naming a range **Profit** rather than **B18:B20**.

Or, **Total Profit = Number Produced*Profit per Unit**
As opposed to **C11=C8*C7**

What do you think is more meaningful?

## 1.2  Guidelines for naming cells and ranges

- The maximum size of the name is 255 characters.

- A range name must begin with a letter or an underscore character. E.g. Sales or _Sales.

- A blank space or hyphen is not permitted but an underscore can be used to separate characters. E.g. Total_Expenses or Salaries_2004.

- A period (full stop) can also be used to separate characters. E.g. VAT.QTR1

- No distinction is made between upper and lower case letters. However if you create a name called Revenue and later create the name REVENUE in the same worksheet, the second name will overwrite the first.

- Names cannot be cell references. E.g. A1, $C$5 and IV65536 are not acceptable.

   If you create an invalid name you will receive a warning. Follow the guidelines and you will never see this warning. If you do get a warning simply choose another name, according to the guidelines.

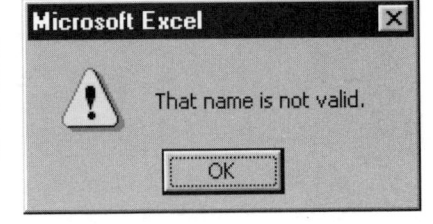

**NOTE**

If you want a practical example where naming ranges are particularly important see Scenarios and Scenario Summary Reports in Chapter 4, Section 2.

## 1.3 Naming Cells and Ranges (4.1.1.1)

- Open the file **Lighting Sales Qtr1**.

    The table shows the sales of five salespersons of Lighting Up Ireland, during the first quarter of 2003. We are going to name cells and ranges within the table.

- Highlight the range **B6:B10**. This range indicates the sales during the month of January.

|    | A | B | C | D |
|----|---|---|---|---|
| 1  | **Lighting Up Ireland** | | | |
| 2  | | | | |
| 3  | | **Sales 2003** | | |
| 4  | | | | |
| 5  | | January | February | March |
| 6  | James Reilly | 5680 | 5900 | 6300 |
| 7  | Ann O' Neill | 7800 | 8400 | 8100 |
| 8  | Darren Quinn | 7500 | 4800 | 5100 |
| 9  | Gina Macari | 6590 | 8900 | 5800 |
| 10 | Noel Higgins | 3400 | 2300 | 4100 |
| 11 | | | | |
| 12 | Total Sales | | | |

- Select **Insert** followed by **Name**. Choose **Define** from the sub-menu.

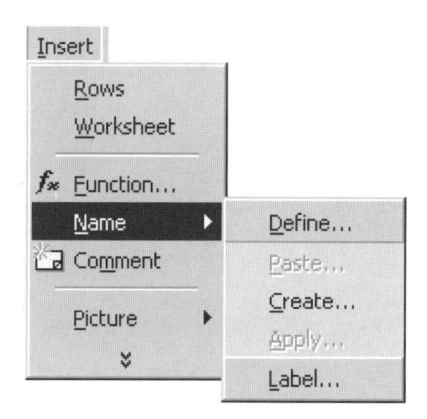

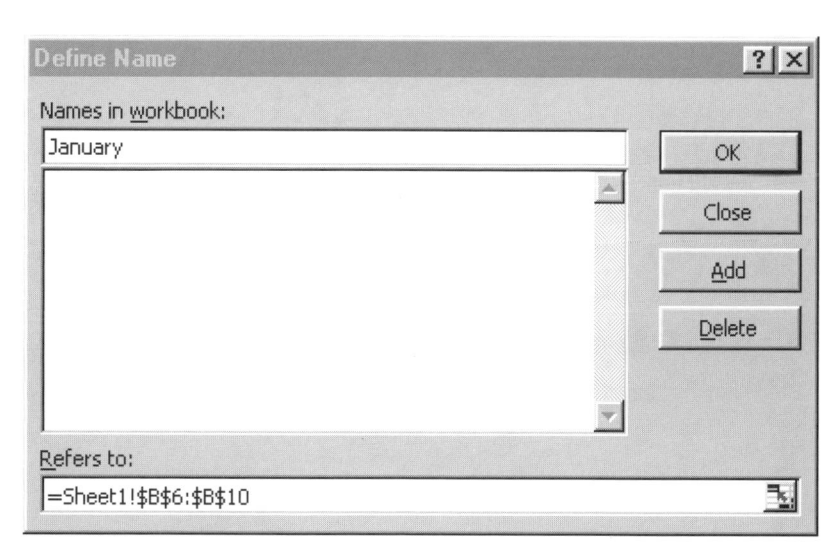

The **Define Name** dialog box opens with a suggested name for the range, January, and a precise reference for the range. **=Sheet1!$B$6:$B$10**. This name is acceptable.

- Click on **OK**.

We have successfully named one range. Let's check to make sure!

- Click on the **Name** box. The drop-down menu shows **January**.

- Click on **January** and the named range **B6:B10** is highlighted.

|   | B |
|---|---|
| 4 |   |
| 5 | January |
| 6 James Reilly | 5680 |
| 7 Ann O' Neill | 7800 |
| 8 Darren Quinn | 7500 |
| 9 Gina Macari | 6590 |
| 10 Noel Higgins | 3400 |

We will now create a **February** and a **March** range.

- Highlight the range **C6:C10**. This range indicates the sales during the month of February.

- Select **Insert** followed by **Name**. Choose **Define** from the sub-menu. The **Define Name** dialog box opens and suggests **February** as the name. This is what we want.

- Click **OK**.

- Repeat the procedure for the range **D6:D10** which should be named **March**.

- Click on the **Name box** to view all three named ranges.

- Save the file at this stage, but do not close.

## 1.4 Labels in formulas

If you require labels to be used in formulas then the **Accept labels in formulas** box must be ticked.

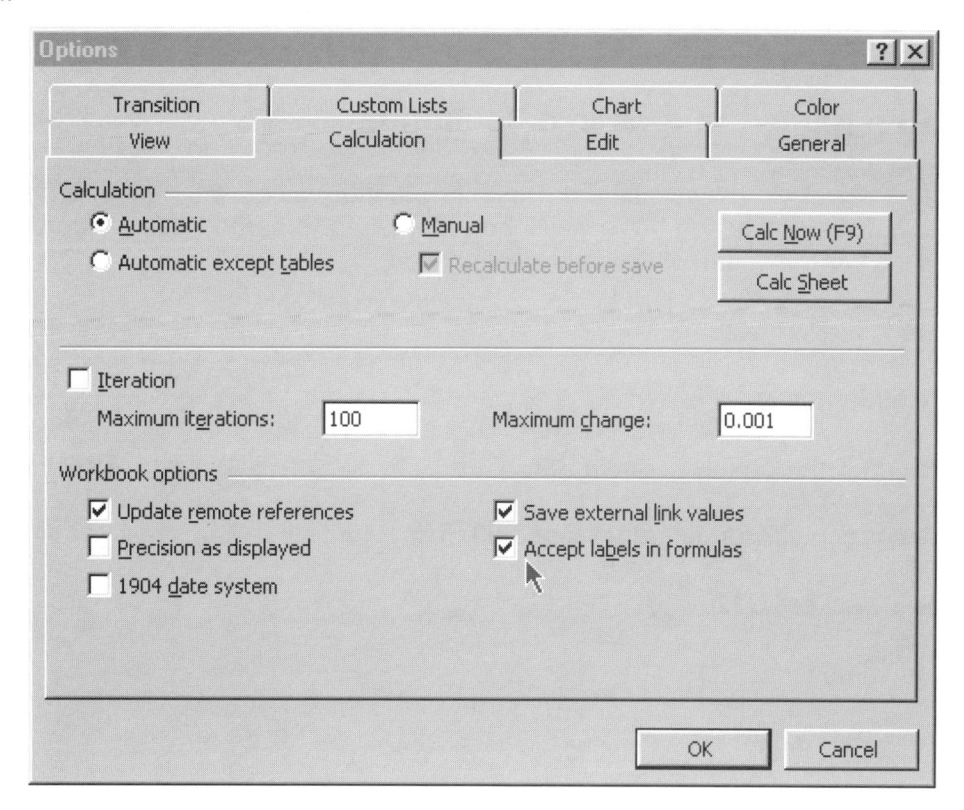

- Select **Tools**, **Options** and select the **Calculation** tab. Click on **Accept labels in formulas** if it is not already selected.

- Click **OK**.

---

The practice exercises contained in this section relate solely to this manual and do not constitute, or imply, certification by the European Driving Licence Foundation in respect of any ECDL examinations. For details on sitting ECDL examinations in your country please contact the local ECDL/ICDL licensee or visit the European Computer Driving Licence Foundation Ltd web site at http://www.ecdl.com

## Exercise 1A

1. Highlight the range **B7:D7**. Select **Insert** followed by **Name**. Choose **Define** and the **Define name** dialog box opens. The suggested name is **Ann_O_Neill**. Click **OK** to accept. (Notice that underscore _ is used in name).

2. Highlight the range **B9:D9**. Choose **Name** from the **Insert** menu. Choose **Define** and the **Define name** dialog box opens. The suggested name is **Gina_Macari**. Click **OK** to accept.

3. Select the single cell **C6**. Choose **Name** from the **Insert** menu. Choose **Define** and the **Define name** dialog box opens. No suggestion as to how the cell should be named is made. Name the cell **Feb_JR**. Click **OK** to accept.

4. Click on cell **C10**. Following the above method name this cell **Feb_NH**.

Click on the **Name** box and check all cells and ranges have been named correctly. You can now name cells and ranges.

5      Now save the file again but do not close.

## 1.5   Using named ranges in calculations

- Select cell **B12**. To calculate the total for January sales we would normally use the **AutoSum** function. We have however already named this range **January** and we will make use of this in our calculation.

- Type in the formula:

    **=SUM(January)**

- Click on **Enter** on the Formula Bar.

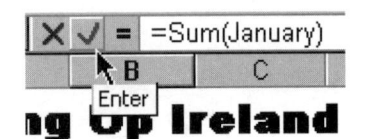

    The correct total for January sales, **30970**, is returned.

- Now select cell **C12**.

- Type in the formula:

    **=SUM(February)**

- Click on **Enter** on the Formula Bar.

    The correct total for February sales, **30300,** is returned.

- Select cell **D12** and repeat the procedure for **March**.

    The formula to use is **=SUM(March)** and **29400** the correct total for March sales is returned.

    We can use the formula to calculate the total quarterly sales.

- Select cell **D14**, and enter the following formula:

    **=SUM(January)+SUM(February)+SUM(March)**

    (Observe that **=** is used only at start of formula)

- Click on **Enter** in the Formula Bar. The total sales for the quarter, **90670** is given.

    Can you think of a faster way of calculating this figure? Of course you can.

- Highlight the range **B12:D12**. Name the range **Sales**. (You may be prompted to use **Total_Sales** as the name which is fine, but we suggest you just type in **Sales**).

- In cell **D16**, insert the formula:

=SUM(Sales)

The total returned is identical to that obtained in cell **D14**. (**90670**).

*The practice exercises contained in this section relate solely to this manual and do not constitute, or imply, certification by the European Driving Licence Foundation in respect of any ECDL examinations. For details on sitting ECDL examinations in your country please contact the local ECDL/ICDL licensee or visit the European Computer Driving Licence Foundation Ltd web site at http://www.ecdl.com*

## Exercise 1B

1. **Ann O' Neill** and **Gina Macari** work as a team. Using only named ranges we want to calculate their total sales in the first quarter of 2003. If their combined total sales are greater than **45000** they get a bonus.

2. Select cell **D18**. Insert the following.

    =SUM(Ann_O_Neill)+SUM(Gina_Macari)

    You may find it faster to drag across the ranges **B7:D7** and **B9:D9**. (Note you only use the **=** once at start of formula).

3. Click on **Enter** on the Formula Bar and the total returned is **45590**. They get the bonus!

## 1.6 Deleting named cells and ranges

- Select **Insert** followed by **Name**. Choose **Define** and the **Define name** dialog box opens.

- Select the name you wish to delete. In this case it is **Feb_JR**.

- Click on **Delete**.

    The name is deleted.

- Click on **OK** to close the **Define Name** dialog box.

- Save the file but do not close, as we will be using it in **Exercise 1C**.

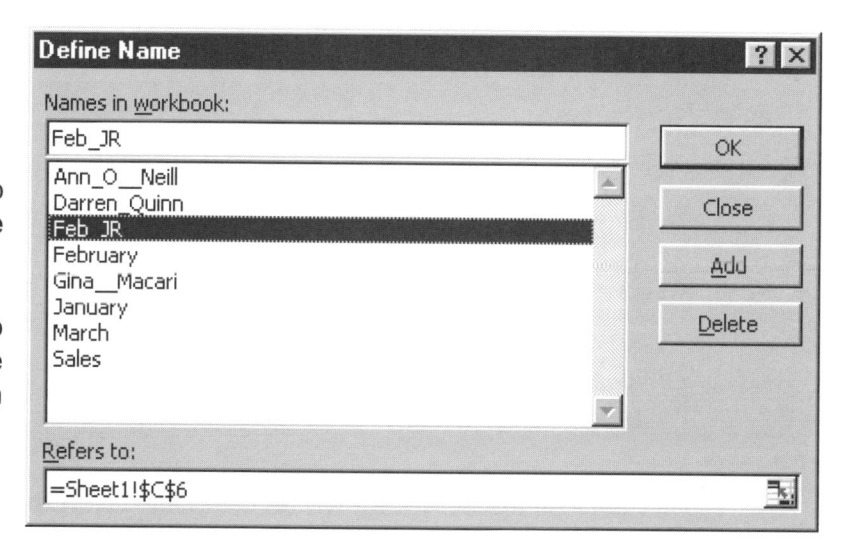

Chapter 1 - Editing

The practice exercises contained in this section relate solely to this manual and do not constitute, or imply, certification by the European Driving Licence Foundation in respect of any ECDL examinations. For details on sitting ECDL examinations in your country please contact the local ECDL/ICDL licensee or visit the European Computer Driving Licence Foundation Ltd web site at http://www.ecdl.com

## Exercise 1C

1  We are going to delete the following named ranges from the worksheet:

   **Ann_O_Neill** and **Gina_Macari.**

2  Choose **Name** from the **Insert** menu. Now select **Define** to open the **Define name** dialog box which will display the named ranges. Click on **Ann_O_Neill** and select the **Delete** button. The name is removed. Repeat for **Gina_Macari**.

   When you have completed these steps, the cell in which the formula appears shows an error reading. Ignore it.

3  **Save** file but do not close.


### 1.7 Naming a number of ranges simultaneously

- Highlight the range **A6:D10**.

- Select **Insert**, **Name** followed by **Create**.

  The **Create Names** option opens. Since our labels are in the left column, that is what we select.

- Click on **Left Column,** if it is not already selected. Now click on **OK**.

- Click on the **Name box**. All five names should be present.

  All the names are added together.

  ```
  Ann_O__Neill
  Darren_Quinn
  Gina__Macari
  James_Reilly
  Noel_Higgins
  ```

  This procedure can also be used for naming items related to **Top Row**, **Bottom Row** and **Right Column**.

  Do not close the file, as we will be using it in **Exercise 1D**.

The practice exercises contained in this section relate solely to this manual and do not constitute, or imply, certification by the European Driving Licence Foundation in respect of any ECDL examinations. For details on sitting ECDL examinations in your country please contact the local ECDL/ICDL licensee or visit the European Computer Driving Licence Foundation Ltd web site at http://www.ecdl.com

## Exercise 1D

Let's look at another example.

Is **Lighting Sales Qtr1** open? If not, open it now.

1   Highlight the range **B5:D10**.

2   Select **Insert**, **Name** followed by **Create**.

   The **Create name** option opens. The labels we want to use are in the top row.

3   Select **Top Row**. Now click on **OK**.

   Three ranges have been named: **January**, **February** and **March**.

4   Click on the **Define name** dialog box to check that the new ranges have been successfully added.

5   Save the file with changes as **Lighting Sales QTR1**.

## 1.8 Applying automatic formatting to a cell range (4.1.1.2)

- Open the file **Lighting Sales Qtr2**.

This is the second quarter sales for **Lighting Up Ireland**.
You will notice that all numbers have been formatted using Accounting Category from Format cells options. (Symbol € and 2 decimal places). You can check this by highlighting the range **B6:D12** and choosing **Format** followed by **Cells**, then **Number**.

- Highlight the range **A5:D12**.

- Select **AutoFormat…** from the **Format** menu.

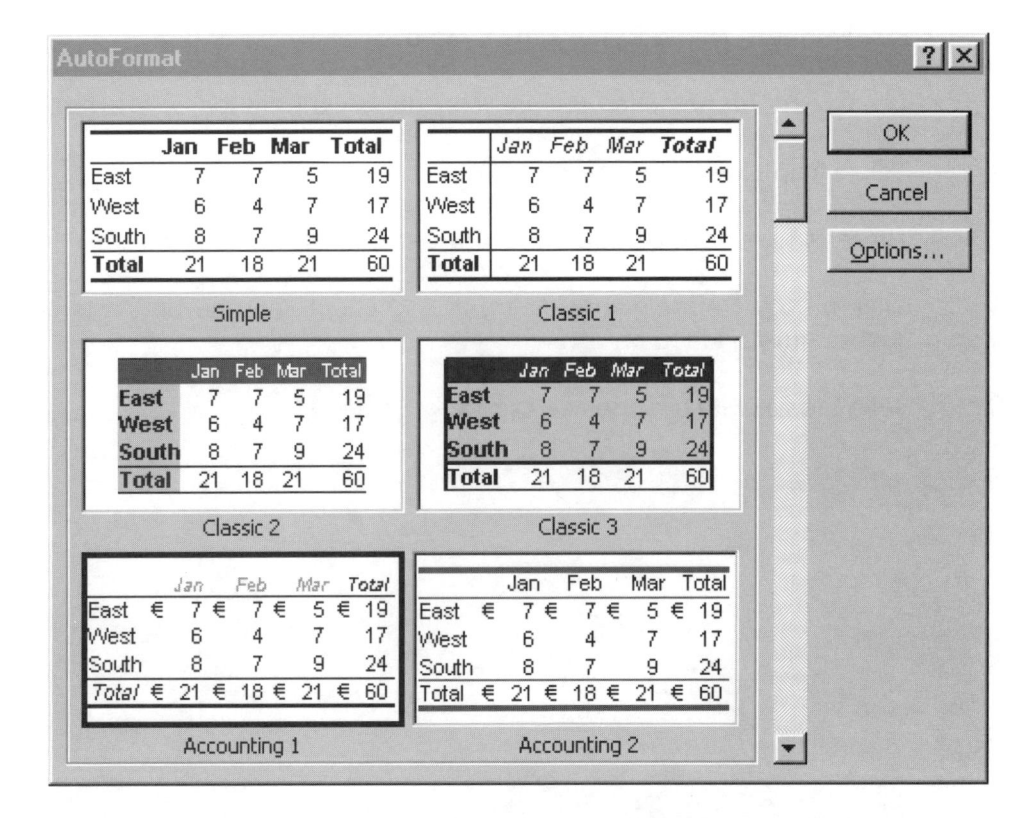

The **AutoFormat** dialog box opens offering a number of alternative formats.

- Select any one of the seventeen choices (except of course the last choice).

- Click **OK**.

In the above case **Classic 3** was applied.

## 1.8.1 Using Options in AutoFormat

- Highlight the range **A5:D12** again and select **Format** followed by **AutoFormat**. Choose the same AutoFormat again.

- Click on the **Options...** button.

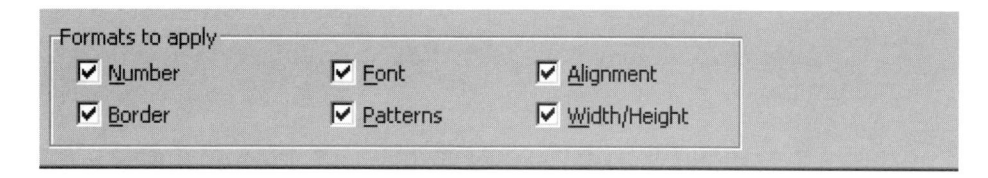

```
Formats to apply
  ☑ Number       ☑ Font        ☑ Alignment
  ☑ Border       ☑ Patterns    ☑ Width/Height
```

By default all six options are applied. If you wish to remove a format you must uncheck it here.

- **Uncheck** each of the six options in turn and note singular effects.

- Make no changes at this stage and leave the default selection of all six options ticked.

- Select **Cancel**.

## 1.8.2 Removing the effects of AutoFormat

If you want to remove the effects of **AutoFormat**:

- Highlight the formatted range **A5:D12**.

- Select **Format** followed by **AutoFormat**. When **AutoFormat** options opens, scroll down to the last option.

- Select last option **None** and click **OK**.

  The formatting is removed from the range. Note that the numbers are no longer prefixed by € and no longer show decimal places.

  To retain the original *number* format:

- Select **Edit** followed by **Undo**.

- Choose **Format** followed by **AutoFormat**.

- Choose **Options** and deselect **Number** on the **Formats to apply**.

- Scroll down and select the last option, **None.**

- Click **OK**.

  The numbers retain their original formatting. (Accounting, € symbol and 2 decimal places). Check this by highlighting the range **B6:D12** and choosing **Format** followed by **Cells**.

The practice exercises contained in this section relate solely to this manual and do not constitute, or imply, certification by the European Driving Licence Foundation in respect of any ECDL examinations. For details on sitting ECDL examinations in your country please contact the local ECDL/ICDL licensee or visit the European Computer Driving Licence Foundation Ltd web site at http://www.ecdl.com

## Exercise 1E

1      Open the file **Lighting Sales Qtr2**.

        The numbers have already been formatted in **Accounting**, two decimal places with € prefix.

2      Highlight the range **A5:D12**. Select **Format**, **AutoFormat** and choose option **Accounting 3**.

        You can click on **OK** here to produce an acceptable table. However you want to retain the original number format!

3      Choose **Options**.

4      Under **Formats to apply**, uncheck **Number**, to keep the original format.

5      Click **OK**.

        Although AutoFormat has successfully been applied, the original number formats have been retained.

**NOTE**

> You may wish to repeat the exercise but leave the Number option unchecked. The numbers will take up the default of Accounting 3. Only the first row of numbers and total Sales will have the prefix €. You may think that this is a neater presentation? Only you can decide that.
> Options are all about choice! Sadly you cannot define your own AutoFormats but there is enough scope within the choices offered to produce a large and attractive number of formats.

6      Save the file as **Lighting Sales Qtr2 Solution**.

## 1.9 Creating Custom Number Formats (4.1.1.3)

Excel offers a large number of formats for numbers, time, dates and text. You will be familiar with many of them. Suppose you wish to format a range of cells and none of those available is suitable. There is a solution. You create your own custom formats.

- Open the file **Custom Number Formats**.

- Click on any cell.

- Choose **Format** followed by **Cells** (or **Ctrl + 1**).

- Choose the **Number** tab and click on **Custom**. The **Type** section offers a number of options – somewhere in the region of sixty.

  We will devise a custom format for cells and ranges. Firstly, what are the main code areas?

- Click **Cancel**.

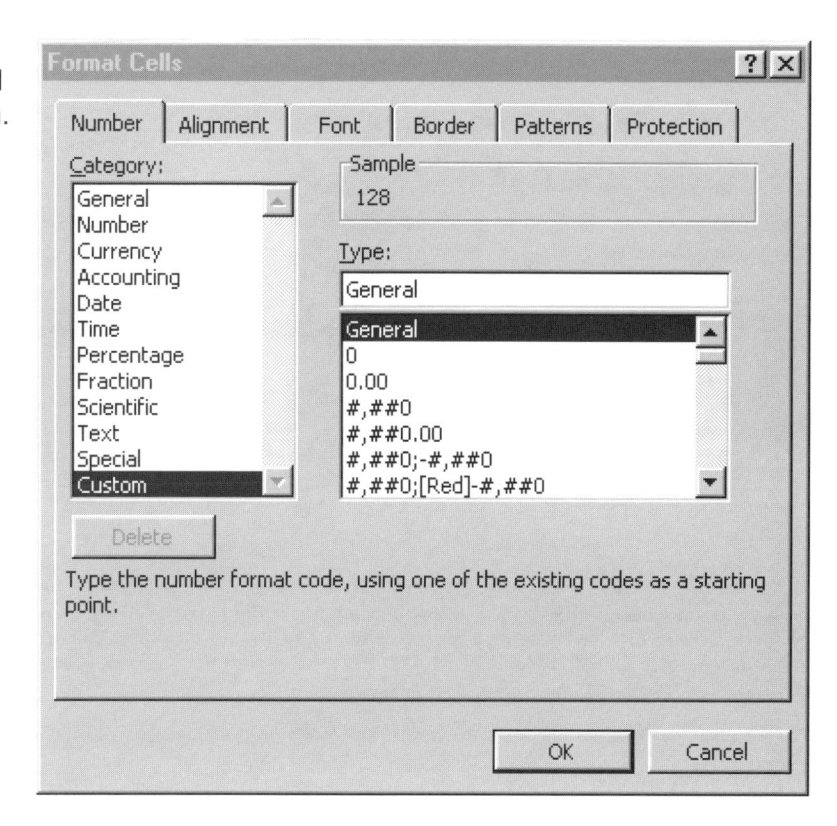

### 1.9.1 Examining the Main Code Sections

There are four main code sections. A semicolon separates one code section from another.

**#.###.00_); [Red] (#,###.00 ;0.00; "profit"@**

The table below shows what each code is responsible for.

| Section one | Section two | Section three | Section four |
|---|---|---|---|
| Format for **positive** numbers | Format for **negative** numbers | Format for **Zeros** | Format for **text** |
| #.###.00_); | [Red] (#,###.00 ; | 0.00; | "profit"@ |

The table below shows the function of the code formats, #, 0 and ?

| Code Format | Result |
|---|---|
| # | Displays only significant digits – insignificant zeros are not displayed |
| 0 | Displays insignificant zeros |
| ? | Spaces are added for insignificant zeros. Decimal points line up if using `Courier New`, a fixed-width (non-proportional font) |

- Select cell **E5**.

- Choose **Format** followed by **Cells**. (Or **Ctrl + 1**). The **Format Cells** dialog box opens.

- Choose the **Number** tab and click on **Custom**.

- In the **Type** box insert the following code:

    **#,###**

- Select **OK**.

- The cell content **42000** changes to **42,000**.

In the next exercise we will apply different format codes to a number and note the result.

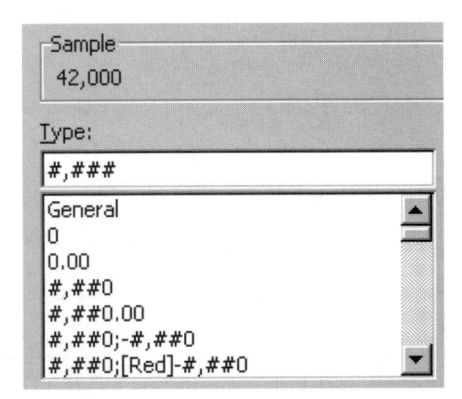

The practice exercises contained in this section relate solely to this manual and do not constitute, or imply, certification by the European Driving Licence Foundation in respect of any ECDL examinations. For details on sitting ECDL examinations in your country please contact the local ECDL/ICDL licensee or visit the European Computer Driving Licence Foundation Ltd web site at http://www.ecdl.com

## Exercise 1F

1   Examine the table which shows **Format Code** before the Format Code has been applied.

2   Select cell **C5** and choose **Format** followed by **Cells** then **Custom**. The Format Code is **General**. Click on **OK**. The number remains unchanged.

3   Select cell **C6**. Choose **Format** followed By **Cells** then **Custom** from the **Category** list. Insert the following code in the Type box.
    **####.#**

4   Click **OK**. This returns **1234.6**

|   | A | B | C |
|---|---|---|---|
| 1 | Custom Number Formats | | |
| 2 | | | |
| 3 | | | |
| 4 | | Format Code | Result |
| 5 | | General | 1234.56 |
| 6 | | ####.# | 1234.56 |
| 7 | | #.000 | 1234.56 |
| 8 | | #,### | 1234.56 |
| 9 | | #,#### | 1234.56 |
| 10 | | [Green]#,### | 1234.56 |
| 11 | | [Red]#,### | 1234.56 |
| 12 | | [Blue]#,### | 1234.56 |

**5** Add the format codes given to the remaining cells in the range **C7:C12**. The results are shown.

|   | A | B | C |
|---|---|---|---|
| 1 | Custom Number Formats | | |
| 2 | | | |
| 3 | | | |
| 4 | | Format Code | Result |
| 5 | | General | 1234.56 |
| 6 | | ####.# | 1234.6 |
| 7 | | #.000 | 1234.560 |
| 8 | | #,### | 1,235 |
| 9 | | #,#### | 1,235 |
| 10 | | [Green]#,### | 1,235 |
| 11 | | [Red]#,### | 1,235 |
| 12 | | [Blue]#,### | 1,235 |

The practice exercises contained in this section relate solely to this manual and do not constitute, or imply, certification by the European Driving Licence Foundation in respect of any ECDL examinations. For details on sitting ECDL examinations in your country please contact the local ECDL/ICDL licensee or visit the European Computer Driving Licence Foundation Ltd web site at http://www.ecdl.com

## Exercise 1G

Choose sheet tab **Exercise 1G**.

**1** We want to set up Employee Numbers to a specific format.
Click on cell **A5**. Select **Format** followed by **Cells**. Choose **Custom**. Insert the following code in the **Type** box.

**"EN" 00-00-000**

Employ the same **Format Code** for cells in range **B6:B8**.

**2** Now type the numbers **0**, **1**, **2** and **3** in cells **A5**, **A6**, **A7** and **A8** respectively. The Format Code will return employee numbers, as **EN00-00-000** to **EN00-00-003**

**3** Save the file as **Custom Number Formats Solution**.

## 1.10 Conditional Formatting (4.1.1.4)

Conditional Formatting is very useful for highlighting important values within a spreadsheet. For example you may want all sales greater than €50,000 to appear blue and emboldened and all sales less than €30,000 to appear red.

We are going to apply conditional formatting to the cell range **B6:D10** so that all sales greater than 6000 will appear in **Green** and **Bold** in our worksheet.

- Open the file **Lighting Sales Qtr3**.

  This is the third quarter sales for **Lighting Up Ireland**.

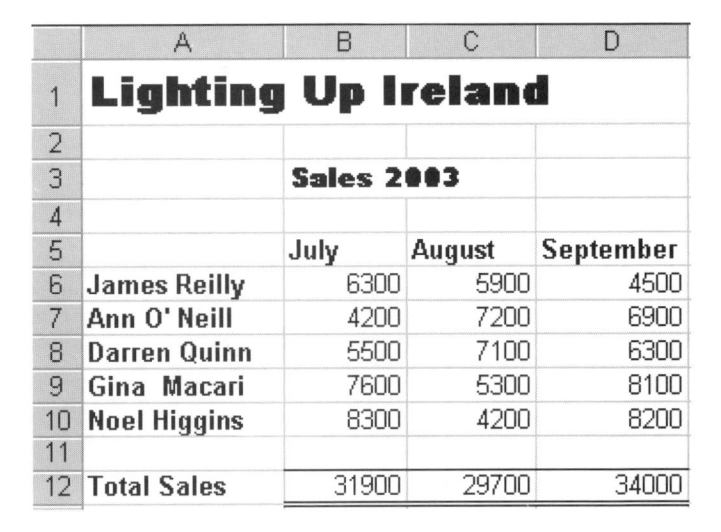

|   | A | B | C | D |
|---|---|---|---|---|
| 1 | **Lighting Up Ireland** | | | |
| 2 | | | | |
| 3 | | **Sales 2003** | | |
| 4 | | | | |
| 5 | | July | August | September |
| 6 | James Reilly | 6300 | 5900 | 4500 |
| 7 | Ann O' Neill | 4200 | 7200 | 6900 |
| 8 | Darren Quinn | 5500 | 7100 | 6300 |
| 9 | Gina Macari | 7600 | 5300 | 8100 |
| 10 | Noel Higgins | 8300 | 4200 | 8200 |
| 11 | | | | |
| 12 | Total Sales | 31900 | 29700 | 34000 |

- Highlight the range **B6:D10**.

- Select **Format** followed by **Conditional Formatting…** from the drop-down menu.

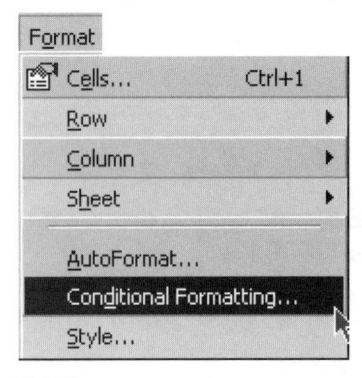

The **Conditional Formatting dialog** box opens.

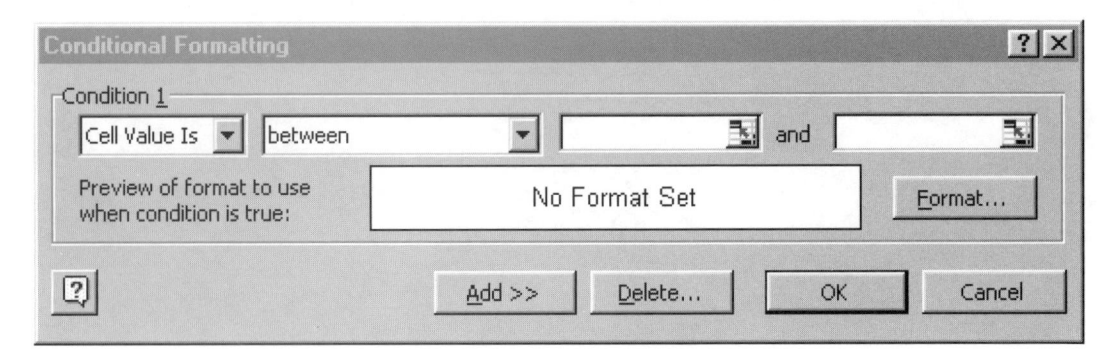

Chapter 1 - Editing

- Now, click on the second drop-down menu and choose **greater than**.

- Insert the value **6000**.

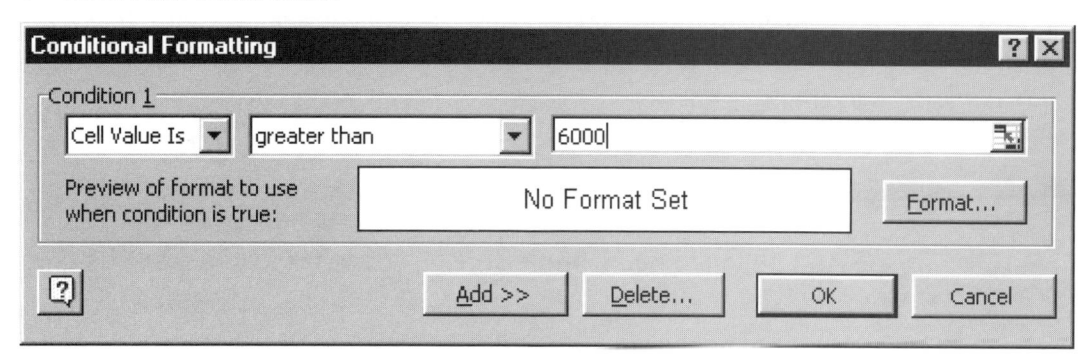

- Click on **Format**....

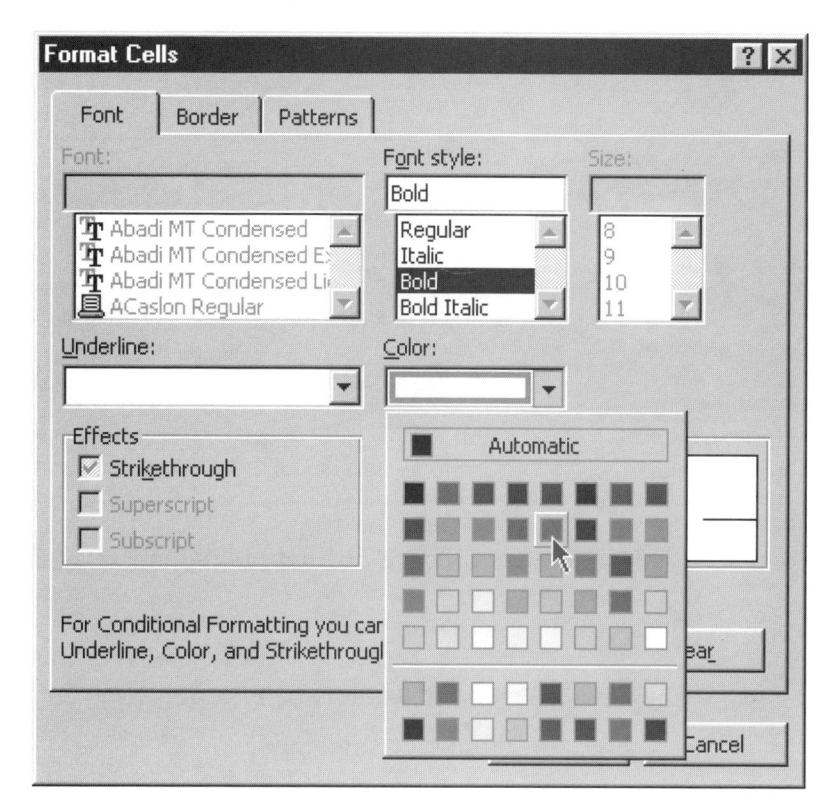

- Select **Bold**, and **Teal (Green)** from the colour option.

- Examine **Preview**, and then click on **OK**, followed by **OK** again to close the **Conditional Formatting dialog** box.

- Deselect the range.

  All sales greater than 6000 are displayed in green.

  | July | August | September |
  |------|--------|-----------|
  | 6300 | 5900   | 4500      |
  | 4200 | 7200   | 6900      |
  | 5500 | 7100   | 6300      |
  | 7600 | 5300   | 8100      |
  | 8300 | 4200   | 8200      |

  There are nine cells highlighted. Cells **B6**, **B9:B10**; **C7:C8**, and **D7:D10**.

You will have noticed that the **Format Cells** dialog box also offers **Border** and **Patterns** options that can be applied to the conditional formatting.

Suppose we still want sales greater than 6000 to be displayed in green but sales less than 5000 to be displayed in red? Well, we can add more than one condition.

- Highlight the range **B6:D10**.

- Choose **Format** followed by **Conditional Formatting…**

- Click on the **Add** button to add **Condition 2**. Choose **less than** from the drop-down menu and type in **5000**.

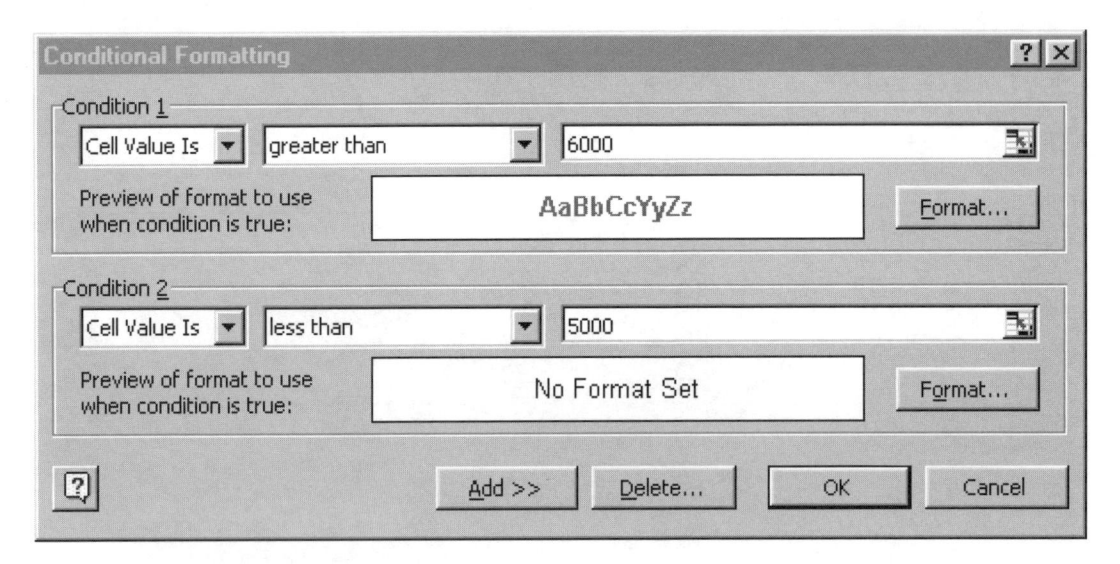

- Click on the **Condition 2 Format** button and select **Red**, **Bold Italics**.

- Click on **OK**, then **OK** again.

    The table is displayed with the conditional formatting applied.

    | July | August | September |
    |------|--------|-----------|
    | 6300 | 5900   | *4500*    |
    | *4200* | 7200 | 6900      |
    | 5500 | 7100   | 6300      |
    | 7600 | 5300   | 8100      |
    | 8300 | *4200* | 8200      |

    The contents of cells **B7**, **C10** and **D6** are **red** with **Bold** *italics*.

- Close the file but do not save changes.

Chapter 1 - Editing

*The practice exercises contained in this section relate solely to this manual and do not constitute, or imply, certification by the European Driving Licence Foundation in respect of any ECDL examinations. For details on sitting ECDL examinations in your country please contact the local ECDL/ICDL licensee or visit the European Computer Driving Licence Foundation Ltd web site at http://www.ecdl.com*

## Exercise 1H

1      Open the file **Lighting Sales Qtr3**.

You are going to apply conditional formatting to the range **B6:D10** so that all sales *greater than or equal to* 8300 are displayed in *blue* and all sales *less than or equal to* 4200 are displayed in *orange*.

2      Highlight the range **B6:D10**, and select **Format** followed by **Conditional Formatting....**

3      In **Condition 1**, choose **greater than or equal to** from the drop-down menu and type in **8300**. Select **Format** and choose the options **Bold** and **Blue**. Select **OK**.

4      Click on **Add** to select our second set of criteria for **Condition 2**. Choose **less than or equal to** from the drop-down menu and insert **4200**. Choose **Format** and select **Bold** and **Orange**. Click on **OK**, followed by **OK**.

       Conditional formatting has been applied to the range.
       To make changes to the conditional formatting simply highlight the range and choose **Format** followed by Conditional **Formatting**. Make the changes.

5      Save file as **Lighting Sales Qtr Solution**, but do not close.

*The practice exercises contained in this section relate solely to this manual and do not constitute, or imply, certification by the European Driving Licence Foundation in respect of any ECDL examinations. For details on sitting ECDL examinations in your country please contact the local ECDL/ICDL licensee or visit the European Computer Driving Licence Foundation Ltd web site at http://www.ecdl.com*

## Exercise 1I

In this exercise we will apply conditional formatting but also apply border and pattern options.

1      Highlight the range **B12:D12**. Choose **Format, Conditional Formatting....**

2      In **Condition 1**, choose **equal to** and insert **34000**. Select **Format** and choose **Violet**. Select the **Border** tab and select **Outline**. Select the **Patterns** tab and choose **Yellow**. (Yellow appears as Sample). Select **OK**, followed by **OK**.

       The cell **D12** is outlined, filled with yellow and the text is the colour violet.

3      Save the file as **Lighting Sales Qtr3 Solution**.

**NOTE**

When applying conditional formatting keep it as simple and clear as possible. Select colours that are clear on screen. If you use lighter colour options, the cell contents can be difficult to view.

## 1.11 Paste Special Options

The Paste Special Option allows you to select specific elements to paste from source to destination. You may wish to copy only number formats or comments from one cell to another.

- Open the file **Lighting Sales Qtr4**.

This is the fourth quarter sales for **Lighting Up Ireland**.

### 1.11.1 Applying paste special options (4.1.1.5)

The cells in the range **B6:D10** have been formatted **Dark Blue**, **Bold**, **Italics**, € Currency to **2** decimal places. Using the paste special option we can paste this format to other cells.

- Highlight the range **B6:B10**. Select **Edit** followed by **Copy** (or use **Ctrl + C**).

- Click on cell **G6**. Select **Edit** followed by **Paste Special**. The **Paste Special** dialog box opens.

There are eight **Paste options**, and five **Operation options**. There is also an option to **Skip blanks** or **Transpose**.

In our case we want to **Paste All**.

- Select **OK**.

- Deselect the range.

The range **B6:D6** is pasted into **G6:G10** with all formatting characteristics intact.

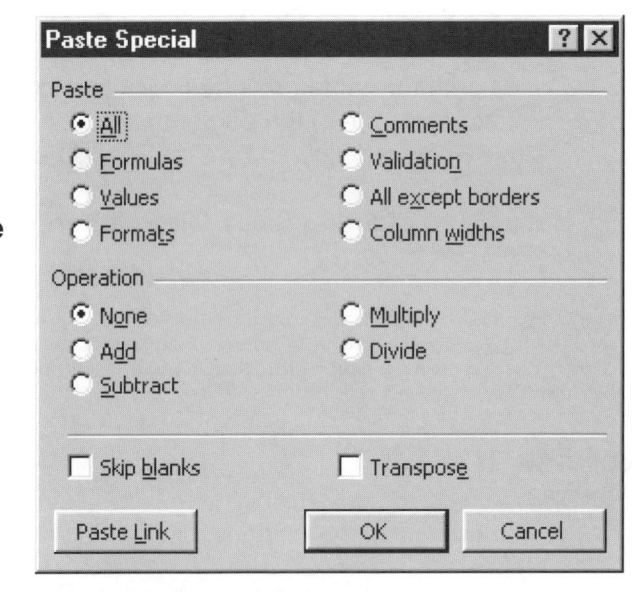

- Now highlight the range **C6:C10**. Select **Copy** from the **Edit** menu. Click on cell **H6** and choose **Paste Special** from the **Edit** menu. Make sure that the **Paste All** radio button is clicked. Click **OK** and the range is successfully pasted.

- Repeat the process for the range **D6:D10**, **A6:A12** and **B5:D5**, but deselect the range when each copy has been completed.

- Perform a **Paste Special** for range **B12:D12** but click on **All except borders** box.

You should have an identical copy of **Qtr4** apart from the absence of borders in **G12:I12**.

### 1.11.2 Transposing Data using Paste special.

The Transpose option is useful if you want to transpose columns to rows and rows to columns.

- Highlight range **A5:D12**. Select **Edit** followed by **Copy**.

- Choose tab **Orientation** and click on cell **A5**.

- Select **Paste Special** from the **Edit** menu.

    We do not want to include the borders.

- Select **All except borders** and **Transpose**.

- Click **OK**.

    The information appears with original rows and columns transposed. Let's make it more presentable.

- Widen columns widths where necessary.

- Delete any empty columns.

    The final result should look similar to that below.

|           | James Reilly | Ann O'Neill | Darren Quinn | Gina Macari | Noel Higgins | Total Sales |
|-----------|--------------|-------------|--------------|-------------|--------------|-------------|
| October   | €7,500.00    | €3,200.00   | €6,700.00    | €8,700.00   | €8,500.00    | €34,600.00  |
| November  | €9,100.00    | €8,500.00   | €6,900.00    | €5,500.00   | €4,300.00    | €34,300.00  |
| December  | €5,300.00    | €7,900.00   | €9,500.00    | €9,300.00   | €9,100.00    | €41,100.00  |

- Save the file as **Light Sales Qtr4 Solution** but do not close.

**Paste Special**

| Paste | What it does |
|-------|--------------|
| All | Copies content and format |
| Formulas | Only formulas are copied |
| Values | Results of formulas only copied |
| Formats | Only formatting copied |
| Comments | Only cell comments are copied |
| Validation | Copies validation criteria |
| All except Borders | All except cell borders copied |
| Column widths | Column width information copied |
| None | No operations carried out |
| Add | Adds pasted data |
| Subtract | Subtracts pasted data |
| Multiply | Multiplies pasted data |
| Divide | Divides pasted data |
| Skip Blanks | Prevents overwriting in paste area with blanks |
| Transpose | Changes orientation of copied rows or columns |

The practice exercises contained in this section relate solely to this manual and do not constitute, or imply, certification by the European Driving Licence Foundation in respect of any ECDL examinations. For details on sitting ECDL examinations in your country please contact the local ECDL/ICDL licensee or visit the European Computer Driving Licence Foundation Ltd web site at http://www.ecdl.com

## Exercise 1J

1. Ensure the file **Lighting Sales Qtr4 Solution** is open. Select tab **Exercise 1J.**

2. Highlight the range **A1:C8**. Select **Copy** from the **Edit** menu and select cell **A14**.

3. Select **Paste Special** from the **Edit** menu. Choose **Values** from the **Paste option** and select the **Transpose** option. Click **OK**.

4. Adjust column widths to view.

    Only the values are copied and not the formatting. The cells and rows are transposed. Delete any blank spaces that have been copied.

5. Save the file as **Lighting Sales Qtr4 Solution**.

## 1.12 Text Files

One advantage of Excel is that data created in different applications, can be imported into an Excel spreadsheet. These other applications include spreadsheets such as Lotus 1-2-3, database and accountancy packages.
If on opening a file, Excel recognises that it is not in standard format, then it will open a Wizard dialog box to assist in 'parsing' the file.

The file we are going to open is from a database. The information listed on the database is employee number, name and work location (either Paris, Hamburg or Dublin).

### 1.12.1 Importing a text file into a worksheet and delimiting by space, comma or tab (4.1.1.6)

- Open the file **Clients**. Since it is not an Excel file, in **Files of type**: select **Text Files**.

    **Text Import Wizard - Step 1 of 3** opens. Excel has deduced that the data is delimited, i.e. characters such as commas or tabs separate the fields. We will start to import at **row 1**. If there were any unnecessary header lines present then you might skip these and start import at e.g. row 4. The file origin is Windows (ANSI) but there is an option for Macintosh files and for MS-DOS (PC-8) files.

- Click on **Next**.

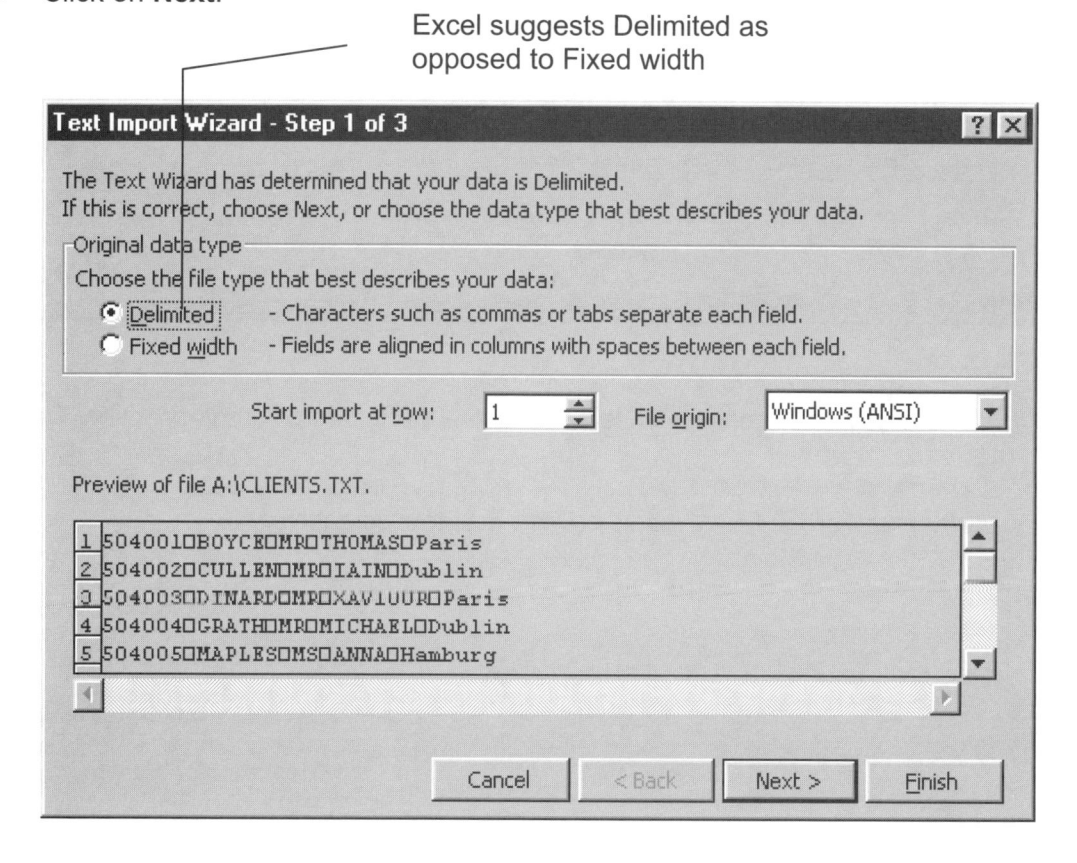

Excel suggests Delimited as opposed to Fixed width

**Text Import Wizard - Step 2 of 3** opens and presents a number of options.

# Chapter 1 - Editing

The next stage is to set the delimiters. **Tab** is set by default. Some experimentation is required here and it can be unrealistic to expect all data to be separated neatly and elegantly into columns!

- Click on delimiter **Space** and note the effect in Data preview.

- Click on delimiter **Comma** and note effect in Data preview.

- Deselect **Tab** and note effect. Now select it again.

    Check each of Delimiters in turn and note effect.

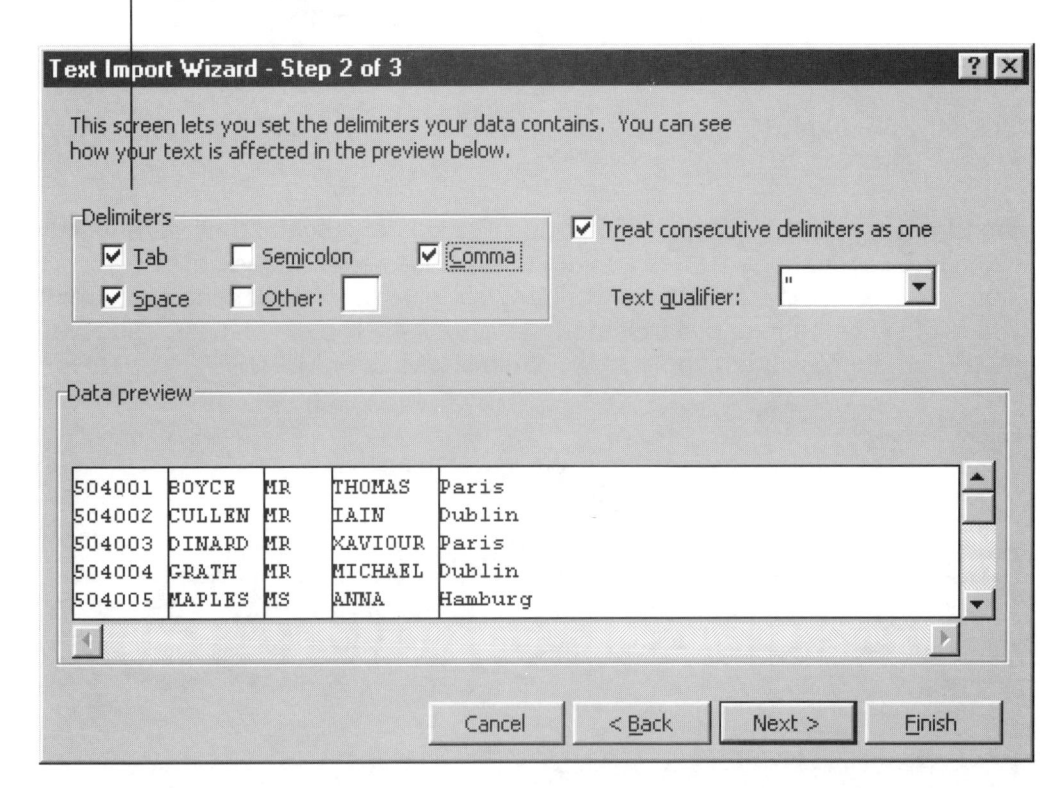

Leave selected those Delimiters that leave the text in columns-probably Tab and Space.

- When you are satisfied with the **Data preview** select **Next**.

# Chapter 1 - Editing

**Text Import Wizard - Step 3 of 3** opens.

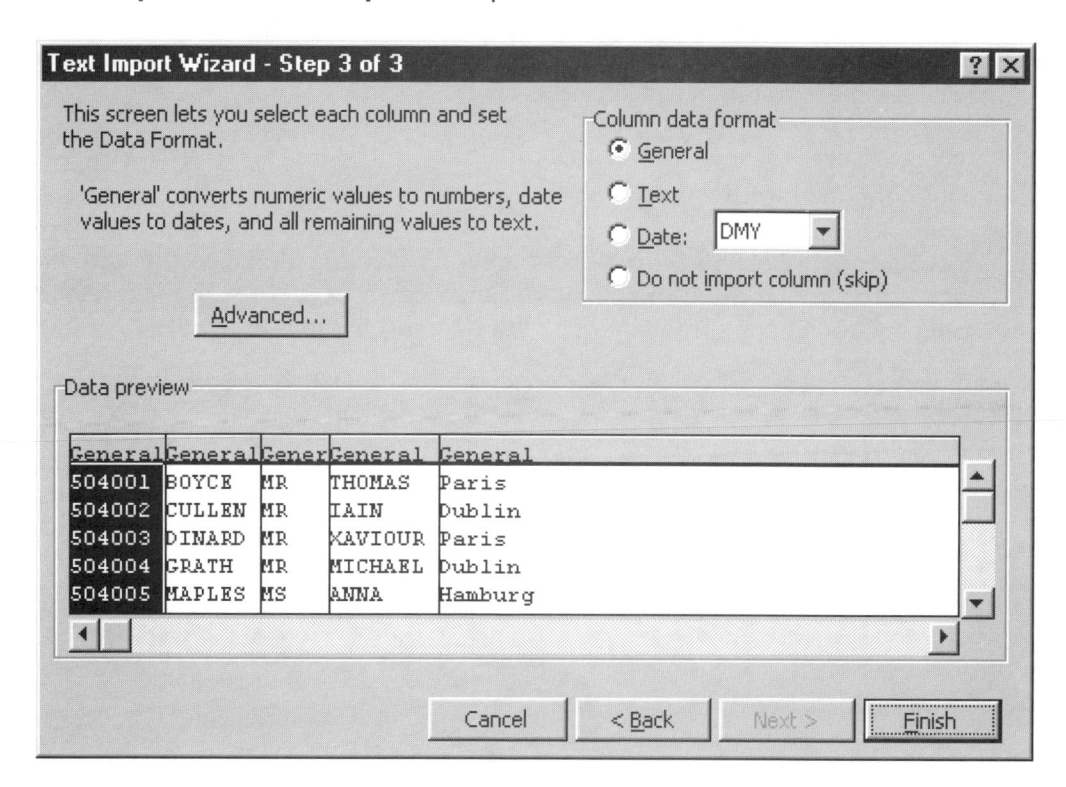

[Screenshot of Text Import Wizard - Step 3 of 3 dialog box showing Data preview with columns: 504001 BOYCE MR THOMAS Paris; 504002 CULLEN MR IAIN Dublin; 504003 DINARD MR XAVIOUR Paris; 504004 GRATH MR MICHAEL Dublin; 504005 MAPLES MS ANNA Hamburg]

You can select the **Column data format**. It is set to **General** by default in all the columns. If you decide that you do not require a column, for example the first column, employee number then you would select **Do not import column (skip)**, for that particular column.
In this case we will leave the Column data format as General.

- Select **Finish**.

The text is imported into the worksheet. If any material or information appears that is unnecessary, delete it. Adjust column widths and format the information to a high standard.

|   | A | B | C | D | E |
|---|---|---|---|---|---|
| 1 | 504001 | BOYCE | MR | THOMAS | Paris |
| 2 | 504002 | CULLEN | MR | IAIN | Dublin |
| 3 | 504003 | DINARD | MR | XAVIOUR | Paris |
| 4 | 504004 | GRATH | MR | MICHAEL | Dublin |
| 5 | 504005 | MAPLES | MS | ANNA | Hamburg |
| 6 | 504006 | NERING | MS | EMMA | Hamburg |
| 7 | 504007 | SLATTERY | MS | BRID | Dublin |
| 8 | 504008 | TRUMP | MR | PHIL | Paris |
| 9 | 504009 | VOLLER | MS | CIARA | Hamburg |

- Save the file as an Excel file, **Clients.xls**.

## 1.12.2 Importing a fixed width text file (4.1.1.6)

The file we are going to import is an accounts report with the following headings: Client account number, client name, credit limit and payments made.

- Open the file **Lighting.rep**

    **Text Import Wizard - Step 1 of 3** opens. Excel has identified that the data is appearing in **Fixed-width** columns. Scroll down to **row 7**. The first few lines are not required in our spreadsheet so we will start the import at **row 7**.

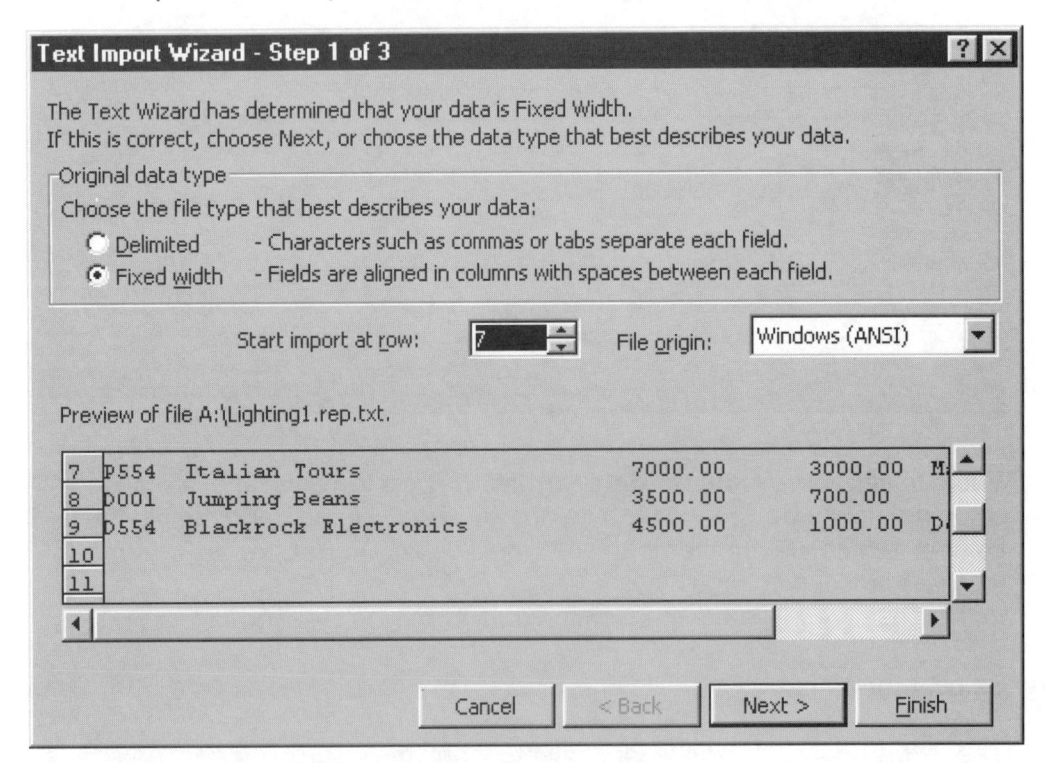

- Scroll down **Start import at** so that import starts at **row 7**.

- Click on **Next**.

    **Text Import Wizard - Step 2 of 3** opens.
    Excel attempts to divide the data into columns. Each line with arrows is a column break. Each line of information at this stage is a single stream of text.

    You will notice that a column division mark appears between each word in Italian Tours and Blackrock Electronics plc. We want these to form one heading. We have to delete the lines which are not relevant.

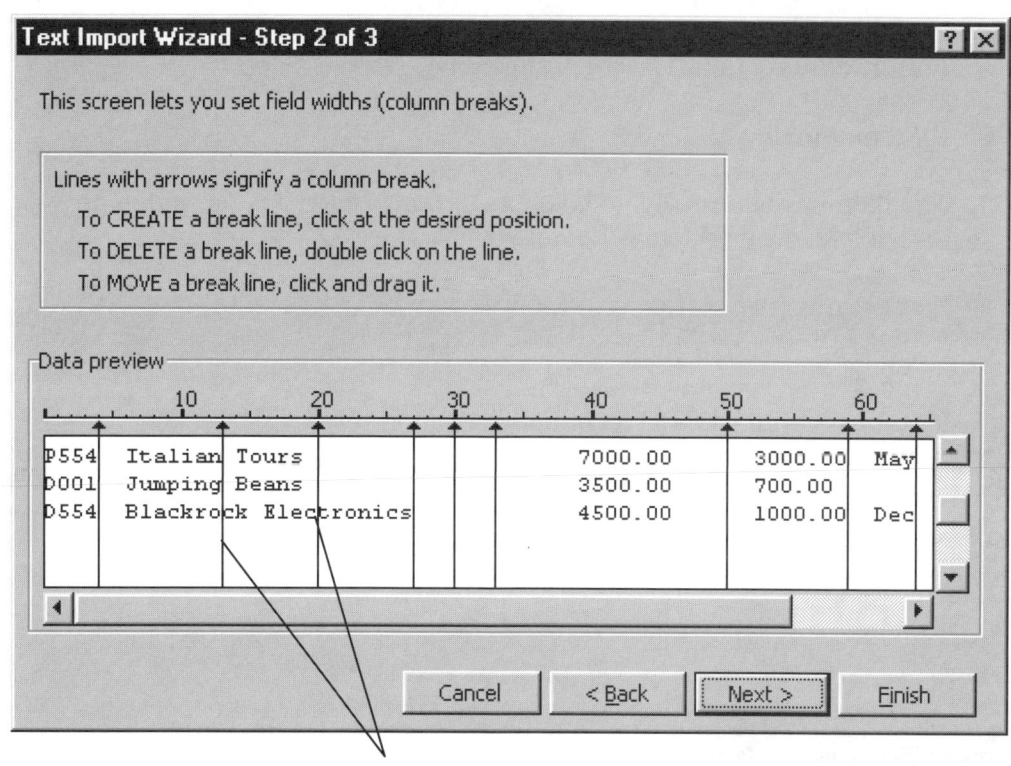

Delete irrelevant break lines

- Double-click on lines to delete them.

- Click on **Next**.

  Change to Skip

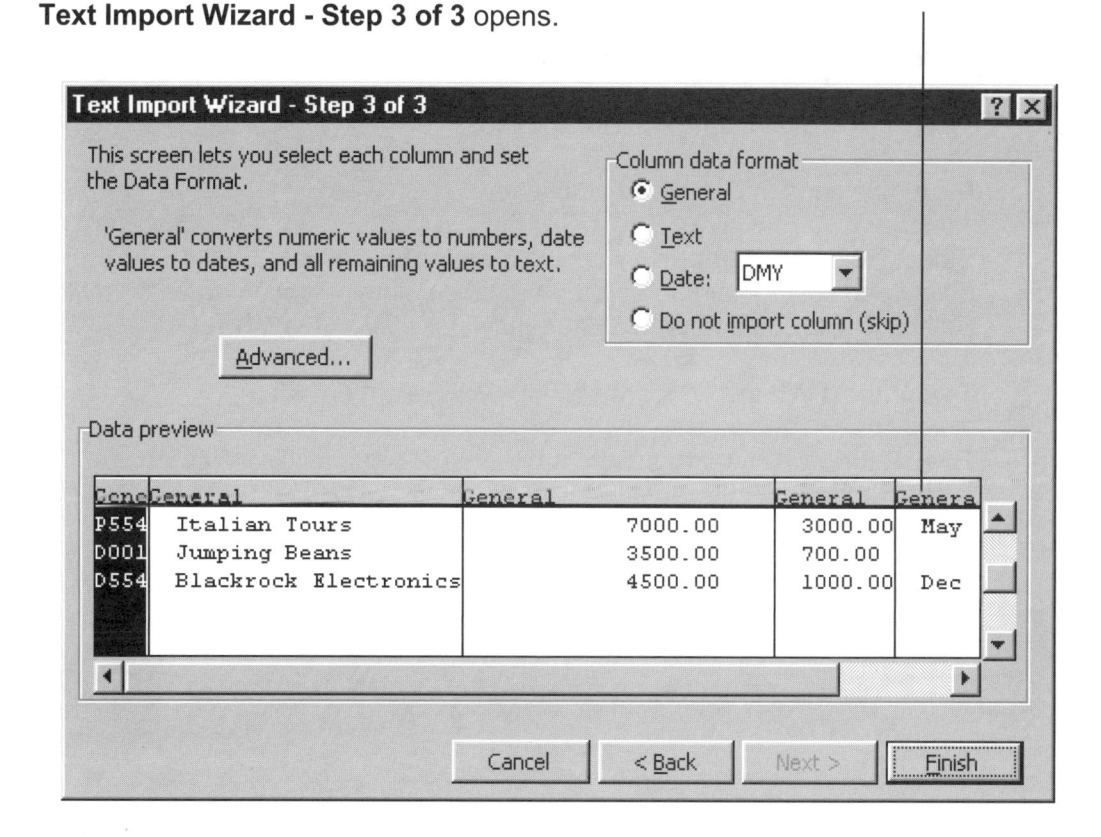

  **Text Import Wizard - Step 3 of 3** opens.

- Leave **General** as the column heading with one exception. Choose **Do not import column (skip)** for the last column. **Skip** will appear as heading.

- Click on **Finish**.

  The data has been split into columns. Format the columns, widen as appropriate and delete any data that is not relevant.

  |   | A | B | C | D |
  |---|---|---|---|---|
  | 1 | P554 | Italian Tours | 7000 | 3000 |
  | 2 | D001 | Jumping Beans | 3500 | 700 |
  | 3 | D554 | Blackrock Electronics | 4500 | 1000 |

- Save as an Excel file, **Lighting.xls**

The practice exercises contained in this section relate solely to this manual and do not constitute, or imply, certification by the European Driving Licence Foundation in respect of any ECDL examinations. For details on sitting ECDL examinations in your country please contact the local ECDL/ICDL licensee or visit the European Computer Driving Licence Foundation Ltd web site at http://www.ecdl.com

## Exercise 1K

You are required to import the text file **Institute** into a worksheet and delimit by space, comma or tab.

1 Open the file **Institute**. In **Fields of type:** select **Text Files**.

2 **Text Import Wizard - Step 1 of 3** opens.

  Excel has chosen **Delimited** as file type.

3 Select **Next**. **Text Import Wizard - Step 2 of 3** opens. Experiment with the delimiters, space, comma and tab until the columns look in an acceptable format. Selecting **Tab** (default) and **Space** may just do it. Select **Next**.

4 **Text Import Wizard - Step 3 of 3** opens. Select **Finish**.

5 Format the worksheet to a high standard and save as Excel worksheet, **Institute.xls**.

## Section 2    Display

It is possible to freeze row and column titles so that they are visible throughout the worksheet. We will look at freezing column titles first.

### 2.1    Freezing Column Titles (4.1.2.1)

- Open the file **Lighting Up Ireland**.

The spreadsheet is made up of two parts – a **Table of Variable Data** and a **Budget for 2003**. The table of variable data is separate from but linked to the budget. The comment in cell B6 refers to an exercise on Macros in Chapter 5 and you can ignore it at present.

The main **column titles** in this spreadsheet are **QTR1 – QTR4**. The main **row titles** are **SALES, COST OF SALES, OVERHEADS** and the sub-headings within each of these groups.

|   | A | B | C | D | E | F |
|---|---|---|---|---|---|---|
| 1 |   |   |   |   |   |   |
| 2 |   | Lighting Up Ireland | | | | |
| 3 |   |   |   |   |   |   |
| 4 |   | Table of Variable Data | | | | |
| 5 |   |   |   |   |   |   |
| 6 |   |   | QTR1 | QTR2 | QTR3 | QTR4 |
| 7 |   |   |   |   |   |   |
| 8 | SALES |   |   |   |   |   |
| 9 |   |   |   |   |   |   |
| 10 | Garden Spot Lights |   | £75,000 | £78,000 | £82,500 | £93,200 |
| 11 | Garden Spot Lights Inc/Dec % |   |   |   |   |   |
| 12 | Outdoor Chinese Lanterns |   | £65,000 | £60,450 | £78,000 | £84,500 |
| 13 | Outdoor Chinese Lanterns Inc/Dec % |   |   | -7.00% | 20.00% | 30.00% |
| 14 | Pagoda Garden Lights |   | £32,000 | £29,120 | £31,158 | £42,064 |
| 15 | Pagoda Garden Lights Inc/Dec |   |   | -9.00% | 7.00% | 35.00% |
| 16 |   |   |   |   |   |   |
| 17 |   |   |   |   |   |   |
| 18 | COST OF SALES |   |   |   |   |   |
| 19 |   |   |   |   |   |   |
| 20 | Garden Spot Lights % |   | 32.00% | 32.00% | 32.00% | 32.00% |
| 21 | Outdoor Chinese Lanterns % |   | 40.00% | 40.00% | 40.00% | 50.00% |
| 22 | Pagoda Garden Lights % |   | 40.00% | 40.00% | 40.00% | 50.00% |

- Click on cell **C7**.

- Scroll down the spreadsheet and the column headings are no longer visible.

    In large spreadsheets this could lead to errors during data entry. We will set the column headings so that they are visible throughout the spreadsheet.

|   |   |   |   |   |   |   |
|---|---|---|---|---|---|---|
| 26 | Rent and Rates |   | £60,000 | £15,000 | £15,000 | £15,000 | £15,000 |
| 27 | Administration |   | £3,000 | £3,000 | £3,000 | £3,000 | £3,360 |
| 28 | Administration Inc/Dec |   |   |   |   |   | 12.00% |
| 29 | Expenses |   | £4,000 | £4,000 | £4,000 | £4,000 | £4,000 |
| 30 | Advertising |   | £4,000 | £4,000 | £4,000 | £4,000 | £4,000 |
| 31 | Other Costs |   | £10,000 | £10,000 | £10,000 | £10,000 | £10,000 |

- Select **row 7**. This is the row **below** the column headings that are on row 6.

- Select **Window** and choose **Freeze Panes** from the drop-down menu.

    A thin black line appears between row 6 and row 7.

- Scroll down the spreadsheet and you will notice that the column titles remain visible.

### 2.1.1 To Unfreeze Column Titles

- Select **Window** and choose **Unfreeze Panes** from the drop-down menu.

    The thin black line disappears.
    *Leave the worksheet with the column title frozen.*

## 2.2 Freezing Row Titles (4.1.2.1)

- Select **Sheet 2**. This contains an identical copy of **Lighting Up Ireland**.

- Select **Column B** which should now be highlighted.

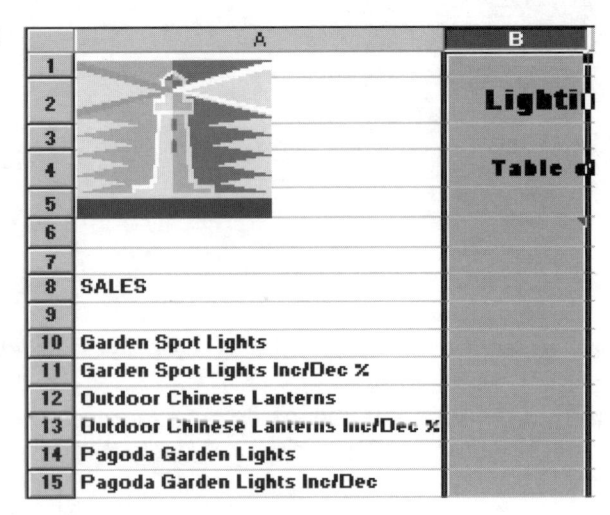

- Select **Freeze Panes** from the **Window** drop-down menu.

A thin black line appears to the right of the row, between column A and Column B.

- Scroll across to the right and the row titles stay visible.

### 2.2.1 To Unfreeze Row Titles

- Select **Window** and choose **Unfreeze Panes** from the drop-down menu. The thin black line disappears.

*Leave the worksheet with the row title frozen.*

## 2.3 To Freeze Row and Column Titles Together

- Select **Sheet3**. This also contains an identical copy of **Lighting Up Ireland**.

- Select cell **B7**.

- Choose **Window** followed by **Freeze Panes**.

A thin black line appears beneath the column titles and a similar line to the right of the row titles.

|    | A | B | C | D | E | F |
|----|---|---|---|---|---|---|
| 1  |   |   |   |   |   |   |
| 2  |   |   | **Lighting Up Ireland** | | | |
| 3  |   |   |   |   |   |   |
| 4  |   |   | **Table of Variable Data** | | | |
| 5  |   |   |   |   |   |   |
| 6  |   |   | QTR1 | QTR2 | QTR3 | QTR4 |
| 7  |   |   |   |   |   |   |
| 8  | SALES |   |   |   |   |   |
| 9  |   |   |   |   |   |   |
| 10 | Garden Spot Lights |   | £75,000 | £78,000 | £82,500 | £93,200 |
| 11 | Garden Spot Lights Inc/Dec % |   |   |   |   |   |
| 12 | Outdoor Chinese Lanterns |   | £65,000 | £60,450 | £78,000 | £84,500 |
| 13 | Outdoor Chinese Lanterns Inc/Dec % |   |   | -7.00% | 20.00% | 30.00% |
| 14 | Pagoda Garden Lights |   | £32,000 | £29,120 | £31,158 | £42,064 |
| 15 | Pagoda Garden Lights Inc/Dec |   |   | -9.00% | 7.00% | 35.00% |

- Scroll down the sheet and across to the right. Both row and column titles remain visible.

|    | A | | QTR2 | QTR3 | QTR4 |
|----|---|---|---|---|---|
| 6  |   |   |   |   |   |
| 24 | OVERHEADS |   |   |   |   |
| 25 |   |   |   |   |   |
| 26 | Rent and Rates |   | £15,000 | £15,000 | £15,000 |
| 27 | Administration |   | £3,000 | £3,000 | £3,360 |
| 28 | Administration Inc/Dec |   |   |   | 12.00% |
| 29 | Expenses |   | £4,000 | £4,000 | £4,000 |
| 30 | Advertising |   | £4,000 | £4,000 | £4,000 |
| 31 | Other Costs |   | £10,000 | £10,000 | £10,000 |

### 2.3.1 To Unfreeze Row and Column Titles

- Select **Window** and choose **Unfreeze Panes** from the drop-down menu.

  *Leave the worksheet with the row and column titles frozen.*

- Save the file as **Lighting Up Ireland Solution**.

The practice exercises contained in this section relate solely to this manual and do not constitute, or imply, certification by the European Driving Licence Foundation in respect of any ECDL examinations. For details on sitting ECDL examinations in your country please contact the local ECDL/ICDL licensee or visit the European Computer Driving Licence Foundation Ltd web site at http://www.ecdl.com

## Exercise 2A

1 Open the file **Getting Better**. Select **row 38** so that it is highlighted.

2 Now select **Widow** followed by **Freeze Panes**. A thin black line appears between row 37 and 38.

3 Scroll down the spreadsheet as far as **row 65**. The column titles remain visible.

4 Now select **Window, Unfreeze Panes.**

5 Select **column B** so that it is highlighted.

6 Choose **Window** followed by **Freeze Panes**. A thin black line appears between column A and column B. Scroll across the page and the row titles remain visible.

Do not close **Getting Better,** as we will be using it in the next exercise.


The practice exercises contained in this section relate solely to this manual and do not constitute, or imply, certification by the European Driving Licence Foundation in respect of any ECDL examinations. For details on sitting ECDL examinations in your country please contact the local ECDL/ICDL licensee or visit the European Computer Driving Licence Foundation Ltd web site at http://www.ecdl.com

## Exercise 2B

1 Select tab **Exercise 2B**. Choose cell **B38**. Now select **Window** followed by **Freeze Panes**. As expected, a thin black horizontal line and a vertical line appear.

2 Scroll down and across the worksheet. The column rows and titles remain visible.

3 Save the file and close.

# Chapter 1 - Editing

## 2.4 Hiding and Unhiding Rows or Columns (4.1.2.2)

It is possible to hide rows and columns in a worksheet.

### 2.4.1 Hiding Rows

- Open the file **Lighting Up Ireland**.

- Select **Row 12**. **Right-click** over **row 12** and select **Hide** from the drop-down menu.

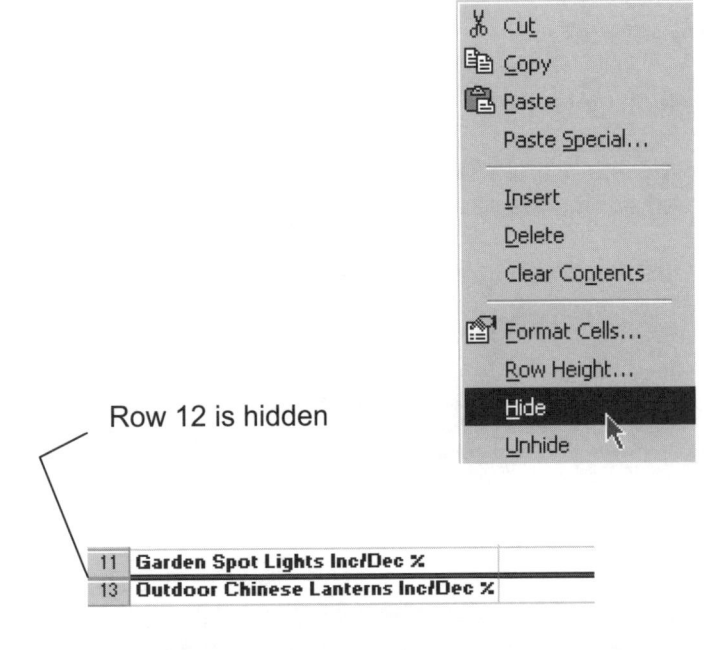

Row 12 is hidden

**Row 12** is now hidden. We can unhide row 12.

### 2.4.2 To Unhide Rows

- Select **rows 11** and **13** – those rows on either side of **row 12**, the hidden row.

- Right-click over these highlighted rows and choose **Unhide** from the drop-down menu.

Row **12** is no longer hidden.

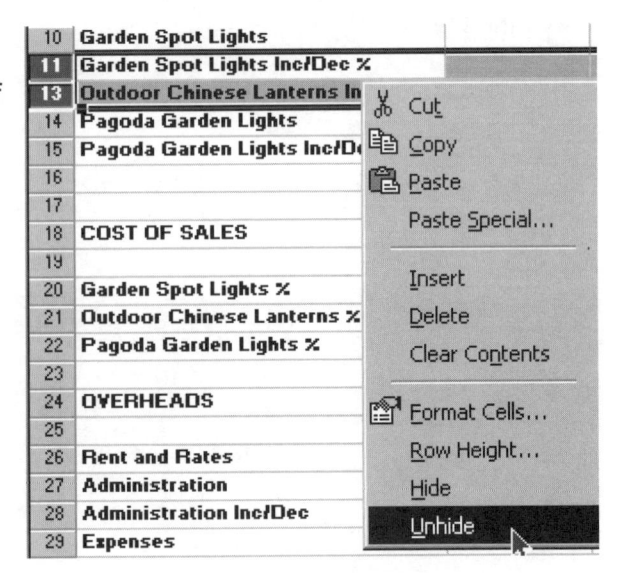

Chapter 1 - Editing

### 2.4.3 Hiding Columns

Is the file **Lighting Up Ireland** open? If not, open it now.

- Select **Column B**. Right-click over column B and choose **Hide** from the drop-down menu.

    **Column B** is no longer visible.

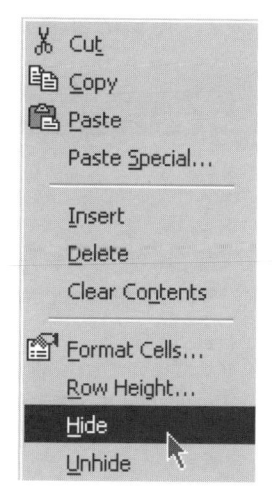

    Column B is hidden

### 2.4.4 To Unhide Columns

- Select **columns A** and **C**, the two columns on either side of the hidden column. Right-click over the highlighted columns and choose **Unhide** from the drop-down menu.

    Column B is now visible.

**NOTE**

If you want to hide more than one column, select the first column to hide then hold the **Shift** key down and select the remaining columns. Similarly you can use the same method to hide more than one row. If the columns are non-contiguous, then hold down the **Ctrl** key to select.

### 2.4.5 Hiding rows and columns by an alternative method

You can hide rows and columns manually.

- Drag the column's border from right to left until the width registers as -**width: 0.00**

- Drag the lower border of a row upwards until height is registered as – **height: 0.00**

    Use **Unhide** as previously explained to view the hidden columns and rows.

**NOTE**
When you create a hidden row you are creating a row of column height equal to zero. Similarly a hidden column is a column of width equal to zero.

The practice exercises contained in this section relate solely to this manual and do not constitute, or imply, certification by the European Driving Licence Foundation in respect of any ECDL examinations. For details on sitting ECDL examinations in your country please contact the local ECDL/ICDL licensee or visit the European Computer Driving Licence Foundation Ltd web site at http://www.ecdl.com

## Exercise 2C

1   Open the file **Getting Better**. Click on tab **Exercise 2C**.

2   Column **E** and row **78** are hidden. Can you unhide the column and row?

3   Highlight columns **D** and **F** and right-click over these highlighted columns. Choose **Unhide** from the drop-down menu. The column is now visible.

4   Highlight row **77** and **79** so that both are highlighted. Right-click over highlighted rows and select Unhide. Row **78** is now visible.

5   Now hide **Columns A** and **D**.

6   Hide **Row 54** and **Row 65**.

    We will be using the file **Getting Better** in a later exercise but you can close the file for now.

## 2.5 Hiding and Unhiding Worksheets (4.1.2.3)

It is possible to hide worksheets in a workbook.

- Open the file **Lighting Up Ireland**.

### 2.5.1 Hiding a worksheet

- Click on tab **Sheet3**.

- Choose **Sheet** from the **Format** menu.

- Now choose **Hide**.

    **Sheet3** is hidden.

Sheet3 is hidden

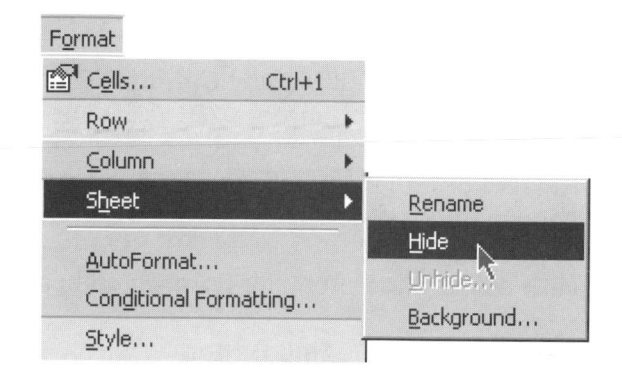

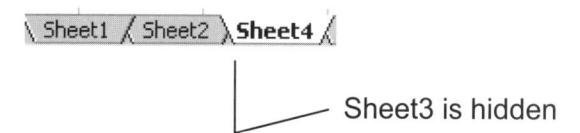

### 2.5.2 Unhiding a worksheet

- To **unhide** Sheet3 select **Format** followed by **Sheet** and select **Unhide**. The **Unhide** dialog box opens listing hidden sheets. **Sheet3** is listed.

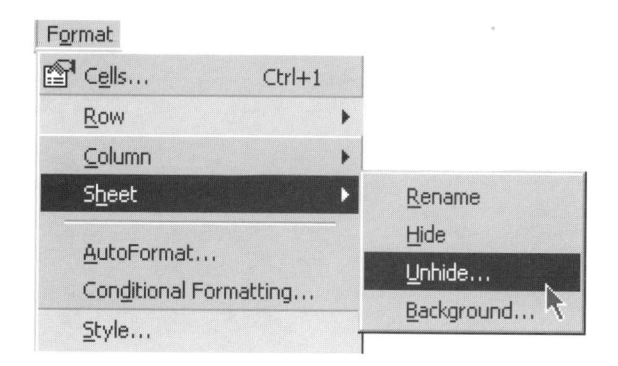

- Click on **OK**.

    **Sheet3** is again visible.

- Close the file **Lighting Up Ireland**.

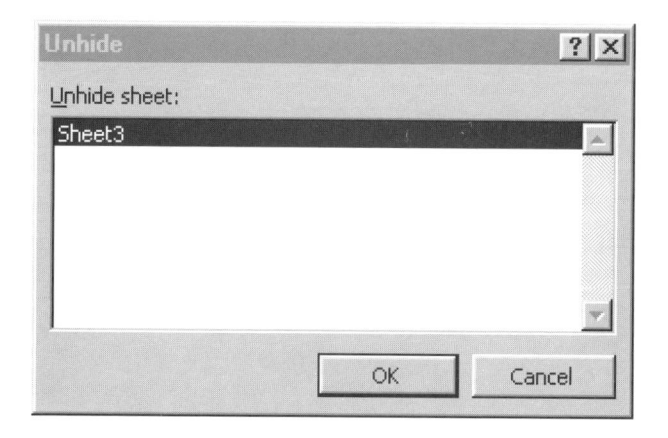

# Chapter 1 - Editing

The practice exercises contained in this section relate solely to this manual and do not constitute, or imply, certification by the European Driving Licence Foundation in respect of any ECDL examinations. For details on sitting ECDL examinations in your country please contact the local ECDL/ICDL licensee or visit the European Computer Driving Licence Foundation Ltd web site at http://www.ecdl.com

## Exercise 2D

Open the file **Getting Better**.

1. The worksheet **EXERCISE 2D** is hidden. Did you notice it when you completed exercises **2A-2C**? Can you now retrieve it?

2. Choose **Format** followed by **Unhide**. The **Unhide dialog** box opens listing the hidden worksheet **Exercise 2D**. Click **OK** and the worksheet opens.

3. Select **Format** sheet, followed by **Rename**. Rename the worksheet – you choose the name.

4. Now select **Sheet** from the **Format** menu and choose **Hide**.

5. Save the file as **Getting Better**.

## 2.6 Using the Subtotal Feature (4.1.2.4)

The Subtotal feature enters formulas with the subtotal function. The list (see NOTE below) must first be sorted.

Syntax of Subtotal function: **SUBTOTAL(function_num,ref)**

**NOTE**

A list is a group of worksheet rows that contain related data. The first row of the list has labels. In the list shown these are **Region**, **Refreshment** and **Sales**. Each column in the list has a label in the first row and contains related information. There should be no blank rows or columns within the list.

### 2.6.1 Creating subtotals in a list

- Open the file **Subtotal**.

    The data we want to subtotal is in a list format.

    The column we want to **subtotal** is headed **Refreshment** and the column we want to obtain the subtotal in, is headed **Sales**.

- Click anywhere in the **Refreshment** column.

- Select **Sort Ascending** or **Sort Descending** from the toolbar.

- Choose **Subtotals** from the **Data** menu.

    The **Subtotal dialog** box opens.

- In the **At each Change in**: box, click drop-down menu and select **Refreshment**.

- In the **Use function**: box we will leave the summary function as **Sum**, but do click the down arrow now to check options available. There are 11 and they are listed in the table. The **function_num** in the formula is **1** to **11** depending on the Function. The number in the **SUM** function is **9**, and in **AVERAGE** is **1** (See table on next page).

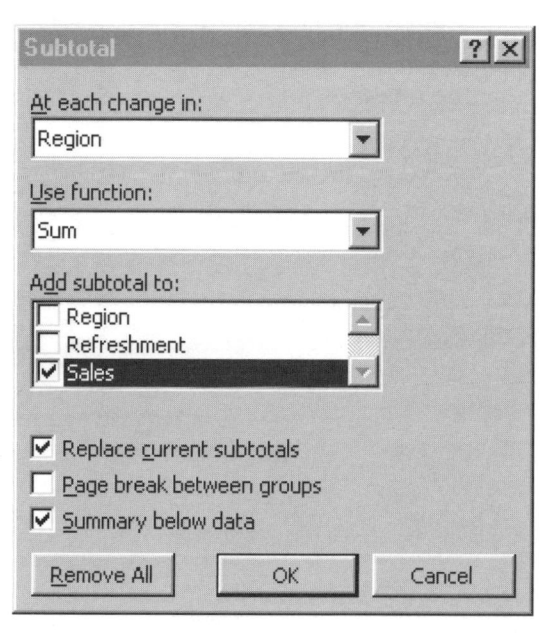

|   | A | B | C |
|---|---|---|---|
| 1 | **Subtotals** | | |
| 2 | | | |
| 3 | | | |
| 4 | Region | Refreshment | Sales |
| 5 | Paris | Tea | 2500 |
| 6 | Paris | Tea | 3200 |
| 7 | Paris | Tea | 2600 |
| 8 | Paris | Tea | 1500 |
| 9 | Paris | Tea | 1700 |
| 10 | Hamburg | Coffee | 5000 |
| 11 | Hamburg | Coffee | 2000 |
| 12 | Hamburg | Coffee | 4000 |
| 13 | Hamburg | Coffee | 1000 |
| 14 | Hamburg | Coffee | 3000 |
| 15 | Dublin | Chocolate | 3000 |
| 16 | Dublin | Chocolate | 1500 |
| 17 | Dublin | Chocolate | 2000 |

| Number | Function Name |
|--------|---------------|
| 1 | AVERAGE |
| 2 | COUNT |
| 3 | COUNTA |
| 4 | MAX |
| 5 | MIN |
| 6 | PRODUCT |
| 7 | STDEV |
| 8 | STDEVP |
| 9 | SUM |
| 10 | VAR |
| 11 | VARP |

- In the **Add subtotal to**: box we will leave **Sales** selected.

- Now click on **OK**.

The list now becomes an outline with titles and subtotals.

The subtotals for each of the cities are given and a **Grand Total** is also given.

Suppose we just want the subtotals and the grand totals – how do we achieve this?

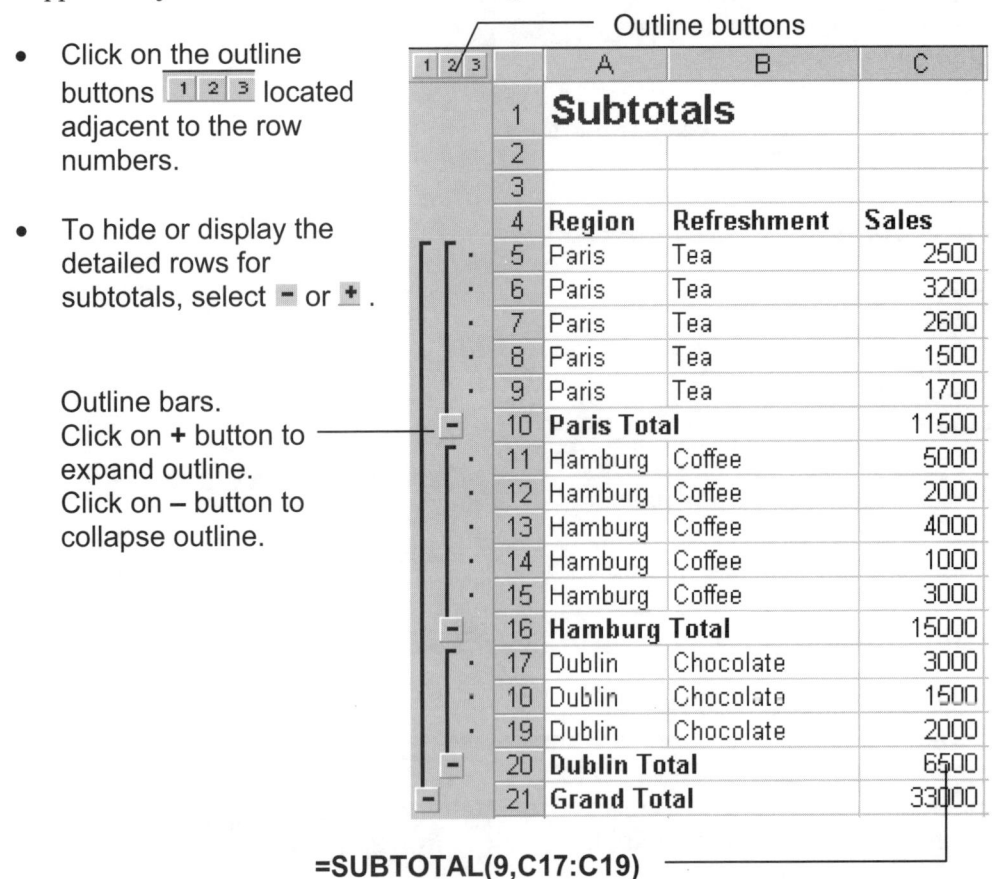

- Click on the outline buttons 1 2 3 located adjacent to the row numbers.

- To hide or display the detailed rows for subtotals, select − or + .

Outline bars.
Click on **+** button to expand outline.
Click on **−** button to collapse outline.

Outline buttons

| | A | B | C |
|---|---|---|---|
| 1 | **Subtotals** | | |
| 2 | | | |
| 3 | | | |
| 4 | **Region** | **Refreshment** | **Sales** |
| 5 | Paris | Tea | 2500 |
| 6 | Paris | Tea | 3200 |
| 7 | Paris | Tea | 2600 |
| 8 | Paris | Tea | 1500 |
| 9 | Paris | Tea | 1700 |
| 10 | **Paris Total** | | 11500 |
| 11 | Hamburg | Coffee | 5000 |
| 12 | Hamburg | Coffee | 2000 |
| 13 | Hamburg | Coffee | 4000 |
| 14 | Hamburg | Coffee | 1000 |
| 15 | Hamburg | Coffee | 3000 |
| 16 | **Hamburg Total** | | 15000 |
| 17 | Dublin | Chocolate | 3000 |
| 18 | Dublin | Chocolate | 1500 |
| 19 | Dublin | Chocolate | 2000 |
| 20 | **Dublin Total** | | 6500 |
| 21 | **Grand Total** | | 33000 |

=SUBTOTAL(9,C17:C19)

## 2.6.2  Using options in Subtotal

Generally you will use Subtotal with SUM. However you may find other options such as AVERAGE, MAX, MIN and COUNT useful.

- Close the **Subtotals** file, but do not save. Now reopen the file.

- Click anywhere in **Column B**.

- Sort descending.

- Select **Data** followed by **Subtotals**....

  The Subtotal dialog box opens.

- Select **Average** as the **Use function** option.

- The other entries should be as in diagram.

- Select **OK**.

  The average sales for each city is given plus a grand average.

- Click on Outline Button 2.

- Select cell **C20** to check formula.

  It is:
  **=SUBTOTAL(1,C17:C19)**

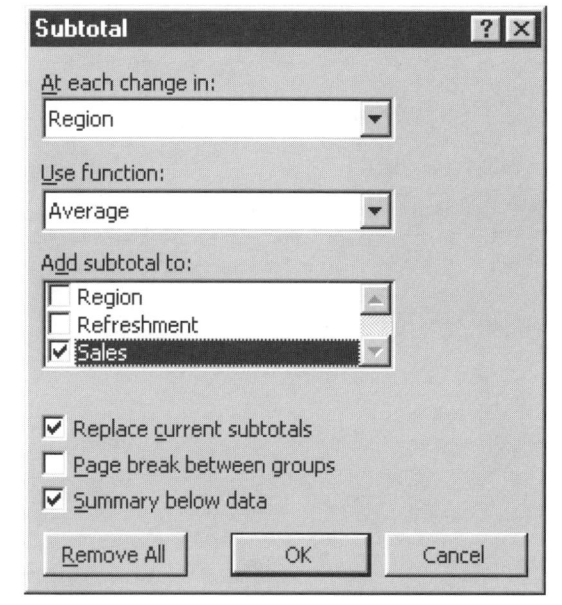

  The **1** in the formula indicates that Subtotal is calculating an **AVERAGE**.

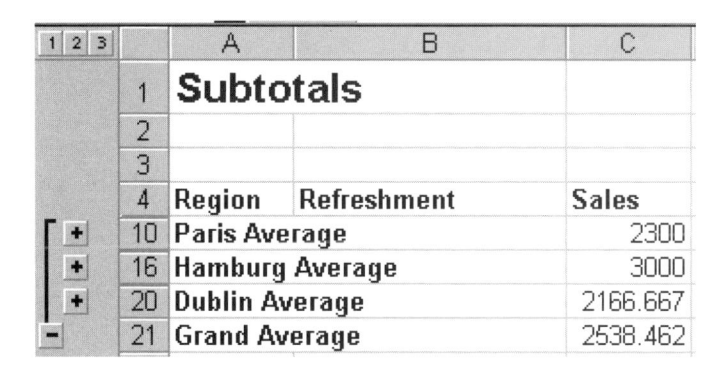

| 1 2 3 | | A | B | C |
|---|---|---|---|---|
| | 1 | **Subtotals** | | |
| | 2 | | | |
| | 3 | | | |
| | 4 | Region | Refreshment | Sales |
| + | 10 | Paris Average | | 2300 |
| + | 16 | Hamburg Average | | 3000 |
| + | 20 | Dublin Average | | 2166.667 |
| − | 21 | Grand Average | | 2538.462 |

- Click on **Column B** again and choose **SUM** from the **Data Menu, Subtotals command** and **Refreshment** from **At each change in**:

  We will now chart the information.

- Click **OK**.

## 2.6.3 Charting Subtotal

- Display only the detailed rows for subtotals by clicking on all – buttons. Click on outline button **2**. The spreadsheet should be the same as in diagram shown to right.

|   | A | B | C |
|---|---|---|---|
| 1 | **Subtotals** | | |
| 2 | | | |
| 3 | | | |
| 4 | Region | Refreshment | Sales |
| 10 | | Tea Total | 11500 |
| 16 | | Coffee Total | 15000 |
| 20 | | Chocolate Total | 6500 |
| 21 | | Grand Total | 33000 |

- Select **Chart Wizard** and proceed through the steps until you have a chart. It should look similar to that below.

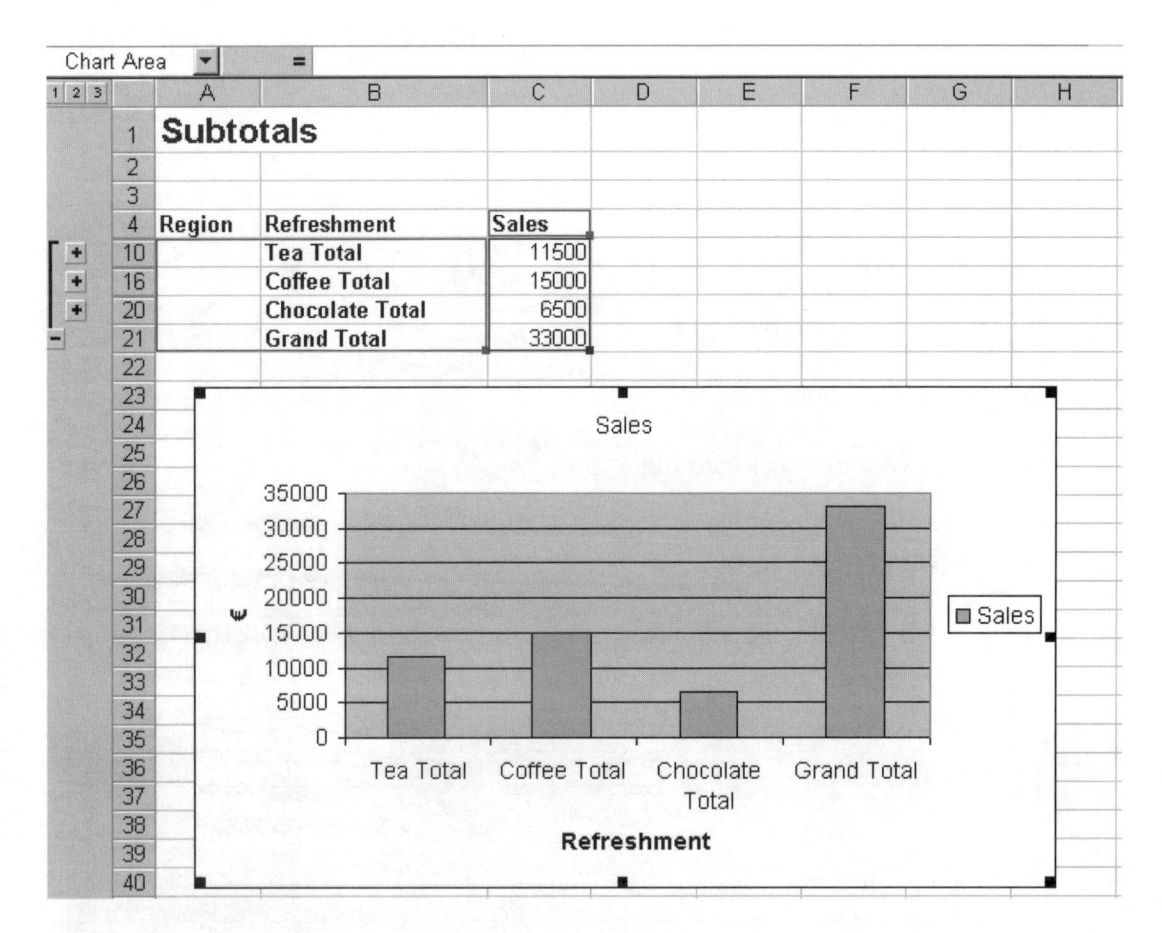

## 2.6.4 Removing Subtotals

- Click on any cell in the list that contains subtotals.

- Choose **Subtotals** from the **Data** menu.

- Click **Remove All**.

- Close the file **Subtotal**.

The practice exercises contained in this section relate solely to this manual and do not constitute, or imply, certification by the European Driving Licence Foundation in respect of any ECDL examinations. For details on sitting ECDL examinations in your country please contact the local ECDL/ICDL licensee or visit the European Computer Driving Licence Foundation Ltd web site at http://www.ecdl.com

## Exercise 2E

1   Open the file **University**. Click on the column **Department** and sort the table in ascending or descending order. Again select the column Department and choose **Data** followed by **Subtotals…**.

2   Select the following options.

   At each change in: **Department**
   Use function: **Sum**
   Add subtotal to: **Salary**

3   Click **OK**.

   Subtotals for each of the nine university departments are given. Click on the outline buttons and note the changes.

4   Save the file as **University**.

## 2.7 DATA TABLES

The Data Table is useful in **What-If Analysis**. In our next example we can use the One-Input Data Table to calculate the monthly payments on a loan against a list of different interest rates. The Data Tables use the PMT function. You should read the note that follows on this function. PMT is covered in Chapter 3.

### 2.7.1 Creating a one-input data table (4.1.2.5)

- Open the file **Mortgage**

We are going to input a series of different interest rates. You can enter the rates from the figure (see next page) directly into the range **A8:A15** and format in percentage to 2 decimal places or, you may want to follow the instructions below.

- Move cursor to cell **A8**.

- Type **0.03** (When we format the cells this will be 3.0%).

- Move cursor to cell **A9**.

- Type **0.035** (When we format the cells this will be 3.5%).

- Format cells **A8:A9** as percentage to two decimal places.

    Choose **Format** followed by **Cells**, then **Percentage** from **Category** list and **2** decimal places. Then click **OK**.

- Now we will use **AutoFill** to complete the rest of the labels.
    Highlight the range **A8:A9** and place the cursor over the fill handle. When the black cross appears drag down to cell **B15** and release.
    The interest rates should vary from **3.00% to 6.50%,** as in figure (see next page).

- Highlight the range **A7:B15**

- Choose **Data** followed by **Table**.

    The **Table Dialog** box opens.

- Drag the Table by its title bar so that it is adjacent to the range of interest rates.

## Chapter 1 - Editing

|   | A | B | C | D | E |
|---|---|---|---|---|---|
| 1 | Home Loan Analysis (One Input Data Table) | | | | |
| 2 | Down Payment | 0 | | | |
| 3 | Interest rate | 4.25% | | | |
| 4 | Term (months) | 240 | | | |
| 5 | Loan Amount | 160,000 | | | |
| 6 | | | | | |
| 7 | | €990.78 | | | |
| 8 | 3.00% | | | | |
| 9 | 3.50% | | | | |
| 10 | 4.00% | | | | |
| 11 | 4.50% | | | | |
| 12 | 5.00% | | | | |
| 13 | 5.50% | | | | |
| 14 | 6.00% | | | | |
| 15 | 6.50% | | | | |

Table dialog:
Row input cell: 
Column input cell: $B$3

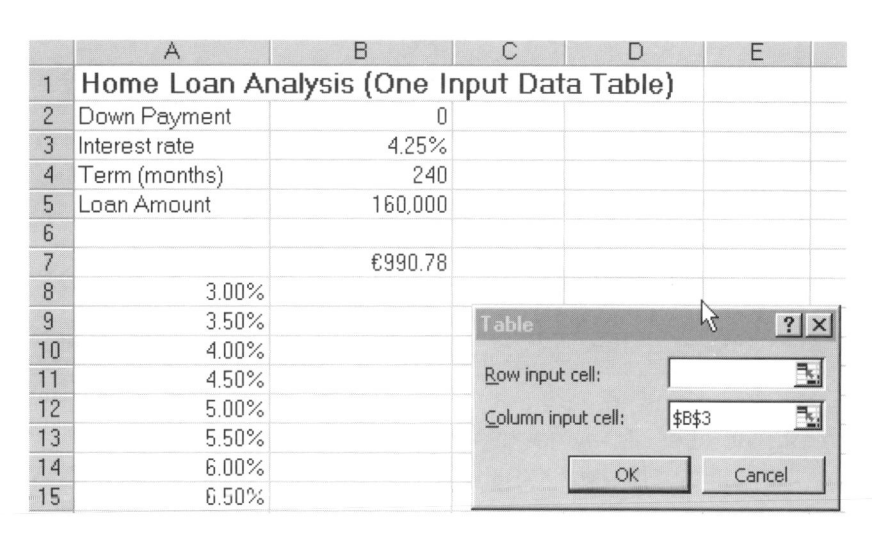

- Place the cursor in the **Column input** cell.

- Click on cell **B3** (Interest Rate).

- Now click **OK** button.

B15  = {=TABLE(,B3)}

|   | A | B | C | D |
|---|---|---|---|---|
| 1 | Home Loan Analysis (One Input Data Table) | | | |
| 2 | Down Payment | 0 | | |
| 3 | Interest rate | 4.25% | | |
| 4 | Term (months) | 240 | | |
| 5 | Loan Amount | 160,000 | | |
| 6 | | | | |
| 7 | | €990.78 | | |
| 8 | 3.00% | 887.36 | | |
| 9 | 3.50% | 927.94 | | |
| 10 | 4.00% | 969.57 | | |
| 11 | 4.50% | 1,012.24 | | |
| 12 | 5.00% | 1,055.93 | | |
| 13 | 5.50% | 1,100.62 | | |
| 14 | 6.00% | 1,146.29 | | |
| 15 | 6.50% | 1,192.92 | | |

The completed **Data Table** shows the monthly repayment amounts related to the interest rate.

- Save the file as **Mortgage Solution**.

**NOTE**

You may be tempted to check your current mortgage (If any) with the One-Input Data Table. Or if you are taking out a loan or mortgage in the future, the Two-Input Data Table may prove useful.

## NOTE

The Data Tables you will be working with utilise the function PMT. Click on cell **B7** to view the formula.

    =PMT(rate,nper,pv,fv,type)

    =PMT(B3/12,B4,-B5)

**PMT** calculates the payments for a loan based on constant payments and a constant interest rate.
**Rate** is the interest rate for the period. If monthly payments, then divide by 12.
**Nper** is the total number of payments made. In our example this is 240.
**PV** is the present value. In our example it is -160,000 – the loan amount with a – (minus sign)
**Fv** is the future value.
**Type** is **0** or **1**. Payment at end of period = 0, or omitted. Payment at beginning of period = 1.

You will find further information and examples of **PMT** in **Chapter 3**.

---

The practice exercises contained in this section relate solely to this manual and do not constitute, or imply, certification by the European Driving Licence Foundation in respect of any ECDL examinations. For details on sitting ECDL examinations in your country please contact the local ECDL/ICDL licensee or visit the European Computer Driving Licence Foundation Ltd web site at http://www.ecdl.com

## Exercise 2F

In this exercise we will calculate the repayments due on a property loan of **€1.2m** over **30** years with a range of interest rates indicated below:

**3.25%, 3.75%, 4.25%, 4.75%, 5.25%, 5.75%, 6.25%, 6.75%**

1 Open the file **Mortgage**.

2 Select the **One Input Data Table Exercise** tab.

3 The range of values is displayed.

4 Highlight the range **A7:B15**. Select **Data** followed by **Table**. The **Table Dialog box** opens. Select **Column input cell** and click on cell **B3**. Click **OK**.

   The table is complete.

5 Save the file as **Mortgage Solution**.

=PMT(B3/12,B4,-B5)

## NOTE

Examine cell **B3** as it contains the **PMT** formula.

## 2.72 Creating a Two-Input Data Table (4.1.2.5)

We have examined the payments due on a mortgage by looking at different interest rates. Now we look at repayments over differing periods. In this situation we use a two-input data table. The data table is useful in **What-If** analysis.

- Open the file **Loan**.

  The table has been set up with the various interest rates and the time of the loan from 120 months to 360 months. Check the formula in cell **B7**. This figure was calculated using the PMT function so you should be familiar with it.

- Highlight the range **B7:G13**

- Use the command **Data** followed by **Table**.

  The Row input cell is **B4** (loan term) and the Column input cell is **B3** (Interest rate).

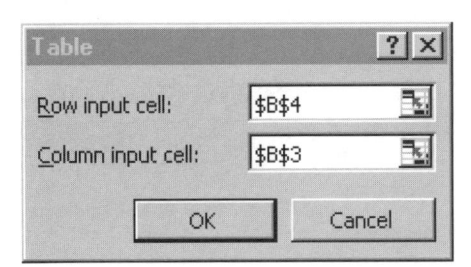

- Input these values now. Click **OK**.

  The two input data table is generated.

|   | A | B | C | D | E | F | G |
|---|---|---|---|---|---|---|---|
| 1 | Home Loan Analysis (Two Input Data Table) | | | | | | |
| 2 | Down Payment | 0 | | | | | |
| 3 | Interest rate | 4.25% | | | | | |
| 4 | Term (months) | 240 | | | | | |
| 5 | Loan Amount | 160,000 | | | | | |
| 6 | | | | | | | |
| 7 | | €990.78 | 120 | 180 | 240 | 300 | 360 |
| 8 | | 4.00% | €1,619.92 | €1,183.50 | €969.57 | €844.54 | €763.86 |
| 9 | | 5.00% | €1,697.05 | €1,265.27 | €1,055.93 | €935.34 | €850.91 |
| 10 | | 6.00% | €1,776.33 | €1,350.17 | €1,146.29 | €1,030.88 | €959.28 |
| 11 | | 7.00% | €1,857.74 | €1,438.13 | €1,240.48 | €1,130.85 | €1,064.48 |
| 12 | | 8.00% | €1,941.24 | €1,529.04 | €1,338.30 | €1,234.91 | €1,174.02 |
| 13 | | 9.00% | €2,026.81 | €1,622.83 | €1,439.56 | €1,342.71 | €1,287.40 |
| 14 | | | | | | | |

B7 = =PMT(B3/12,B4,-B5)

**NOTE**

You may wish to compare the figures in the One-Input Data Table. The loan amount is the same, 160,000. Look under the 240-month column and at comparable interest rates, 4, 5 and 6%.

Notice formula     {=TABLE(B4,B3)}
in data table

- Click on any cell within the range **C8:G13**.

- Check the formula in the cells above. Those in the main body of the table are the same: **{=TABLE(B4,B3)}**

- Save the file as **Loan Solution**

The practice exercises contained in this section relate solely to this manual and do not constitute, or imply, certification by the European Driving Licence Foundation in respect of any ECDL examinations. For details on sitting ECDL examinations in your country please contact the local ECDL/ICDL licensee or visit the European Computer Driving Licence Foundation Ltd web site at http://www.ecdl.org

## Exercise 2G

Open the file **College Investment Club**.

In this exercise we will consider the options open to a **College Investment Club** which has up to **€5,000** of members' cash to invest over a period of one year.

The sums of money they may invest are as follows:
**€1000, €2000, €3000, €4000, €5000**

The interest rates on offer are:
**1.5%, 1.75%, 2.0%, 2.25%, 2.5%, 3.0%, 3.25%** and **3.5%**

Calculate the return by using a **Two-Input Data Table**.

1   Highlight the range **A8:F15**. Select **Data** followed by **Table**.

2   For **Row input cell**: select cell **B4**. For **Column input cell**: select cell **B5**.

3   Now click on **OK**.

    The table fills with the relevant data.

4   Save the file as **College Investment Club Solution**.

**NOTE**

You will have noted the PMT formula in cell B6. You will recognise how useful the two-input data table is when it comes to calculating annuities and mortgages.

## Section 3    Protection

### 3.1    Protecting a Worksheet (4.1.3.1)

**Musical Eggs** is a small Internet company set up earlier this year. The first selection of eggs play popular pieces of classical music including Mozart's Symphony No. 40, Debussy's Claire de Lune and Bach's Brandenburg Concerto No. 3. So tune in and read on!

- Open the file **Musical Eggs**.

- Select **Protection** from the **Tools** menu and **Protect Sheet...** from the sub-menu.

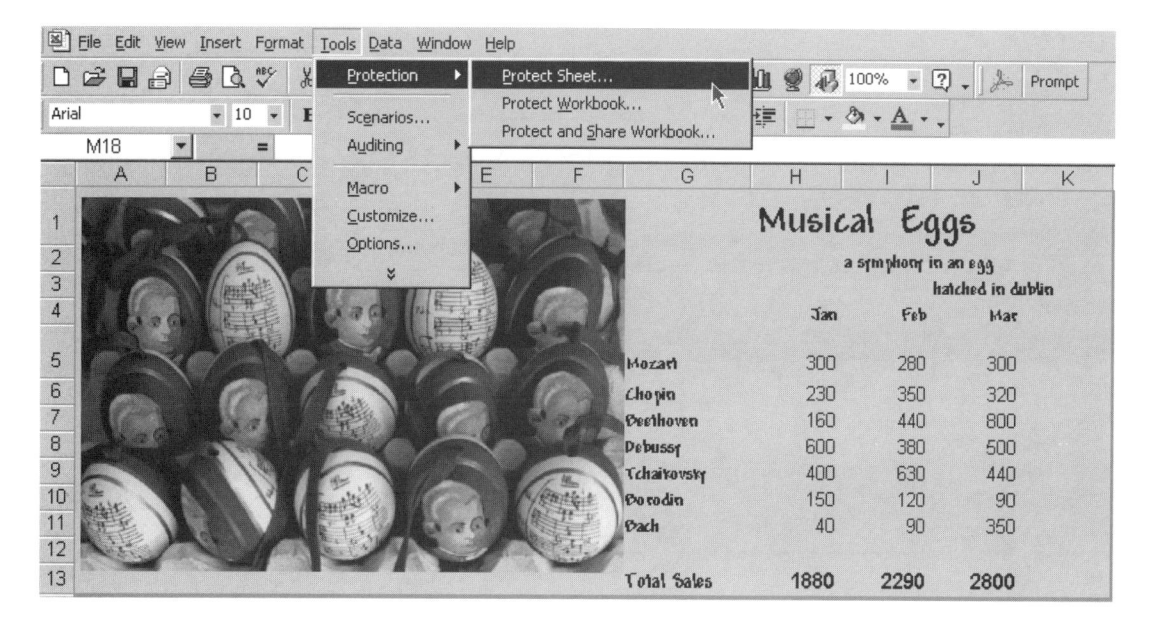

The **Protect Sheet dialog** box opens. There is an option to protect worksheet for Contents, Objects and Scenarios. The password is optional.
We will insert a password.

You can choose any password you like but to keep in the spirit of musical eggs, we will use **mozart40** (lower case). This is the only password we will use. If you choose your own password, use only that one password for all of the exercises that follow. Write your own password down now.

- Insert the optional password: **mozart40**     mozart40 is password

- Click **OK**.

**NOTE**

Passwords can be up to 255 characters in length. Use alphanumeric passwords, which are harder to 'crack'. Keep passwords safe in a personal diary or store in Word with a password - which should be written down safely. There is no easy way!

The **Confirm Password dialog** box opens.

- Re-enter the password: **mozart40**

- Click **OK**.

Let us see if the worksheet is protected.

- Select cell **H10** and attempt to change the number of **Borodin Musical Eggs** sold from **150** to **200**.

The following message is received.

We are unable to make the changes in the worksheet as the sheet is protected. To make the changes we have to unprotect the worksheet.

## 3.2 Unprotecting a Worksheet

- Select **Tools** followed by **Protection** and choose **Unprotect Sheet** from the sub-menu.

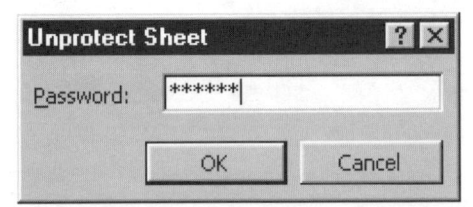

The **Unprotect Sheet dialog** box opens.

- Insert the password: **mozart40** and click **OK**.

- Now go back to cell **H10** and replace the figure of **150** with **200**.

There should be no problem changing the sales figure as the worksheet is no longer protected.

## 3.3 Protecting designated cells in a worksheet with a password
(4.1.3.2)

The cells we want to protect is the range **H13:J13**. (Total Sales range).

- Highlight the range **H13:J13**.

- Choose **Format** followed by **Cells**. Select the **Protection** tab.

- Cells are **Locked** by default.

- Leave **Hidden** unchecked at present.

- Click **OK**.

  The range is not protected. You can change any of the values. The worksheet has to be protected first.

- Choose **Tools** followed by **Protection** and **Protect Sheet**. If you wish, you can insert a password. (**Musical Eggs** suggest **mozart40** as the password).

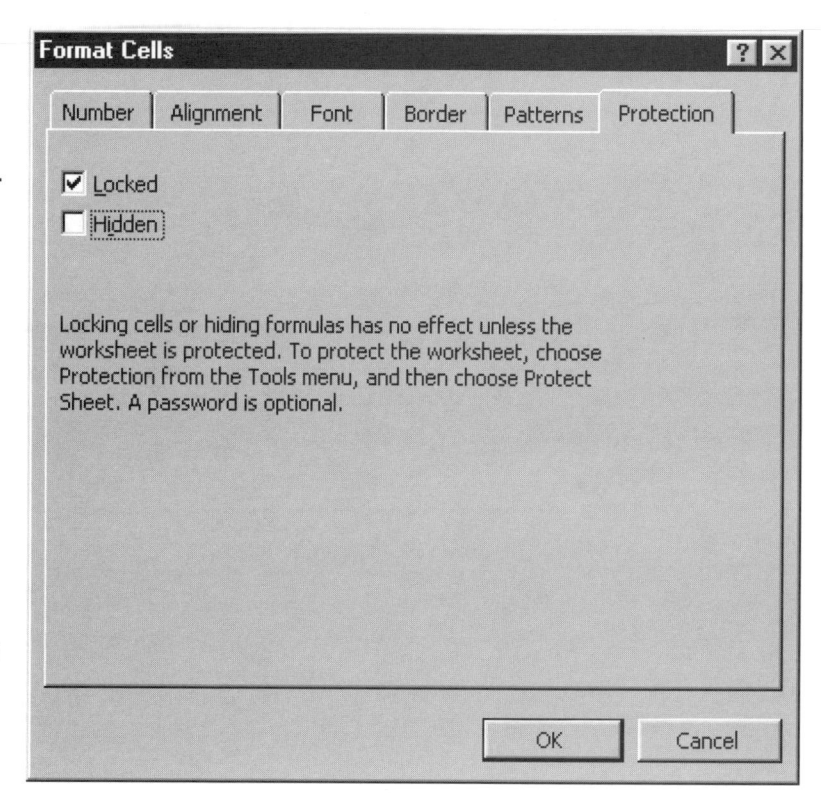

To remove the password, choose **Tools** followed by **Protection** followed by **Unprotect Sheet**. Insert password and click **OK**.

## 3.4 Unprotecting Cells (4.1.3.2)

- Select **Format** followed by **Cells…**. Choose the **Protection** tab. Uncheck the **Locked** option.

- Click **OK**.

## 3.5 Protecting formula in a cell

Click on the tab **Egg Testing Unit**.

Cell **F23** contains the formula which calculates the **Selling Price** of a Musical egg

- Click on cell **F23**. The formula is not visible in the Formula Bar.

- Select **Format** followed by **Cells**. Cells is greyed out and we are unable to access **Format cells Protection** tab.

- Select **Tools** followed by **Protection** and select **Unprotect Sheet** from the sub-menu.

- Type in **mozart40** (remember lower case).

The formula for the cell is now visible in the formula Toolbar.

- Save the file as **Musical Egg** and close.

The practice exercises contained in this section relate solely to this manual and do not constitute, or imply, certification by the European Driving Licence Foundation in respect of any ECDL examinations. For details on sitting ECDL examinations in your country please contact the local ECDL/ICDL licensee or visit the European Computer Driving Licence Foundation Ltd web site at http://www.ecdl.com

## Exercise 3A

1   Open the file **Seaside Garden Centre**.

2   Cell **D27** gives **520** as the bulb sales for **2004**. The figure is inaccurate. Insert the true figure of **630**.

3   You receive the message that the worksheet is protected.

4   Following the advice given, **unprotect** the worksheet and make the required change to the sales figure. (The password is **mozart40**).

5   Now select **Protection** from the **Tools** menu and **Protect Sheet...**

6   Choose a password and save and close the file.

## Section 4    Security

### 4.1    Setting a password to open a workbook (4.1.4.1)

- Open the file **Musical Eggs**.

- Select **Save As** from the **File** drop-down menu.

- Click on the **Tools icon** and select **General Options**....

If you want to create a backup file then select, **Always create backup**. Also, a password can be specified to **open** the workbook and a password to **modify** the workbook.
Do not select **Always create backup**.

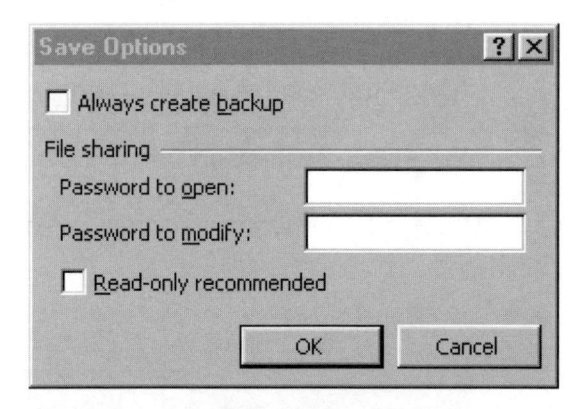

- Select the password **mozart40** as the **Password to open** and use the same password as **Password to modify**.

- Also click on **Read-only recommended**.

- Click **OK**.

    You will be asked to confirm your password.

- Confirm password as **mozart40** and click **OK**.

- Save the file with the passwords.

- Close the file.

    We will now reopen the file and see what protection the worksheet has.

Chapter 1 - Editing

- Open the file **Musical Eggs**.

    We are informed that Musical Eggs is protected and a Password is required.

- Insert the password and click **OK**.

    You are informed that Musical Eggs is reserved by user.

- Enter the required password and click **OK**.

    Since we selected the **Read-only recommended** box we receive the following message. You can encourage your colleagues to open the document as **read-only**.

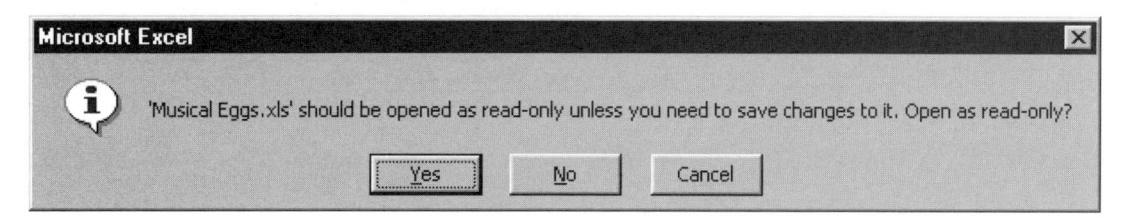

- You can select either **Yes** or **No**.

- In this case, select **No**.

    The document opens.

## 4.2 Using a Password to protect a workbook

- Select **Tools** followed by **Protection**, then, **Protect Workbook**.

  The password is optional but we will insert our password.

- Insert the password and click **OK**.

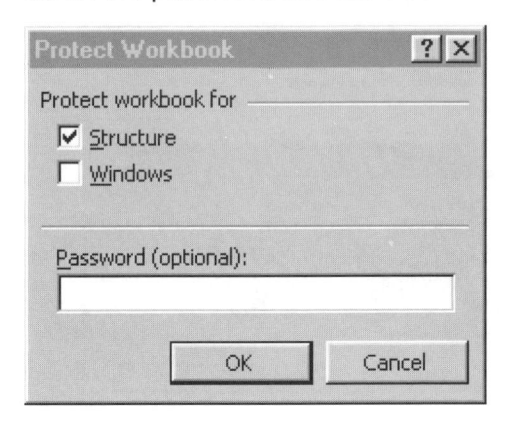

  You are asked to Confirm Password.

- Confirm password and click **OK**.

- Save the file and close. When you open the file again you are prompted for a password.

## 4.3 Removing Password protection from a worksheet (4.1.4.2)

- Open **Musical Eggs**.

- Select **Save as** from the **File** drop-down menu.

- Select **Tools** followed by **General Options**.

  The **Save Options dialog** box opens.

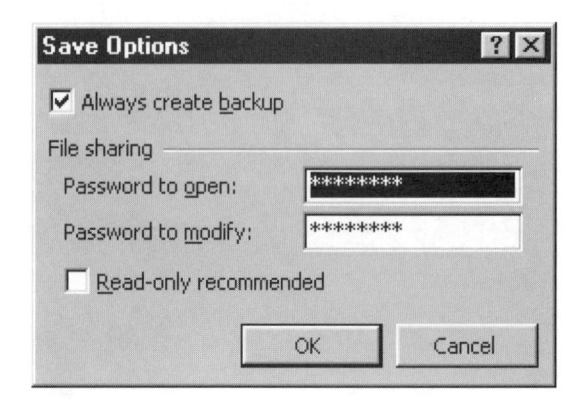

- Delete the Password from the **Password to open** option and also from the **Password to modify** option.

  All the **asterisks** should be deleted.

- Click **OK** and save the file with the changes.

The practice exercises contained in this section relate solely to this manual and do not constitute, or imply, certification by the European Driving Licence Foundation in respect of any ECDL examinations. For details on sitting ECDL examinations in your country please contact the local ECDL/ICDL licensee or visit the European Computer Driving Licence Foundation Ltd web site at http://www.ecdl.com

## Exercise 4A

When prompted the password is **mozart40**.

1.  Open the file **Seaside Garden Sales**.

2.  Type in password.

3.  Remove protection from the worksheet.

4.  Remove protection from the workbook.

5.  Save the file and close.

## Self Check Exercises

1. If you wanted to calculate the monthly repayments on a mortgage, given a range of rates and varying time periods, -you would use a two-input data table. - True or False?
   - ☐ True
   - ☐ False

2. What is the correct procedure for naming a range in a worksheet?
   - ☐ Choose Insert, Name, Define - and then type name in Define Name dialog box.
   - ☐ Choose Insert, Create, Define – and then type name in Define Name dialog box.
   - ☐ Choose Format, Insert, Define – and then type name in Define Name dialog box.

3. How do you freeze row and column titles?
   - ☐ Select Window and choose Split.
   - ☐ Select Window and choose Freeze Panes.
   - ☐ Select Window followed by Arrange, and choose Tiled from the available options.

4. When a text file is being imported into Excel, delimiters are used in the procedure. Which of the following are delimiters?
   - ☐ Tab, Comma
   - ☐ Space, semicolon
   - ☐ Windows (ANSI), Fixed width

5. There are 17 possible options when you apply automatic formatting to a cell range. - True or False?
   - ☐ True
   - ☐ False

6. How will the following custom number format return the value 25000?

   Code:  #,###
   - ☐ 25000
   - ☐ 25,000
   - ☐ 2.5,000
   - ☐ 2.500

7. In the following formula, what function name does 1 refer to?

   =SUBTOTAL(1, B10:B24)
   - ☐ AVERAGE
   - ☐ COUNTA
   - ☐ SUM

8. What cell names would return the message above?
   - ☐ Profit.QTR1
   - ☐ Profit_QTR1
   - ☐ Profit-QTR1
   - ☐ D24

The practice exercises contained in this section relate solely to this manual and do not constitute, or imply, certification by the European Driving Licence Foundation in respect of any ECDL examinations. For details on sitting ECDL examinations in your country please contact the local ECDL/ICDL licensee or visit the European Computer Driving Licence Foundation Ltd web site at http://www.ecdl.com

## Practical Exercises

### Exercise 1

1   Open the file **Car Loan** and click on the **Loan 1** tab. We are going to calculate the monthly repayments on a car loan over a fixed term.

2   Select cell **D8**. We will insert the **PMT** function in this cell. Type in the formula as follows:

   **=PMT(C8/12,D5,-D4)** and select enter. This returns a value of **354.29**.

3   Now, highlight the range **C8:D17**. Choose the **Table** command from the **Data** menu. The Table dialog box opens. Select the **Column input** cell and select cell **C8**. Now click on **OK**. The one-input data table is completed showing the repayments due at the varying interest rates.

4   Save the file as **Car Loan Solution** but do not close.

### Exercise 2

1   Open the file **Car Loan** and click on the **Loan 2** tab. Select cell **C7**. The PMT formula is already inserted. Highlight the range **C7:H17**. Now choose **Table** from the **Data** menu. The **Table dialog** box opens. This is a two-input data table so we have two entries to make.

   In the Row input cell: **D5**
   In the Column input cell: **D6**

2   The two-input data table displays the **what-if** values.

3   Save the file as **Car Loan Solution**

# Chapter 2

## Data Handling

## Chapter 2 – Data Handling

**AM4.2.1 Sorting** — Page
- AM4.2.1.1    Sort data by multiple columns    67
- AM4.2.1.2    Perform custom sorts    69

**AM4.2.2 Querying / Filtering**
- AM4.2.2.1    Create a single or multiple criteria query using available options    74-78
- AM4.2.2.2    Use advanced query / filter options    81

**AM4.2.3 Linking**
- AM4.2.3.1    Link data / chart within a worksheet    83
- AM4.2.3.2    Link data / chart between worksheets    84
- AM4.2.3.3    Link data / chart / between spreadsheets    87
- AM4.2.3.4    Link data / chart into a word processing document    89
- AM4.2.3.5    Consolidate data in adjacent worksheets using a 3D sum function    92

**AM4.2.4 Templates**
- AM4.2.4.1    Use a template    94
- AM4.2.4.2    Edit a template    96

**AM4.2.5 Charts & Graphs**
- AM4.2.5.1    Change angle of pie chart slices    98
- AM4.2.5.2    Format chart axes numbers or text    100
- AM4.2.5.3    Re-position title, legend, or data labels in a chart    103
- AM4.2.5.4    'Explode' all the segments in a pie chart    107
- AM4.2.5.5    Delete a data series in a chart    109
- AM4.2.5.6    Modify the chart type for a defined data series    111
- AM4.2.5.7    Widen the gap between columns / bars in a 2D chart    114
- AM4.2.5.8    Insert an image in a 2D chart    116, 118

# Section 1     Sorting

**Lighting Stock** is an Excel list that records the sales of lamps and lights. The list is a flat-file database with the following characteristics:

- Each **column** is a **field**. E.g. Stock Code, Description and Location are all fields.

- Each **row** is a **record**.

- The entire **database**, field names and records are referred to as a **list**.

There is a limitation on the size of a list. It can have 256 fields (columns) and 65,535 records (rows). Although there are 65,536 rows in a spreadsheet, the first row is used for field names. You can if you wish format the first row containing the field names in a different manner from the rest of the rows, which contain the information.

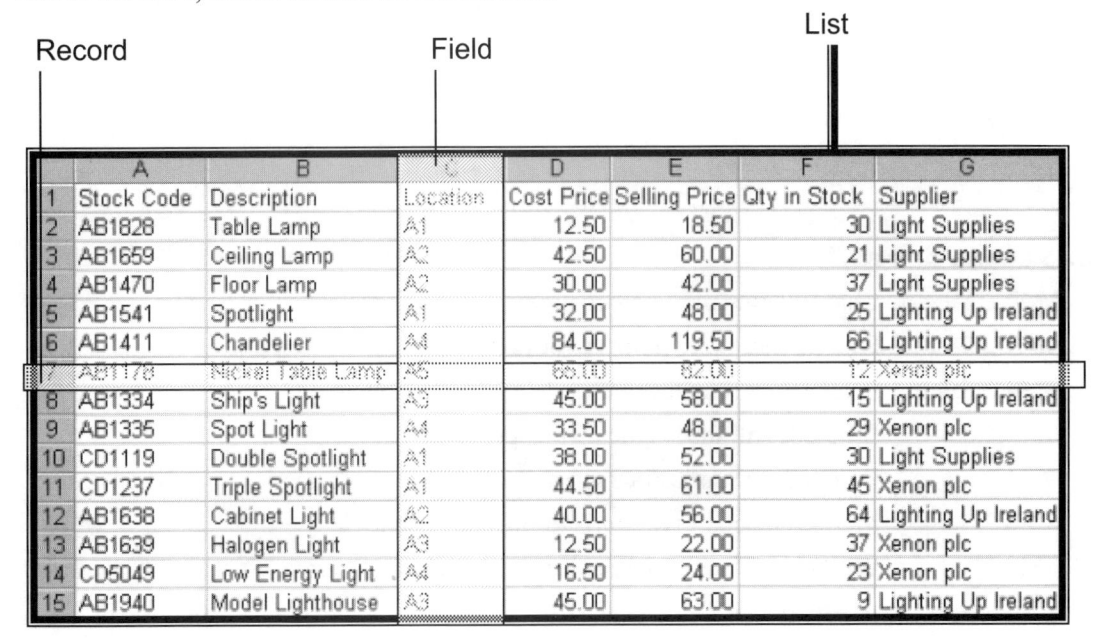

|  | A | B | C | D | E | F | G |
|---|---|---|---|---|---|---|---|
| 1 | Stock Code | Description | Location | Cost Price | Selling Price | Qty in Stock | Supplier |
| 2 | AB1828 | Table Lamp | A1 | 12.50 | 18.50 | 30 | Light Supplies |
| 3 | AB1659 | Ceiling Lamp | A2 | 42.50 | 60.00 | 21 | Light Supplies |
| 4 | AB1470 | Floor Lamp | A3 | 30.00 | 42.00 | 37 | Light Supplies |
| 5 | AB1541 | Spotlight | A1 | 32.00 | 48.00 | 25 | Lighting Up Ireland |
| 6 | AB1411 | Chandelier | A4 | 84.00 | 119.50 | 66 | Lighting Up Ireland |
| 7 | AB1178 | Nickel Table Lamp | A5 | 65.00 | 82.00 | 12 | Xenon plc |
| 8 | AB1334 | Ship's Light | A3 | 45.00 | 58.00 | 15 | Lighting Up Ireland |
| 9 | AB1335 | Spot Light | A4 | 33.50 | 48.00 | 29 | Xenon plc |
| 10 | CD1119 | Double Spotlight | A1 | 38.00 | 52.00 | 30 | Light Supplies |
| 11 | CD1237 | Triple Spotlight | A1 | 44.50 | 61.00 | 45 | Xenon plc |
| 12 | AB1638 | Cabinet Light | A2 | 40.00 | 56.00 | 64 | Lighting Up Ireland |
| 13 | AB1639 | Halogen Light | A3 | 12.50 | 22.00 | 37 | Xenon plc |
| 14 | CD5049 | Low Energy Light | A4 | 16.50 | 24.00 | 23 | Xenon plc |
| 15 | AB1940 | Model Lighthouse | A3 | 45.00 | 63.00 | 9 | Lighting Up Ireland |

## 1.1    Sorting data by a single column

We will do a sort on a single field, the Stock Code field.

- Open the file **Lighting Stock**.

- Select any cell in the **Stock Code** field. i.e. in the range **A1:A15**.

- Select **Data** followed by **Sort**. The **Sort dialog** box opens.

    The first field name, **Stock Code** has been selected in the **Sort by** box. (If not click the drop-down arrow and select **Stock Code**).

Chapter 2 – Data Handling

**Primary** sort

**Then by** boxes are used if the **Primary** sort field has more than one record with the same value.

Ensure that **Header row** is selected otherwise the header will be sorted along with the data.

Select Options… for Custom Sorts

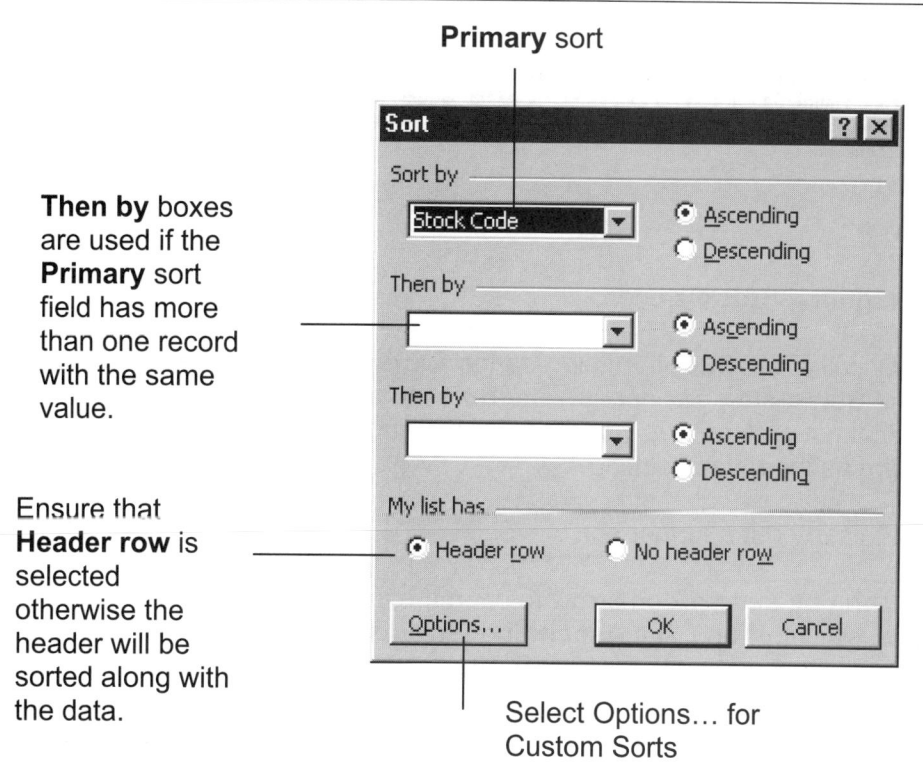

- Click **OK**. The list is sorted in **Ascending** (low to high) order of **Stock Code**.

  To sort in descending (high to low) order of Stock Code you would select the **Descending** option.

  Do not save or close file.

## 1.2 Sorting data by multiple columns (4.2.1.1)

It is possible to sort by up to **three** fields by using **Sort by** and both **Then by** options.

- Place cursor in **List** i.e. any cell in the range **A1:G15**.

- Select **Data** followed by **Sort**.

  The Sort dialog box opens. Choose **Description** as the **Sort by** option. Ensure **Ascending** is selected. Now choose **Then by** and select **Location** from the drop-down menu. **Ascending** should also be selected. The Second **Then by** entry should be blank (None).

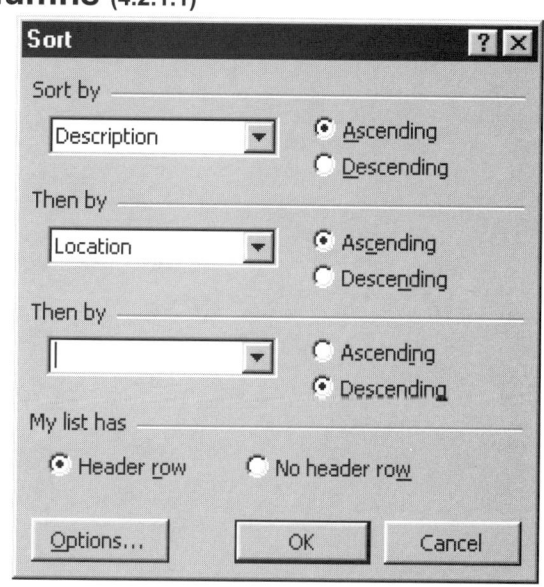

- Now click **OK**.

  The list is sorted on two columns (fields).

- Close the file but do not save changes.

The practice exercises contained in this section relate solely to this manual and do not constitute, or imply, certification by the European Driving Licence Foundation in respect of any ECDL examinations. For details on sitting ECDL examinations in your country please contact the local ECDL/ICDL licensee or visit the European Computer Driving Licence Foundation Ltd web site at http://www.ecdl.com

## Exercise 1A

Ensure the File **Lighting Stock** is open.

1   Select any cell in the **Supplier** field – range **G1:G15**. Choose **Data** followed by **Sort**. The **Sort dialog** box opens. The **Sort by** box will contain the word **Supplier**. If not click on arrow of drop-down menu and select **Supplier**. Accept **Ascending** as the default setting.

   We want to carry out a further sort.

2   Choose **Then by** and click on arrow to open the drop-down menu. From the menu choose **Location**. The **Ascending** button should be selected. In the next **Then by** option leave blank or select **(none)**. Choose **OK**.

   The list is sorted first by **Supplier** in alphabetic order, then by **Location**, also in alphabetic order.

3   Close the file but do not save changes.

## 1.3 Performing Custom Sorts (4.2.1.2)

- Open the file **Lighting Stock** and select the tab for sheet **Custom Sort**.

It is possible to carry out custom sorts. The list shows the monthly sales of Low Energy Lights in the year 2002, by three salespersons, Maria, Jason and John.
We want to view Maria's sales with the highest month's sales first and the lowest sales last.

- Select any cell in the field **Maria** – cell range **B4:B16**.

- Choose the **Sort Descending** icon on the Standard toolbar.

- The data is sorted from highest sales to lowest sales.

- Now choose the **Sort Ascending** button on the Standard toolbar. The data is sorted from the lowest sales to the highest sales.

|    | A         | B     | C     | D    |
|----|-----------|-------|-------|------|
| 1  |           |       |       |      |
| 2  |           | Low Energy Light Sales | | |
| 3  |           |       |       |      |
| 4  | Month     | Maria | Jason | John |
| 5  | June      | 24    | 77    | 12   |
| 6  | September | 30    | 43    | 19   |
| 7  | January   | 28    | 55    | 24   |
| 8  | July      | 18    | 58    | 33   |
| 9  | August    | 30    | 78    | 45   |
| 10 | November  | 38    | 52    | 50   |
| 11 | December  | 35    | 88    | 63   |
| 12 | April     | 22    | 67    | 66   |
| 13 | February  | 32    | 76    | 68   |
| 14 | May       | 12    | 43    | 77   |
| 15 | October   | 56    | 60    | 80   |
| 16 | March     | 60    | 70    | 85   |

Maria's sales sorted in Ascending order.

|    | A         | B     | C     | D    |
|----|-----------|-------|-------|------|
| 1  |           |       |       |      |
| 2  |           | Low Energy Light S. | | |
| 3  |           |       |       |      |
| 4  | Month     | Maria | Jason | John |
| 5  | May       | 12    | 43    | 77   |
| 6  | July      | 18    | 58    | 33   |
| 7  | April     | 22    | 67    | 66   |
| 8  | June      | 24    | 77    | 12   |
| 9  | January   | 28    | 55    | 24   |
| 10 | August    | 30    | 78    | 45   |
| 11 | September | 30    | 43    | 19   |
| 12 | February  | 32    | 76    | 68   |
| 13 | December  | 35    | 88    | 63   |
| 14 | November  | 38    | 52    | 50   |
| 15 | October   | 56    | 60    | 80   |
| 16 | March     | 60    | 70    | 85   |

Suppose we want to view Maria's sales chronologically in order of month, e.g. from January to December?

- Click on any cell in the **Month** field – range **A4:A16**, and choose the **Sort Ascending** icon. The months are arranged in *alphabetic* order and not in *chronological* order.

|    | A | B |
|----|---|---|
| 1  |   |   |
| 2  |   | Low E. |
| 3  |   |   |
| 4  | Month | Maria |
| 5  | April | 22 |
| 6  | August | 30 |
| 7  | December | 35 |
| 8  | February | 32 |
| 9  | January | 28 |
| 10 | July | 18 |
| 11 | June | 24 |
| 12 | March | 60 |
| 13 | May | 12 |
| 14 | November | 38 |
| 15 | October | 56 |
| 16 | September | 30 |

To arrange the months in chronological order we must perform a custom sort.

- Select any cell in the **Month** field - Range **A4:A16**.

- Choose **Data** followed by **Sort**.

    The **Sort by** box should have **Month** as entry. Both **Then by** boxes should be empty.

- Click on the **Options** button to display the **Sort Options** dialog box. Now choose the down arrow of the **First key sort order** section of the dialog box. Choose **January, February, March** etc. Then click on the **OK** button to select.

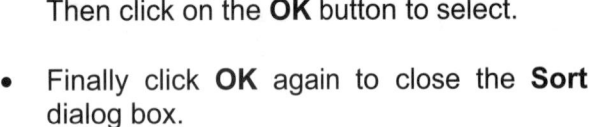

- Finally click **OK** again to close the **Sort** dialog box.

    The months are sorted in chronological order and Maria's sales can be read from January to December.

- Save the file and close.

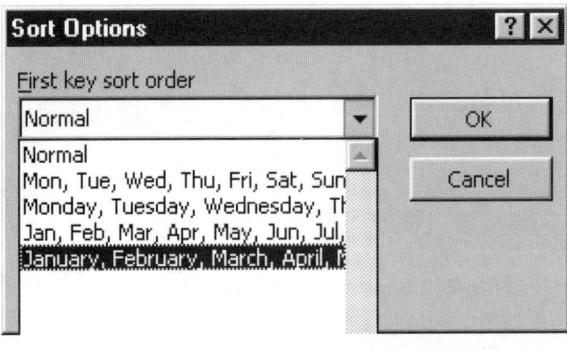

|    | A | B | C | D |
|----|---|---|---|---|
| 1  |   |   |   |   |
| 2  |   | Low Energy Light S |   |   |
| 3  |   |   |   |   |
| 4  | Month | Maria | Jason | John |
| 5  | January | 28 | 55 | 24 |
| 6  | February | 32 | 76 | 68 |
| 7  | March | 60 | 70 | 85 |
| 8  | April | 22 | 67 | 66 |
| 9  | May | 12 | 43 | 77 |
| 10 | June | 24 | 77 | 12 |
| 11 | July | 18 | 58 | 33 |
| 12 | August | 30 | 78 | 45 |
| 13 | September | 30 | 43 | 19 |
| 14 | October | 56 | 60 | 80 |
| 15 | November | 38 | 52 | 50 |
| 16 | December | 35 | 88 | 63 |

**NOTE**

You can create your own custom sorts: For example you may want to sort in the following order: Low, Medium, High *or* North, South, East, West or Ulster, Leinster, Munster, Connaught or Spring, Summer, Autumn, Winter.

### 1.3.1 Creating an original custom sort

We are going to create a custom sort involving the terms **Low**, **Medium** and **High**.

- Ensure file **Lighting Stock** is open.
- Select the sheet tab **Original Custom Sort**.
- Select **Tools** followed by **Options** and select the tab **Custom Lists**. In **List** entries add **Low**, **Medium**, **High**.
- Click **Add** followed by **OK**.

We will use the custom sort we have just created in the next exercise, Exercise 1B.

---

The practice exercises contained in this section relate solely to this manual and do not constitute, or imply, certification by the European Driving Licence Foundation in respect of any ECDL examinations. For details on sitting ECDL examinations in your country please contact the local ECDL/ICDL licensee or visit the European Computer Driving Licence Foundation Ltd web site at http://www.ecdl.com

## Exercise 1B

The sales data for three persons is shown.

1. Select any cell in the **Sales** field. (**Range A3:A6**) Choose **Data** followed by **Sort**. The **Sort by** box should indicate **Sales**. Click on the **Options...** button.

2. The **First key sort order** will indicate **Normal**. Select the drop-down arrow key and choose **Low, Medium, High**. Click **OK**, followed by **OK**.

   The sales are sorted in the order Low, Medium, High.

3. Save your work and close.

# Section 2   Querying / Filtering

The **AutoFilter** feature puts drop-down menus in the titles of each column. The menus are used to select criteria in the column so that only those records that meet the criteria are displayed. The AutoFilter is quite straightforward to use but has limitations.
The **Advanced Filter** lets you specify even more criteria than the AutoFilter.
First, we will look at AutoFilter.

- Open the file **Lighting Stock** and select sheet tab **List**.

- Click on any cell within the list. (Range **A1:G15**)

- Select **Data**, followed by **Filter**, followed by **AutoFilter**.

    **AutoFilter arrows** are displayed next to each column title.

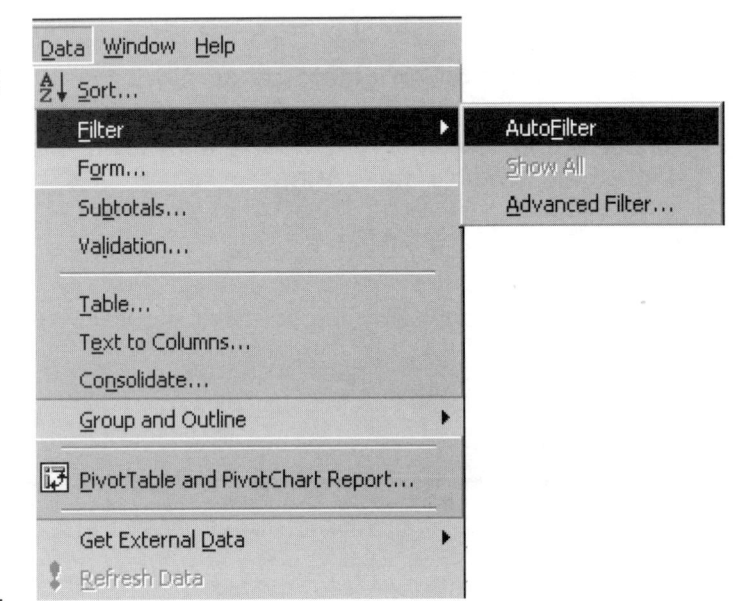

AutoFilter arrow

Clicking on the AutoFilter arrow will show one entry for each category in the column

| | A | B | C | D | E | F | G |
|---|---|---|---|---|---|---|---|
| 1 | Stock Code | Description | Location | Cost Price | Selling Price | Qty in Stock | Supplier |
| 2 | AB1638 | Cabinet Light | A2 | 40.00 | 56.00 | 64 | Lighting Up Ireland |
| 3 | AB1659 | Ceiling Lamp | A2 | 42.50 | 60.00 | 21 | Light Supplies |
| 4 | AB1411 | Chandelier | A4 | 84.00 | 119.50 | 66 | Lighting Up Ireland |
| 5 | CD1119 | Double Spotlight | A1 | 38.00 | 52.00 | 30 | Light Supplies |
| 6 | AB1470 | Floor Lamp | A2 | 30.00 | 42.00 | 37 | Light Supplies |
| 7 | AB1639 | Halogen Light | A3 | 12.50 | 22.00 | 37 | Xenon plc |
| 8 | CD5049 | Low Energy Light | A4 | 16.50 | 24.00 | 23 | Xenon plc |
| 9 | AB1940 | Model Lighthouse | A3 | 46.00 | 63.00 | 9 | Lighting Up Ireland |
| 10 | AB1178 | Nickel Table Lamp | A3 | 65.00 | 82.00 | 12 | Xenon plc |
| 11 | AB1334 | Ship's Light | A3 | 45.00 | 58.00 | 15 | Lighting Up Ireland |
| 12 | AB1541 | Spotlight | A1 | 32.00 | 48.00 | 25 | Lighting Up Ireland |
| 13 | AB1828 | Table Lamp | A2 | 12.50 | 18.50 | 30 | Light Supplies |
| 14 | CD1237 | Triple Spotlight | A1 | 44.50 | 61.00 | 45 | Xenon plc |
| 15 | AB1335 | Wall Light | A4 | 33.50 | 48.00 | 29 | Xenon plc |

- Click on the **AutoFilter** arrow for the field **Description**.

Chapter 2 – Data Handling

The drop-down menu shows one entry for each category in the column such as Cabinet Light, Ceiling Lamp etc. Note the All, (Top 10…) and (Custom…) options.

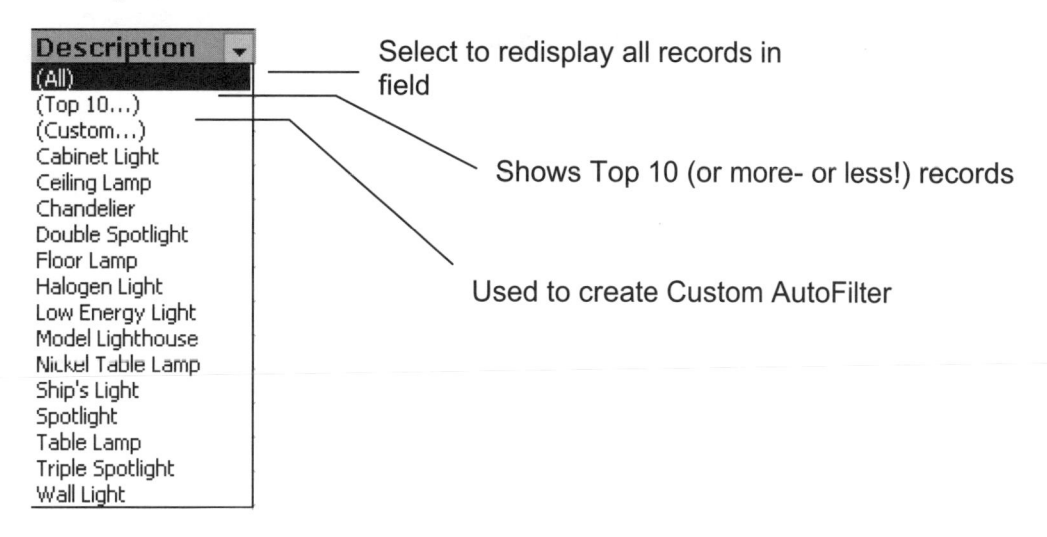

| Description ▼ | |
|---|---|
| (All) | Select to redisplay all records in field |
| (Top 10…) | |
| (Custom…) | Shows Top 10 (or more- or less!) records |
| Cabinet Light | |
| Ceiling Lamp | |
| Chandelier | |
| Double Spotlight | Used to create Custom AutoFilter |
| Floor Lamp | |
| Halogen Light | |
| Low Energy Light | |
| Model Lighthouse | |
| Nickel Table Lamp | |
| Ship's Light | |
| Spotlight | |
| Table Lamp | |
| Triple Spotlight | |
| Wall Light | |

- Choose **Data** followed by **Filter** and **AutoFilter** to remove AutoFilter.

- Click on any cell not in the list – i.e *outwith* the range **A1:G15**.

- Select **Data**, **Filter** followed by **AutoFilter**.

    An error message is given.

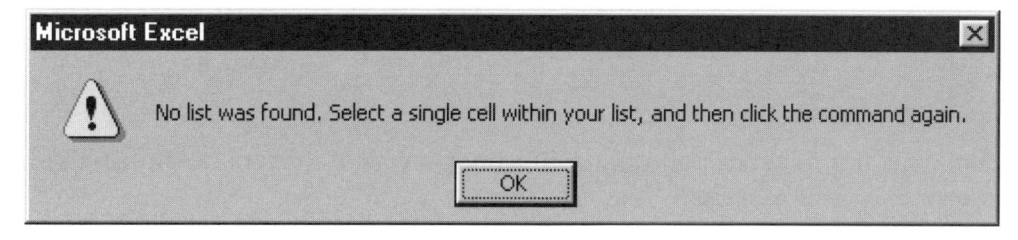

**Microsoft Excel**

⚠ No list was found. Select a single cell within your list, and then click the command again.

[ OK ]

You receive this message if a cell from the list is *not* selected prior to using filters.

Chapter 2 – Data Handling

## 2.1 Using AutoFilter to find records using a single criteria query (4.2.2.1)

- Display the AutoFilter by selecting **Data** followed by **Filter** then **AutoFilter**.

    We want to display only the records of the supplier Xenon plc.

- Click on the **AutoFilter arrow** of **Supplier**.

- Select **Xenon plc**.

    Supplier
    (All)
    (Top 10…)
    (Custom…)
    Light Supplies
    Lighting Up Ireland
    Xenon plc

    Only the records that meet the criteria we choose are displayed. You will notice that the **AutoFilter arrow** for **Supplier** is now **Blue** in colour. Also, only those Suppliers that meet the criteria are present. The row numbers are also **Blue** in colour.

    Row Numbers and AutoFilter arrows are blue in colour

|    | A | B | C | D | E | F | G |
|----|---|---|---|---|---|---|---|
|  1 | Stock Code | Description | Location | Cost Price | Selling Price | Qty in Stock | Supplier |
|  7 | AB1639 | Halogen Light | A3 | 12.50 | 22.00 | 37 | Xenon plc |
|  8 | CD5049 | Low Energy Light | A4 | 16.50 | 24.00 | 23 | Xenon plc |
| 10 | AB1178 | Nickel Table Lamp | A3 | 65.00 | 82.00 | 12 | Xenon plc |
| 14 | CD1237 | Triple Spotlight | A1 | 44.50 | 61.00 | 45 | Xenon plc |
| 15 | AB1335 | Wall Light | A4 | 33.50 | 48.00 | 29 | Xenon plc |

    To redisplay all the records click on the **Supplier** arrow and choose **All**. All the records should now be visible.

- To redisplay all the records choose **Data** followed by **Filter**, and then choose **AutoFilter** from the menu. Note the tick to the left of **AutoFilter** which indicates that it is active. This is the preferred method to redisplay all the records.

    ✓ AutoFilter
    Show All
    Advanced Filter…

The practice exercises contained in this section relate solely to this manual and do not constitute, or imply, certification by the European Driving Licence Foundation in respect of any ECDL examinations. For details on sitting ECDL examinations in your country please contact the local ECDL/ICDL licensee or visit the European Computer Driving Licence Foundation Ltd web site at http://www.ecdl.com

## Exercise 2A

Suppose we want to find only those lamps that are stored in location **A3**?

1    Click on the **AutoFilter arrow** for **Location**. Choose **A3** from the drop-down menu. Only the records that meet this criterion are displayed.

2    To redisplay all the records, select the **Location** arrow (It is **blue** in colour) and choose **All** from the drop-down menu. All the records are again displayed.

Now, we want to find only the information on **Stock Code 1334**.

3    Click on the **Stock Code AutoFilter arrow**. Choose **AB1334** from the drop-down menu. Only the information that meets this criterion is displayed. In this case it is a single record.

4    To redisplay all the records, choose the **Stock Code arrow** (It is **blue** in colour) and choose **All** from the drop-down menu. All the records are redisplayed.

## 2.2  Creating a multiple criteria query (4.2.2.1)

Suppose we want to filter data using more than one criterion. Say we want to sort the data in our list to display items in location **A4** from **Supplier, Lighting Up Ireland**.

- Select the **AutoFilter arrow** of **Supplier**. Choose **Lighting Up Ireland** from the drop-down menu.

  Only the records that meet the criteria are listed.

- Now choose the **AutoFilter arrow** of **Location** and select **A3** from the drop-down menu.

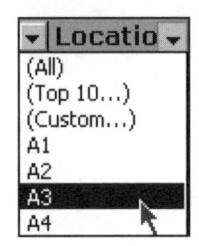

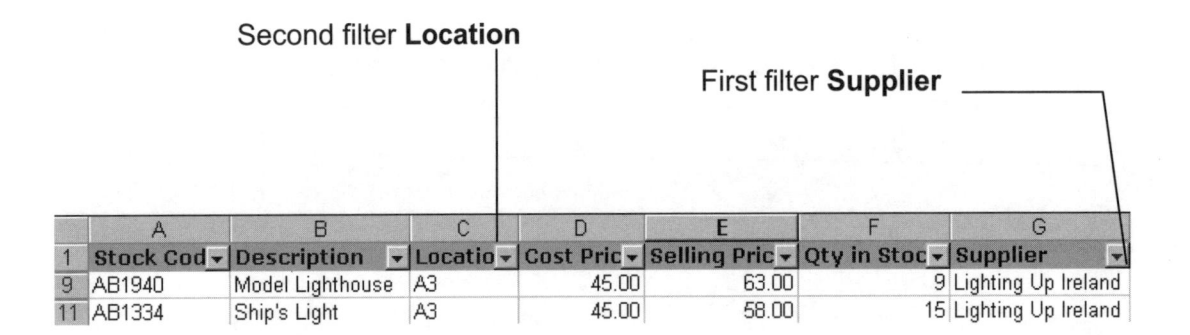

Second filter **Location**

First filter **Supplier**

| | A | B | C | D | E | F | G |
|---|---|---|---|---|---|---|---|
| 1 | Stock Cod | Description | Locatio | Cost Pric | Selling Pric | Qty in Stoc | Supplier |
| 9 | AB1940 | Model Lighthouse | A3 | 45.00 | 63.00 | 9 | Lighting Up Ireland |
| 11 | AB1334 | Ship's Light | A3 | 45.00 | 58.00 | 15 | Lighting Up Ireland |

The records that meet this multiple criteria are shown above.

- Select **Data** followed by **Filter** and then choose **AutoFilter** to remove AutoFilter options.

- Save file and close.

Chapter 2 – Data Handling

## 2.3 Creating a multiple criteria query with a custom filter (4.2.2.1)

If we want to find those items supplied by Lighting Up Ireland whose cost price is greater than or equal to 40.00, we do it as follows.

- Open the file **Lighting Stock**. Then select **Data** followed by **Filter**. From the drop-down menu choose **AutoFilter**.

- Click the **Supplier AutoFilter arrow** and from the drop-down menu choose **Lighting Up Ireland**.

    The items that meet this criterion are displayed.

- Select the **AutoFilter arrow** of the field **Cost Price**.

    You will note that the cost prices are listed including 40.00 but we require Cost Prices *greater than or equal to* 40.00 so we must use the Custom option. If we required only an item equal to 40.00 we would simply select 40.00.

- Choose **Custom** from the drop-down menu.

    The **Custom AutoFilter** dialog box opens.

- Click on the drop-down menu for **Cost Price** and choose the option **is greater than or equal to**.

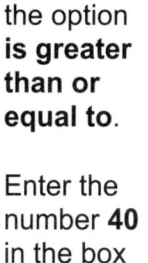

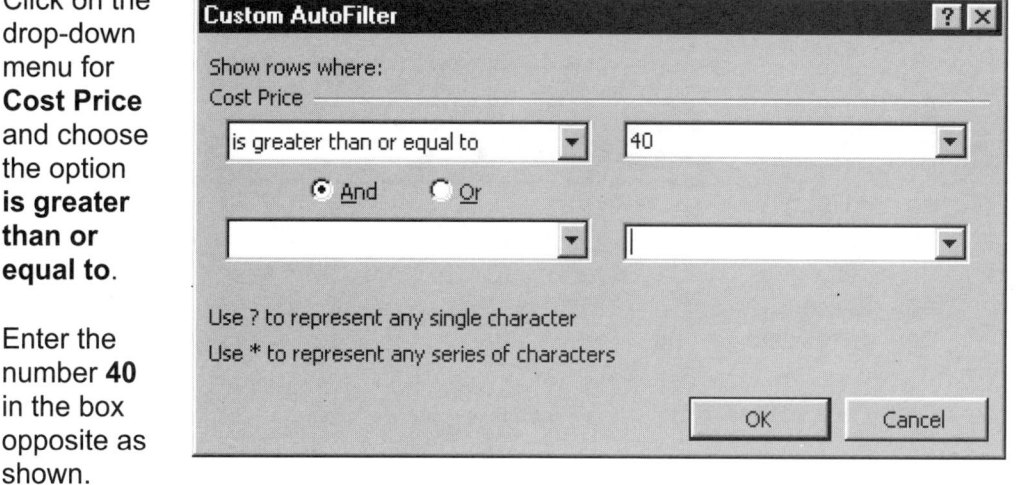

- Enter the number **40** in the box opposite as shown.
    Then click on **OK**.

    Only those items supplied by Lighting Up Ireland with a Cost Price greater than or equal to 40.00 are shown. (The order below may differ but it should contain the same items).

| Stock Code | Description | Location | Cost Price | Selling Price | Qty in Stock | Supplier |
|---|---|---|---|---|---|---|
| AB1638 | Cabinet Light | A2 | 40.00 | 56.00 | 64 | Lighting Up Ireland |
| AB1411 | Chandelier | A4 | 84.00 | 119.50 | 66 | Lighting Up Ireland |
| AB1940 | Model Lighthouse | A3 | 45.00 | 63.00 | 9 | Lighting Up Ireland |
| AB1334 | Ship's Light | A3 | 45.00 | 58.00 | 15 | Lighting Up Ireland |

- Choose **Data** followed by **Filter** then **Show All** to return the list to its original state.

Custom AutoFilter Operators

| Operator | Effect |
|---|---|
| = | Equal to |
| > | Greater than |
| < | Less than |
| >= | Greater than or equal to |
| <= | Less than or equal to |
| <> | Not equal to |

## 2.4 Creating a multiple criteria query using the And /Or Filters
(4.2.2.1)

Suppose we want to create a list of items whose Cost Price is greater than 32.00 and less than or equal to 44.50. We use the Custom AutoFilter for this. We also utilise the **And** filter.

- Click on any cell within the list.

- Now choose **Data** followed by **Filter** then **AutoFilter** from the drop-down menu.

- Click on the **AutoFilter arrow** in the **Cost Price** and select **Custom** from the drop-down menu.

    The **Custom AutoFilter** dialog box opens.

- Choose **is greater than** from the **Cost Price** drop-down dialog box. Click on the adjacent box (to the right) and from the drop-down menu choose **32.00**. (Alternatively you can simply type 32.00 in this box).

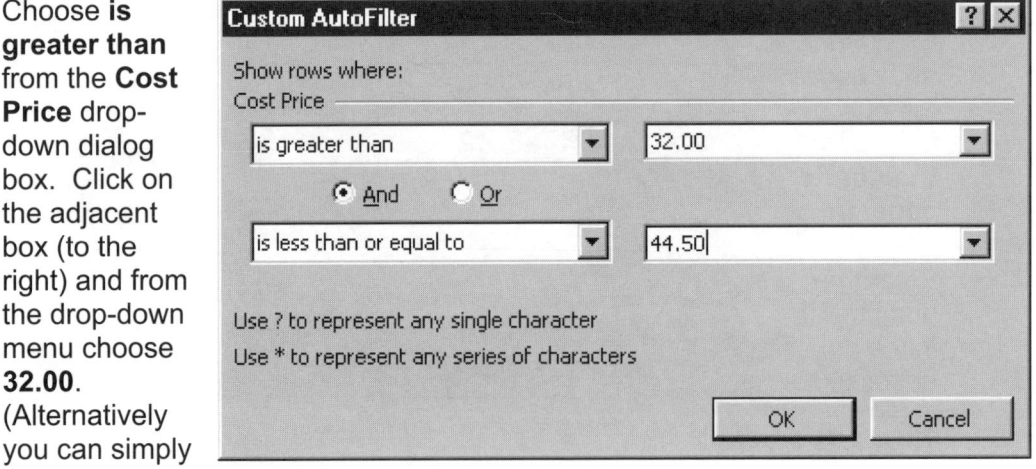

- Ensure **And** is selected. Now select **is less than or equal to** from the drop-down menu. Choose **44.50** from the drop-down menu adjacent (to the right of) this box.

- Click on **OK**.

# Chapter 2 – Data Handling

| Stock Code | Description | Location | Cost Price | Selling Price | Qty in Stock | Supplier |
|---|---|---|---|---|---|---|
| AB1638 | Cabinet Light | A2 | 40.00 | 56.00 | 64 | Lighting Up Ireland |
| AB1659 | Ceiling Lamp | A2 | 42.50 | 60.00 | 21 | Light Supplies |
| CD1119 | Double Spotlight | A1 | 38.00 | 52.00 | 30 | Light Supplies |
| CD1237 | Triple Spotlight | A1 | 44.50 | 61.00 | 45 | Xenon plc |
| AB1335 | Wall Light | A4 | 33.50 | 48.00 | 29 | Xenon plc |

The results are displayed above. (The order above may differ but it should contain the same items).

- To remove the AutoFilters select **Data** followed by **Filter** and **AutoFilter**.

The practice exercises contained in this section relate solely to this manual and do not constitute, or imply, certification by the European Driving Licence Foundation in respect of any ECDL examinations. For details on sitting ECDL examinations in your country please contact the local ECDL/ICDL licensee or visit the European Computer Driving Licence Foundation Ltd web site at http://www.ecdl.com

## Exercise 2B

In this example we want to find those objects produced by **Light Supplies** whose **Selling Price** is greater than **52.00** but *less than or equal to* **60.00**.

1   Select the AutoFilter arrow of **Selling Price** and choose **Custom...** from the drop-down menu. The Custom AutoFilter dialog box opens. Click on the drop-down menu of Selling Price and choose option – **is greater than**. Insert 52.00 in the adjacent box to right. Ensure the **And** radio button is selected. Choose **is less than or equal to** from the drop-down menu of the lower box. In the box to the right, either type in **60.00** or select 60.00 from the drop-down menu.

2   Select **OK**.

The result shows all those records that meet the criterion. These are the **Ship's Light**, **Ceiling Lamp** and **Cabinet Light**.

3   Choose **Data**, **Filter** followed by **Show All**.

## 2.5 Using the Top 10 AutoFilter

The **Top 10 AutoFilter** allows you to filter data in a greater number of ways than the name suggests.

- Choose **Data** followed by **Filter** then **AutoFilter**. Select the **AutoFilter arrow** of the **Qty in Stock** field then select **(Top 10…)**.

    The **Top 10 AutoFilter** dialog box opens with a number of options.

- Examine each of the drop-down menus in turn.

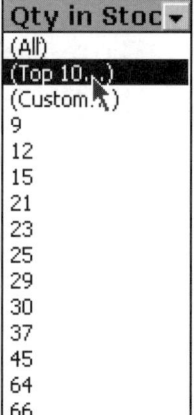

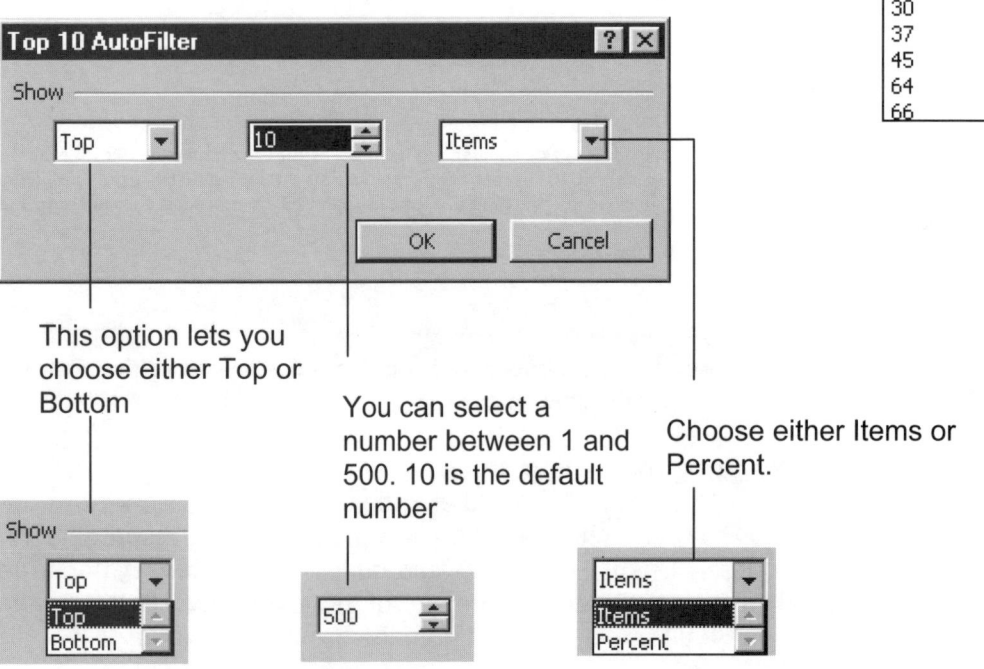

This option lets you choose either Top or Bottom

You can select a number between 1 and 500. 10 is the default number

Choose either Items or Percent.

- In the **Show** option select **Top**, in the next option choose **7** (though remember it can be the top 500 in a large list) and in the final option choose **Items**. Click **OK**.

| | A | B | C | D | E | F | G |
|---|---|---|---|---|---|---|---|
| 1 | Stock Code | Description | Location | Cost Price | Selling Price | Qty in Stock | Supplier |
| 2 | AB1828 | Table Lamp | A1 | 12.50 | 18.50 | 30 | Light Supplies |
| 4 | AB1470 | Floor Lamp | A2 | 30.00 | 42.00 | 37 | Light Supplies |
| 6 | AB1411 | Chandelier | A4 | 84.00 | 119.50 | 66 | Lighting Up Ireland |
| 10 | CD1119 | Double Spotlight | A1 | 38.00 | 52.00 | 30 | Light Supplies |
| 11 | CD1237 | Triple Spotlight | A1 | 44.50 | 61.00 | 45 | Xenon plc |
| 12 | AB1638 | Cabinet Light | A2 | 40.00 | 56.00 | 64 | Lighting Up Ireland |
| 13 | AB1639 | Halogen Light | A3 | 12.50 | 22.00 | 37 | Xenon plc |

You will notice that only the **Top 7** items are listed for **Qty in Stock**.

(The order above may differ but it should contain the same items).

- Remove the filter.

## 2.6 Using Advanced Query / Filter Options (4.2.2.2)

The Advanced Filter option is used for more complex filters. For example, to filter the list so that only those lamps located in **Location** A2 and A3, whose **Cost Price** is greater than 20 but less than 40 are listed. The last criterion required is that the **Qty in Stock** is greater than or equal to 37. It sounds complex but we are able to do this by using the Advanced Filter Option.

The first step is to list the relevant fields *below* the list. (Or above the list if there is space).

- First open the file **Lighting Stock**.

- List the field names, **Location**, **Cost Price** and **Qty in Stock** below the list in the locations shown in the figure below.

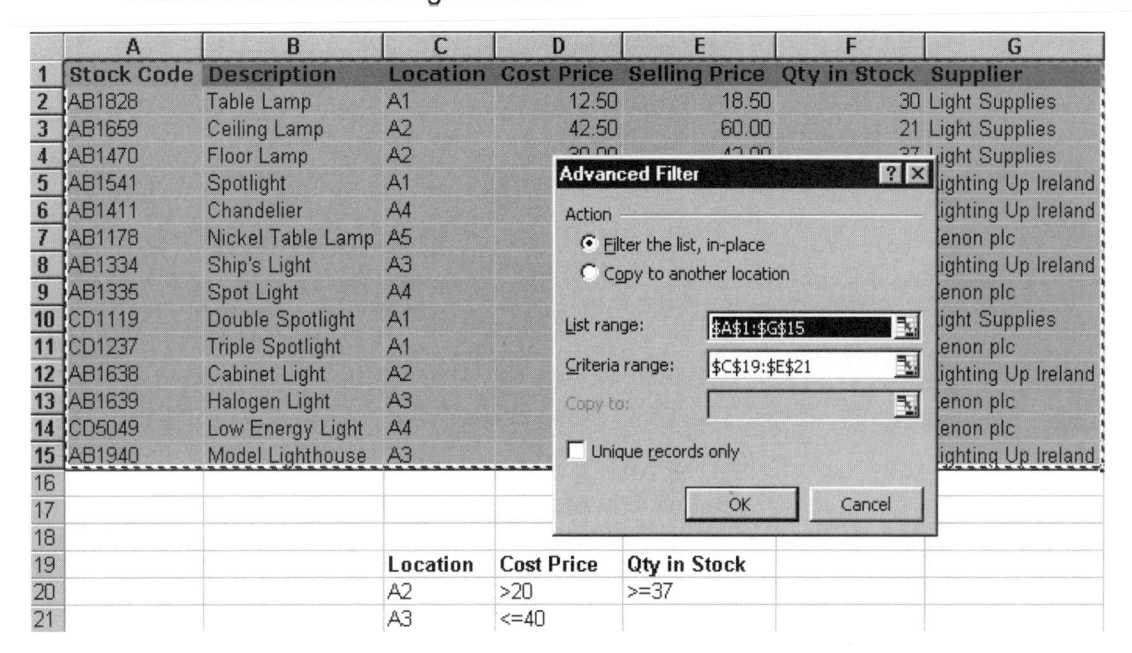

|    | A | B | C | D | E | F | G |
|----|---|---|---|---|---|---|---|
| 1  | Stock Code | Description | Location | Cost Price | Selling Price | Qty in Stock | Supplier |
| 2  | AB1828 | Table Lamp | A1 | 12.50 | 18.50 | 30 | Light Supplies |
| 3  | AB1659 | Ceiling Lamp | A2 | 42.50 | 60.00 | 21 | Light Supplies |
| 4  | AB1470 | Floor Lamp | A2 |  |  |  | Light Supplies |
| 5  | AB1541 | Spotlight | A1 |  |  |  | Lighting Up Ireland |
| 6  | AB1411 | Chandelier | A4 |  |  |  | Lighting Up Ireland |
| 7  | AB1178 | Nickel Table Lamp | A5 |  |  |  | enon plc |
| 8  | AB1334 | Ship's Light | A3 |  |  |  | Lighting Up Ireland |
| 9  | AB1335 | Spot Light | A4 |  |  |  | enon plc |
| 10 | CD1119 | Double Spotlight | A1 |  |  |  | Light Supplies |
| 11 | CD1237 | Triple Spotlight | A1 |  |  |  | enon plc |
| 12 | AB1638 | Cabinet Light | A2 |  |  |  | Lighting Up Ireland |
| 13 | AB1639 | Halogen Light | A3 |  |  |  | enon plc |
| 14 | CD5049 | Low Energy Light | A4 |  |  |  | enon plc |
| 15 | AB1940 | Model Lighthouse | A3 |  |  |  | Lighting Up Ireland |
| 16 |  |  |  |  |  |  |  |
| 17 |  |  |  |  |  |  |  |
| 18 |  |  |  |  |  |  |  |
| 19 |  |  | Location | Cost Price | Qty in Stock |  |  |
| 20 |  |  | A2 | >20 | >=37 |  |  |
| 21 |  |  | A3 | <=40 |  |  |  |

Advanced Filter dialog:
- Action: Filter the list, in-place / Copy to another location
- List range: $A$1:$G$15
- Criteria range: $C$19:$E$21
- Copy to:
- Unique records only

- Now insert the locations **A2** and **A3** under the field **Location**. Insert **>20** and **<=40** under the **Cost Price** field. Finally Insert **>=37** under the **Qty in Stock** field.

- Click on any cell within the list. Choose **Data** followed by **Filter**. Select **Advanced Filter...** and the **Advanced Filter** dialog box opens.

    The **List range** is already inserted in the List range box. You must now insert the **Criteria range**.

- Click in the **Criteria range** box. Drag over the filter criteria range **C19:E21** and the range is entered in the box.

- Click **OK**.

    The list is filtered showing the records that match the criteria listed.

**NOTE**

The **Unique records only** checkbox in the Advanced Filter dialog box is clicked to ensure no duplicate records are included in the filter.

|   | A | B | C | D | E | F | G |
|---|---|---|---|---|---|---|---|
| 1 | Stock Code | Description | Location | Cost Price | Selling Price | Qty in Stock | Supplier |
| 5 | AB1470 | Floor Lamp | A2 | 30.00 | 42.00 | 37 | Light Supplies |
| 8 | AB1638 | Cabinet Light | A2 | 40.00 | 56.00 | 64 | Lighting Up Ireland |
| 12 | AB1639 | Halogen Light | A3 | 12.50 | 22.00 | 37 | Xenon plc |
| 16 | | | | | | | |
| 17 | | | | | | | |
| 18 | | | | | | | |
| 19 | | | Location | Cost Price | Qty in Stock | | |
| 20 | | | A2 | >20 | >=37 | | |
| 21 | | | A3 | <40 | | | |

**NOTE**

The three items listed may be in a different order to that shown since you have already carried out a number of exercises on the list. However, only these three items should be listed.

The practice exercises contained in this section relate solely to this manual and do not constitute, or imply, certification by the European Driving Licence Foundation in respect of any ECDL examinations. For details on sitting ECDL examinations in your country please contact the local ECDL/ICDL licensee or visit the European Computer Driving Licence Foundation Ltd web site at http://www.ecdl.com

## Exercise 2C

In this exercise we are going to use the **Advanced Filter** option to determine those items located in **A3** whose **Cost Price** is greater than or equal to 40 and whose **Selling Price** is less than or equal to 60.

1  First open the file **Lighting Stock**. Then, list the field names **Location**, **Cost Price** and **Selling Price** below the list in any order.

2  Below the **Location** name insert: **A3**; below the **Cost Price** name insert: **>=40** and below the **Supplier Name** insert: **<=60**.

3  Click on any cell in the list. Select **Data** followed by **Filter** then **Advanced Filter…**. The **Advanced Filter dialog** box opens with the **List range** in the **list box**.

4  Insert the **Criteria range** by dragging across and down with the mouse. Now click **OK** to complete the **Advanced Filter**.

   Only one item meets the criteria, the **Ship's Light**.

5  Close the file but do not save.

## Section 3     Linking

A **link** can be created between one cell in a worksheet and another. When the source cell is changed the dependent cell is automatically changed. The link can also be between cells in different worksheets of the same workbook or the link can be between two different workbooks. The advantage of the link is that when the source cell is changed the dependent cell changes also. Using links it is possible to update charts from the data used to create them.

When an object from the source file is **embedded** in another file, the destination file, the object becomes part of the destination file. When the source file is changed the destination file remains the same. The embedded object has no links to the source file. Double-click on the destination file to open it in the source program.

### 3.1    Linking data / chart within a worksheet (4.2.3.1)

We are going to create a link between cells **B3** and cell **D9**.

- Open the file **Link**.

- Select cell **D9**. Insert the formula **=B3**. Select **Enter** on the toolbar.

  The contents of cell B3 are inserted in cell D9. Cell D9 is now linked to cell B3 and if any change is made to cell B3, then the contents of cell D9 are automatically updated.

|   | A | B | C | D | E |
|---|---|---|---|---|---|
| 1 |   | Linking data within a worksheet | | | |
| 2 |   |   |   |   |   |
| 3 |   | 20 |   | Sales |   |
| 4 |   |   |   | 12 |   |
| 5 |   |   |   | 24 |   |
| 6 |   |   |   | 18 |   |
| 7 |   |   |   | 30 |   |
| 8 |   |   |   | 16 |   |
| 9 |   |   |   | =B3 |   |
| 10|   |   | Total |   |   |

- Change the contents of cell **B3** to **30**. The content of cell **D9** is updated to **30**.

The table on **Sheet1** shows the number of visitors to a Guesthouse from Germany, France, Denmark and Ireland.

The chart on this worksheet is based on the data in the table.

- Select the **Chart Area**. The links to the table are clearly outlined in colour, (green, blue and purple). Any change to the data in the table is reflected immediately in the chart.

- Change the number of visitors from Denmark for 2003 from **50** to **70**.

  The chart changes to reflect the increased number of visitors.

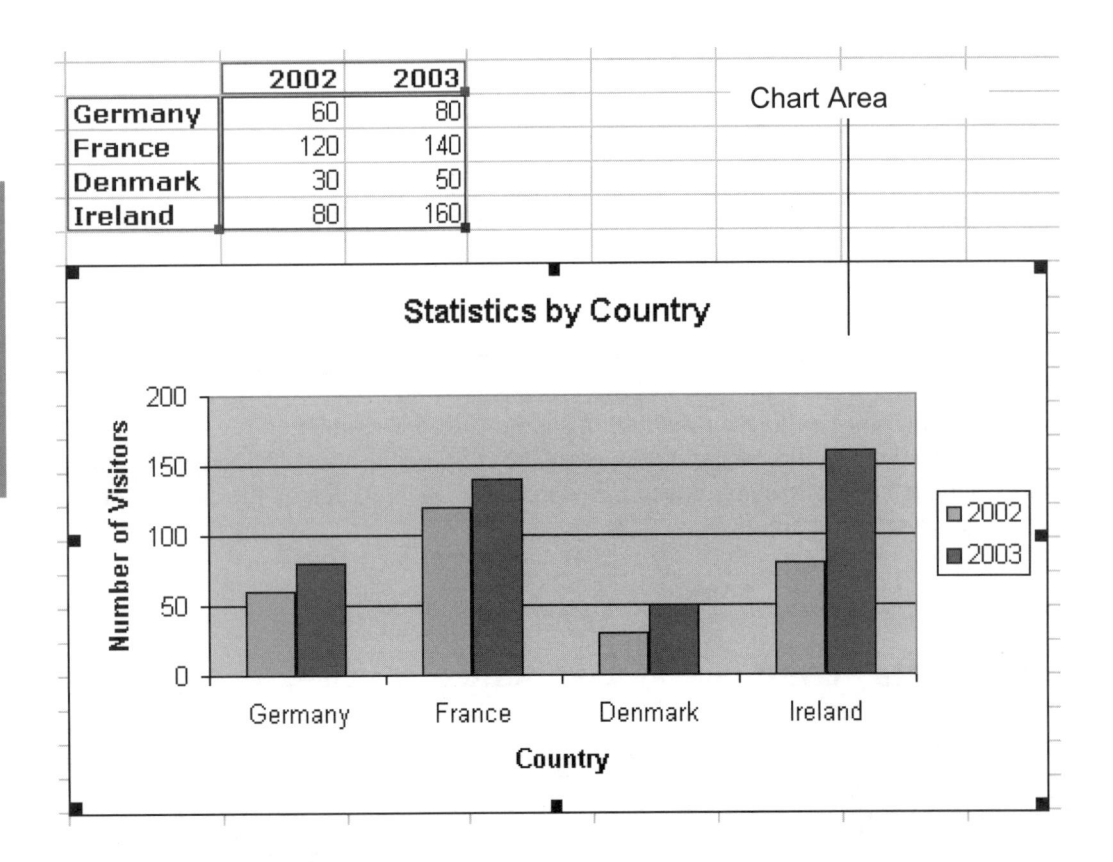

|         | 2002 | 2003 |
|---------|------|------|
| Germany | 60   | 80   |
| France  | 120  | 140  |
| Denmark | 30   | 50   |
| Ireland | 80   | 160  |

**Statistics by Country**

*(Bar chart showing Number of Visitors by Country for 2002 and 2003)*

## 3.2 Linking data / chart between worksheets (4.2.3.2)

In this section we are going to link the data range **G4:I8** to the worksheet **Sheet2**.

- Highlight the range **G4:I8** on **Sheet1**. Choose **Edit** followed by **Copy** (or **Ctrl + C**) to copy the data. Or use the Copy button on Standard toolbar.

- Select the tab for **Sheet 2** and click on cell **A1**.

- Choose **Edit** followed by **Paste Special** from the drop-down menu.

  The **Paste Special dialog** box opens.

- Choose the **Paste Link** button.

- Click on cell **B1** to view the linking formula that is shown below.

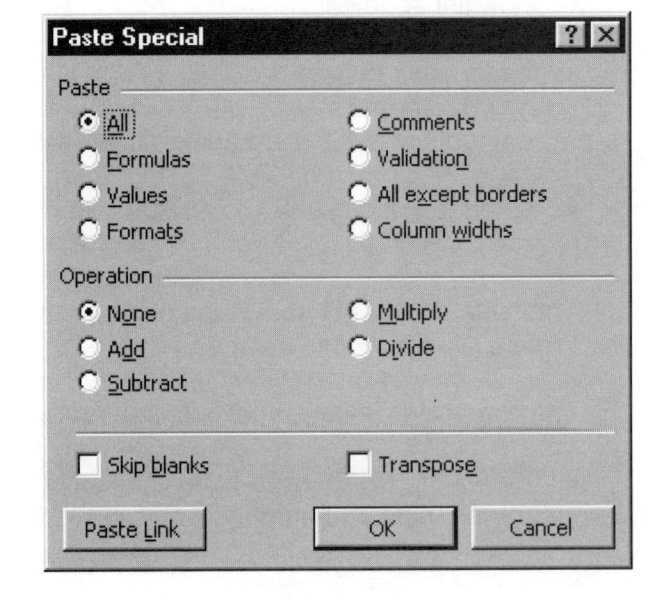

    =Sheet1!H4

  Select any of the other data cells and the linking formula is shown.

- Go back to **Sheet1** and click on **Esc** to remove marquee from selected cells.

### 3.2.1 Linking data / chart between worksheets (4.2.3.2)

In this section we are going to use the data on **Sheet1** to create a chart on **Sheet3**.

- Select the tab for **Sheet3**. Choose the **Chart Wizard** icon. **Chart Wizard – Step 1 of 4 – Chart Type** dialog box opens.

- Choose the **Chart type Column** and **Chart sub-type Clustered Column** (default setting) and click on the **Next** button.

- **Chart Wizard – Step 2 of 4 – Chart source Data** dialog box opens.

  We are required to select the **Data range** that is present on **Sheet1**.

- Click in **Data range** box, if cursor is not already present.

- Select tab for **Sheet1**.

- Using the mouse highlight the range **G4:I8**.

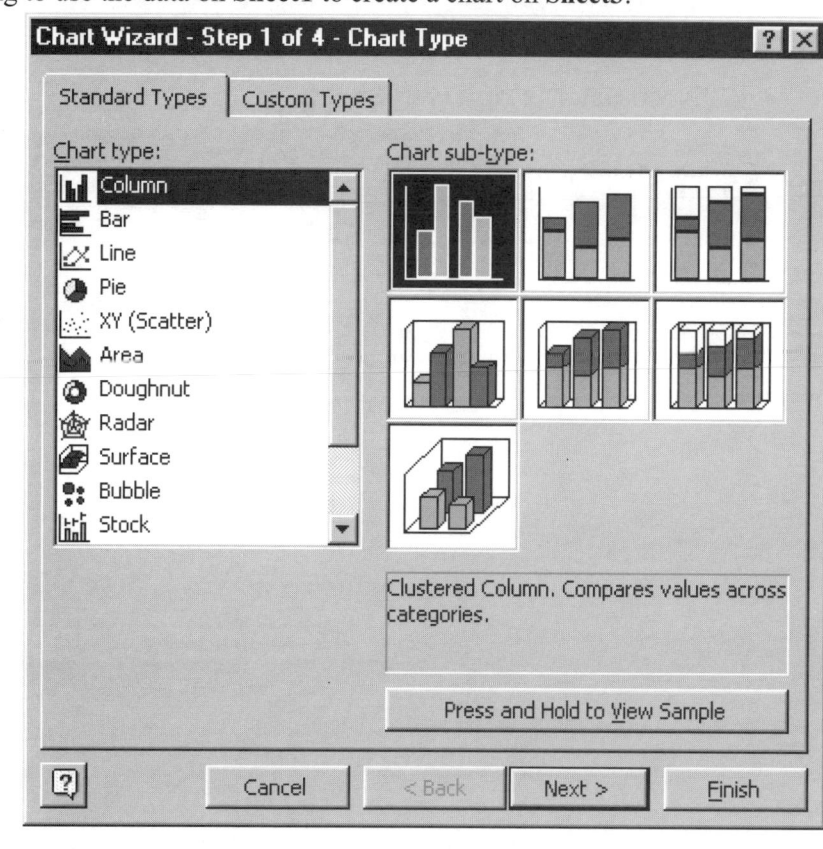

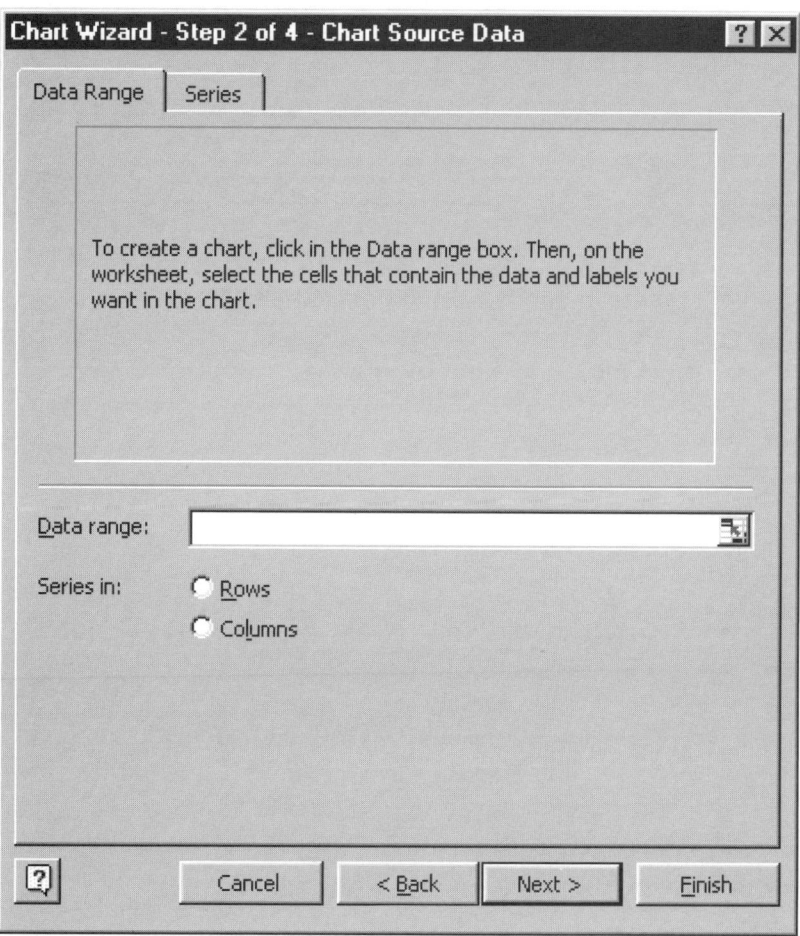

Chapter 2 – Data Handling

This range is entered in the **Data range box** as shown in **Source Data** dialog box.

- Select **Next** and proceed through the **Chart Wizard Step 3 of 4 – Chart Options** and **Chart Wizard – Step 4 of 4.**

- Choose **Save as object in Sheet.**

- Click on the **Finish** button.

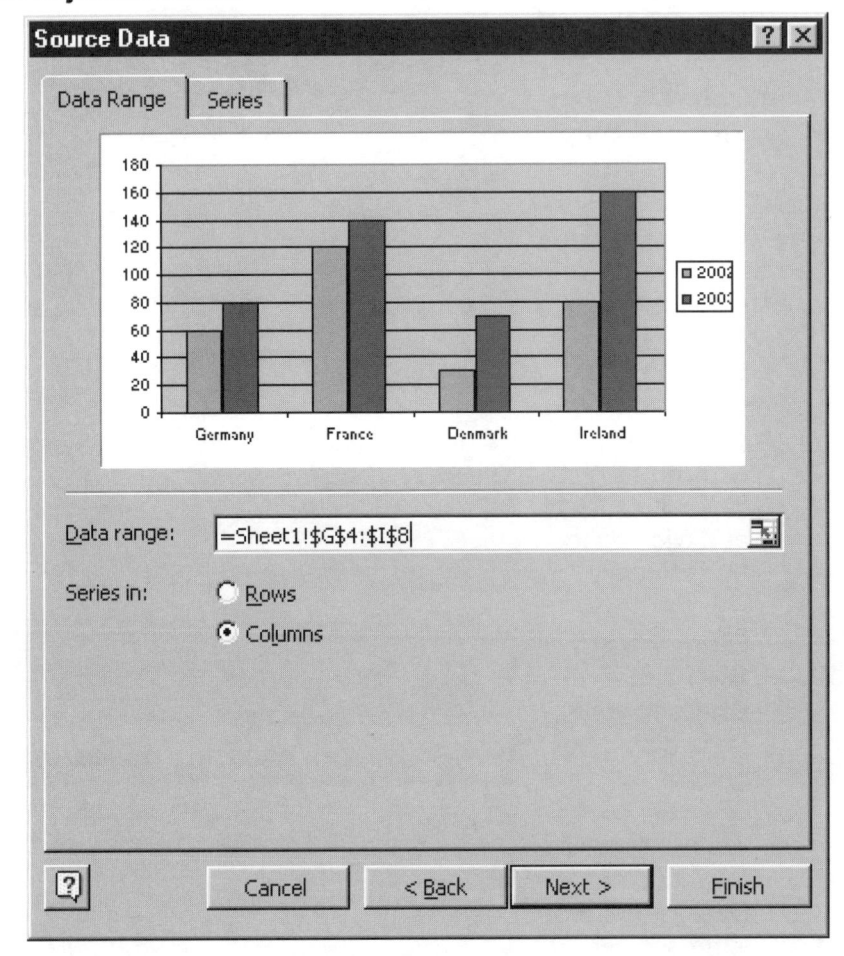

You have successfully created a chart in one worksheet (Sheet3) using the data present in another worksheet (Sheet1).

- Save the file as **Link Solution**.

## 3.3 Linking data / chart between spreadsheets (4.2.3.3)

In this section we are going to link data from one Spreadsheet to another Spreadsheet using the Paste Special command and the Paste link button.

- Open **Workbook1** and **Workbook2**.

- In **Workbook1** highlight the range **C4:D9**. Choose **Edit** followed by **Copy** (or **Ctrl + C**) to copy the data. Or use the Copy button on Standard toolbar.

- Select **Workbook2** and click on cell **A1**.

- Choose the **Paste Special** command from the **Edit** menu.

- Click on the **Paste Link** button. Now click on the **OK** button.

  The formula is shown in the Formula bar.

  =''[Workbook 1.xls]Sheet1'!C4

### 3.3.1 Linking a chart between spreadsheets (4.2.3.3)

- Open **Workbook1** and select the **Chart Area**. Choose **Edit** followed by **Copy** (or **Ctrl + C**). Or select the Copy button on Standard toolbar.

- Select **Start** followed by **Programs** followed by **Microsoft Excel** to open *another* copy of Excel. (Or use any alternative method to open another copy of Excel).

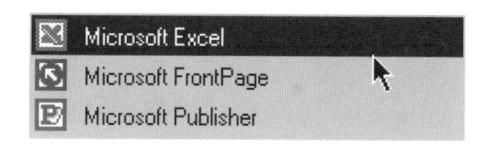

- Select cell **A1** in the blank worksheet.

- Choose **Edit** followed by **Paste Special**.

  The **Paste Special** dialog box opens.

- Select **Microsoft Excel Chart Object** in the **As:** section.

- Click on the **Paste Link** radio button.

  This creates a link to the source file – Workbook1. Any changes made to the source file will be reflected in the new document.

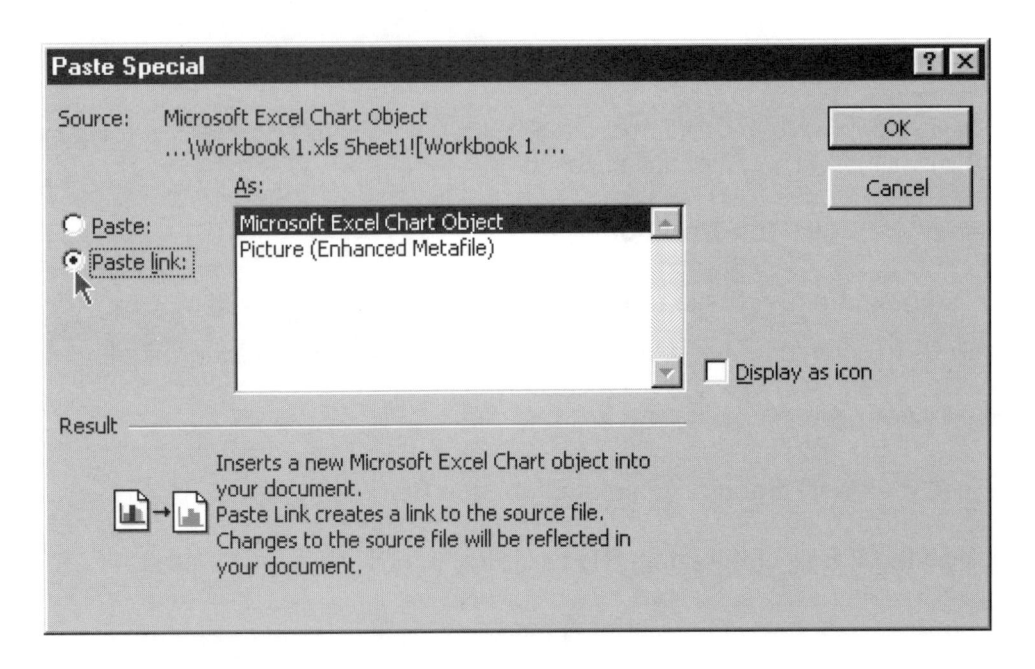

- Click **OK**.

  The chart from **Workbook1** is pasted into **Sheet1**. The formula in the Formula bar reflects the link between Workbook1 and Sheet1 in the recently opened copy of Excel. Your own formula may differ slightly.

  =Excel.Chart.8|'A:\Workbook 1.xls'!Sheet1![Workbook 1.xls]Sheet1 Chart 1'

  Remember, Paste link has created a link to the source file. Any changes in **Workbook1** are reflected in **Book1**. We will test this now.

- Change the figure for **Dublin** in **Workbook1** from **400** to **1000**.

  The change in the chart has been made from the source file - Workbook1.

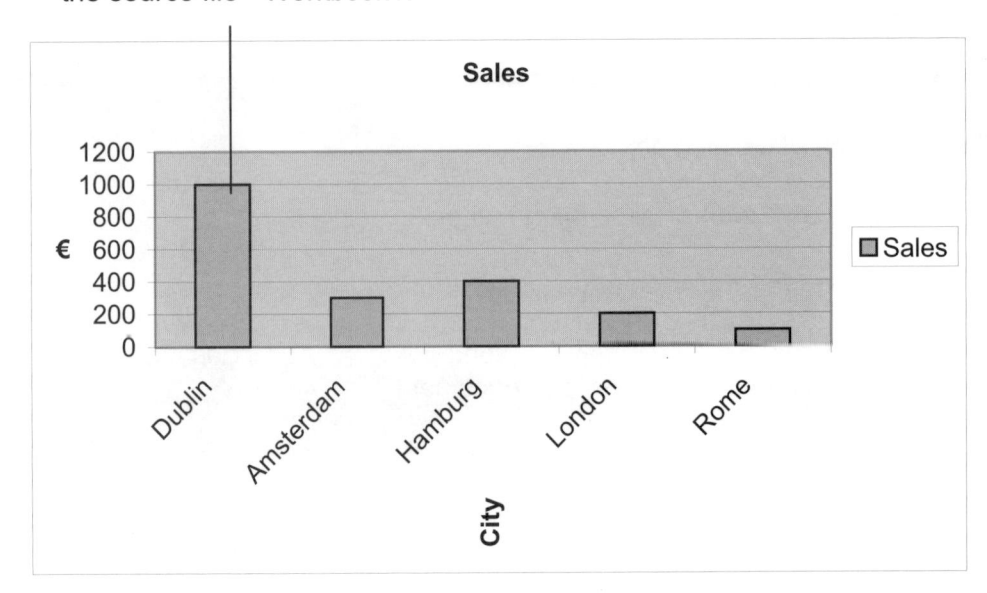

  The change in data is reflected in **Sheet1**.

## 3.4 Linking Data / Chart into a word processing document
(4.2.3.4)

- Open Excel file **Workbook 4** and Word document **Report**.

- Click on the chart area and select **Edit** followed by **Copy** (or **Ctrl + C**) or click on **Copy** icon on Standard toolbar.

- Switch to **Report** document and click at point indicated.

- Choose **Edit** followed by **Paste Special**.

- Click on **Paste link** radio button.

- Click **OK**.

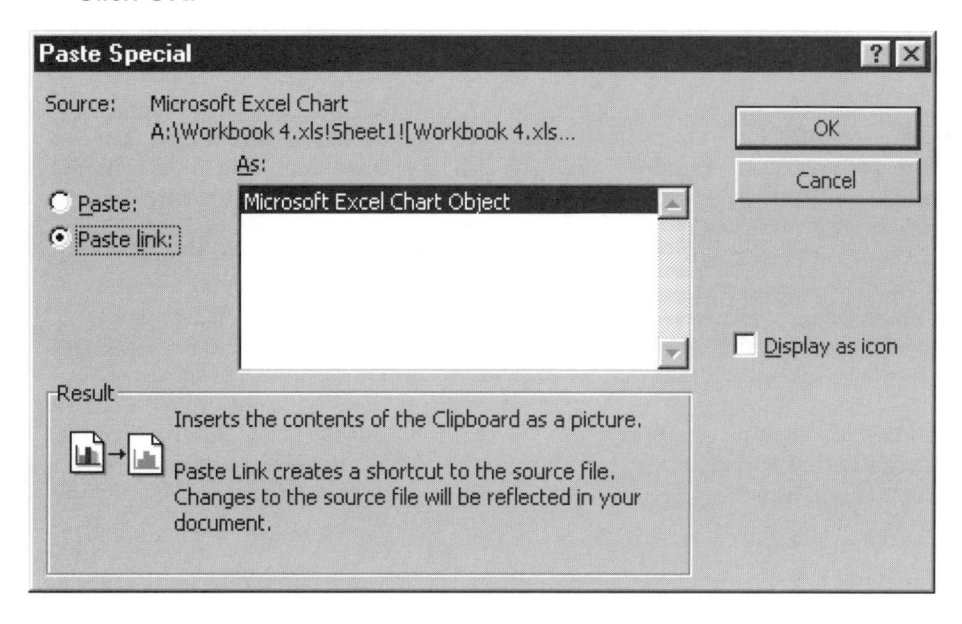

The chart is copied to Word document **Report**.

Any changes made in the Excel document **Workbook 4** are reflected in the Word document **Report**.

- Change the number of vistors from Germany in 2003 from **80** to **200** in **Workbook 4**.

The change is reflected in the word document **Report**.

- Close the Word file Report but do not save.

## 3.5 Embedding a chart into a word processing document

In this exercise we are going to **embed** an Excel chart into a Word document.

- Open the Excel file **Workbook 4** and the Word file **Report**.

- Click on the chart area.

- Select **Edit** followed by **Copy** (Or **Ctrl + C**) or use copy icon. Or select the Copy button on Standard toolbar.

- Switch to Word document **Report** and insert cursor at point indicated.

### Guesthouse Report 2003

The Guesthouse was renovated late in 2001 at a cost of €30,000. It reopened in 2002 and has had a steady throughput of visitors. Our adverts in European Travel Guide have brought us over 80 enquiries per month on average and an estimated 100 visitors. We are still assessing the effectiveness of our web site but will be going ahead with online booking from Jan 2004.

The breakdown of visitors from four European countries, Germany, France, Denmark and Ireland is given in the chart below.

We are fully booked for March 2004. The Welsh Hitec Group is holding their conference in town. All hotels are full so we are benefiting here.

Two of our staff have just successfully completed their **ECDL** so we are confident about their ability to handle online booking when our web site opens in January 2004. Both are keen to complete the Advanced Spreadsheets for ECDL (AM4) and Advanced Word Processing for ECDL (AM3). We have purchased the Training Manuals from Blackrock Education Centre.

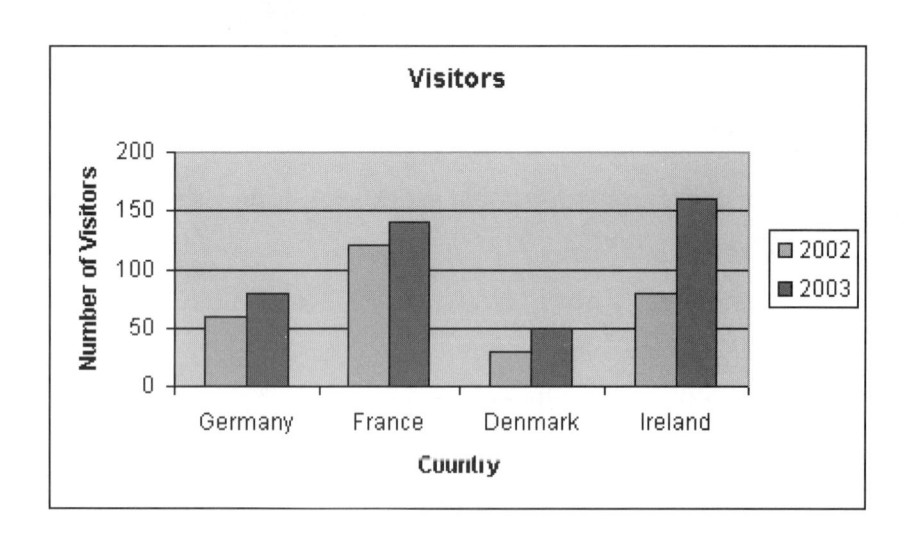

**Visitors**

| Country  | 2002 | 2003 |
|----------|------|------|
| Germany  | 60   | 80   |
| France   | 120  | 140  |
| Denmark  | 30   | 50   |
| Ireland  | 80   | 160  |

- Select **Edit** followed by **Paste** (Or **Ctrl +V**) or use paste icon.

    The chart is **embedded** in the document Report. Changes made to the data or chart in Workbook 4 have no effect on the chart in Report1 as the charts are **not linked**.

- Save the file as **Report Solution**.

The practice exercises contained in this section relate solely to this manual and do not constitute, or imply, certification by the European Driving Licence Foundation in respect of any ECDL examinations. For details on sitting ECDL examinations in your country please contact the local ECDL/ICDL licensee or visit the European Computer Driving Licence Foundation Ltd web site at http://www.ecdl.com

## Exercise 3A

1 Open the file **Link Exercise**. Highlight the range **D2:E7**. Select **Edit** followed by **Copy** (or Ctrl + C) or click on Copy button on the Standard toolbar. Select the tab for **Sheet2** and click on cell **A1**.

2 Choose **Paste Special** from the **Edit** menu and when the **Paste Special dialog** box opens, click on the **Paste Link** button.

3 Click on any of the cells to view the linking formula.

4 Select **Sheet1** and press Esc to remove marquee. Click on cell **E3**. The sales for **Germany** have increased to **700**. Make the entry now.

Since the cells are linked, any changes made in the source cells (Sheet1) are reflected in the dependent cells (Sheet2). Clicking on Sheet2 will confirm this. The sales figure for Germany is now shown as 700.

The practice exercises contained in this section relate solely to this manual and do not constitute, or imply, certification by the European Driving Licence Foundation in respect of any ECDL examinations. For details on sitting ECDL examinations in your country please contact the local ECDL/ICDL licensee or visit the European Computer Driving Licence Foundation Ltd web site at http://www.ecdl.com

## Exercise 3B

1 Open the file **Link Exercise**. Select the **Chart Area** by clicking on it. Choose **Edit** followed by **Copy** to copy the chart area.

2 We are now going to open another copy of Excel. Choose **Start** followed by **Programs** followed by **Microsoft Excel**. Select cell **A1** in **Sheet1** of the new copy of Excel. Now, choose **Paste Special** from the **Edit** menu and the **Paste Special dialog** box opens. In the **As:** section select **Microsoft Excel Chart Object**. Click on the **Paste Link** radio button. Click **OK**.

3 Now click on **Link Exercise**. Press **Esc** to remove marquee around chart.

4 Change the sales figure for **Italy** from **350** to **175** in the **Link Exercise** worksheet.

Since both spreadsheets are linked the change is also made in the recently opened copy of Excel. Examine it now to confirm this is the case.

## 3.6 Consolidating data in adjacent worksheets using a 3D sum function (4.2.3.5)

It is possible to combine data from many sources and consolidate it in a single worksheet.

- Open the file **Consolidation**.

**Lighting Up Ireland** has produced a limited range of lamps, which it sells in Dublin, Milan and Barcelona. The Projected (Project) and Actual Sales for the three cities are given. The sales for each city are contained in separate named worksheets. A separate worksheet named **Consolidation** is where the data is consolidated.

We are going to use the **3D Sum function** to consolidate the **projected** and **actual totals** in the worksheet to verify the figures already calculated. i.e. **22350** and **25810**.

- Click on the tabs for **Dublin**, **Milan** and **Barcelona**. You will notice that each worksheet is set up in an identical manner with respect to layout - headings, total, format etc.

- Click on the **Consolidation** tab. It is in this worksheet that we want to consolidate the **total** data from the three cities.

- Select cell **H22**. Click on AutoSum Σ icon.

- Select the tab **Dublin** and click on cell **B19**.

- Hold down the **Shift** key and click on the tab **Milan** and select cell **B19**.

- Keeping the **Shift** key depressed select the tab **Barcelona** and click on cell **B19**.

- Press **Enter** and the total for the three cities is entered in cell **H22**.

    The **Total** in cell **H22** should be the same as the total in cell **H19** that has been previously calculated using the **AutoSum** function.

- Select cell **C22** to examine the formula in the formula bar.

    It should read:  H22  =SUM(Dublin:Barcelona!B19)

    The Dublin:Barcelona range includes Dublin, Milan and Barcelona.

- Select cell **I22**.

    Repeat the exercise to consolidate the **Actual Sales** total for Dublin, Milan and Barcelona.

    The final total should be the same as that in cell **I19**. The figure is shown below.

|   | A | B | C | D | E | F | G | H | I |
|---|---|---|---|---|---|---|---|---|---|
| 1 | **Lighting Up Ireland** | | | | | | | | |
| 2 | | | | | | | | | |
| 3 | | Dublin | | Milan | | Barcelona | | TOTAL | |
| 4 | | | | | | | | | |
| 5 | Month | Project | Actual | Project | Actual | Project | Actual | Project | Actual |
| 6 | Jan | 500 | 630 | 550 | 435 | 560 | 880 | 1610 | 1945 |
| 7 | Feb | 480 | 875 | 330 | 525 | 480 | 555 | 1290 | 1955 |
| 8 | Mar | 700 | 850 | 600 | 620 | 600 | 630 | 1900 | 2100 |
| 9 | Apr | 730 | 720 | 780 | 710 | 730 | 730 | 2240 | 2160 |
| 10 | May | 700 | 860 | 500 | 745 | 810 | 945 | 2010 | 2550 |
| 11 | Jun | 600 | 550 | 550 | 660 | 630 | 740 | 1780 | 1950 |
| 12 | Jul | 830 | 750 | 570 | 860 | 820 | 740 | 2220 | 2350 |
| 13 | Aug | 800 | 810 | 845 | 810 | 790 | 920 | 2435 | 2540 |
| 14 | Sep | 890 | 990 | 725 | 650 | 770 | 660 | 2385 | 2300 |
| 15 | Oct | 600 | 500 | 550 | 670 | 440 | 800 | 1590 | 1970 |
| 16 | Nov | 720 | 430 | 540 | 390 | 500 | 420 | 1760 | 1240 |
| 17 | Dec | 900 | 880 | 950 | 890 | 450 | 980 | 2300 | 2750 |
| 18 | | | | | | | | | |
| 19 | TOTAL | 8450 | 8845 | 7490 | 7965 | 7580 | 9000 | 23520 | 25810 |
| 20 | | | | | | | | | |
| 21 | | | | | | | | Project | Actual |
| 22 | | | | Consolidating data using 3D sum function | | | | 23520 | 25810 |

Calculated using 3D sum function

Calculated using AutoSum

- Save the file as **Consolidation Solution**.

The practice exercises contained in this section relate solely to this manual and do not constitute, or imply, certification by the European Driving Licence Foundation in respect of any ECDL examinations. For details on sitting ECDL examinations in your country please contact the local ECDL/ICDL licensee or visit the European Computer Driving Licence Foundation Ltd web site at http://www.ecdl.com

## Exercise 3C

1  Open the file **ConsolExports**.

   We are going to use the **3D sum function** to consolidate the export sales in the years 2002 – 2004.

2  Select the tab **Consol Exports** and click on cell **F4**. Choose the **AutoSum** function and select tab **2002**. Click on cell **F4**. Whilst depressing the **Shift** key select the tab for worksheet **2003** and click on cell **F4**. Continue to hold down the **Shift** key and select the tab for **2004** and choose cell **F4**. Now click **OK**.

   The total export figures for **Iron** in the years **2002 – 2004** are consolidated.

3  Repeat the procedure for **Steel**, **Cobalt** and **Nickel**.

   Alternatively you can copy the range in cell **F4** down through **F5:F7**.

4  Save the file as **ConsolExports Solution**.

## Section 4    Templates

All documents created in Excel are based on a ***template***.  A Template is a special master worksheet that contains custom settings but no data.

The templates may contain predetermined settings for styles, custom formats, formulas, pictures, row and column settings, page headers, charts, macros and any other information you wish to include.

A template is particularly useful if a worksheet is used regularly.  A company invoice template could be designed so that all the main details, such as logo, business address, telephone, Email, Web address are present.  This saves time as only customer details and transactions have to be added.  Another advantage of using a template is that a series of business forms such as Expense statement or Purchase Orders or Annual Reports can be created with the same formatting or style.

**NOTE**
Remember to install the sample templates that come with the Excel program.

### 4.1    Using a Template (4.2.4.1)

When Excel is opened the workbook is based on the normal template that has predefined settings.

There are a number of templates available with predefined settings.  These are useful as they can be modified to suit your own requirements.

To use an Excel template:

- Select **File** followed by **New**. (Or **Ctrl + N**).

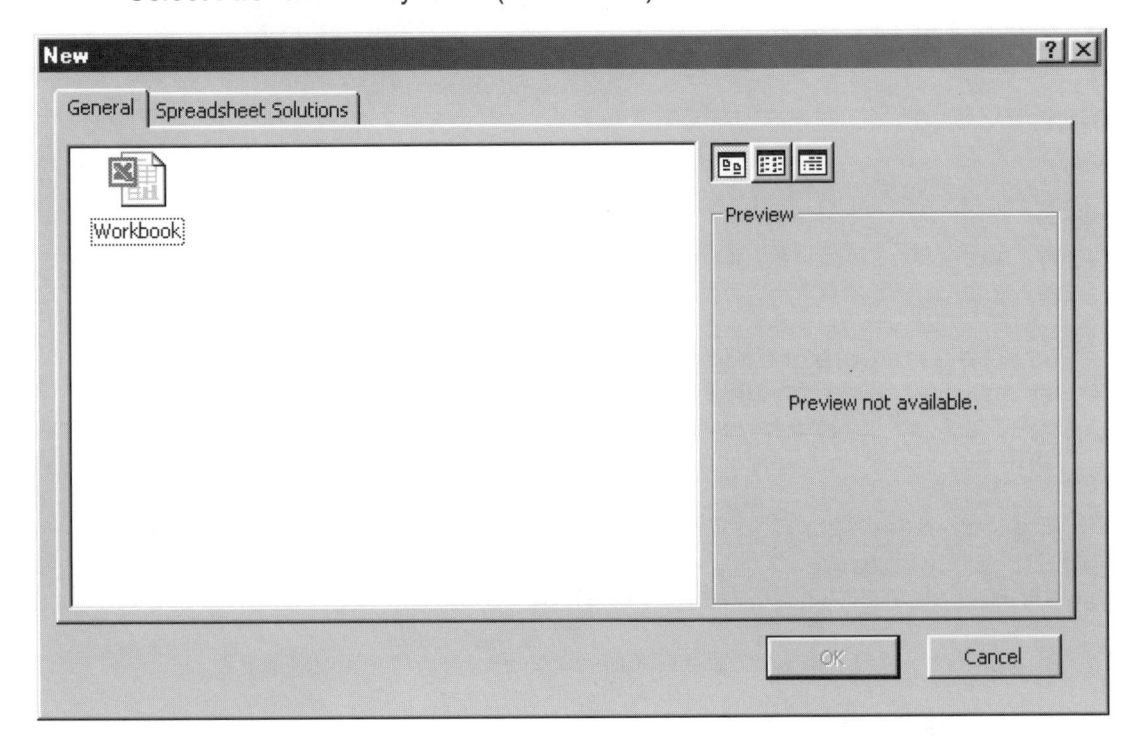

The **New dialog** box opens.

- Check the tabs for **General** and **Spreadsheet Solutions**

- Choose any of the available templates that are of particular interest to you.

- Click **OK**. You now have a copy of the template.

- Examine the template in detail. Look at structure and layout. Are there headers and footers present? Are there formulas present in cells? Make *no* changes at this stage.

- If you want to check structure and content select **Format** followed by **Style** and the **Style dialog** box opens and gives the relevant details. Make *no* changes at this stage.

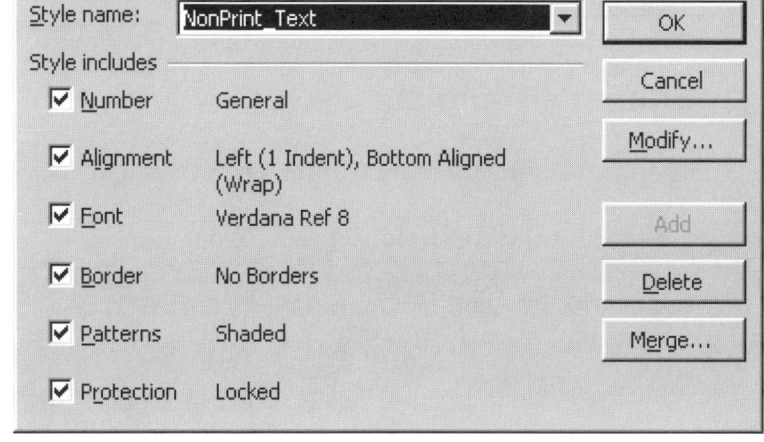

- Make a *small* number of changes to the template. For example if you have chosen the **Invoice** Template, change the **Company Name** to a name of your choosing.

We will now save the template with the changes you have made under a different name.

- Choose **Save as** in the **File** menu. The **Save as** window opens.

- **Save** the template under a different name in the **File name** box. E.g. **Lighting Invoice**

- Click on the **Save as type** drop-down arrow and select **Template**.

- Click on the **Save** button to save the template.

To locate the template:

- Select **File** followed by **New** (or choose **Ctrl + N**).

  The new **Template** appears under the **General** tab.

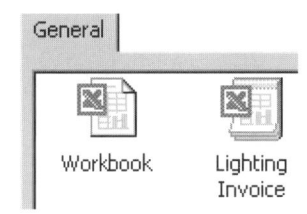

The practice exercises contained in this section relate solely to this manual and do not constitute, or imply, certification by the European Driving Licence Foundation in respect of any ECDL examinations. For details on sitting ECDL examinations in your country please contact the local ECDL/ICDL licensee or visit the European Computer Driving Licence Foundation Ltd web site at http://www.ecdl.com

## Exercise 4A

1. Create new documents based on the available templates in the **New** window. Choose from the **Spreadsheet Solutions**. Examine the structure and content of the template by using **Format** followed by **Style**.

2. Familiarise yourself and experiment with a selection of the available templates.

3. Do not save any changes.

## 4.2 Editing a Template (4.2.4.2)

We will open the template **Lighting Up Ireland Invoice** and make selective changes to it.

Locate the file **Lighting Up Ireland Invoice**, or:

- Select **File** followed by **Open** (Or use **Ctrl + O**).

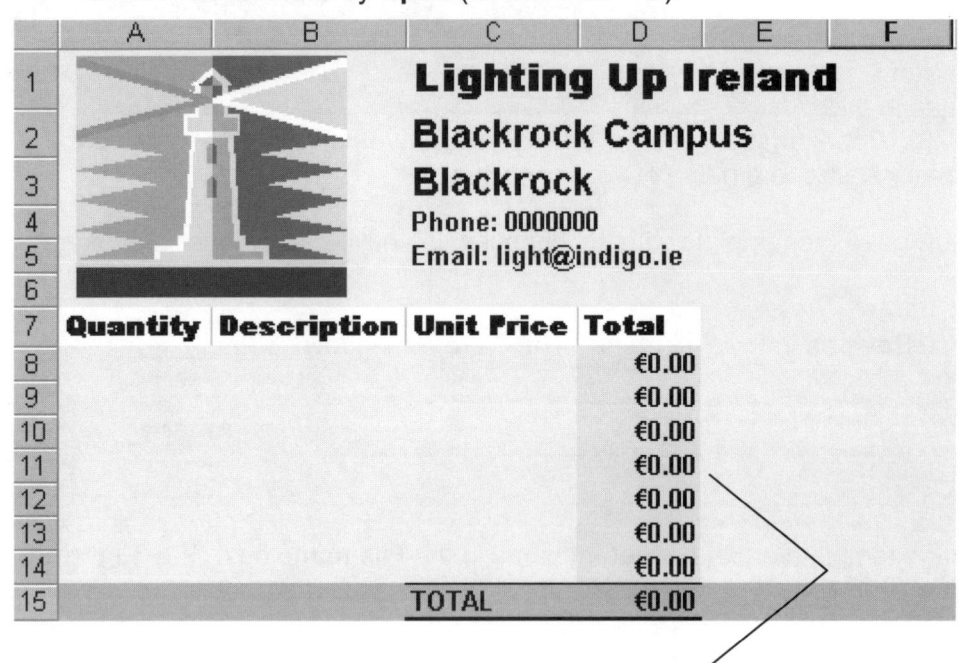

Cells in range **D8:D15** contain formula

- Make the following changes to the template:

    Insert a telephone number; add a web address; assign areas for customer details; change any of the font formats and background colours. (Do not remove any formula, as you will be using them in the next exercise).

- Save the template with changes as **Lighting Up Ireland Invoice**.

    When the template is next used all the changes made will be present.

## 4.3 Saving a Template

Templates are saved in a separate folder and this location may vary. One possibility is:

**C:\Windows\Applications Data\Microsoft…\Templates**

The practice exercises contained in this section relate solely to this manual and do not constitute, or imply, certification by the European Driving Licence Foundation in respect of any ECDL examinations. For details on sitting ECDL examinations in your country please contact the local ECDL/ICDL licensee or visit the European Computer Driving Licence Foundation Ltd web site at http://www.ecdl.com

## Exercise 4B

Open the template **Lighting Up Ireland Invoice**.

1   We are going to invoice the following to a purchaser.

| Quantity | Description | Unit Price |
|---|---|---|
| 3 | Ship's Light | 58.00 |
| 2 | Chandelier | 119.50 |
| 4 | Floor Lamp | 42.00 |

The **Total** cost of each item is automatically calculated since the formula is present in the template.

2   Insert details of the person or company to whom the invoice is being sent.

3   Save the invoice as **Invoice1**.

The Lighting Up Ireland Invoice template remains unchanged and can be used to process the next order.

The practice exercises contained in this section relate solely to this manual and do not constitute, or imply, certification by the European Driving Licence Foundation in respect of any ECDL examinations. For details on sitting ECDL examinations in your country please contact the local ECDL/ICDL licensee or visit the European Computer Driving Licence Foundation Ltd web site at http://www.ecdl.com

## Exercise 4C

Create your own template from scratch using **Workbook** which is located by selecting the **General** tab of **New** window. Use the information from the file **Lighting Stock** to create a *sales list* that is sent out to clients on a regular basis.

1   Include any five items and their selling price in the list.

2   Add a picture. Format data and use a colourful background.

3   Add a Discount Column adjacent to the Selling Price Column.

4   In the Discount Column include a formula that will discount the items by 25%.

5   Save the template as **Lighting Stock Discount**.

## Section 5   Charts & Graphs

**NOTE**
The exercises in Section 5 are present in the file **Charts & Graphs**. Each exercise is present on a separate worksheet. The tab label indicates the purpose of the exercise.

> Change angle of pie chart slice / Format axes numbers or text / Title legend & labels / Explode

### 5.1   Changing the angle of a pie chart slice (4.2.5.1)

- Open the file **Charts & Graphs**.

- Select the tab **Change angle of pie chart slice**.

- Click on the pie chart to select it.

- Right-click on pie chart and choose **Format Data Series…**.

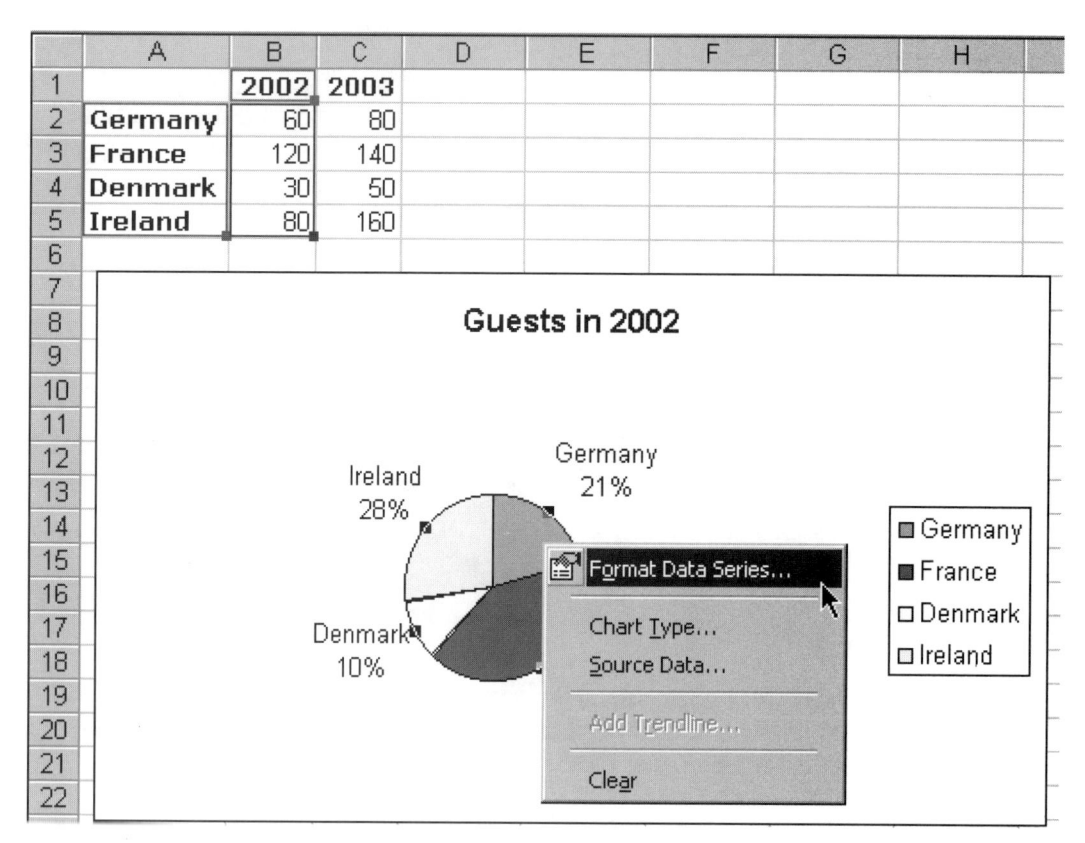

|   | A | B | C |
|---|---|---|---|
| 1 |   | 2002 | 2003 |
| 2 | Germany | 60 | 80 |
| 3 | France | 120 | 140 |
| 4 | Denmark | 30 | 50 |
| 5 | Ireland | 80 | 160 |

Guests in 2002

- Germany 21%
- Ireland 28%
- Denmark 10%

Legend: Germany, France, Denmark, Ireland

Context menu: Format Data Series…, Chart Type…, Source Data…, Add Trendline…, Clear

The Format Data Series dialog box opens.

- Choose the **Options** tab.

- Click on the box **Angle of first slice**.

Chapter 2 – Data Handling

Each click increases the angle by ten degrees

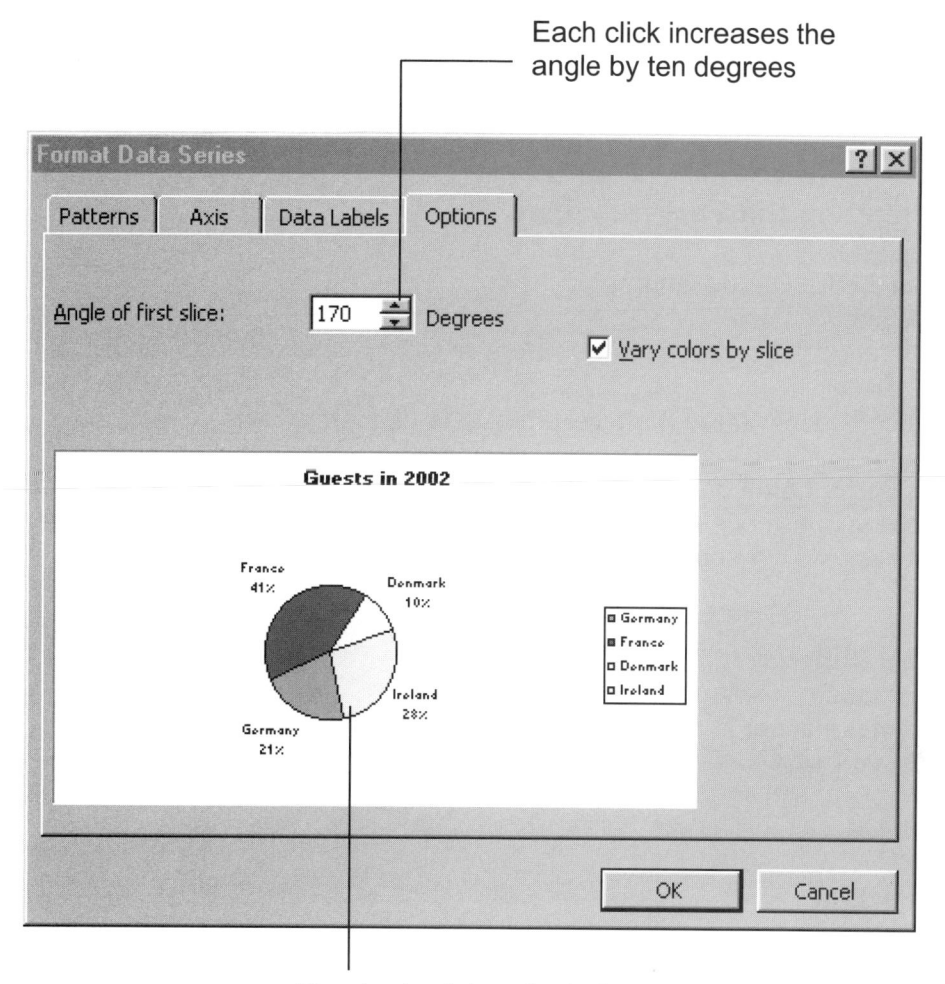

Pie chart rotates clockwise as angle increases, anti-clockwise as angle decreases

You can increase the angle gradually by clicking on the upper arrow to the left of the Degrees label. The angle increases by ten degrees for each click and you will note that the pie chart rotates clockwise.

- Set the angle to **170** degrees. (Or choose your own angle).

- Click on **OK**.

- Save the chart as **Charts & Graphs Solution**.

We will now look at how to format chart axes, numbers and text.

## 5.2 Formatting chart axes, numbers and text (4.2.5.2)

In this section we will format chart axes, numbers and text.

### 5.2.1 Formatting chart axis numbers

- Open the file **Charts & Graphs**.

- Select the tab **Format axes numbers or text**.

- Double click on **Value (Left Vertical) Axis** of chart.

    The **Format Axis** dialog box opens. Choose the **Number** tab. In our example involving guesthouse visitors we wish to leave the numbers as they are. However, we will select **Currency** and note the change. Then we will undo the change.

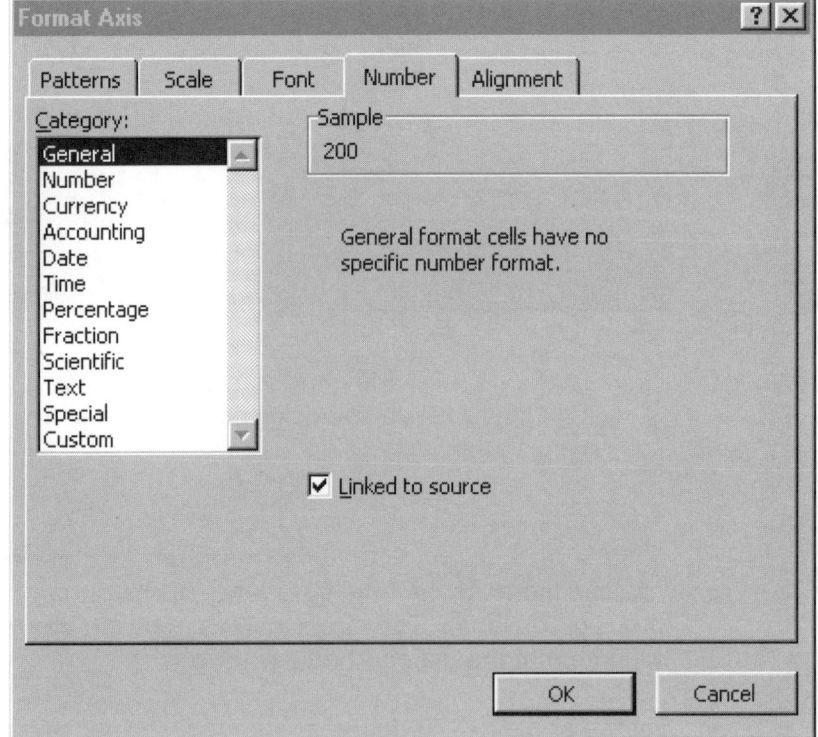

- Select **Currency** and choose **Decimal places: 2** and **Symbol: €**

- Click **OK**.

    The Axis is formatted in currency to two decimal places. You will note the other options available including Custom option.

- Select **Edit** followed by **Undo Format Axis (or Ctrl + Z)**.

    This returns the axis numbers to their original state.

## 5.2.2 Formatting chart axis scales

In this exercise we will make changes to the Major unit in the Scale dialog box. This changes the Major gridlines on the chart.

- Double click on **Value** (Left Vertical) **Axis** of the chart.

- When the **Format Axis** dialog box opens choose the **Scale** tab.

- Click on **Major unit**: and change the figure from **50** to **40**.

- Click **OK**.

Examine the chart and you will notice that the Y axis (vertical) scale has changed from 50 to 40. The *major gridlines* are now set at 40.

Leave the Major unit at 40. We will now change the chart axis text.

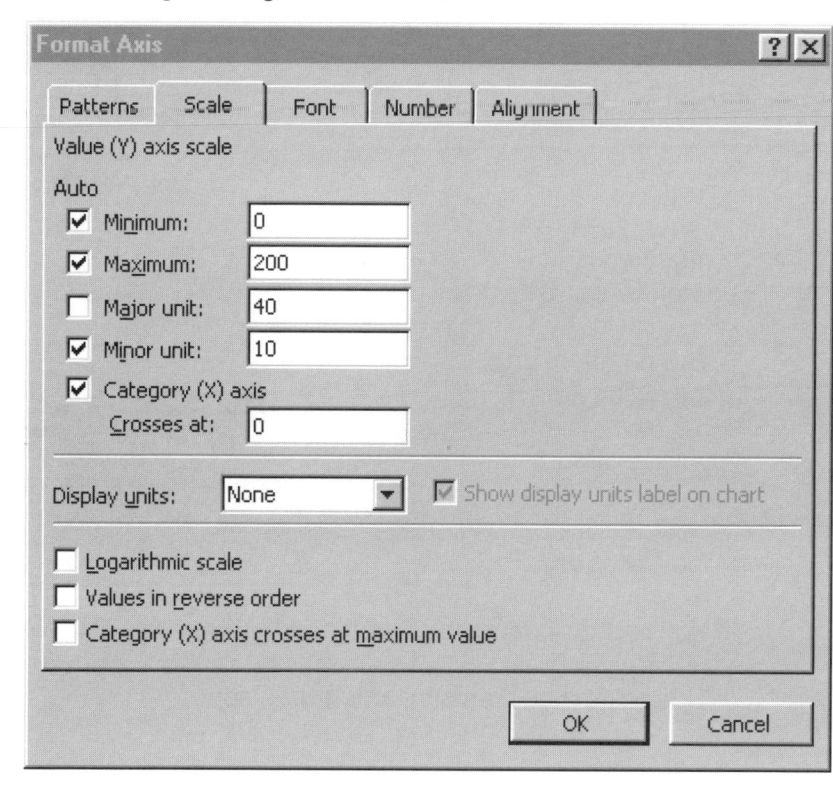

**NOTE**

If the boxes in Format Axis, Scale are ticked Excel automatically determines their value.

| Value (Y) axis scale | |
|---|---|
| Minimum | The minimum value on the scale – usually 0 |
| Maximum | The maximum value on the scale – usually set to a round number above the largest value plotted |
| Major unit | Corresponds to major gridlines |
| Minor unit | Corresponds to minor gridlines |
| Category (X) axis, crosses at | The axis can be positioned at a different location |
| Logarithmic scale | Uses a log scale for axis |
| Values in reverse order | Scale values extend in opposite direction |
| Category (X) axis crosses at maximum value | Axis located at maximum value of perpendicular axis – usually located at minimum value |

### 5.2.3 Formatting the chart axis text

- Double click on **Value** (Left Vertical) **Axis** of chart.

- When the **Format Axis** dialog box opens choose the **Font** tab.

- Choose a **Font**, **Font Style**, **Size** and **Colour**.

    We have chosen **Andy**, **Bold Italic**, **11** point and **Dark Blue** as our choice.

- When you have made your choice click **OK**.

    The numbers on the Value Axis are formatted to your choice.

- Double-click on the **Category** (Lower Horizontal) **Axis** so that the country names are also formatted.

The chart should be similar to that below.

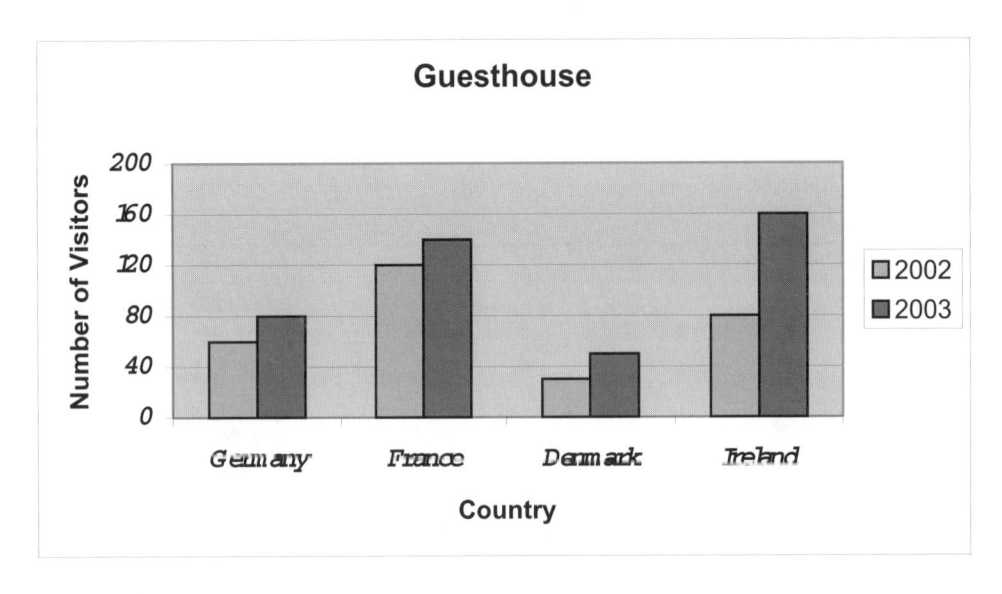

**Guesthouse**

- Save the file as **Charts and Graph Solution**.

We will now look at how to re-position chart title, legend and data labels.

## 5.3 Re-positioning title, legend or data labels in a chart (4.2.5.3)

- Open the file **Charts & Graphs**.

- Select the tab **Title legend & labels**.

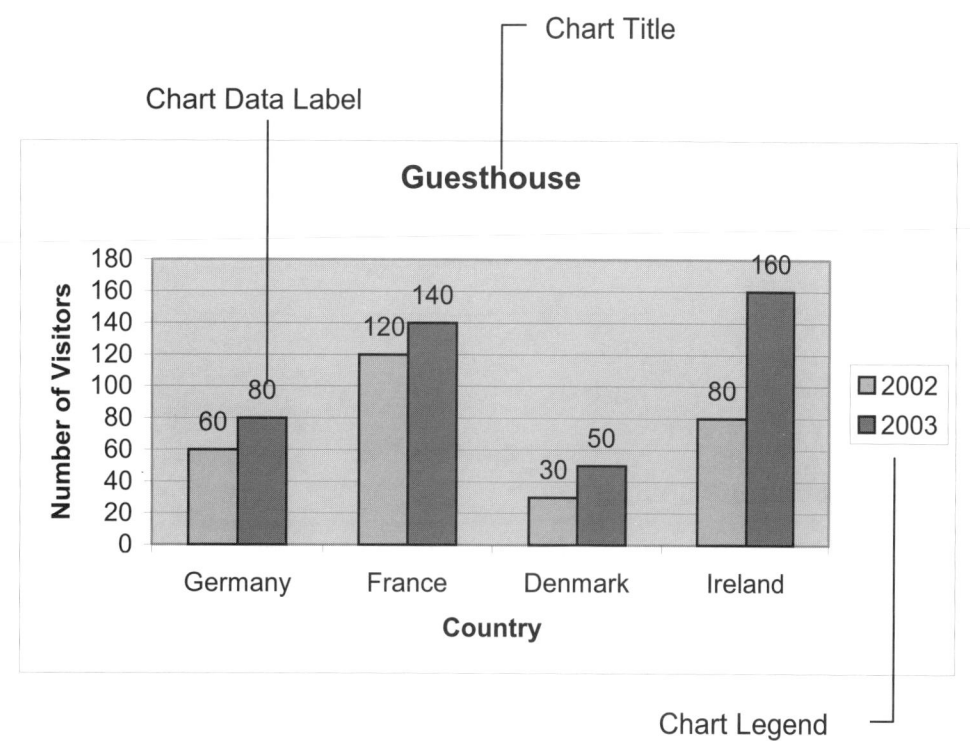

*Chart Title* — points to "Guesthouse"
*Chart Data Label* — points to the "80" label
*Chart Legend* — points to the 2002/2003 legend

Chart: **Guesthouse** — Number of Visitors by Country (Germany, France, Denmark, Ireland) for 2002 and 2003.
- Germany: 60 (2002), 80 (2003)
- France: 120 (2002), 140 (2003)
- Denmark: 30 (2002), 50 (2003)
- Ireland: 80 (2002), 160 (2003)

### 5.3.1 Re-positioning a chart title

The chart title is **Guesthouse**.

- Select the chart by clicking on it.

    Eight handles appear around the chart.

- Click on **Chart Title**.

    [Guesthouse]

    Eight handles appear as shown in diagram.

- With the mouse button depressed *drag* the Chart Title and *drop* in location shown in the next diagram.

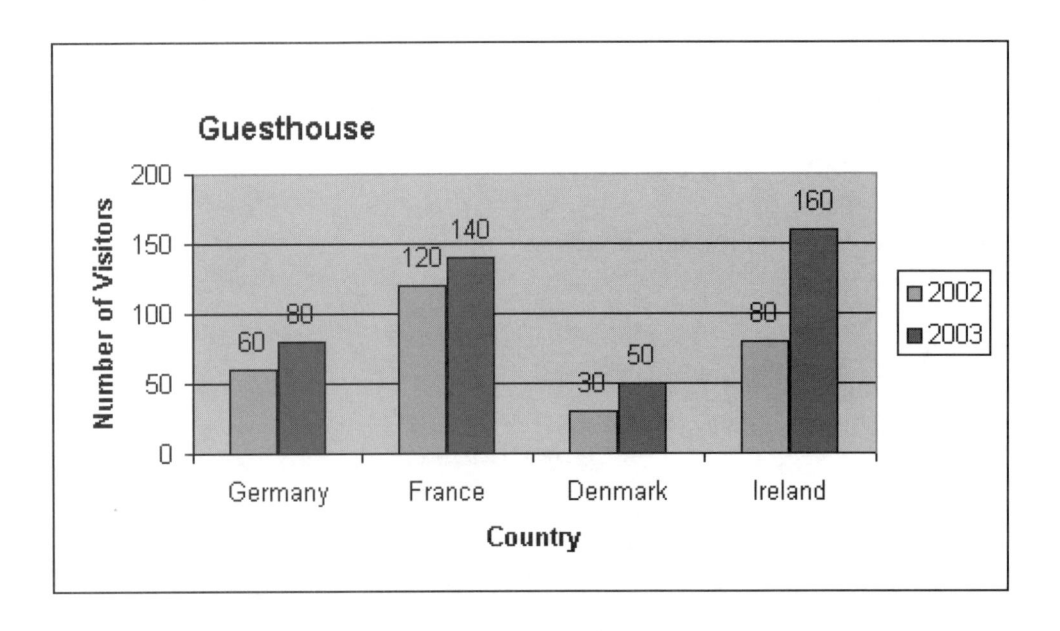

# Chapter 2 – Data Handling

[Bar chart: Guesthouse – Number of Visitors by Country (2002, 2003). Germany: 60, 80. France: 120, 140. Denmark: 30, 50. Ireland: 80, 160.]

We will now re-position the chart legend.

## 5.3.2 Re-positioning a chart legend

- Select the **chart** by clicking on it.
- Choose the **chart legend** by clicking on it.

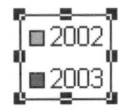

[Legend showing 2002, 2003 with selection handles]

Eight handles appear around object.

- With the mouse button depressed *drag* the Chart Legend and *drop* in location shown.

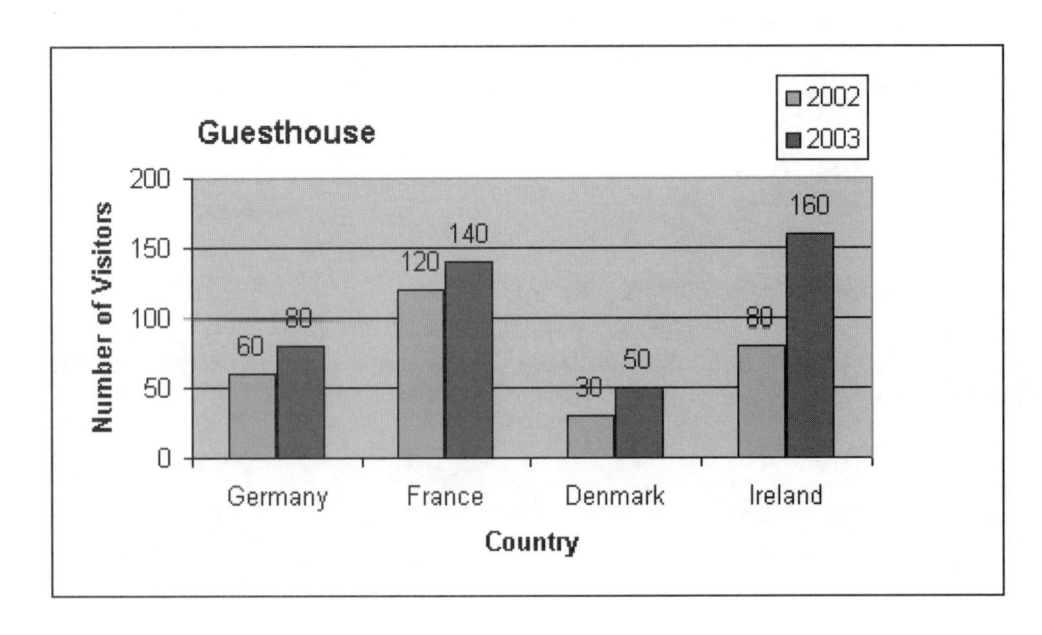

[Bar chart: Guesthouse with legend repositioned to top right – Number of Visitors by Country (2002, 2003). Germany: 60, 80. France: 120, 140. Denmark: 30, 50. Ireland: 80, 160.]

### 5.3.3 Re-positioning a chart data label

- Select the **chart** by clicking on it.

- Select the **chart options** by clicking right button of mouse.

- Select **Data labels** tab.

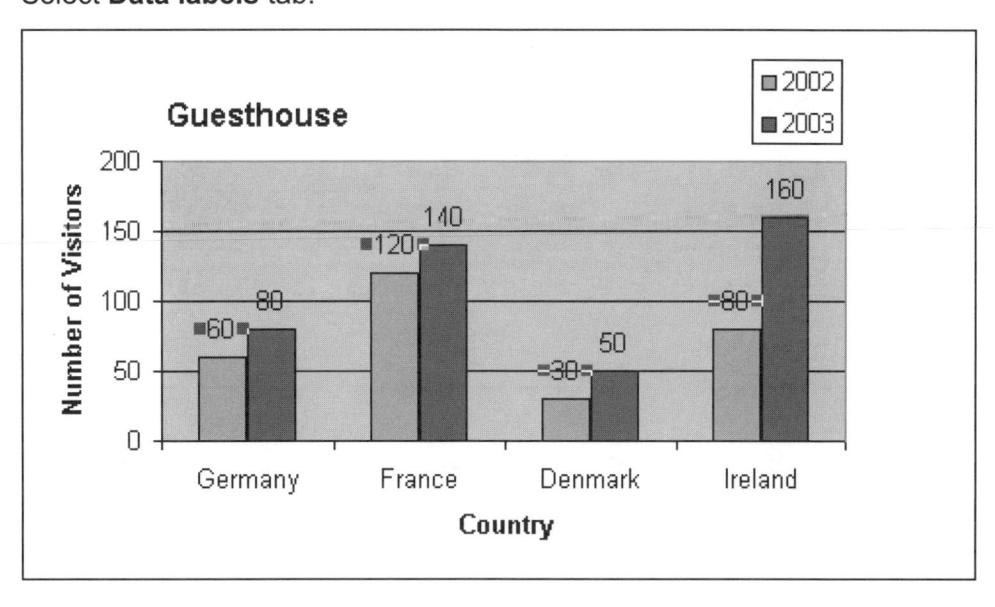

- Select value.

    Two small black squares appear on either side of data label when you click on any one of the values showing.

- Double-click on data label.

    The **Format Data Labels** dialog box opens.

- Choose **Alignment** tab

- Drag the text pointer to **45 Degrees** (or type 45 in the Degrees box)

- Click **OK**.

    The data labels are located at 45 degrees to the horizontal.

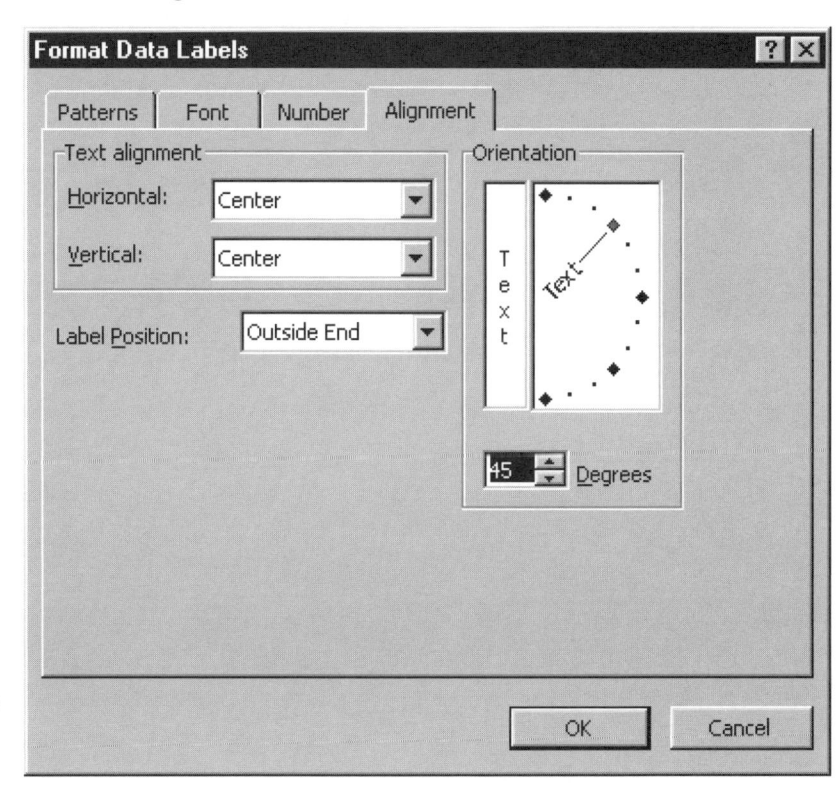

- Repeat these steps for the second set of data labels.

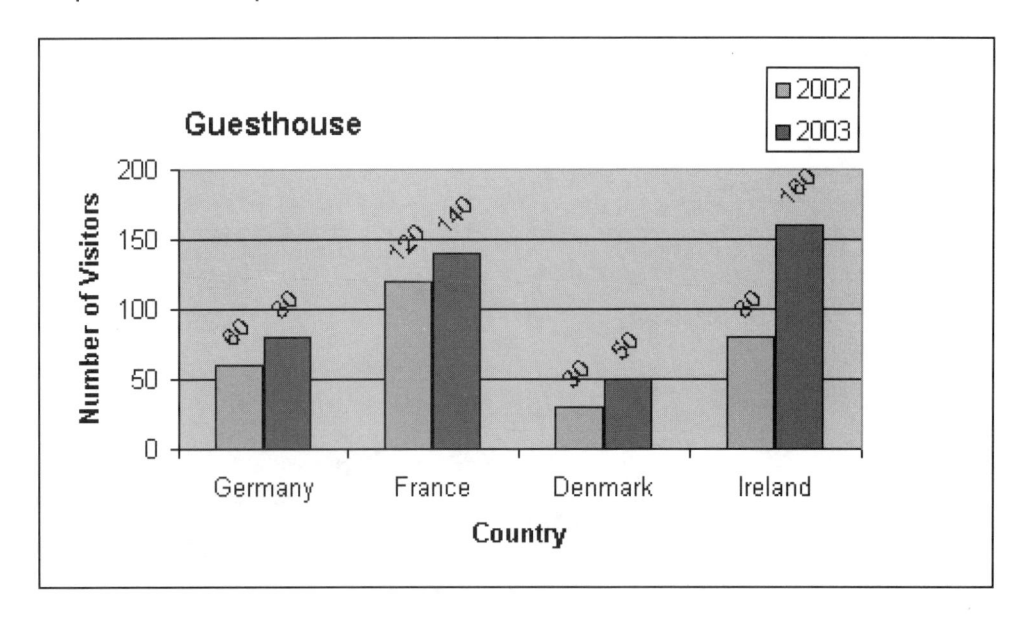

**Guesthouse**

(Bar chart showing Number of Visitors by Country for 2002 and 2003)

| Country | 2002 | 2003 |
|---|---|---|
| Germany | 60 | 80 |
| France | 120 | 140 |
| Denmark | 30 | 50 |
| Ireland | 80 | 160 |

The diagram above gives an indication as what to expect.

In the next section we will find out how to 'explode' the segments in a pie chart.

## 5.4 'Exploding' all the segments in a pie chart (4.2.5.4)

- Open the file **Charts & Graphs**.

- Select the tab **Explode pie chart segments**.

- Click on the pie chart to select it.

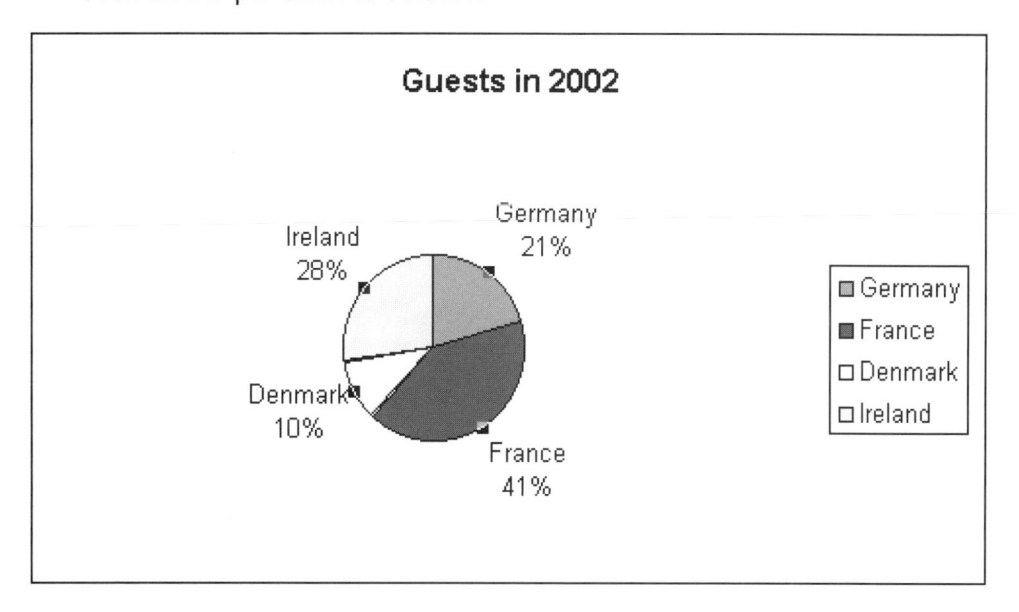

*Guests in 2002*

Germany 21%
Ireland 28%
Denmark 10%
France 41%

The four segments in the pie chart each have a handle – a small black square.

- Click on one of the handles, e.g. France and drag outwards.

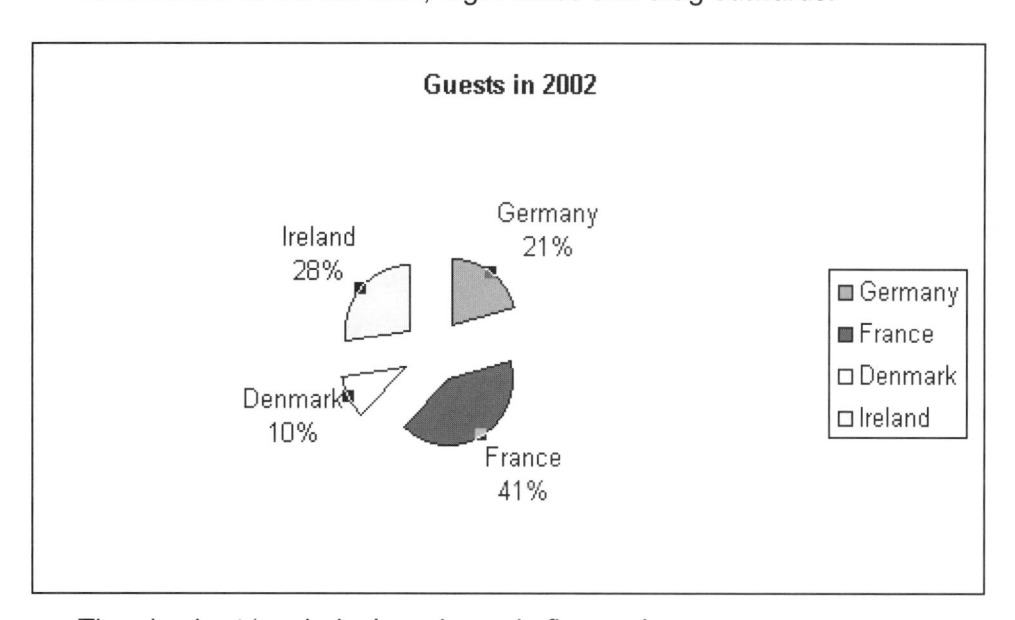

*Guests in 2002*

Germany 21%
Ireland 28%
Denmark 10%
France 41%

The pie chart 'explodes' as shown in figure above.

**NOTE**

To 'explode' a single segment, click on pie chart. Next click on a single segment, e.g. Germany. Click on the Germany handle and drag out the Germany segment.

In the next section we will look at deleting and adding a data series in a chart.

The practice exercises contained in this section relate solely to this manual and do not constitute, or imply, certification by the European Driving Licence Foundation in respect of any ECDL examinations. For details on sitting ECDL examinations in your country please contact the local ECDL/ICDL licensee or visit the European Computer Driving Licence Foundation Ltd web site at http://www.ecdl.com

## Exercise 5A

1. Open the file **Healthcare**. The data shows the sales of a Healthcare product in the year 2003. Select the tab **Pie Chart Explode**. Click on the pie chart to select it. Grab one of the boxes on any of the segments and drag outwards. The pie chart 'explodes'.

2. Now select the tab **Pie Chart**. Click on the pie chart to select it. Right-click on the pie chart and choose **Format Data Series…**. Choose the **Options** tab. Click on the box **Angle of first slice**. Change the angle to **250 degrees**.

3. Click on **OK**.

The practice exercises contained in this section relate solely to this manual and do not constitute, or imply, certification by the European Driving Licence Foundation in respect of any ECDL examinations. For details on sitting ECDL examinations in your country please contact the local ECDL/ICDL licensee or visit the European Computer Driving Licence Foundation Ltd web site at http://www.ecdl.com

## Exercise 5B

1. Select the tab **Healthcare Products**.

   We are going to format the chart numbers and text.

2. Double-click on the **Value Axis**. When the Format Axis dialog box opens, choose **Number**. Choose **Currency** and **0** (zero) **Decimal Places**. Click **OK**.

3. Double-Click on the **Value-Axis** again and choose the **Font** tab from the **Format Axis dialog** box. Choose an appropriate Font, Font Style, Size and Colour. Click **OK**.

4. Repeat 3, for the **Chart Title** and **Legend** and any other labels.

5. Save the file as **Healthcare Solution**.

## 5.5 Deleting a data series in a chart (4.2.5.5)

- Open the file **Charts & Graphs**.

- Select the tab **Delete data series.**

There are two data series represented by the columns in the chart, one for 2002 (blue in colour) and one for 2003 (plum in colour). We are going to delete the data series for 2003.

|         | 2002 | 2003 |
|---------|------|------|
| Germany | 60   | 80   |
| France  | 120  | 140  |
| Denmark | 30   | 50   |
| Ireland | 80   | 160  |

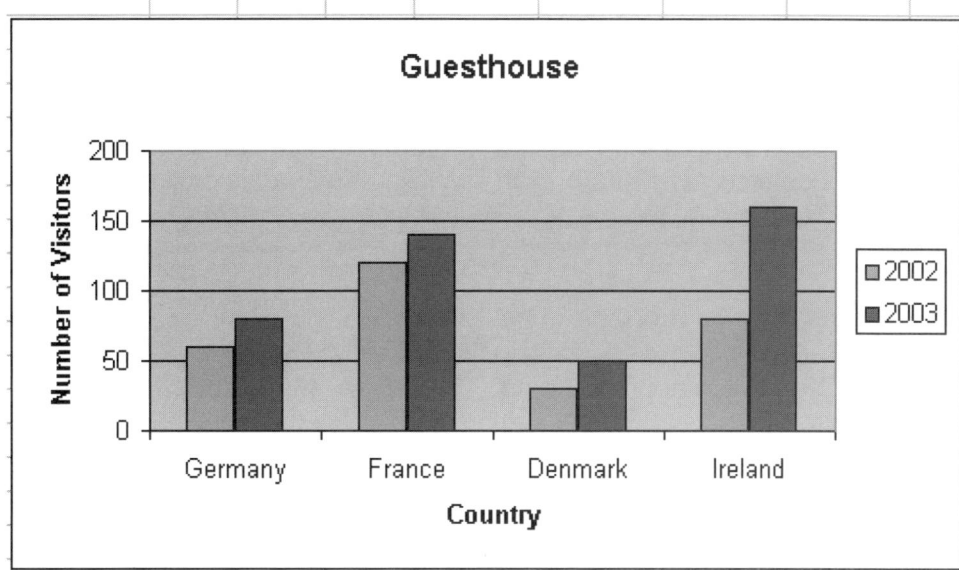

- Click on any of the columns for the year **2003**. The presence of a black box indicates they are selected.

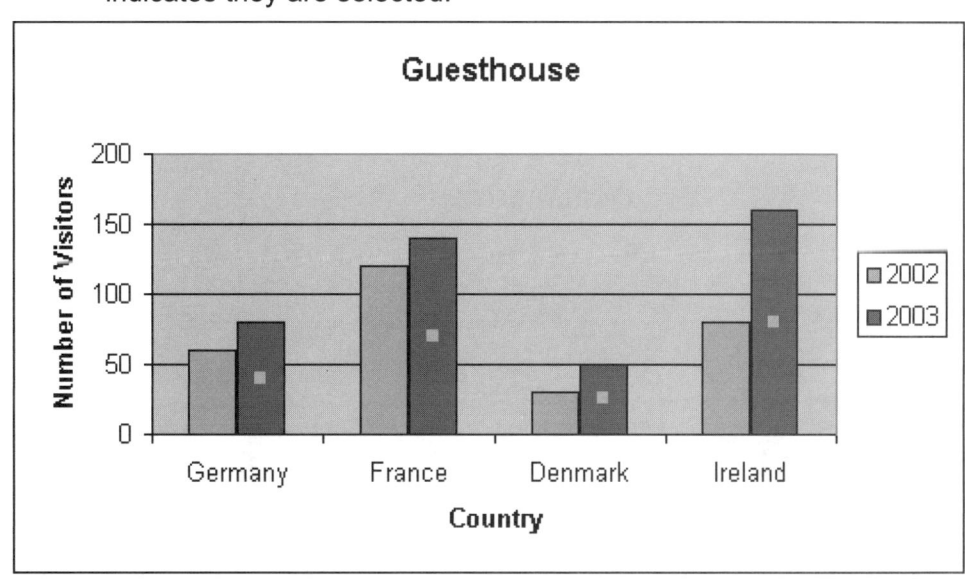

- Click on the **Del** key.

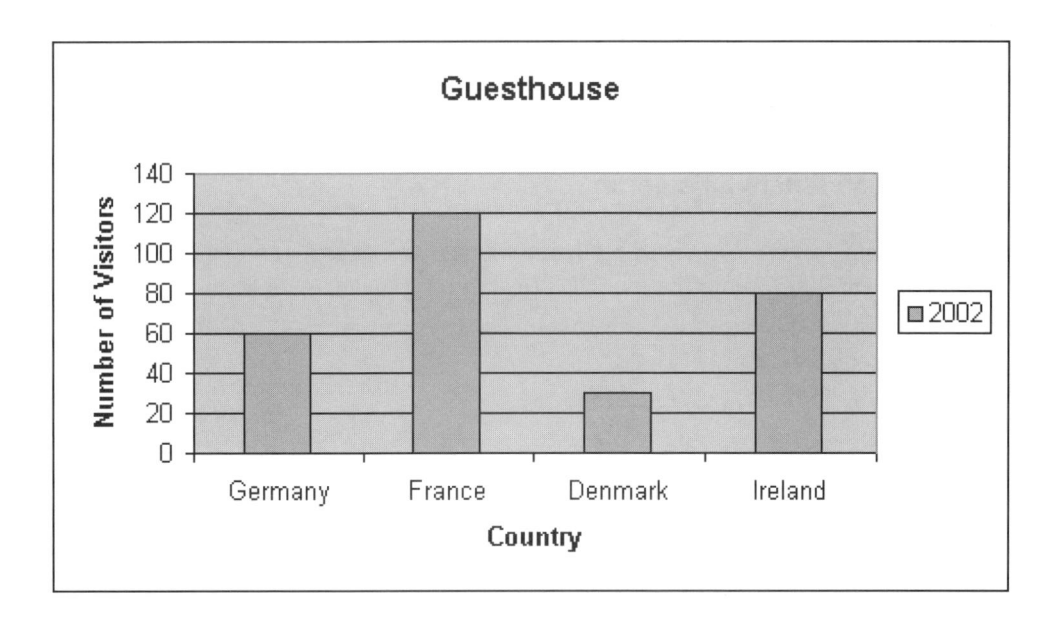

The chart now displays only the data series for 2002. Notice that only the data series for 2003 is deleted. The information on which the chart is based has not been changed! (Range A1:C5).

### 5.5.1 Adding a data series to a chart

We have successfully deleted a data series from a chart. We will now **add** a data series for **2004**. The data for 2004 is present in the range **J1:J5**.

- Cut (**Ctrl + X**) the range in **J1:J5** and paste (**Ctrl + V**) into cell **D1**.

The figure below shows how it should look.

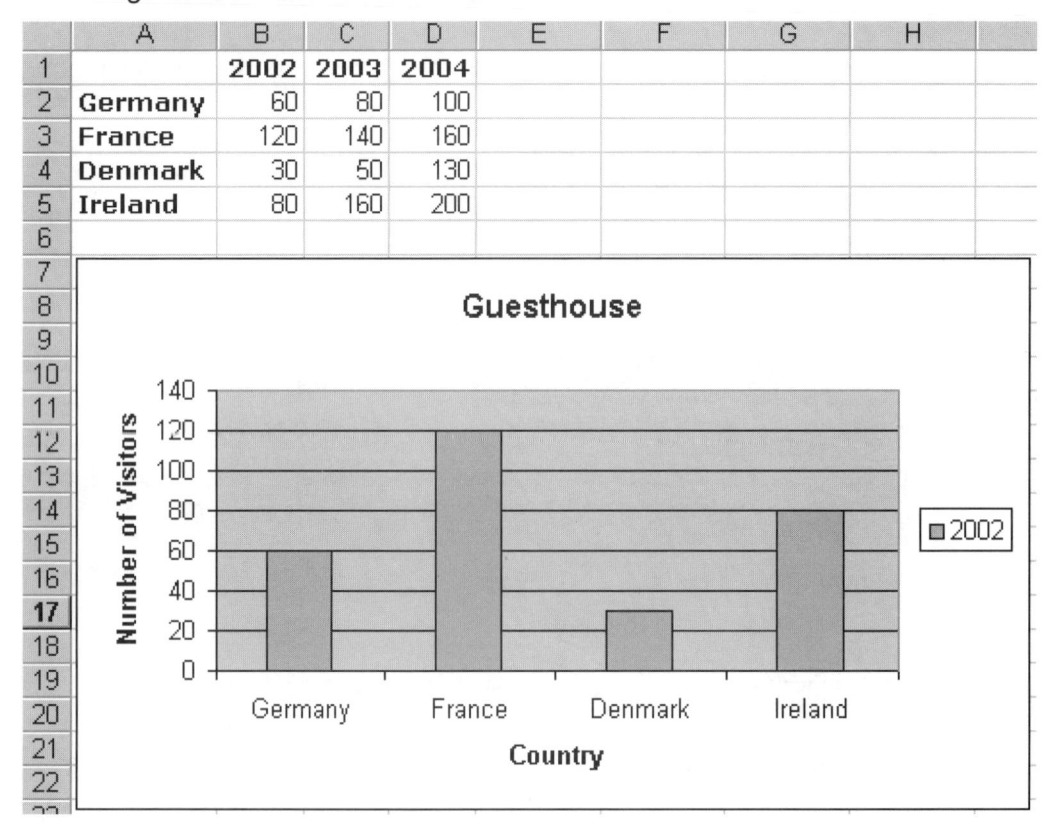

|   | A | B | C | D |
|---|---|---|---|---|
| 1 |   | 2002 | 2003 | 2004 |
| 2 | Germany | 60 | 80 | 100 |
| 3 | France | 120 | 140 | 160 |
| 4 | Denmark | 30 | 50 | 130 |
| 5 | Ireland | 80 | 160 | 200 |

Chapter 2 – Data Handling

- Highlight the data for **2004** in the range **D1:D5**.
- Copy the data using **Edit** followed by **Copy** (or **Ctrl + C**).
- Click on the **Plot Area** of the chart.
- Select **Edit** followed by **Paste** (or **Ctrl + V**).

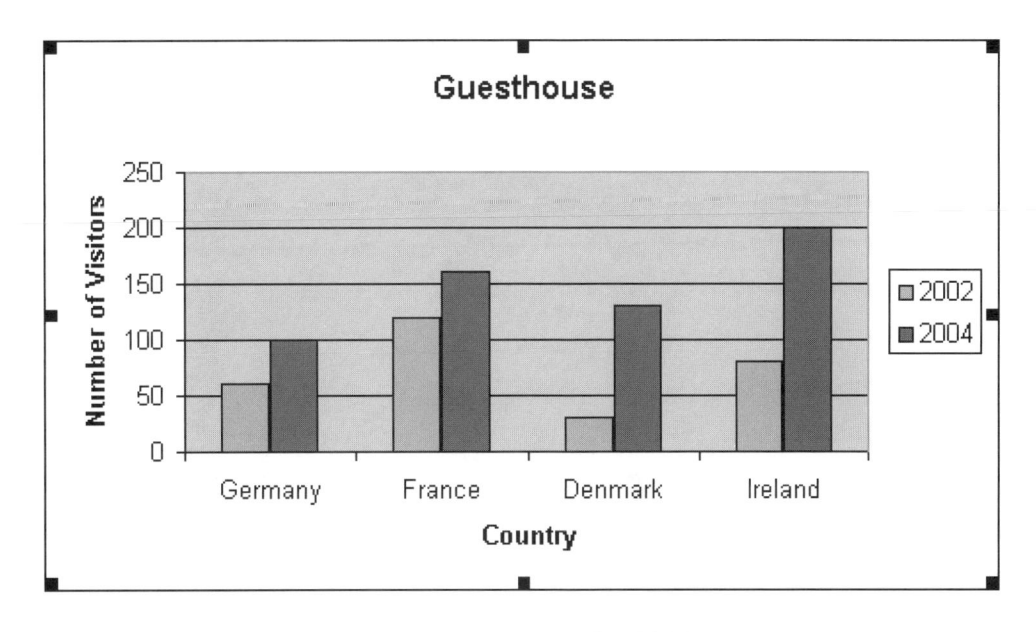

**Guesthouse**

*(Bar chart showing Number of Visitors by Country for 2002 and 2004: Germany, France, Denmark, Ireland)*

The chart now includes the data series for 2004.

Next we will modify a chart for a defined data series.

## 5.6 Modifying a chart type for a defined data series (4.2.5.6)

- Open the file **Charts & Graphs**.
- Select the tab **Modify chart type.**
- Click on the data series for **2003**.
- Right-click on the chart and choose **Chart Type ...** from the menu.

Chapter 2 – Data Handling

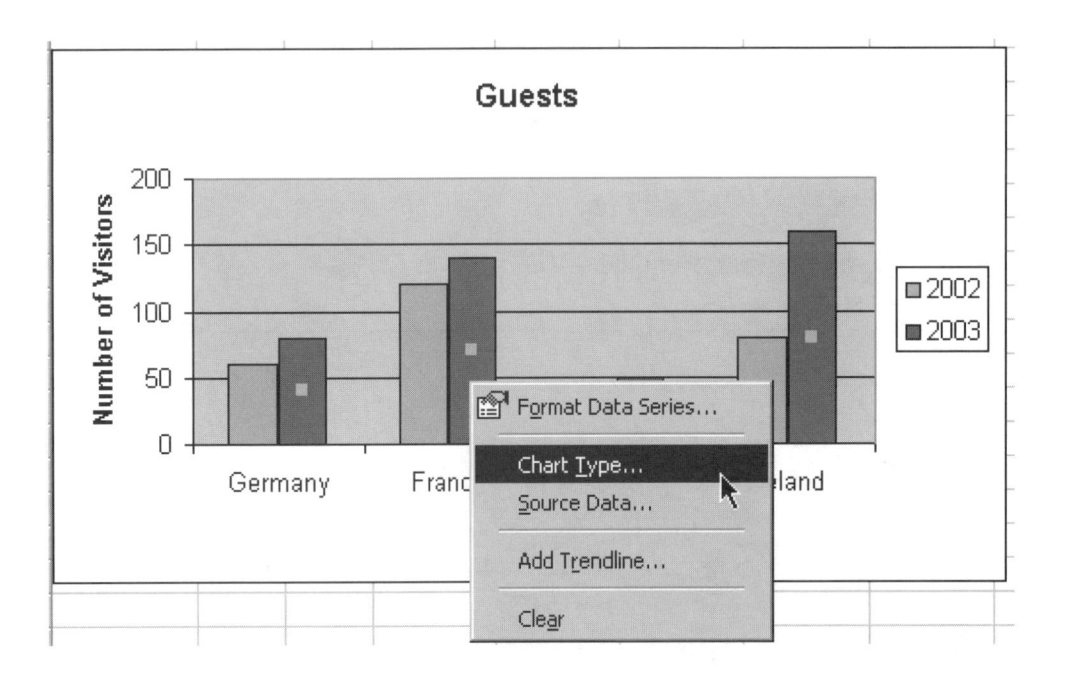

- The **Chart Type** dialog box opens. Select **Line-Chart** from the options available.

- Choose one of the **Chart sub-types**. (Not all are suitable).

- Click **OK**.

  The chart type is changed as shown on the next page.

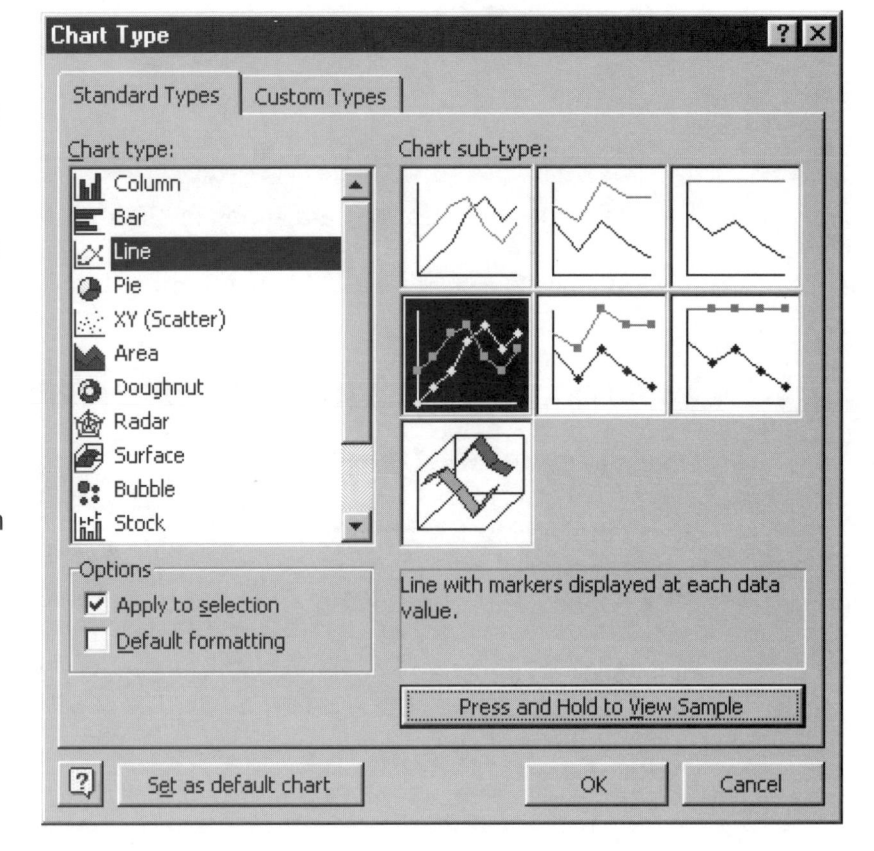

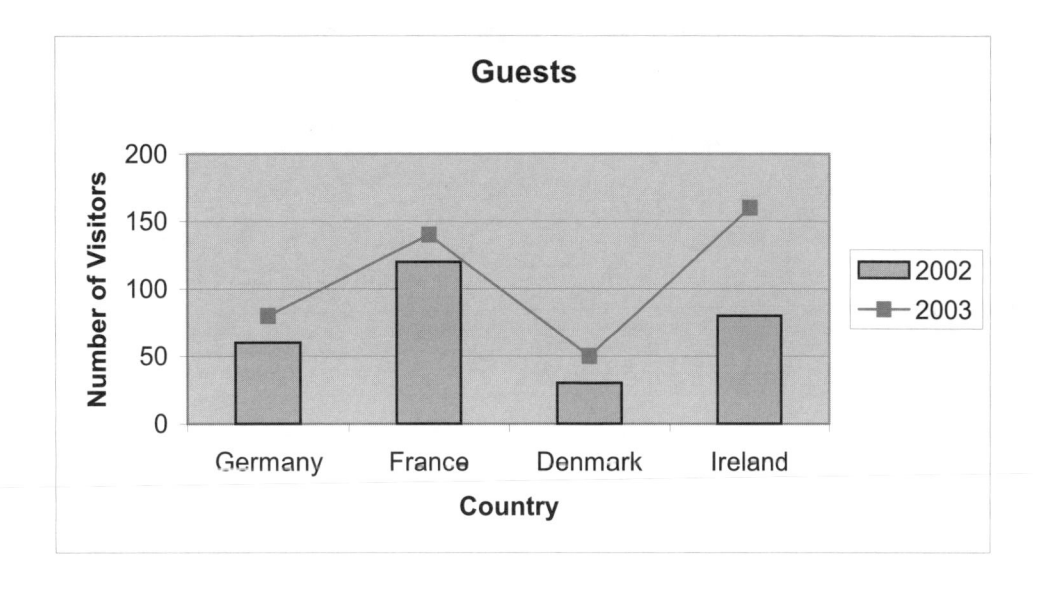

In the next section we will look at how to widen the gap between columns and bars in a 2D chart.

## 5.7 Widening the gap between columns / bars in a 2D chart
(4.2.5.7)

- Open the file **Charts & Graphs**.

- Select the tab **Widen gap in 2D chart**

- Right-click on one of the columns for **2003**. Small squares indicate that the data markers are selected.

- Select **Format Data Series** from the menu.

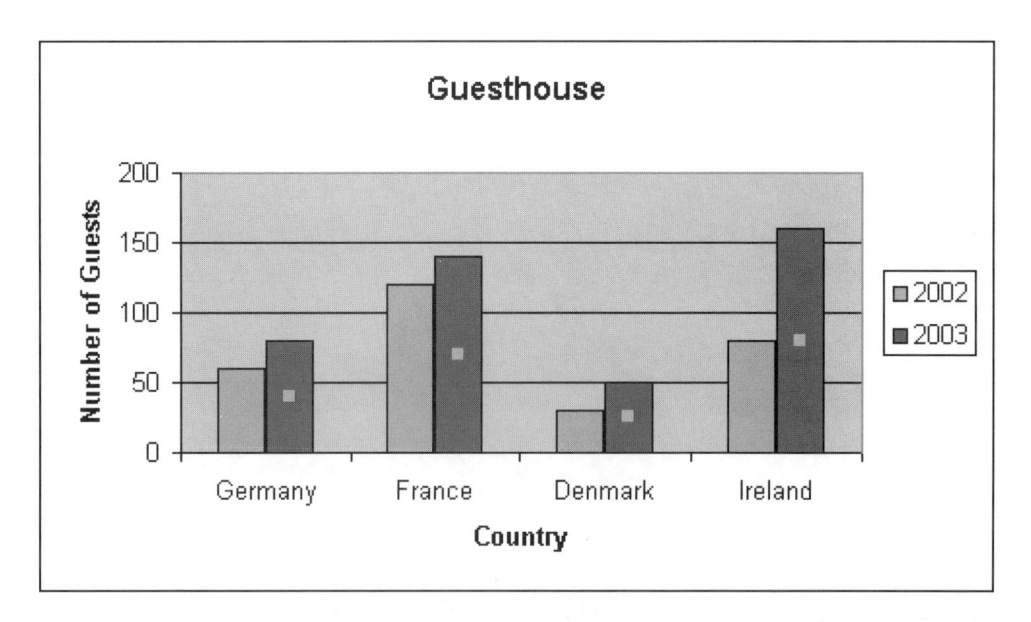

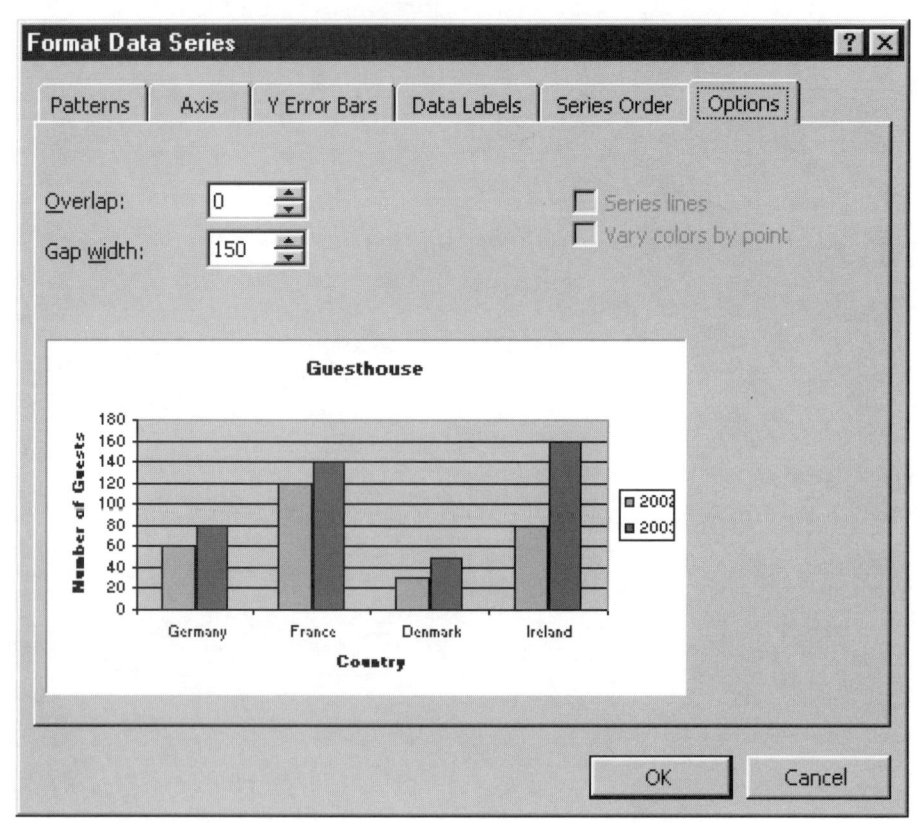

Chapter 2 – Data Handling

The **Format Data Series** dialog box opens.

- Choose the **Options** tab.

- Double click on the **Overlap** box.

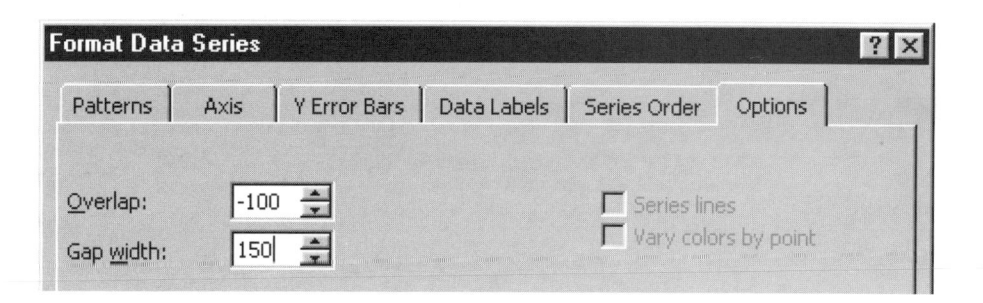

- Change the Overlap value to **–100 (minus 100).**

- Click on **OK**.

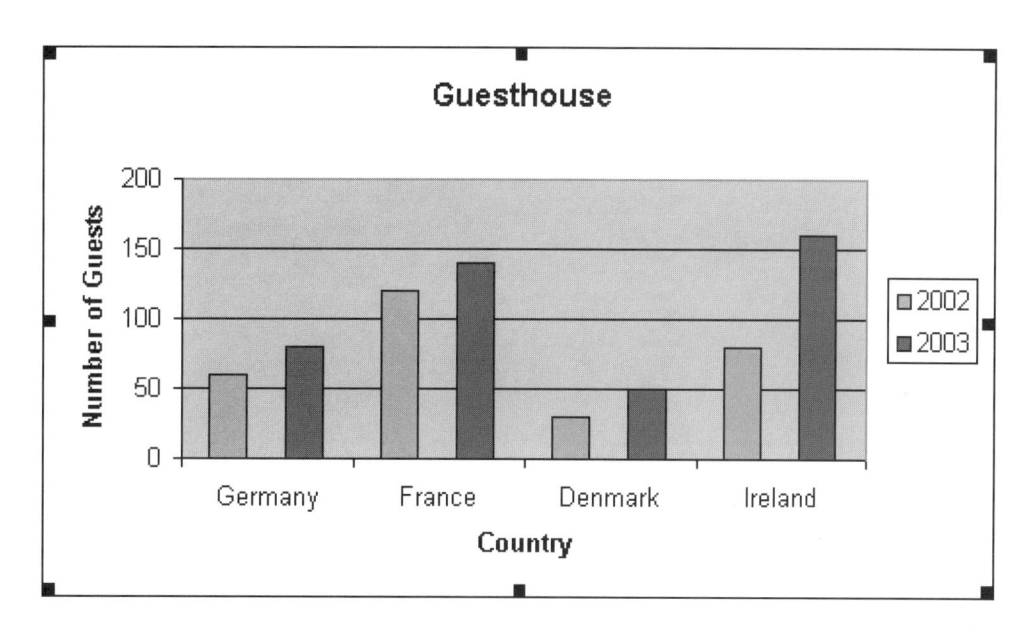

The gap between the columns increases.
You may wish to experiment with other values.

In the next section we will look at how to insert a background image in a 2D chart.

Chapter 2 – Data Handling

## 5.8 Inserting a background image in a 2D chart (4.2.5.8)

- Open the file **Charts & Graphs**.

- Select the tab **Insert image in 2D chart.**

- Double-click on the **Plot Area**.

    The **Format Plot Area** dialog box opens.

- Select the **Patterns** tab.

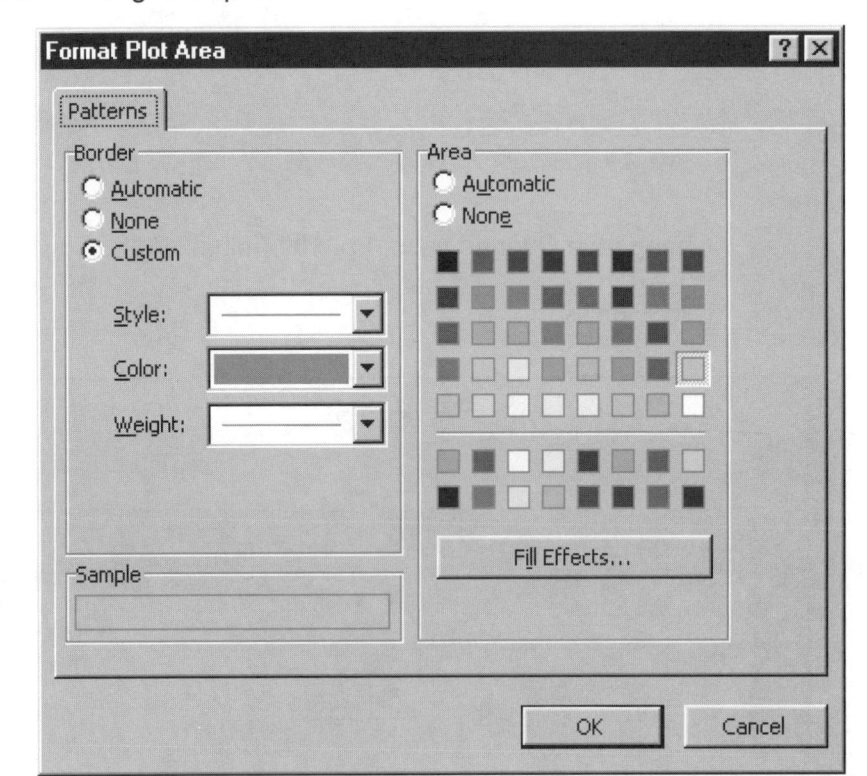

- Now click **Fill Effects...** button.

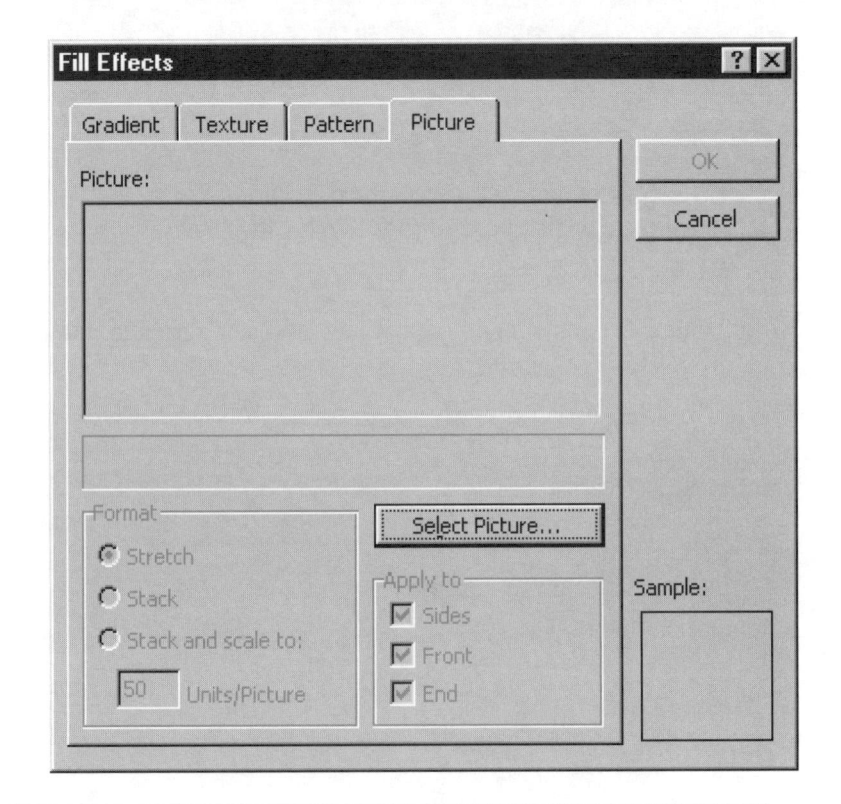

- Click on **Select Picture....**

Chapter 2 – Data Handling

The **Select Picture** dialog box opens. You must locate the picture you intend to insert. You will have access to the two listed, **Guesthouse** or **Tourist**.

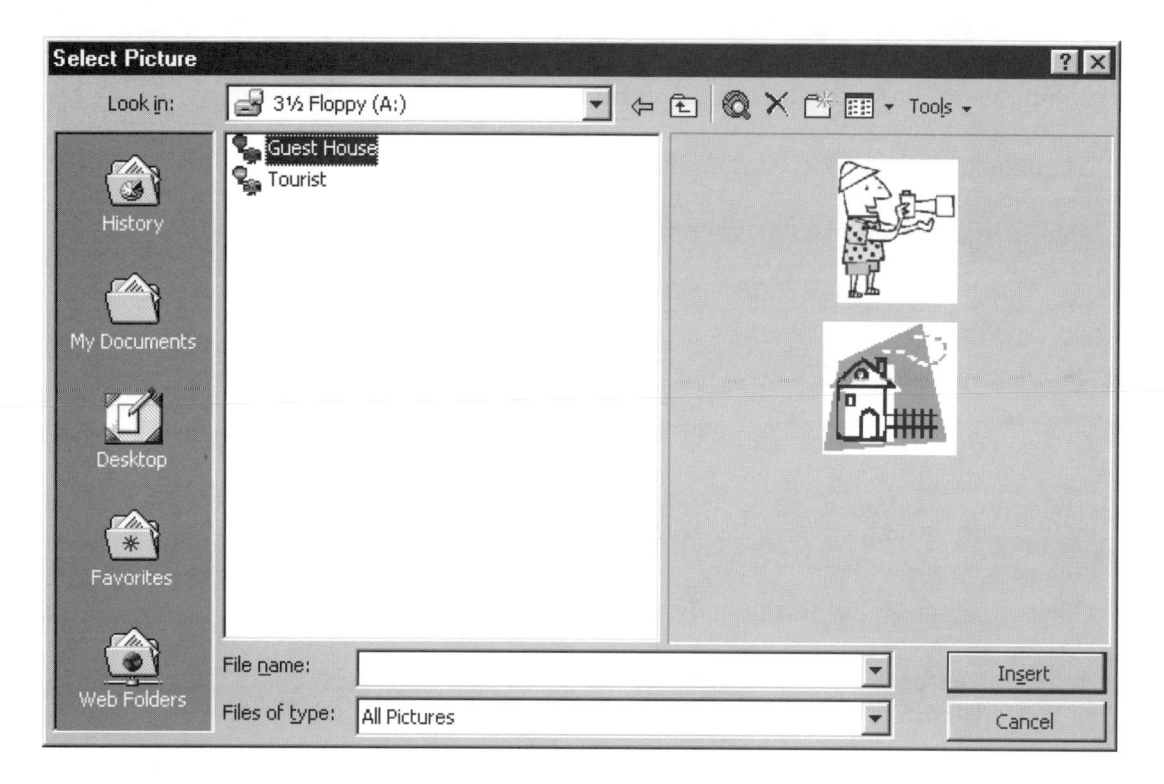

- Click on your picture choice and then select **Insert**.

- When the **Fill Effects** dialog box opens with your choice select **OK**.

- Click **OK** again to close remaining dialog boxes.

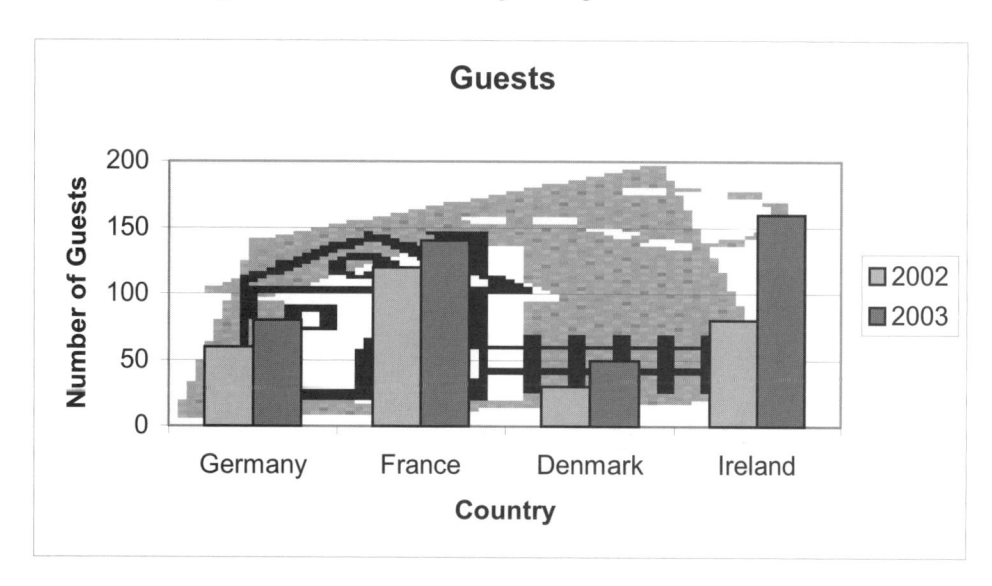

The selected picture appears in the background.

## 5.9 Inserting an image in a 2D chart bar (4.2.5.8)

- Open the file **Charts & Graphs**.

- Select the tab **Insert image in 2D chart.**

- Double-click on any of the columns.

  The **Format Chart Area** dialog box opens.

- Select the **Patterns** tab and click on the **Fill Effects** button.

- Choose the **Picture** tab.

- Click on **Select Picture** button to open the **Select Picture** dialog box.

You will have to find your picture. You have two options **Guesthouse** or **Tourist**. (There may be alternative pictures in your folders that you prefer to use).

- Click on either **Guesthouse** or **Tourist**.

- In the **Fill Effects** options click on **Stack and scale** and insert **50** as the number of **Units/Picture**.

- Select **OK**, followed by **OK**.

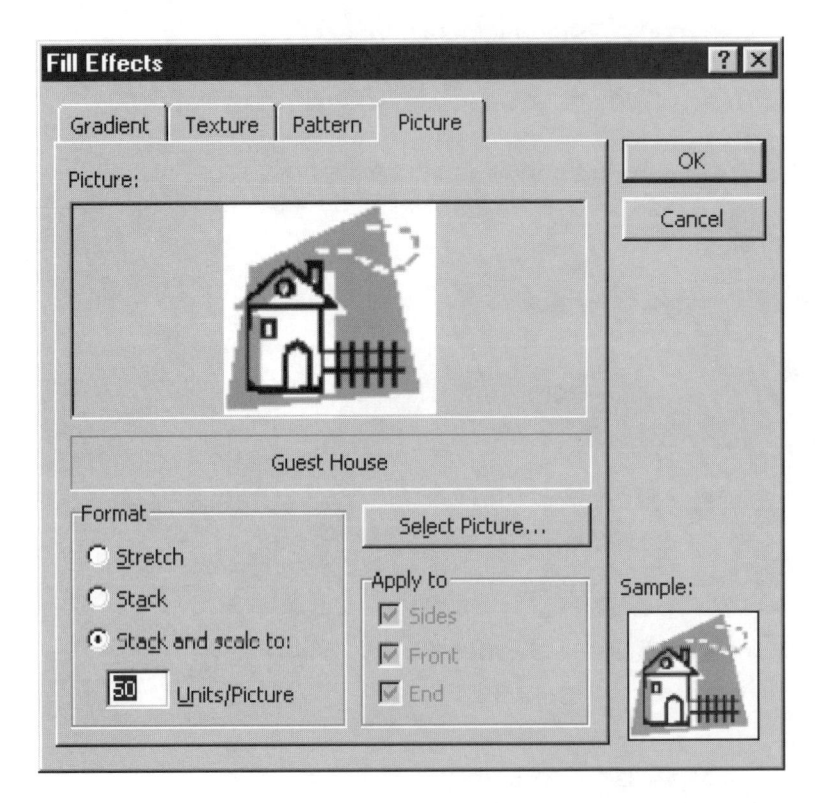

# Chapter 2 – Data Handling

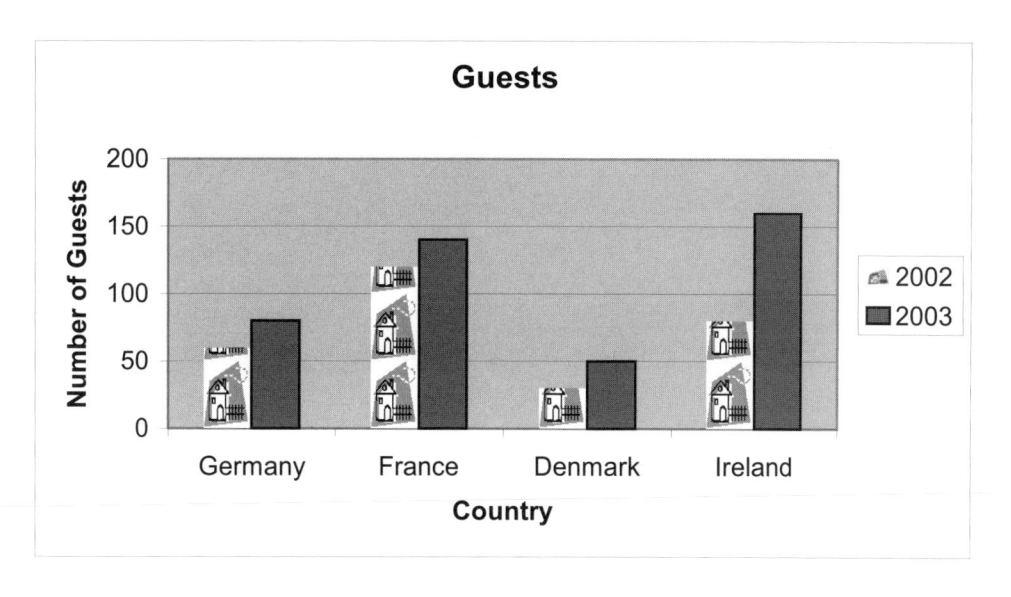

[Bar chart titled "Guests" showing Number of Guests by Country for 2002 and 2003: Germany (~55, 80), France (~120, 140), Denmark (~25, 50), Ireland (~80, 160)]

The final chart should look like the one above.

- Save the file as **Charts & Graphs Solution**.

The practice exercises contained in this section relate solely to this manual and do not constitute, or imply, certification by the European Driving Licence Foundation in respect of any ECDL examinations. For details on sitting ECDL examinations in your country please contact the local ECDL/ICDL licensee or visit the European Computer Driving Licence Foundation Ltd web site at http://www.ecdl.com

## Exercise 5C

1   Open the file **Healthcare** and click on the **Healthcare Products** tab. Right-click on the chart and select **Chart Type...** from the menu. The Chart Type dialog box opens. Select a chart of your choice and click **OK**.

## Self Check Exercises

1.  Using the Top 10 AutoFilter permits you to filter only the Top 10 Items or Percent in a list.
    - ☐ True
    - ☐ False

2.  What is the correct procedure for displaying the AutoFilter menu?
    - ☐ Choose Data, followed by Sort and then select AutoFilter.
    - ☐ Choose AutoFilter icon on the Standard toolbar.
    - ☐ Choose Data, followed by Filter and then select AutoFilter.

3.  How do you 'explode' all the segments in a pie chart?
    - ☐ Click on pie chart to select it, click on a segment, choose a handle and drag outwards.
    - ☐ Click on pie chart to select it, double click on segment, select a handle and drag outwards.
    - ☐ Double click on pie chart to select it, choose a handle and drag outwards.

4.  To save a workbook as a template you must choose File followed by Save As, type in a name for the template, click the Save as type drop-down arrow and choose Template?
    - ☐ True
    - ☐ False

5.  Templates cannot contain formulas - True or False?
    - ☐ True
    - ☐ False

6.  Ready-made templates are available from which tabs in the New dialog box?
    - ☐ Spreadsheet Solutions
    - ☐ Business Planner Templates
    - ☐ General
    - ☐ All of the above

7.  To consolidate data in adjacent worksheets you could use a:
    - ☐ 2D sum function
    - ☐ 3D sum function
    - ☐ 4D sum function

8.  By examining the box above what procedure is being carried out?
    - ☐ A multiple criteria query
    - ☐ A custom sort
    - ☐ A single criteria query
    - ☐ An advanced filter

The practice exercises contained in this section relate solely to this manual and do not constitute, or imply, certification by the European Driving Licence Foundation in respect of any ECDL examinations. For details on sitting ECDL examinations in your country please contact the local ECDL/ICDL licensee or visit the European Computer Driving Licence Foundation Ltd web site at http://www.ecdl.com

## Practical Exercises

### Exercise 1

In this exercise, you will reposition the Chart Title and Chart Legend.

1 Open the file **Healthcare** and select the **Practical Exercise** tab. You are required to reposition the **Chart Title** (Product Sales) and **Chart Legend** (Product A, Product B, Product C). Place them in a suitable location.

You are required to delete the data series for Product B.

2 Click on any of the columns for **Product B**. The black box indicates they are selected. Now click on the **Del** key. The data series is deleted.

You are required to modify the chart type for **Product C**.

3 Click on data series for **Product C**. Right-click on chart and choose **Chart Type...** from the menu. When the **Chart Type dialog** box opens, select **Line Charts** from the available options. Choose a **Chart sub-type** and click **OK**.

4 Save the file as **Healthcare Solution**.

# Chapter 3

Functions

# Syllabus
## Module AM4
## Spreadsheets – Advanced Level

**AM 4.3.1 Using Functions**     Page

| | | |
|---|---|---|
| AM4.3.1.1 | Use date and time functions:<br>TODAY; DAY; MONTH; YEAR | 131 |
| AM4.3.1.2 | Use mathematical functions:<br>SUMIF; SUMPOSITIVE; ROUND | 140 |
| AM4.3.1.3 | Use statistical functions:<br>COUNT; PURECOUNT; COUNTA; COUNTIF | 145 |
| AM4.3.1.4 | Use text functions:<br>PROPER; UPPER; LOWER; CONCATENATE | 150 |
| AM4.3.1.5 | Use Financial Functions:<br>FV; NPV; PMT; PV; RATE | 156 |
| AM4.3.1.6 | Use lookup and reference functions:<br>HLOOKUP; VLOOKUP | 169 |
| AM4.3.1.7 | Use logical functions:<br>IF; AND; OR; ISERROR | 174 |
| AM4.3.1.8 | Use available database functions:<br>DSUM; DMIN; DMAX; DCOUNT | 182 |
| AM4.3.1.9 | Use nested functions: | 186 |

# Functions

A **function** performs a predetermined operation on a cell or a range of cells, such as adding the values or calculating the average of a range of cell values. For example, the function =SUM(A1:A12) calculates the sum of all the values in the range A1 to A12. If any of the values in this range are changed, then the sum is recalculated.

Functions facilitate the writing of formulas. If for example you wished to add numbers in the range A1 to A7, you could write the formula as:

=A1 + A2 + A3 + A4 + A5 + A6 + A7

This formula uses cell references separated by arithmetic operators, in this case plus(+).
It takes much less time and makes more sense to use the formula:

=SUM(A1:A7)

Also, using a formula reduces the chances of error which can happen easily when inputting data manually.

## Structure of a function

A *function* has two main parts, the function name and the arguments.

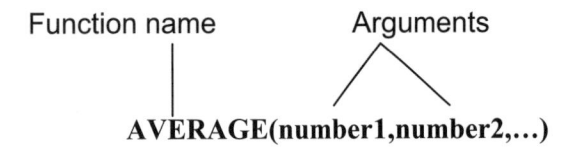

Function name     Arguments

AVERAGE(number1,number2,...)

The functions in Excel follow a similar design. The function name is followed by a set of parentheses. The arguments are inside the parentheses. If there is more than one argument, then the arguments are separated by commas.
The function name indicates what the function does. An argument is text or numerical value used by the function. Excel has over 200 functions, which are grouped in the following categories: *Financial*, *Date & Time*, *Math & Trig*, *Statistical*, *Lookup & Reference*, *Database*, *Text*, *Logical*, *Information* and *User Defined*. In order to use the function properly you must know about the values used in the function. Also, you have to know which function to use as there are a large number of them. We will be looking at examples from many of these categories.

**NOTE**
If you have knowledge of Visual Basic for Applications (VBA) you can create your own complex functions. Functions can also be bought commercially.

## Arguments

**Functions with one argument**

Some functions use only a single argument. These can be represented as follows.

=function_name(argument)

The table below shows some of these.

| Function | Result |
|---|---|
| =SUM(A1:A10) | Adds the sum of values in range A1:A10 |
| =AVERAGE(B6:B12) | Calculates the average of values in the range B6:B12 |
| =MAX(C1:C10) | Shows the highest value in the range C1:C10 |
| =MIN(F12:H16) | Shows the minimum value in the range F12:H16 |
| =COUNT(A1:A12) | Counts the number of entries in the range A1:A12 |

**Functions with more than one argument**

Some functions have more than one argument. These can be represented as follows:

=function_name(argument,argument)

=SUM(A1:A10, B1) adds the values in the range A1 to A10 then adds on the contents of cell B1. We will examine functions with more than one argument. These include:

**CONCATENATE(text1,text2,...)**

**PV(rate,nper,fv,type)**

**AND(logical1,logical2,...)**

**Functions with no arguments**

Some functions have no arguments. These can be represented as:

=function_name()

Below are three functions without arguments.

=**TODAY()** displays the serial number of today's date.

=**NOW()** returns the current date and time in the cell containing the formula.

=**PI()** returns the value of PI accurate to nine decimal places by default.

Although the above examples have no argument, the parentheses must be present.

## Entering a Function

You can enter a function in two ways:

- Using the Formula Palette.
- Typing and clicking.

## Using the Formula Palette

Select **Function** from the **Insert** menu or click the **Paste Function** on the **Standard toolbar**.

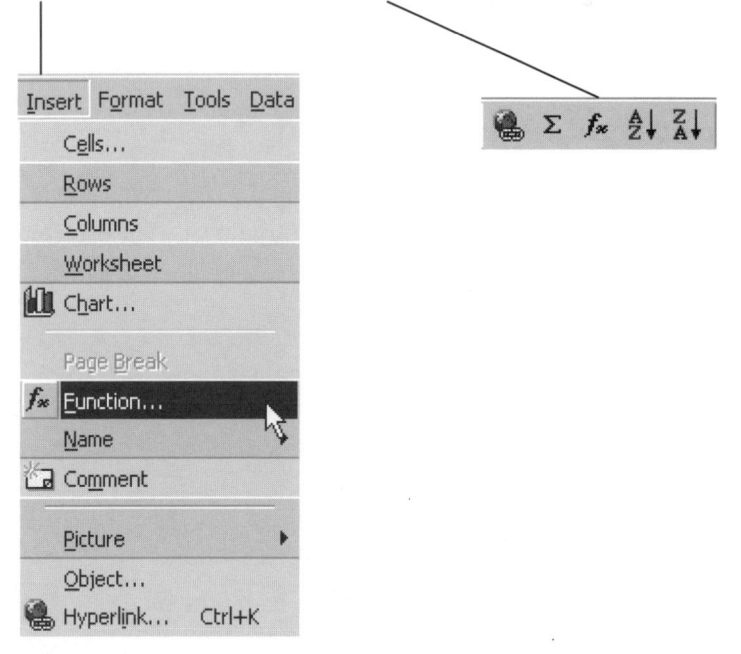

The **Paste Function** dialog box opens with a list of **Function categories**. You scroll down the categories to select the one you wish to use and then select the function name. For example if you are going to use a **Financial** function select it from the **Function category**, then scroll down the **Function name** list to the function you are going to use, in this case **PMT**.
The Paste function box states what the function does and also gives the name of the function with its arguments.

**=PMT(rate,nper,pv,fv,type)**

We will be using this function in **Section 5** of this chapter.

Click **OK**.

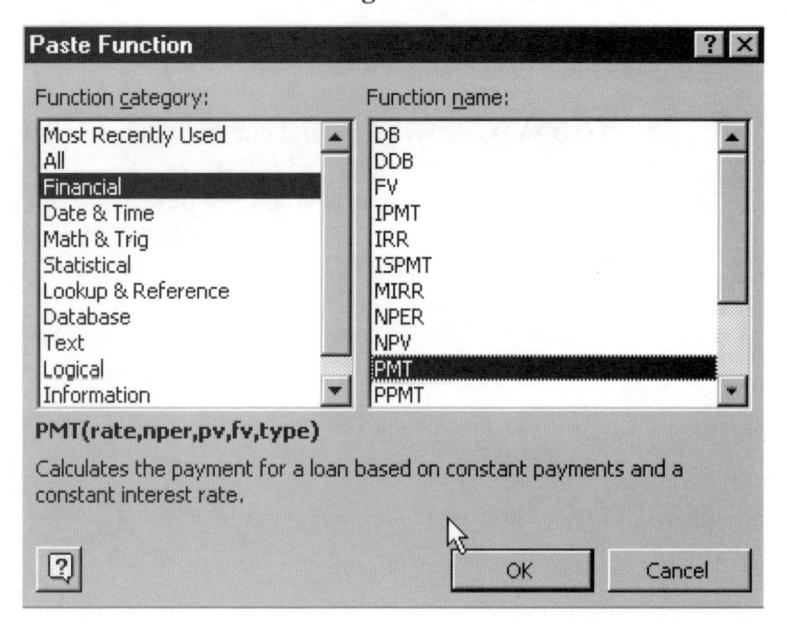

# Chapter 3 - Functions

The **Formula Palette** opens below the **Formula bar**. It includes areas where the argument entries may be added. Those emboldened, in this case **Rate**, **Nper** and **Pv** require an entry. Those greyed out are optional entries. Information on the function is also given and when all entries are complete the Formula result will display the solution.

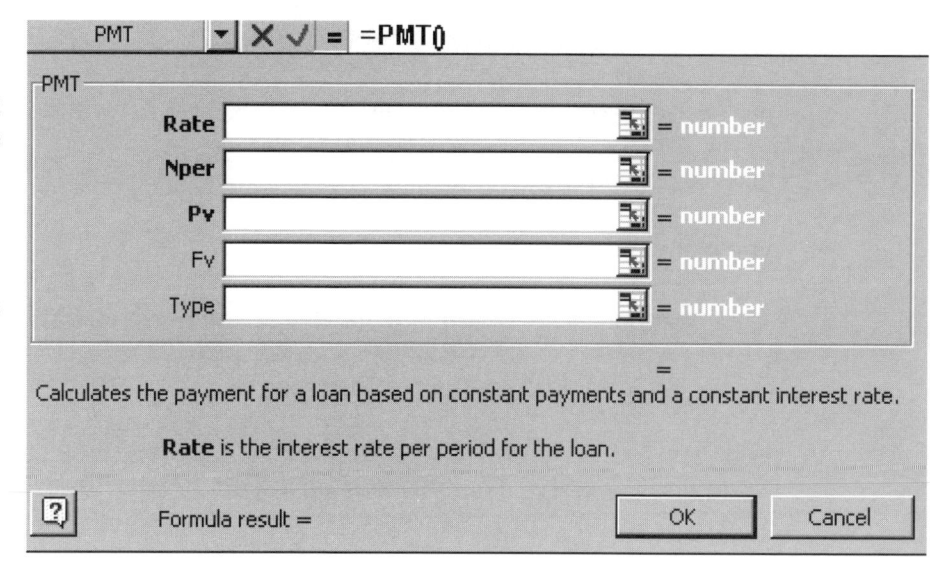

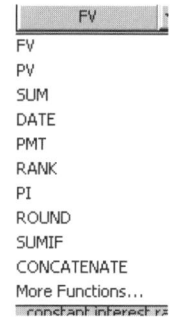

Functions can also be chosen from the **Functions menu** by clicking on the drop down menu. This also gives access to More Functions.

## Typing and Clicking

You can enter a function by typing and clicking. The formula always starts with an = (equals) sign.

   =ROUND(F6,2)

   =FV(rate,nper,pmt,fv,type)

   =CONCATENATE(text1,text2,...)

Refer to any of the above functions, ROUND, FUTURE VALUE, CONCATENATE as you complete the exercise below.

- Select the cell where you wish to enter function.
- Type in an **=** (equals) sign.
- Insert open parenthesis **(**

- Type in reference for first argument.

- Insert second argument, if any, and separate by a **,** (comma).

- Insert remaining arguments, if any.

- Type close parenthesis **)**

- Click Enter on the keyboard or Enter ✓ on the Formula bar.

Remember the formula does not contain spaces.

As you become more familiar and indeed confident with formulas you may decide to use this method of entry. The choice is up to you.

Now that we have completed the introduction to functions, let's have a look at **DATE** and **TIME** functions.

# Chapter 3 - Functions

## Section 1    Date and Time Functions (4.3.1.1)

**TODAY, DAY, MONTH, YEAR**
Also **DATE, TIME, NOW** and **WEEKDAY**

### 1.1    DATE

**Syntax:** DATE(year,month,day)

**What it does:** Returns the serial number of a particular date in date-time code.

Excel considers dates and times as numbers. When a date or time is inserted in a worksheet, Excel converts it to a number in Microsoft Excel Date-Time Code. A DATE is a serial number that indicates the number of days since January 1, 1900.
Let's check how Excel interprets the date.

- Select **Insert** followed by **Function** or click on **Paste Function** button $f_x$ on the Standard toolbar. Choose **Date & Time** from the **Function category** and **DATE** as the **Function name**. Click **OK**. The Date dialog box opens.

- Input **1900** as the year, **1** (January) as the month and **1** as the day.

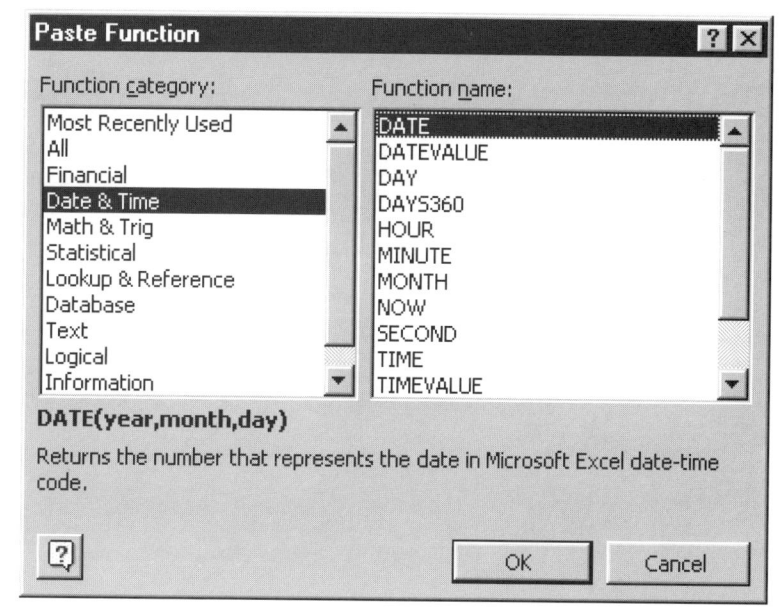

- Excel returns the number 1.

  All DATES are simply the number of days since January 1, 1900.

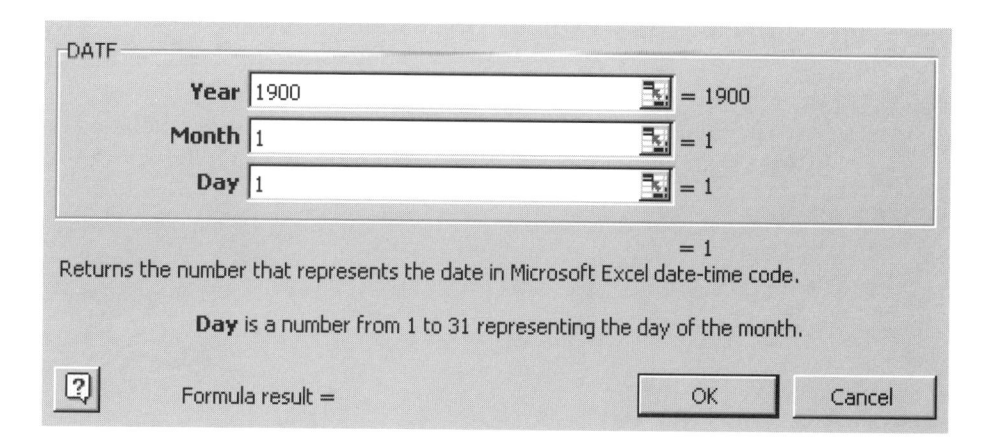

The practice exercises contained in this section relate solely to this manual and do not constitute, or imply, certification by the European Driving Licence Foundation in respect of any ECDL examinations. For details on sitting ECDL examinations in your country please contact the local ECDL/ICDL licensee or visit the European Computer Driving Licence Foundation Ltd web site at http://www.ecdl.com

## Exercise 1A

1    Open the file **Date & Time** and select the **DATE** tab.

2    Check the following: St. Patrick's Day (March 17$^{th}$) 2002, Christmas Day (December 25$^{th}$) 2010, Bastille Day (July 14) 2005 and American Independence Day (July 4$^{th}$) 1945.

3    Your own birthday. (We promise not to look).

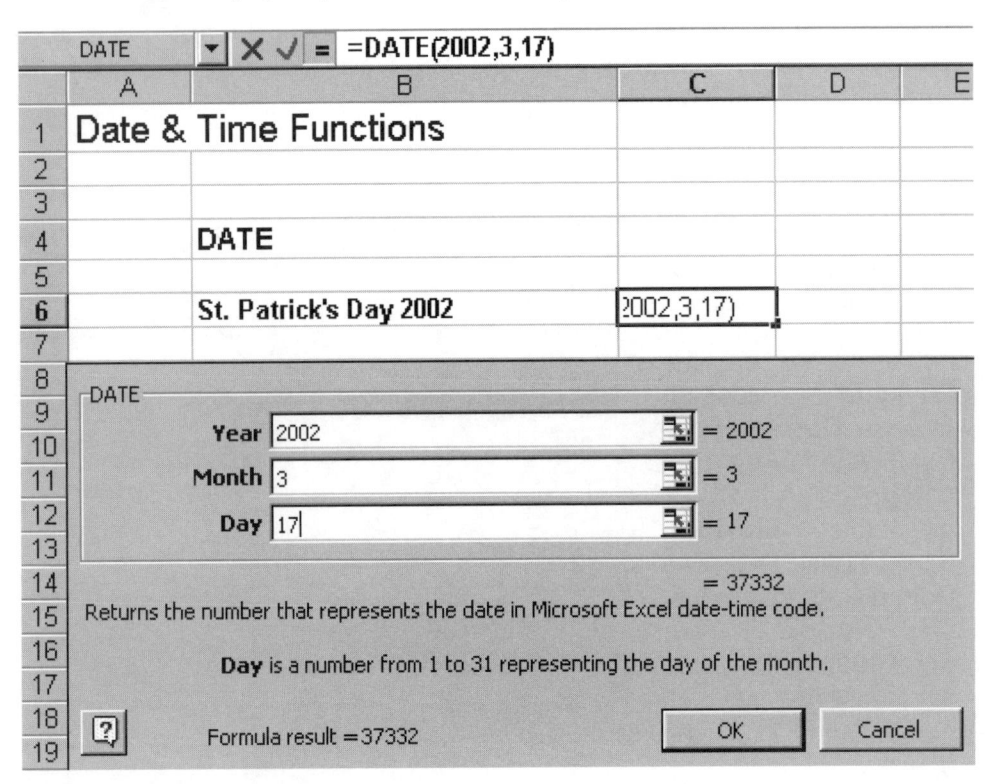

The first example St. Patrick's Day 2002 returns a value of 37332, indicating the number of days since January 1, 1900.

The table gives some of the expected results.

The other results are listed in the table below. Also included are some TIME entries that we shall look at next.

= 7/20/2002
Formula Bar

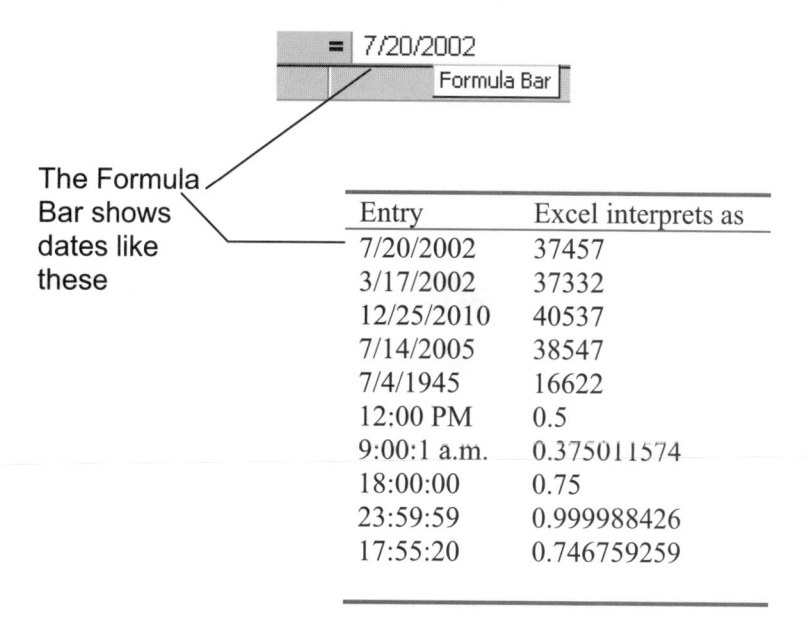

The Formula Bar shows dates like these

| Entry | Excel interprets as |
|---|---|
| 7/20/2002 | 37457 |
| 3/17/2002 | 37332 |
| 12/25/2010 | 40537 |
| 7/14/2005 | 38547 |
| 7/4/1945 | 16622 |
| 12:00 PM | 0.5 |
| 9:00:1 a.m. | 0.375011574 |
| 18:00:00 | 0.75 |
| 23:59:59 | 0.999988426 |
| 17:55:20 | 0.746759259 |

### 1.1.1 Windows 1900 date system and Mac OS 1904 date system

- Select **Tools** followed by **Options** and click on the **Calculation** tab

Excel supports two date systems. The Windows 1900 date system and the Mac Operating System 1904 date system. Clicking on the 1904 date system allows compatibility with Mac Operating System.

- Make no changes and click **Cancel**.

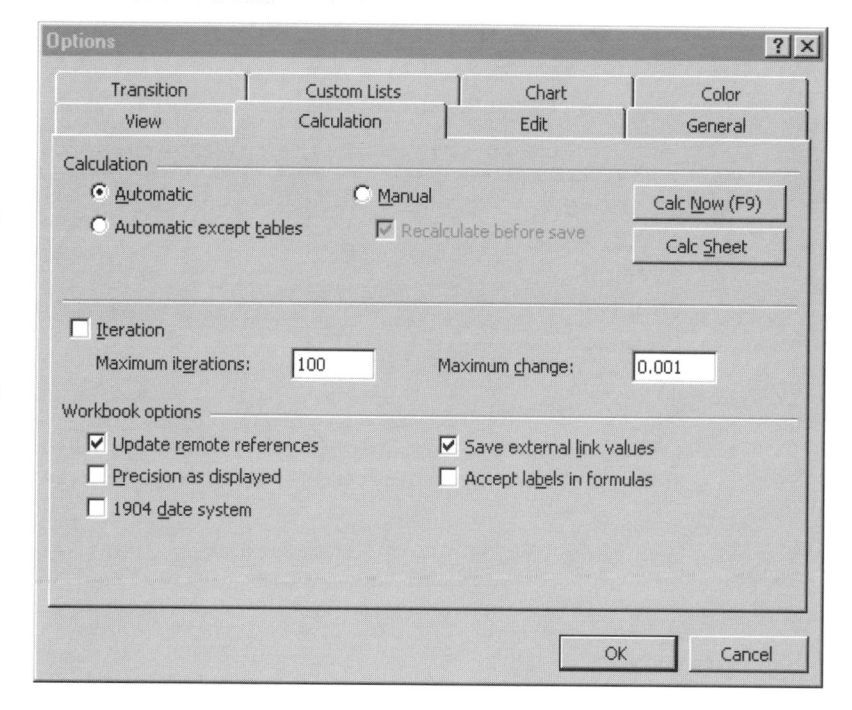

## 1.2 TIME

**Syntax: TIME(hour,minute,second)**

**What it does:** Returns the serial number that represents a particular time.
TIME is represented as a decimal fraction from 0 to 0.99999999. We will check what 12.00 p.m. is represented by.

- Select **Insert** followed by **Function** or click on Paste Function button *fx* on the Standard toolbar. Choose **Date & Time** from the **Function category** and **TIME** as the **Function name**. Click **OK**. The **TIME** dialog box opens.

- In the Hour box insert **12**. In the Minute and Second boxes insert **0** and **0**.

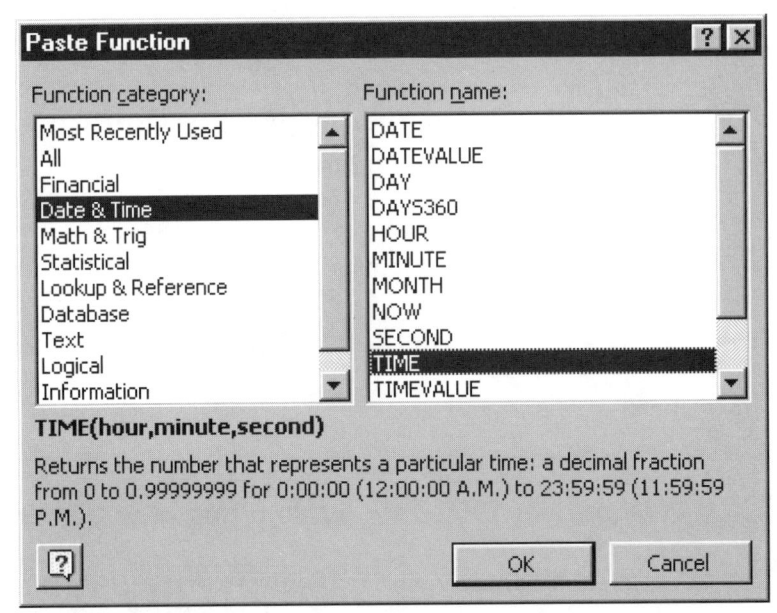

Can you predict what the answer will be?

This returns an answer of **0.5**. You have no doubt predicted this.

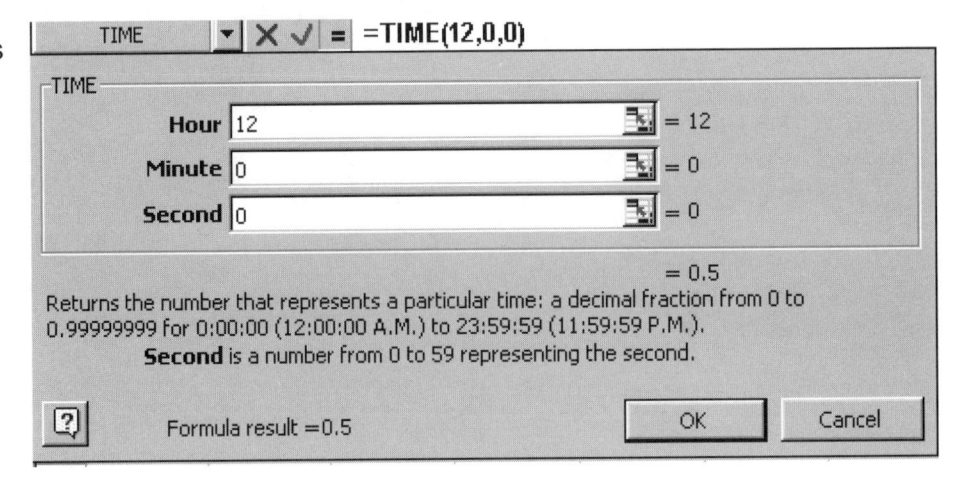

## Exercise 1B

1.  Open the file **Date & Time** and select the **TIME** tab.

    What number values do the following times return? Can you predict any of the values in advance?

2.  17:55:20, 9:00:1 AM.

3.  23:59:59 and 18:00:00

## Exercise 1C

**Calculating the number of days between two dates**

1.  Is the file **Date & Time** open? If not, open it now and click on the **DATE** tab. You are going to choose any two dates but must make sure that you enter them in the same format.

2.  Click on cell **C27**. Insert the first date.
    Now click on cell **C28** and insert the second date.
    In cell **C29** insert the formula **= C28 - C27**
    Select **Enter.**
    This returns the number of days between the dates.

    If the number of days does *not* appear make sure the format for cells is set to **General**.

A worked example is given for reference. You may find the calculation useful in problems where you are calculating interest over a non-regular period.

| Calculating the number of days between two dates | |
| --- | --- |
| Date one | 25/01/01 |
| Date two | 15/07/04 |
| Number of days = | 1267 |

## 1.3 NOW

Syntax: NOW()

**What it does:** Returns the serial number of the current date and time.
When NOW is entered into a cell, Microsoft Excel formats the number as a date.
Although the NOW function has no arguments the parentheses must be added.

The practice exercises contained in this section relate solely to this manual and do not constitute, or imply, certification by the European Driving Licence Foundation in respect of any ECDL examinations. For details on sitting ECDL examinations in your country please contact the local ECDL/ICDL licensee or visit the European Computer Driving Licence Foundation Ltd web site at http://www.ecdl.com

## Exercise 1D

1. Open the file **Date & Time**. Click on tab **NOW & TODAY**.

    The spreadsheet shows the revenue over a six-month period of a wildlife sanctuary.

2. Click on cell **J3**.

    The comment indicates what is to be inserted.

3. Type =**NOW()**

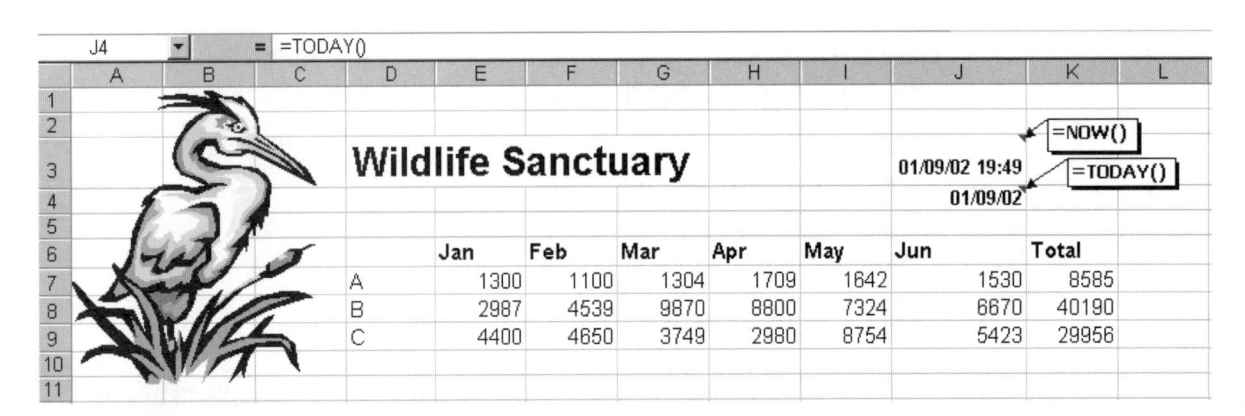

The current date and time are entered in the cell.

It is important to remember that the NOW function only changes when the worksheet is calculated. It will also change if a macro containing the function is executed.

**NOTE**
You are asked to create such a macro in Chapter 5, Practical Exercises: Exercise 3.

## 1.4 TODAY

**Syntax: TODAY()**

**What it does:** Returns a number that represents today's date, In Microsoft Excel date-time code. When TODAY is entered into a cell, Microsoft Excel formats the number as a date.

The practice exercises contained in this section relate solely to this manual and do not constitute, or imply, certification by the European Driving Licence Foundation in respect of any ECDL examinations. For details on sitting ECDL examinations in your country please contact the local ECDL/ICDL licensee or visit the European Computer Driving Licence Foundation Ltd web site at http://www.ecdl.com

### Exercise 1E

1. Ensure the file **Date & Time** is open and click on tab **NOW & TODAY**. Click on cell **J4**.

   The comments indicate what is to be inserted.

2. Insert **=TODAY()**

   The current date is entered in the cell.

3. Re-save the file **Date & Time**.

   You may consider using the **NOW()** and **TODAY()** functions in some of your future spreadsheets.

## 1.5 DAY

Syntax: **DAY(serial_number)**

**What it does:** Returns the day of the month (a number from 1 to 31) corresponding to a number that represents a date.

Example: 25 September 2002 will return **25**.

## 1.6 WEEKDAY

Syntax: **WEEKDAY(serial_number)**

**What it does:** Converts a serial number to a day of the week.

Example: 25/09/2000 will return **4**. (Fourth day of the week-a Wednesday)

## 1.7 MONTH

Syntax: **MONTH(serial_number)**

**What it does:** Returns the month, an integer from 1(January) to 12(December) corresponding to a serial number.

Example: March 12, 2003 will return **3**. (The third month in year)

## 1.8 YEAR

Syntax: **YEAR(serial_number)**

**What it does:** Returns the year, an integer in the range 1900 – 9999, corresponding to a number that represents a date.

Example: June 8, 2005 will return **2005**.

The practice exercises contained in this section relate solely to this manual and do not constitute, or imply, certification by the European Driving Licence Foundation in respect of any ECDL examinations. For details on sitting ECDL examinations in your country please contact the local ECDL/ICDL licensee or visit the European Computer Driving Licence Foundation Ltd web site at http://www.ecdl.com

### Exercise 1F

| | A | B | C | D | E |
|---|---|---|---|---|---|
| 1 | DAY, WEEKDAY, MONTH & YEAR Functions | | | | |
| 2 | | | | | |
| 3 | | | 30/09/02 00:00 | | |
| 4 | | | | | |
| 5 | | DAY | 30 | | |
| 6 | | | | | |
| 7 | | WEEKDAY | 2 | | |
| 8 | | | | | |
| 9 | | MONTH | 9 | | |
| 10 | | | | | |
| 11 | | YEAR | 2002 | | |

1. Open the file **Date & Time**
2. Select tab **Day Weekday Month & Year.**
3. Click on cell **C5**.
4. Insert **=DAY(C3)**

This returns the day of the month as **30**.

**5**   Click on cell **C7**

**6**   Type in **=WEEKDAY(C3)**

This returns the weekday **2** (Second day of week, a Monday)

Now select cell **C9**

**7**   Insert **=MONTH(C3)**

This returns the month as **9** (September)

Finally select cell **C11**.

**8**   Insert the formula **=YEAR(C3)**

This returns the year **2002**.

**9**   Save file as **Date & Time Solution**.

We will now look at some useful mathematical functions.

## Section 2    Mathematical Functions (4.3.1.2)

SUMIF, ROUND

### 2.1  SUMIF

Syntax: **SUMIF(range,criteria,sum_range)**

**What it does:** Adds the cells specified by a given condition or criteria.

- Open the file **Sumif**.

- Select cell **D12**.

We wish to determine the **sum** of the Commissions for Sales Values over 60,000.  The Sales Value column list sales from 30,000 to 110,000.  Commission is paid on the sales, the greater the sales the larger the commission.

- Select **Insert** followed by **Function** or click on **Paste Function** button $f_x$ on the Standard toolbar.

- Choose **Math & Trig** from the Function category and **SUMIF** as the Function name. Click **OK**.

    The **SUMIF Formula Palette** opens.  We will add our information now.

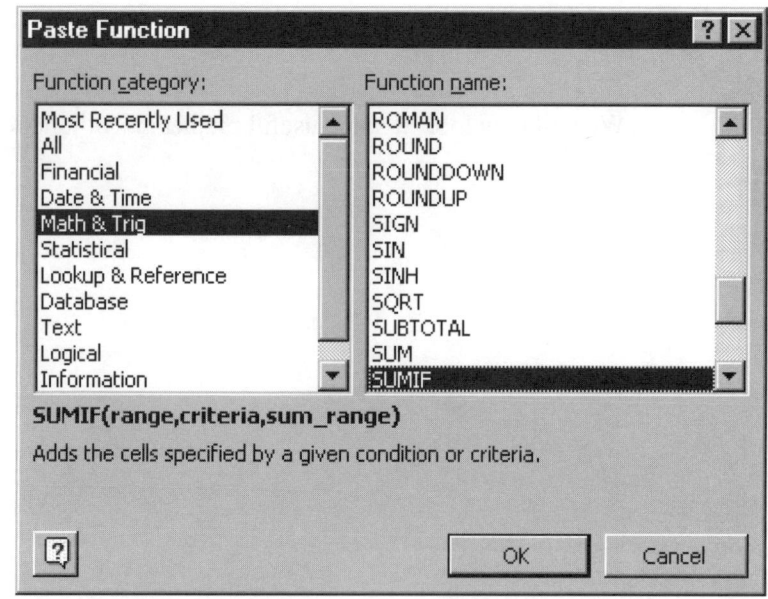

- Click on **Range** box (if cursor is not already inside).

- Drag along the range **C5:C9**.

- Click on **Criteria** box.

    The criterion is sales over 60000. This is written as > (greater than) 60000.

- Insert **>60000** in the **Criteria** box.

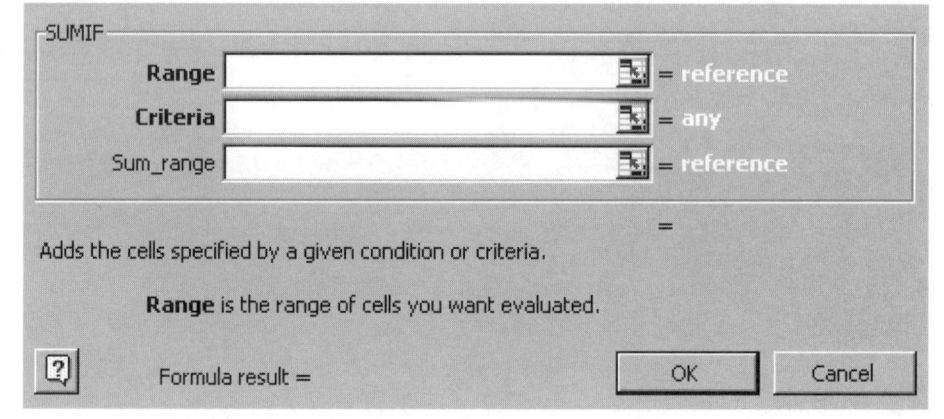

- Now click on the **Sum_range**.

    This is the range of commissions.

- Drag down the range **D5:D9**

    You will observe the value of commission appears before you click OK.

- Click **OK**.

|  | D12 | = =SUMIF(C5:C9,">60000",D5:D9) |  |
|---|---|---|---|
| | A | B | C | D |

**Mathematical Functions(SUMIF)**

| Name | Region | Sales Value | Commission |
|---|---|---|---|
| Alison O'Neill | A | 30000 | 1650 |
| Brian Joyce | A | 50000 | 2750 |
| Tim Blaney | C | 70000 | 3850 |
| Mary Menton | B | 90000 | 4950 |
| Claude Gazin | C | 110000 | 6050 |
| | | | 14850 |

The total is returned as **14850**.

Only those sales persons whose sales value was greater than 60,000 are included(i.e. Blaney, Menton and Gazin). It is these three commissions that are added to give the total 14850.

*The practice exercises contained in this section relate solely to this manual and do not constitute, or imply, certification by the European Driving Licence Foundation in respect of any ECDL examinations. For details on sitting ECDL examinations in your country please contact the local ECDL/ICDL licensee or visit the European Computer Driving Licence Foundation Ltd web site at http://www.ecdl.com*

## Exercise 2A

We will now calculate the sum of the commissions for Sales Values less than or equal to 30000. In this case we are going to type in the formula – we will not use the formula palette.

1   Click on cell **D14** and type in the **=** sign

2   Now type in the function name, **SUMIF**

3   Type in open parenthesis character **(**

4   We now add the first argument, the Range

5   Drag along the range **C5:C9** then add a **,** (comma)

6   Insert **"** followed by **<= 30000**(less than sign followed by equals sign followed by 30000) with no spaces.

7   Insert **"**, followed by a **,** (comma). We now add range of commission.

8   Drag down the range **D5:D9** and finish by closing parenthesis **)**

    The formula should be the same as:

    **=SUMIF(C5:C9,"<=30000",D5:D9)**

9   Press **Enter** or click on **OK** ✓

    A result of **1650** is returned.

## 2.2 ROUND

**Syntax: ROUND(number,num_digits)**

**What it does:** Rounds a number to a specified number of digits

Example: 2.3457 rounded to two decimal places is 2.35, 1.89375 rounded to three decimal places is 1.894.

The ROUND function is useful in spreadsheets as it can be used to ROUND the results of other functions or formula.

E.g. **=ROUND(A1:C20),2)** will round all numbers in the range **A1:C20** to two decimal places.

- Open the file **ROUND** and click on the sheet **PI**.

We will ROUND the number in **B4** to two decimal places.

- Click on cell **C4**

- Write the following:

    **=ROUND(B4,2)**

    This rounds the figure to two decimal places. Can you predict by examining cells B5 and B6, the formula in cells C5 and C6?

The table below shows a selection of numbers rounded to a specified number of digits.

| =ROUND(number,num_digits) | Resultant Number |
|---|---|
| =ROUND(698.356,2) | 698.36 |
| =ROUND(698.354,2) | 698.35 |
| =ROUND(5000.999,1) | 50001 |
| =ROUND(860.930,0) | 861 |
| =ROUND(1266.5044,2) | 1266.5 |
| =ROUND(3.14159265358979,2) | 3.14 |

We can use the ROUND function to return another function to a required number of decimal places.
In this case we will look at **PI** which relates the circumference of a circle to the radius or diameter.
First we will generate the function **PI**.

The function **PI** has no arguments but it does require parenthesis – **PI()**

- Place the cursor in cell **C12**

- Click on the **Paste** function on the Standard toolbar or select **Insert** followed by **Function**.

- Choose **Math & Trig** from the **Function** category and **PI** as the **Function** name.

- Click on **OK**

The value of **PI** is returned accurate to 15 decimal places.
PI() = 3.141592653589790

**Using Nested Functions**

**NOTE**
Section 9 of this Chapter deals with Nested Functions in detail.

We can link the two functions, **ROUND** and **PI**, to return the value of PI in the cell in which it is located:

- Insert the following in cell **C14**

    =ROUND(PI(),2)

- Press return. This gives the value of PI to two decimal places.

    3.14

The practice exercises contained in this section relate solely to this manual and do not constitute, or imply, certification by the European Driving Licence Foundation in respect of any ECDL examinations. For details on sitting ECDL examinations in your country please contact the local ECDL/ICDL licensee or visit the European Computer Driving Licence Foundation Ltd web site at http://www.ecdl.com

## Exercise 2B

In this exercise we will calculate the bonus due to four employees. Then we will round the bonus to two decimal places.

1. Open the Sheet **Round**. Select cell **F6**.

    The bonus is calculated as **(Actual Sales – Target Sales) *1.532%**

2. Write in the formula:

    =(E6-D6)*0.01532

3. Now press return. This gives the value

    **1929.5540** as the bonus.

4. Copy the formula to cells **F7:F9**.

|   | A | B | C | D | E | F | G |
|---|---|---|---|---|---|---|---|
| 1 | **ROUND** | | | | | | |
| 2 | | | | | | | |
| 3 | | | | | | | |
| 4 | | | | | | | |
| 5 | Surname | First Name | Region | Target Sales | Actual Sales | Bonus | Rounded |
| 6 | Barnes | Liam | Ulster | 300000 | 425950 | 1929.5540 | 1929.55 |
| 7 | Connor | Felicity | Leinster | 270000 | 345780 | 1160.9496 | 1160.95 |
| 8 | Farrell | Cara | Munster | 221000 | 476580 | 3915.4856 | 3915.49 |
| 9 | Melon | Paul | Connought | 350000 | 432670 | 1266.5044 | 1266.5 |
| 10 | | | | | | | |

We will now ROUND the bonus figures to two decimal places.

5   Select cell **G6** and insert the following:

   =ROUND(F6,2)

6   Press return to get a value of **1929.55**

7   Copy the formula to cell range **G7:G9**

   The Bonus is rounded to two decimal places.

## Combining the ROUND function with another function or formula

We can combine the ROUND function with other functions so that the required response is in the actual cell where the information is required and not in the adjacent cell. In a practical situation you would not have a separate column of rounded figures?

8   Click on cell **F6**

   We will re-enter the formula as follows:

   =ROUND((E6-D6)*0.01532,2)

It is the same formula but prefixed by ROUND and the number of decimal places indicated.

9   Complete the column and save the file as ROUND.

Hint: Check that the number of parentheses matches left and right. (( and ))

It makes sense to *combine* ROUND with other functions.

10   Save the file as **Round Solution**.

NOTE
Once you understand how the ROUND function works you can apply it to any range in your spreadsheet. What is the difference between Rounding and Formatting?

# Chapter 3 - Functions

## Section 3    Statistical Functions (4.3.1.3)

**COUNT, COUNTA, COUNTIF**
Also **SUM, AVERAGE, MIN, MAX, MODE, STDEV, COUNT, MEDIAN** and **RANK**

### 3.1    COUNT

**Syntax: COUNT(value1,value2,...)**

**What it does:** Counts the number of cells that contain numbers, within the list of arguments.

- Open the file **COUNT** and click on sheet **Count**.

- Select cell **B22**.

    Select **Insert** followed by **Function** or click on **Paste Function** button $f_x$ on the Standard toolbar.

    Select **Statistical** from the Function category and **COUNT** as the function name.

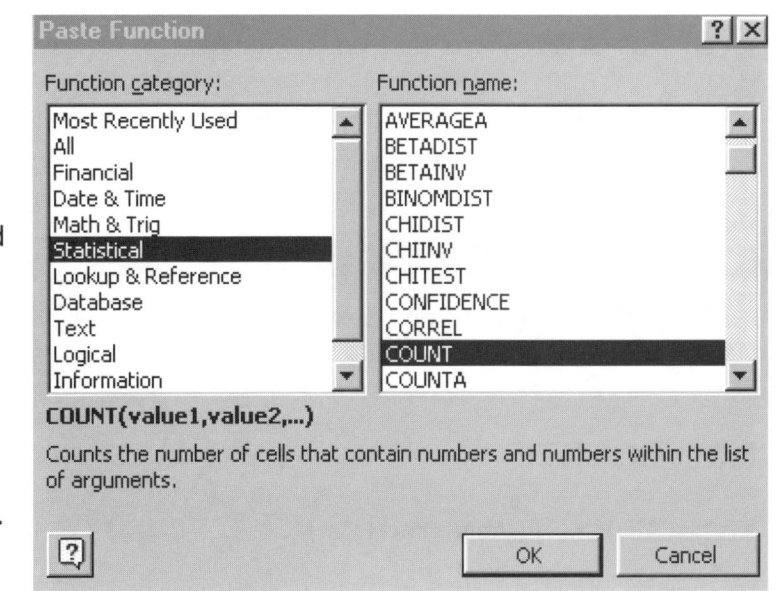

    The **COUNT** Formula palette opens. Click **OK**.

- In the **Value 1** box select cell **A4** and drag down to cell **A19**.

| | A |
|---|---|
| 1 | COUNT |
| 2 | |
| 3 | |
| 4 | Lottery Numbers |
| 5 | |
| 6 | |
| 7 | 15.3 |
| 8 | 0 |
| 9 | 19.5 |
| 10 | 02/09/02 21:46 |
| 11 | |
| 12 | €43,000 |
| 13 | |
| 14 | ECDL ADVANCED |
| 15 | |
| 16 | 3.141592654 |
| 17 | |
| 18 | 18.44159265 |
| 19 | Test Results |

- Click **OK**.

    The value returned is **7**.

    Why is this? Well, COUNT only includes numbers and formulas. Text and empty cells are not included. Check the cells to see which ones contain formulae.

    **A10** as you probably realised contains the **=NOW()** formula, cell **A16** the **PI** formula and cell **A18** is **SUM(A7 + A13).**

    How does the COUNT function differ from the COUNTA function?
    We will look at this now.

## 3.2 COUNTA

Syntax: **COUNTA(value1,value2,...)**

**What it does:** Counts the number of cells that are not empty and the values within the list of arguments.

- Place cursor in cell **B24**.
- Select **Insert** followed by **Function** or click on **Paste Function** button $f_x$ on the Standard toolbar.
- Select **Statistical** from the Function category and **COUNTA** as the function name.

    The **COUNTA** Formula palette opens.

- In the **Value 1** box select cell **A4** and drag down to cell **A19**.
- Click **OK**.

    The result given is **10**.

    COUNTA includes all non-blank cells whereas COUNT includes numbers and formulas that produce numbers only.

## 3.3 COUNTIF

Syntax: **COUNTIF(range,criteria,...)**

**What it does:** Counts the number of cells within a range that meet a given condition.

- Place cursor in cell **B26**.
- Select **Insert** followed by **Function** or click on **Paste Function** button $f_x$ on the Standard toolbar.
- Select **Statistical** from the Function category and **COUNTIF** as the function name.

    The **COUNTIF** Formula palette opens.

- In the Range box drag the range **A4:A19**.

    How many of the entries are greater than 15? To find out:

- In the criteria box insert **>15**

    This returns the result as **5**.

    Repeat this example but choose "**>43000**". The result, as you would expect, is **0**.

The practice exercises contained in this section relate solely to this manual and do not constitute, or imply, certification by the European Driving Licence Foundation in respect of any ECDL examinations. For details on sitting ECDL examinations in your country please contact the local ECDL/ICDL licensee or visit the European Computer Driving Licence Foundation Ltd web site at http://www.ecdl.com

## EXERCISE 3A

In this exercise, we are going to use the **COUNT**, **COUNTA** and **COUNTIF** functions.

1 Open the File **Statistics**.

 The worksheet is set out so that you can enter the functions in the cells provided.

2 **Cell comments** have been used to annotate the cells where you are required to enter functions.

3 Select cell **F4** and calculate **COUNT** in the range specified.

4 This gives the answer **9**.

5 Select cell **F6** and calculate **COUNTA** in the range specified.

6 This returns the answer **9**.

7 Select cell **F8** and calculate the **COUNTIF** in the specified range.

8 The answer is **4**.

9 Save the file as **Statistics Solution**

## 3.4 SUM, AVERAGE, MIN, MAX, MODE, STDEV, COUNT, MEDIAN and RANK

Most of the functions here will be familiar to you so you can regard the exercises below as mainly revision.

- Open the file **Business Test Results**.

The table shows the test results of twenty business students. The maximum mark is 100. In the columns to the right of **Mark(100)** are three columns containing formulae. The **Pass/Fail** and **Grade** columns both contain the **IF** and **nested IF** function which we deal with in **Section 7** and **Section 9**.

You will be pleased to notice that most of the table has been completed for you.

|   | A | B | C | D | E | F |
|---|---|---|---|---|---|---|
| 1 | Business Test Results | | | | | |
| 2 | | | | | | |
| 3 | | | | | | |
| 4 | | | | | | |
| 5 | First Name | Surname | Mark (100) | Pass/Fail | Grade | Rank |
| 6 | Anne | Byrne | 91 | PASS | A | 4 |
| 7 | Leslie | Byrne | 79 | PASS | C | 9 |
| 8 | Paul | Devine | 91 | PASS | A | 4 |
| 9 | Brian | Dunphy | 45 | FAIL | F | 17 |
| 10 | Janet | Fallon | 88 | PASS | B | 6 |
| 11 | Elenor | Fallon | 75 | PASS | C | 11 |
| 12 | James | Finn | 100 | PASS | A | 1 |
| 13 | Maria | Fitzpatrick | 49 | FAIL | F | 16 |
| 14 | Alicia | Granville | 79 | PASS | C | 9 |
| 15 | Seamus | King | 37 | FAIL | No Grade | 19 |
| 16 | Owen | McNulty | 99 | PASS | A | 2 |
| 17 | Sinead | Murphy | 67 | PASS | D | 14 |
| 18 | Jonathan | O'Brien | 45 | FAIL | F | 17 |
| 19 | Yvonne | O'Brien | 69 | PASS | D | 13 |
| 20 | Gavin | O'Brien | 75 | PASS | C | 11 |
| 21 | Kate | O'Connor | 86 | PASS | B | 7 |
| 22 | Rita | O'Donnell | 58 | PASS | E | 15 |
| 23 | Adele | O'Reilly | 95 | PASS | A | 3 |
| 24 | Fergus | Smith | 85 | PASS | B | 8 |
| 25 | Angela | Sinnott | 35 | FAIL | No Grade | 20 |

The practice exercises contained in this section relate solely to this manual and do not constitute, or imply, certification by the European Driving Licence Foundation in respect of any ECDL examinations. For details on sitting ECDL examinations in your country please contact the local ECDL/ICDL licensee or visit the European Computer Driving Licence Foundation Ltd web site at http://www.ecdl.com

## Exercise 3B

However, you are required to determine the appropriate function and use it correctly to complete the range **C28:C35**.

1. Select **Insert** followed by **Function** or click on **Paste Function** button $f_x$ on the Standard toolbar.
   Or, you may enter the function by typing and clicking. You make the decision.

# Chapter 3 - Functions

**NOTE**

If you are involved in an educational establishment, school, college or university you will be familiar with most of the functions and terms. Have you ever used RANK before? There are a number of functions that are not covered in this syllabus that you may find useful.

2   All of the functions are statistical functions, apart from SUM, the details of which are given below.

   Using this information complete the exercise.

3   Save the file as **Business Test Results Solution**.

**SUM(number1,number2,...)**
**What it does:** Adds its arguments.

**AVERAGE(number1,number2,...)**
**What it does:** Returns the average of the arguments.

**MIN(number1,number2,...)**
**What it does:** Returns the minimum value in a list of arguments

**MAX(number1,number2,...)**
**What it does:** Returns the maximum value in a list of arguments.

**MODE(number1,number2,...)**
**What it does:** Returns the most common value in the data set.

**STDEV(number1,number2,...)**
**What it does:** Estimates standard deviation based on a sample but ignoring text and logical values.

**COUNT(value1,value2,...)**
**What it does:** Counts how many numbers there are in a list of arguments.

**MEDIAN(number1,number2,...)**
**What it does:** Returns the median of the given numbers.

**RANK(number,ref,order)**
**What it does:** Returns the rank of the number in a list of numbers.

The solution to this exercise is given below.

| Sum | 1448 |
|---|---|
| Average | 72.4 |
| Minimum | 35 |
| Maximum | 100 |
| Mode | 91 |
| Standard Deviation | 20.911845 |
| Count | 20 |
| Median | 77 |

## Section 4   Text Functions (4.3.1.4)

**PROPER, UPPER, LOWER, CONCATENATE**

The PROPER, UPPER and LOWER functions convert text to lowercase, uppercase and title case respectively. These functions work only on alphabetic characters. All other characters are ignored.

### 4.1   PROPER

**Syntax: PROPER(text)**

**What it does:** Capitalizes the first letter in each word of a string of text and converts all the other letters to lowercase letters.

- Open the file **Text Functions**. Click on Bewley's tab.

- In cell **C3** write the following exactly as it is written here.

  Yesterday I went to Bewley's Café in Grafton Street at around 9.15.

- In cell **C5**, Select **Insert** followed by **Function** or click on **Paste Function** button $f_*$ on the Standard toolbar.

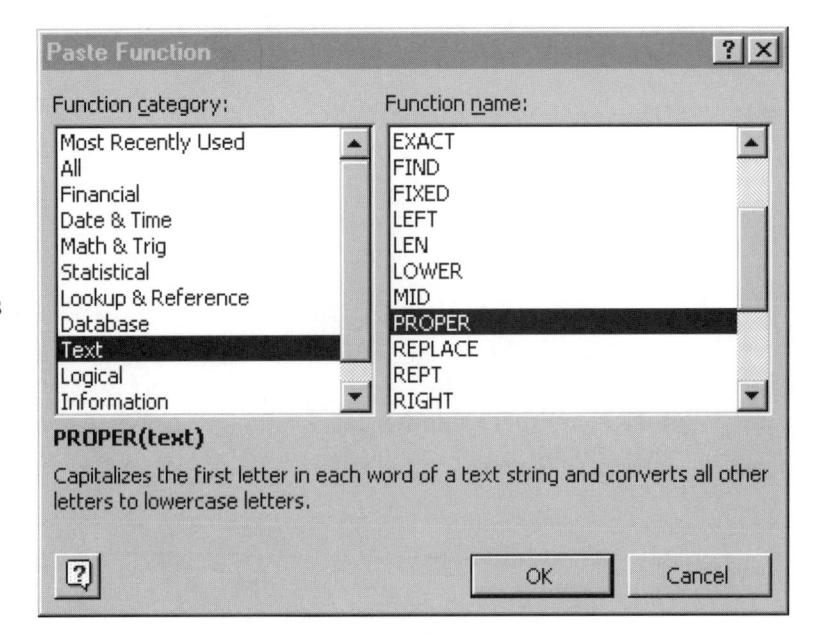

- Choose **Text** as the Function category and **PROPER** as the Function name. Select **C3** for **Text** and click **OK**.

  The result is observed in cell **C5**.

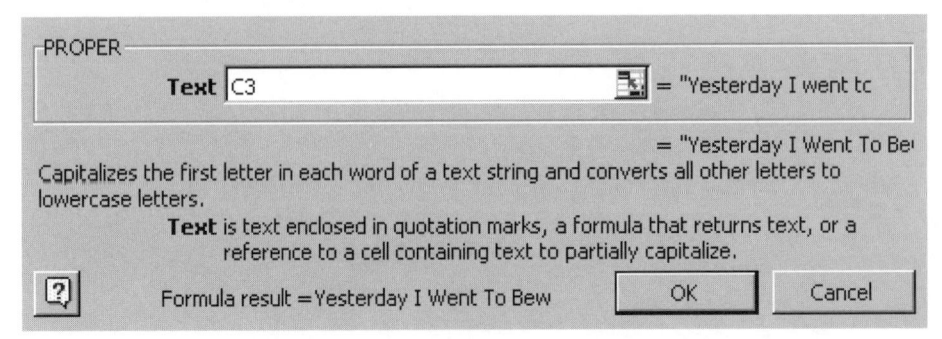

  **Yesterday I Went To Bewley'S Café In Grafton Street At Around 9.15**

  You will notice that 9.15 is unchanged.

## 4.2 UPPER

**Syntax: UPPER(text)**

**What it does:** Converts a text string to upper case.

What effect does UPPER have on the sentence?

- Click on cell **C7** and we'll find out.
- Select **Insert** followed by **Function** or click on **Paste Function** button $f_x$ on the Standard toolbar.
- Choose **Text** from the Function category and **Upper** as the Function name.
- In the Text box select cell **C3**. (This contains the original sentence you typed earlier).

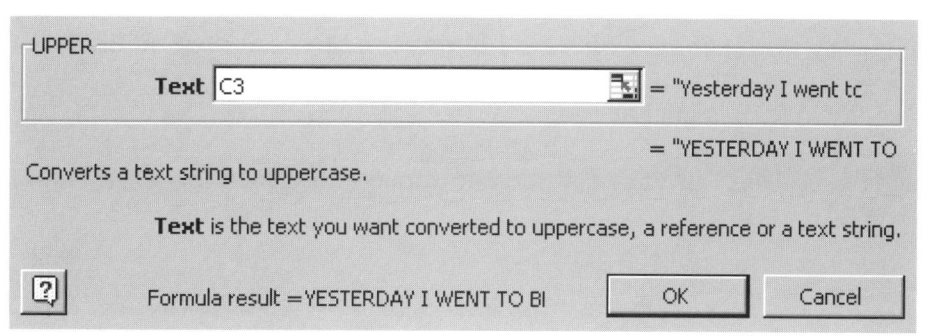

![UPPER dialog box showing Text: C3 = "Yesterday I went to", result = "YESTERDAY I WENT TO". Converts a text string to uppercase. Text is the text you want converted to uppercase, a reference or a text string. Formula result = YESTERDAY I WENT TO BI]

- Now click **OK**.

The result is observed in cell C7.

**YESTERDAY I WENT TO BEWLEY'S CAFÉ IN GRAFTON STREET AT AROUND 9.15**

You will again see that 9.15 is unaffected.

## 4.3 LOWER

**Syntax: LOWER(text)**

**What it does:** Converts all uppercase letters in a text string to lower case.

Can you predict what effect LOWER will have on the original sentence?

- Place cursor in cell **C9**.
- Select the **Paste Function** or choose **Insert** followed by **Function**.
- Choose **Text** from Function category and **Lower** as Function name.

```
┌─LOWER─────────────────────────────────────────────────────────┐
│      Text │C3                                    │ = "Yesterday I went tc│
│                                                                │
│                                              = "yesterday i went to bew  │
│  Converts all uppercase letters in a text string to lowercase.│
│                                                                │
│      Text is the text you want to convert to lowercase. Characters in Text that are│
│                       not letters are not changed.            │
│   [?]   Formula result =yesterday i went to bewle   [ OK ]  [ Cancel ]│
└────────────────────────────────────────────────────────────────┘
```

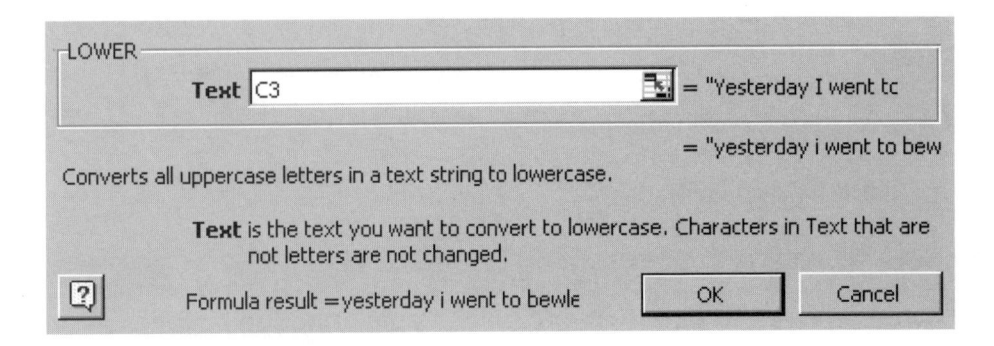

- In the **Text** box select cell **C3**.

- Now click **OK**.

   The result is observed in cell **C9**.

   **yesterday i went to bewley's café in grafton street at around 9.15**

   Once again 9.15 is unchanged.

   Save file as **Text Functions**, but do not close. Let's try a few examples.

---

The practice exercises contained in this section relate solely to this manual and do not constitute, or imply, certification by the European Driving Licence Foundation in respect of any ECDL examinations. For details on sitting ECDL examinations in your country please contact the local ECDL/ICDL licensee or visit the European Computer Driving Licence Foundation Ltd web site at http://www.ecdl.org

## Exercise 4A

1     Ensure the file **Text Functions** is open.

2     Click on tab **BEC**.

   You are required to select the Text Functions that will return the three variant sentences.

   The original sentence is in cell **C4**. You complete the rest.

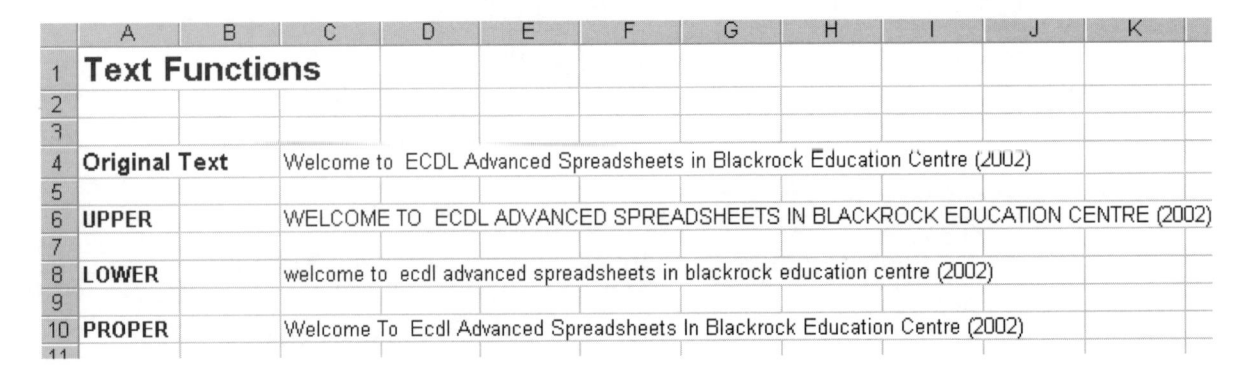

|    | A | B | C | D | E | F | G | H | I | J | K |
|----|---|---|---|---|---|---|---|---|---|---|---|
| 1  | Text Functions | | | | | | | | | | |
| 2  | | | | | | | | | | | |
| 3  | | | | | | | | | | | |
| 4  | Original Text | | Welcome to ECDL Advanced Spreadsheets in Blackrock Education Centre (2002) | | | | | | | | |
| 5  | | | | | | | | | | | |
| 6  | UPPER | | WELCOME TO ECDL ADVANCED SPREADSHEETS IN BLACKROCK EDUCATION CENTRE (2002) | | | | | | | | |
| 7  | | | | | | | | | | | |
| 8  | LOWER | | welcome to ecdl advanced spreadsheets in blackrock education centre (2002) | | | | | | | | |
| 9  | | | | | | | | | | | |
| 10 | PROPER | | Welcome To Ecdl Advanced Spreadsheets In Blackrock Education Centre (2002) | | | | | | | | |
| 11 | | | | | | | | | | | |

3     Save the file on completion of exercise.

The practice exercises contained in this section relate solely to this manual and do not constitute, or imply, certification by the European Driving Licence Foundation in respect of any ECDL examinations. For details on sitting ECDL examinations in your country please contact the local ECDL/ICDL licensee or visit the European Computer Driving Licence Foundation Ltd web site at http://www.ecdl.com

## Exercise 4B

1. Select tab **Mercury Products.**

A report has been received which requires some minor editing.

**Text Functions**

|  |  |
|---|---|
| MERCURY PRODUCTS, | |
| 300 RATHMINES ROAD, | |
| dublin 6 | |
| phone: 01 7322500 | |
| EMAIL: MERCURY@INDIGO.IE | |
| Client List: | |
| Surname | First Name |
| ABBOT | NEIl |
| BELL | Siobhan |
| JOYCE | Stanislaus |
| KELLY | Gavin |
| MORAN | Anne |
| PETRA | Xaviour |

2. Edit the report using **only** the Text Functions **UPPER**, **LOWER** and **PROPER** so that the completed report looks like the one below. You will use each function at least once.

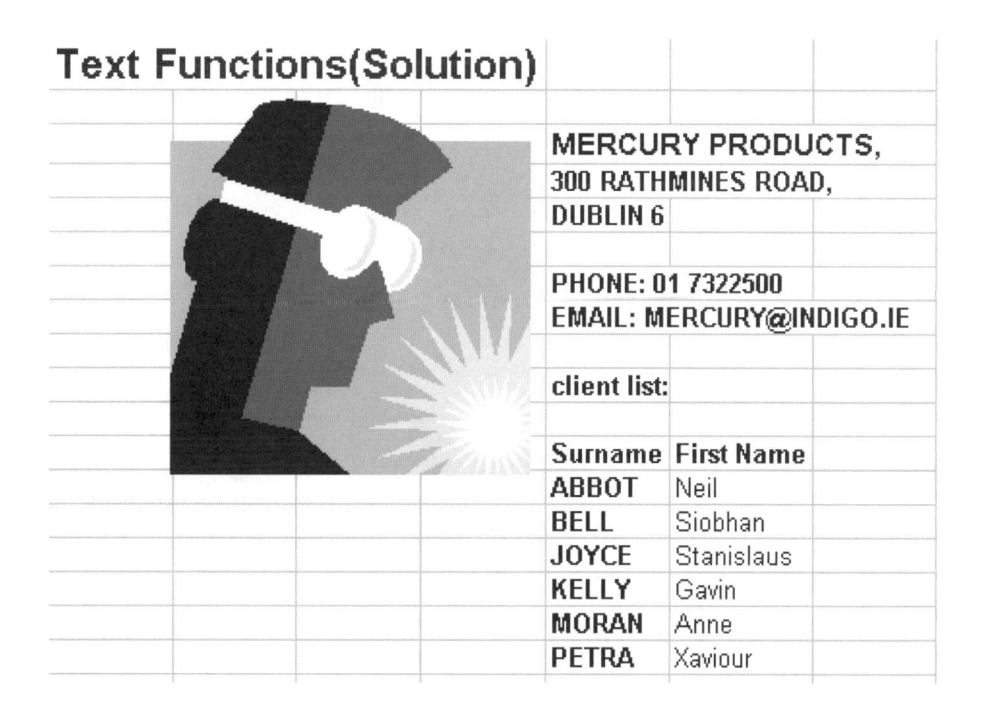

**Text Functions(Solution)**

|  |  |
|---|---|
| MERCURY PRODUCTS, | |
| 300 RATHMINES ROAD, | |
| DUBLIN 6 | |
| PHONE: 01 7322500 | |
| EMAIL: MERCURY@INDIGO.IE | |
| client list: | |
| Surname | First Name |
| ABBOT | Neil |
| BELL | Siobhan |
| JOYCE | Stanislaus |
| KELLY | Gavin |
| MORAN | Anne |
| PETRA | Xaviour |

3. Save the file as **Text Functions Solution**.

**NOTE**

Text functions are useful in 'cleaning up' parts of a worksheet. Skilfully used it may be faster than reformatting. What do you think?

## 4.4 CONCATENATE

**Syntax:** CONCATENATE(text1,text2,...)

**What it does:** Joins several text strings into one text string.

The concatenate function can take up to 30 arguments. It simply joins cell contents together. The **& (ampersand)** operator can be used to join text terms instead of using CONCATENATE.

We will look at the use of **&(ampersand)** first. Then we will do the same example using the CONCATENATE function.

- Open file **Concatenate**.

- Select cell **D4**.

- In this cell write the following:

- **=C4&" "&B4**.

    Since we want a space between the two names we include " " with a space between double quote characters.

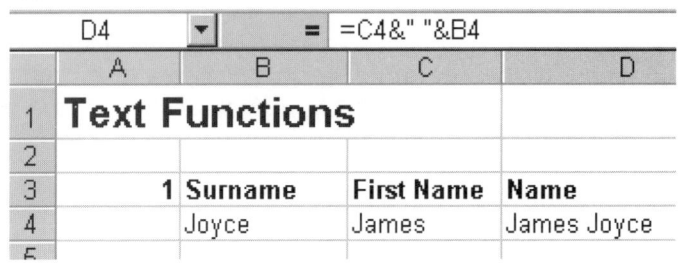

|   | A | B | C | D |
|---|---|---|---|---|
| 1 | Text Functions | | | |
| 2 | | | | |
| 3 | 1 | Surname | First Name | Name |
| 4 | | Joyce | James | James Joyce |

This returns **James Joyce**

How do we complete the exercise using CONCATENATE?

- Ensure cursor is in cell **D6**.

- Select **Insert** followed by **Function** or click on **Paste Function** $f_x$ button on the Standard toolbar.

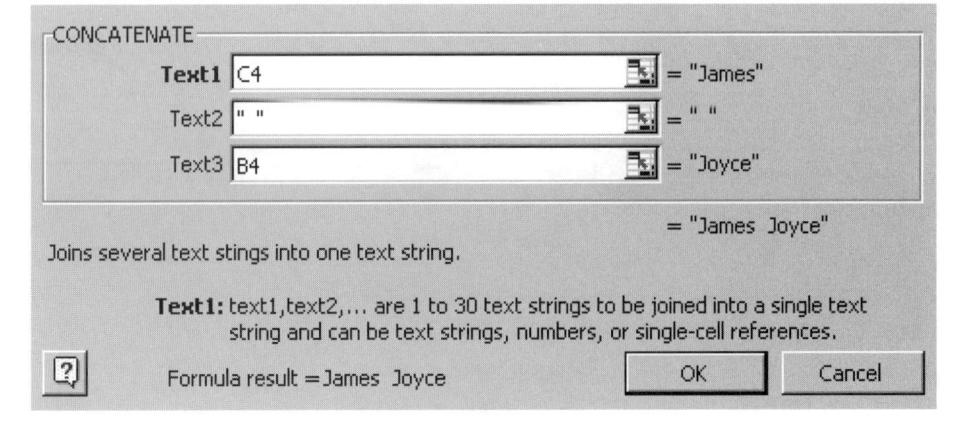

CONCATENATE
- Text1: C4 = "James"
- Text2: " " = " "
- Text3: B4 = "Joyce"

= "James Joyce"

Joins several text stings into one text string.

Text1: text1,text2,... are 1 to 30 text strings to be joined into a single text string and can be text strings, numbers, or single-cell references.

Formula result = James Joyce

- Select **Text** from Function category and **CONCATENATE** as function name.

    The **CONCATENATE** dialog box opens.

- In the **Text1** box click on cell **C4**.

    Since we want a space between James and Joyce, in Text2 box we must leave a space between the double quote " " characters.

- In **Text2** box insert, " followed by space, then "

- In **Text3** box click on cell **B4**.

- Now click **OK**.

    Welcome to **James Joyce** whose name appears in cell **D6**.

We can also complete the above exercise as follows.

- Click on cell **D8**.

- Type in the following, ensuring there is a space between the double quote characters.

    **=CONCATENATE(C4," ",B4)**

    This will return James Joyce again.

- Save file as **CONCATENATE**.

The practice exercises contained in this section relate solely to this manual and do not constitute, or imply, certification by the European Driving Licence Foundation in respect of any ECDL examinations. For details on sitting ECDL examinations in your country please contact the local ECDL/ICDL licensee or visit the European Computer Driving Licence Foundation Ltd web site at http://www.ecdl.com

## Exercise 4C

Using the CONCATENATE function create the following sentences.

1	James Joyce is the author of Ulysses

   =CONCATENATE(C4," ",B4," ","is author of," " ",B9)

2	Total Sales for 2003 will equal €27,000

3	A solution for 1 is given. Now save the file as **Concatenate Solution**.

## Section 5    Financial Functions (4.3.1.5)

FV, NPV, PMT, PV, RATE

### 5.1    FV

**Syntax: FV(rate,nper,pmt,pv,type)**
**What it does:** Returns the future value of an investment based on periodic, constant payments and a constant interest rate. 0 is the default value.

**Rate** – interest rate per period.
**Nper** – total number of periods.
**Pmt** – amount of periodic payments- this is fixed.
**Pv** – present value, assumed to be zero.
**Type** – 0 or 1, 0 if payment due at end of period, 1 if payment is due at beginning of period.

**What is the FV(Future Value) of an investment of €300 per month at an annual interest rate of 5%? The payments are made monthly over a five-year period. (i.e. 60 payments).**

- Open file **Investments**.

- Ensure cursor is in cell **B7**.

- Select **Insert** followed by **Function** or click on **Paste Function** button $f_x$ on the Standard toolbar.

- Select **Financial** from **Function category** and **FV** as Function name.

  The **Paste function** dialog box opens.

- Place cursor in Rate box and click on cell **B3**.

  Remember to divide by 12 (since there are 12 payments per annum).

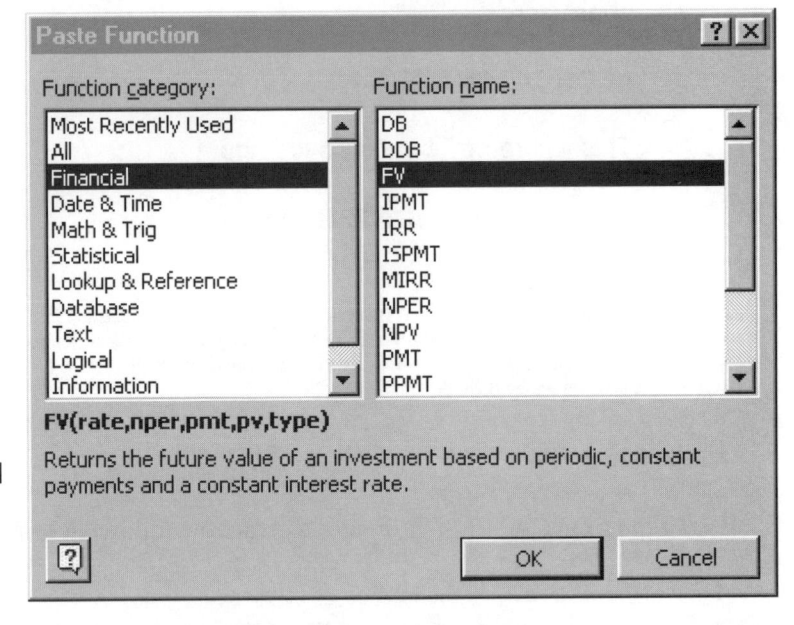

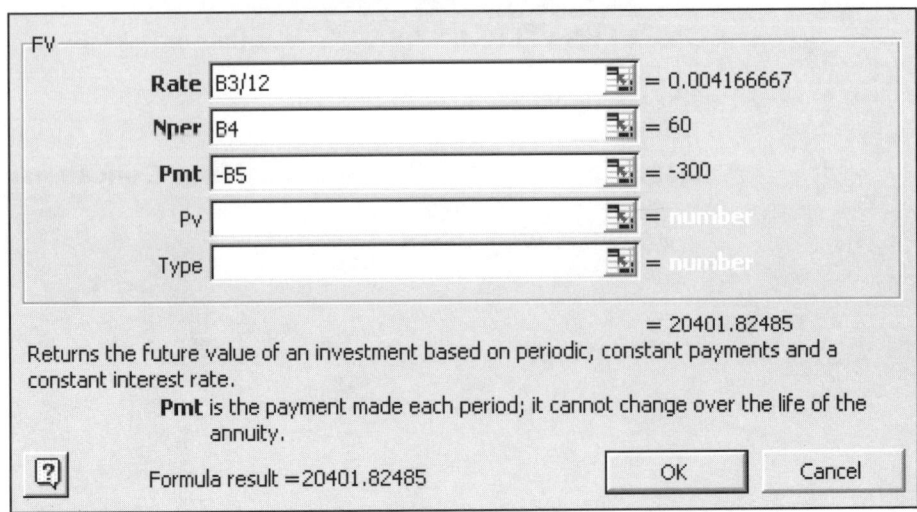

## Chapter 3 - Functions

- The number of payments is **60** so type **B4** in **Nper** box.

- Finally in the **Pmt** box insert – (minus sign) **B5**.

We will assume that the current value is Zero and that payments are paid at the end of the month. If left out Pv = 0 and if Type is left out Type = 0. You can if you wish type 0 in both these boxes.

The Future value of the investment is indicated by the Formula result.

- Click **OK** and the value of the investment is given.

  It is **€20,401.82**.

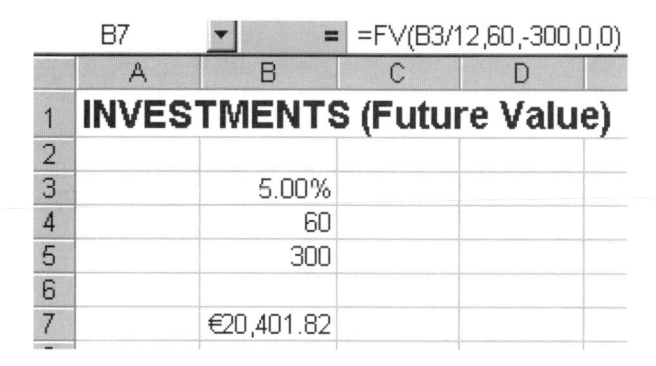

|   | A | B | C | D |
|---|---|---|---|---|
| 1 | INVESTMENTS (Future Value) | | | |
| 2 | | | | |
| 3 | | 5.00% | | |
| 4 | | 60 | | |
| 5 | | 300 | | |
| 6 | | | | |
| 7 | | €20,401.82 | | |

B7  =FV(B3/12,60,-300,0,0)

The practice exercises contained in this section relate solely to this manual and do not constitute, or imply, certification by the European Driving Licence Foundation in respect of any ECDL examinations. For details on sitting ECDL examinations in your country please contact the local ECDL/ICDL licensee or visit the European Computer Driving Licence Foundation Ltd web site at http://www.ecdl.com

## Exercise 5A

1    Click on tab Exercise 5A which is adjacent to FV tab.
     Using the information given in each of the three cases calculate the Future Value(FV) in all cases.

2    Save the file as **Investments Solution**.

## 5.2 NPV

Syntax: NPV(rate,value1,value2,…)

**What it does:** Returns the **net present value** of an investment based on a discount rate and a series of future payments (negative values) and income (positive values).

**Rate** is the rate of discount over the length of one period.
**Value 1, value 2** are 1 to 29 arguments that represent the payments and income.
Value 1, value 2,… must be equally spaced in time, e.g. yearly.

Discounting suggests that the value of a sum of money today is greater than the same amount a number of years in the future. €1000 in today's terms will not be worth the same in 10 years time. Discounting is used to calculate the present value of an amount, which is the current value of a future sum of money.

**NOTE**
NPV is based on future cash flows.
If the initial investment is made at the beginning of the first period it must be **added** to the NPV result and not included with the values arguments.
If the investment is made at the end of the first period it must be included with the values arguments.

- Open file **NPV**. Click on **NPV 1** tab.

In this example we wish to calculate the NPV on an investment in which €10000 is paid one year from now and on which expect an annual income of €2500, €2900, €3100, €3300 and €5300. The annual discount rate (Cost of capital) is 12%.

- Place cursor in cell reference **D15**.

- Select **Insert** followed by **Function** or click on **Paste Function** button $f_*$ on the Standard toolbar. Select **Financial** from **Function category** and **NPV** as Function name.

- Click on **OK**.

    You will note in the NPV dialog box that **Rate** and **Value1** are emboldened. You are required to input values in these locations. **Value2** is greyed which indicates that adding a value is optional.

- Place cursor in **Rate** box and click on cell **D6**.

- Place cursor in **Value1** box.

    Since the **€10000** payment will be made at end of first year we **must** include this in our range of values.

- Select the range **D8:D13** and click on **OK**.

    The **NPV** is calculated as **€1656.34**.

# Chapter 3 - Functions

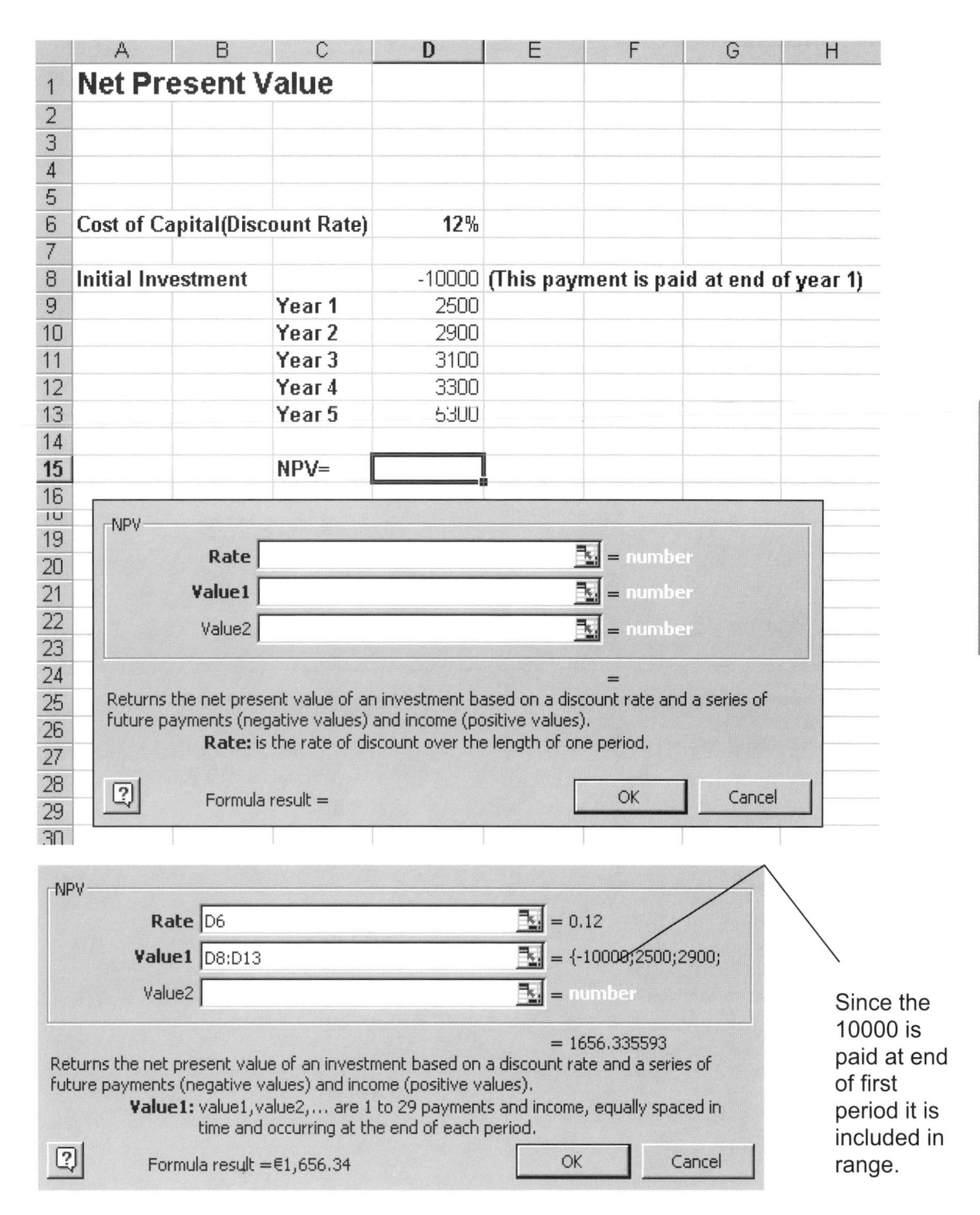

|   | A | B | C | D | E | F | G | H |
|---|---|---|---|---|---|---|---|---|
| 1 | **Net Present Value** | | | | | | | |
| 2 | | | | | | | | |
| 3 | | | | | | | | |
| 4 | | | | | | | | |
| 5 | | | | | | | | |
| 6 | Cost of Capital(Discount Rate) | | | 12% | | | | |
| 7 | | | | | | | | |
| 8 | Initial Investment | | | -10000 | (This payment is paid at end of year 1) | | | |
| 9 | | | Year 1 | 2500 | | | | |
| 10 | | | Year 2 | 2900 | | | | |
| 11 | | | Year 3 | 3100 | | | | |
| 12 | | | Year 4 | 3300 | | | | |
| 13 | | | Year 5 | 5300 | | | | |
| 14 | | | | | | | | |
| 15 | | | NPV= | | | | | |

**NPV**

Rate
Value1
Value2

= number
= number
= number

=

Returns the net present value of an investment based on a discount rate and a series of future payments (negative values) and income (positive values).
Rate: is the rate of discount over the length of one period.

Formula result =      OK      Cancel

---

**NPV**

Rate D6           = 0.12
Value1 D8:D13     = {-10000;2500;2900;
Value2            = number

= 1656.335593

Returns the net present value of an investment based on a discount rate and a series of future payments (negative values) and income (positive values).
Value1: value1,value2,... are 1 to 29 payments and income, equally spaced in time and occurring at the end of each period.

Formula result =€1,656.34      OK      Cancel

Since the 10000 is paid at end of first period it is included in range.

- Save the file as INVESTMENT but do not close file.

- Click on tab **NPV2**.

Say for example you wish to purchase a small outlet in a Shopping Centre and the initial price is €50000. The income for the operation varies from €4000 in year 1 to €22000 in year 7.
In calculating the NPV we must not include the initial price but add it to NPV.

- Place cursor in cell reference **D19**.

- Select **Insert** followed by **Function** or click on **Paste Function** button $f_x$ on the Standard toolbar.

- Select **Financial** followed by **NPV**.

- Choose cost of capital **D6**, for the **Rate** box.

- Choose **D9:D15** as the range (omit **D8**).

- Click on **OK** button.

- This returns a value of **50310.16** in cell **D19**.

- Click on Formula Bar.

- Select **+** (sign) then cell **D8**.

- Click on Enter button ✓ on the Formula Bar.

i.e. **=NPV(D6,D9:D15) + D8**

| | A | B | C | D | E | F | G |
|---|---|---|---|---|---|---|---|
| 1 | **Net Present Value** | | | | | | |
| 2 | | | | | | | |
| 3 | | | | | | | |
| 4 | | | | | | | |
| 5 | | | | | | | |
| 6 | Cost of Capital(Discount Rate) | | | 12% | | | |
| 7 | | | | | | | |
| 8 | Initial Investment | | | -50000 | (This is paid at start of year 1) | | |
| 9 | | | Year 1 | 4000 | | | |
| 10 | | | Year 2 | 7000 | | | |
| 11 | | | Year 3 | 10000 | | | |
| 12 | | | Year 4 | 13000 | | | |
| 13 | | | Year 5 | 14500 | | | |
| 14 | | | Year 6 | 15000 | | | |
| 15 | | | Year 7 | 22000 | | | |
| 16 | | | | | | | |
| 17 | | | | | | | |
| 18 | | | | | | | |
| 19 | | | NPV= | €310.16 | | | |
| 20 | | | | | | | |

Formula Bar: D19 = =NPV(D6,D9:D15)+D8

This returns an **NPV** of **€310.16**

- Save the file as **NPV Solution**.

The practice exercises contained in this section relate solely to this manual and do not constitute, or imply, certification by the European Driving Licence Foundation in respect of any ECDL examinations. For details on sitting ECDL examinations in your country please contact the local ECDL/ICDL licensee or visit the European Computer Driving Licence Foundation Ltd web site at http://www.ecdl.com

## Exercise 5B

In this exercise we want to calculate the NPV for a Business School whose cash flow projections are given between the years 2002-2006.

1 Open the file **NPV**. Select **BUSINESS tab**.

2 Place the cursor in cell **C15**.

3 Select **Insert** followed by **Function** or click on **Paste Function** button $f_x$ on the Standard toolbar.

4 Choose **Financial** from the **Function category** and **NPV** from the **Function name** list.
Or Select **NPV** from the Function category **Most Recently Used**.

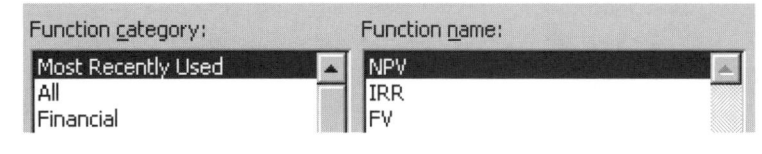

Remember if you were using a function recently you can select it from the **Most Recently Used** Function category.

5 Place cursor in **Rate** box and click on cell **C13**.

The values in this case are represented by the range **C8:G10** that gives the inflows and outflows of money.

6 With cursor in **Value1** box drag across the range **C8:G10**.

The Net Present Value is indicated in **Formula result =.**

7 Click **OK**.

8 Format the answer to zero decimal places.

The **NPV** is given as **€744,431**.

9 Save the file as **NPV Solution**.

## 5.3 PMT

**Syntax: PMT(rate,nper,pv,fv,type)**

**What it does:** Calculates the payments for a loan based on constant payments and a constant interest rate.

**Pmt** – amount of periodic payments- this is fixed.
**Rate** is the interest rate for the period. If payments are made monthly divide it by 12.
**Nper** is the total number of payments made. If a bank loan is taken out over 5 years and monthly repayments are made, the total number of payments is 60 (5 * 12).
**Pv** is the present value.
**Fv** is the future value
**Type** – 0 or 1, 0 if payment is due at end of period, 1 if payment is due at beginning of period.

In this example we will use the PMT function to calculate the periodic payments on a home loan (Mortgage).

- Open the file **Home Loan.**

- Select Home Loan tab.

- Ensure cursor is in cell **B8**.

- Select **Insert** followed by **Function** or click on **Paste Function** button $f_x$ on the Standard toolbar. The **Paste Function** dialog box opens.

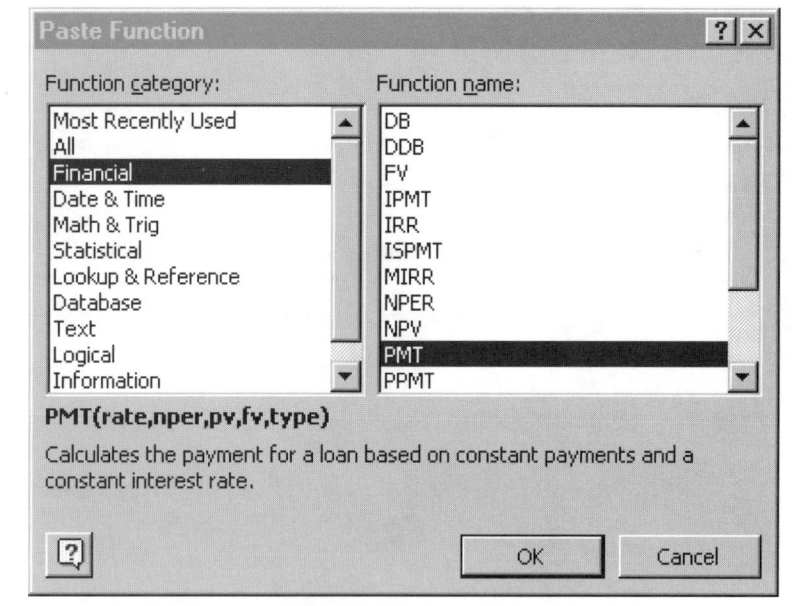

- Select **Financial** as the Function category and **PMT** as the Function name, then click **OK**.

- Drag the Paste Function dialog box to a suitable location so that you can view data in worksheet.

- Place cursor in **Rate** box and click on cell **B5**. B5 appears in the Rate box, but as mortgages are repaid monthly, we must divide this by **12**.

- Place cursor in **Nper** box where we will input the number of payments. Select cell **B6.**

- Move the cursor to cell **Pv** and type – (minus) sign and select cell **B4**.

We ignore **FV** the future value or the value at the end of the period. If omitted, 0 is assumed as value.

Type indicates when payments are due; 1 for the beginning of the month and 0 for the end of month. 0 is displayed by default.

Note that the answer is already displayed.

- Click the **OK** button.

- The answer is displayed in cell **B8**.

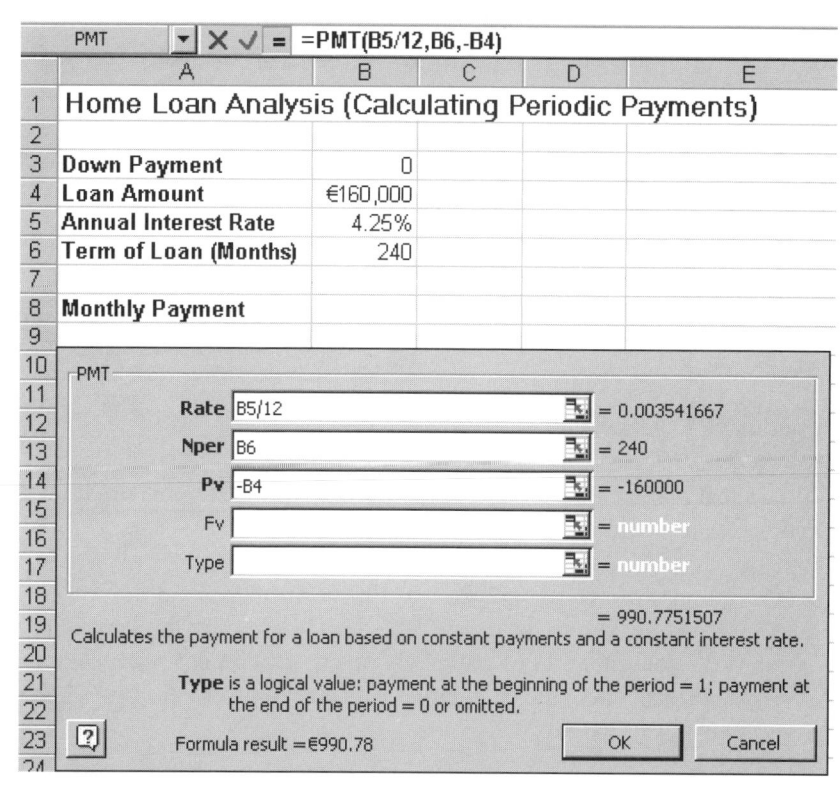

The cost of a €160,000 mortgage at a rate of 4.25%, spread over 20 years is €990.78 per month.

- Save the file as **Home Loan Solution**.

### What If?

The use of the function lends itself to the use of **What If?**
What if the rate of interest increased to 5.25%. How would this affect the monthly repayments?
If the period of the loan is extended to 30 years, what is the new monthly repayment?

The practice exercises contained in this section relate solely to this manual and do not constitute, or imply, certification by the European Driving Licence Foundation in respect of any ECDL examinations. For details on sitting ECDL examinations in your country please contact the local ECDL/ICDL licensee or visit the European Computer Driving Licence Foundation Ltd web site at http://www.ecdl.com

## Exercise 5C

The homebuyers want to check three options:

- What are the new repayments if the interest rate rises by 1% to 5.25%?

- What is the monthly repayment if they spread the loan over 30 years?

- If the loan is increased to €200,00 what are new monthly repayments?

1   Open the File **Home Loan**.

2   Select the tab **Home Loan Exercise**.

3   Using the **PMT** function complete the calculations.

**4**     Save the file as **Home Loan Solution**.

We have found that we can calculate the new monthly payments for changes in the interest rate. Is there a way of calculating monthly payments for a series of interest rates? There is. We use the **One Input Data Table**. See Chapter 1.

## 5.4  PV

**Syntax: PV(rate,nper,pmt,fv,type)**

**What it does:** Returns the present value of an investment: the total amount that a series of future payments is worth now.

**Pmt** – amount of periodic payments- this is fixed.
**Rate** is the interest rate for the period. If payments are made monthly divide it by 12.
**Nper** is the total number of payments made. If a bank loan is taken out over 5 years and monthly repayments are made, the total number of payments are 60 (5 * 12).
**Pv** is the present value.
**Fv** is the future value.
**Type** – 0 or 1, 0 if payment is due at end of period, 1 if payment is due at beginning of period.

You have a money purchase pension and wish to buy an annuity with your fund. You are given an annuity rate of 8% and the annuity pays out €500 per month. Is this a good investment? Let's find out.

- Open the file **PV**.

- Place cursor in cell **B13**.

- Select **Insert** followed by **Function** or click on **Paste Function** button $f_x$ on the Standard toolbar.

- Select **Financial** from Function category and **PV** as Function name.

  The **PV** dialog box opens. Drag it to a suitable location so that you can see exactly what you are entering.

- Place cursor in the **Rate box** and click on cell **B6**. This enters the annual interest rate. We must divide this by **12** since payments are made monthly.

- Place cursor in **Nper** box and click on cell **B8** to enter the number of payments.

- Locate cursor in **Pmt** box and click on cell **B10** to input the monthly payment.

## Chapter 3 - Functions

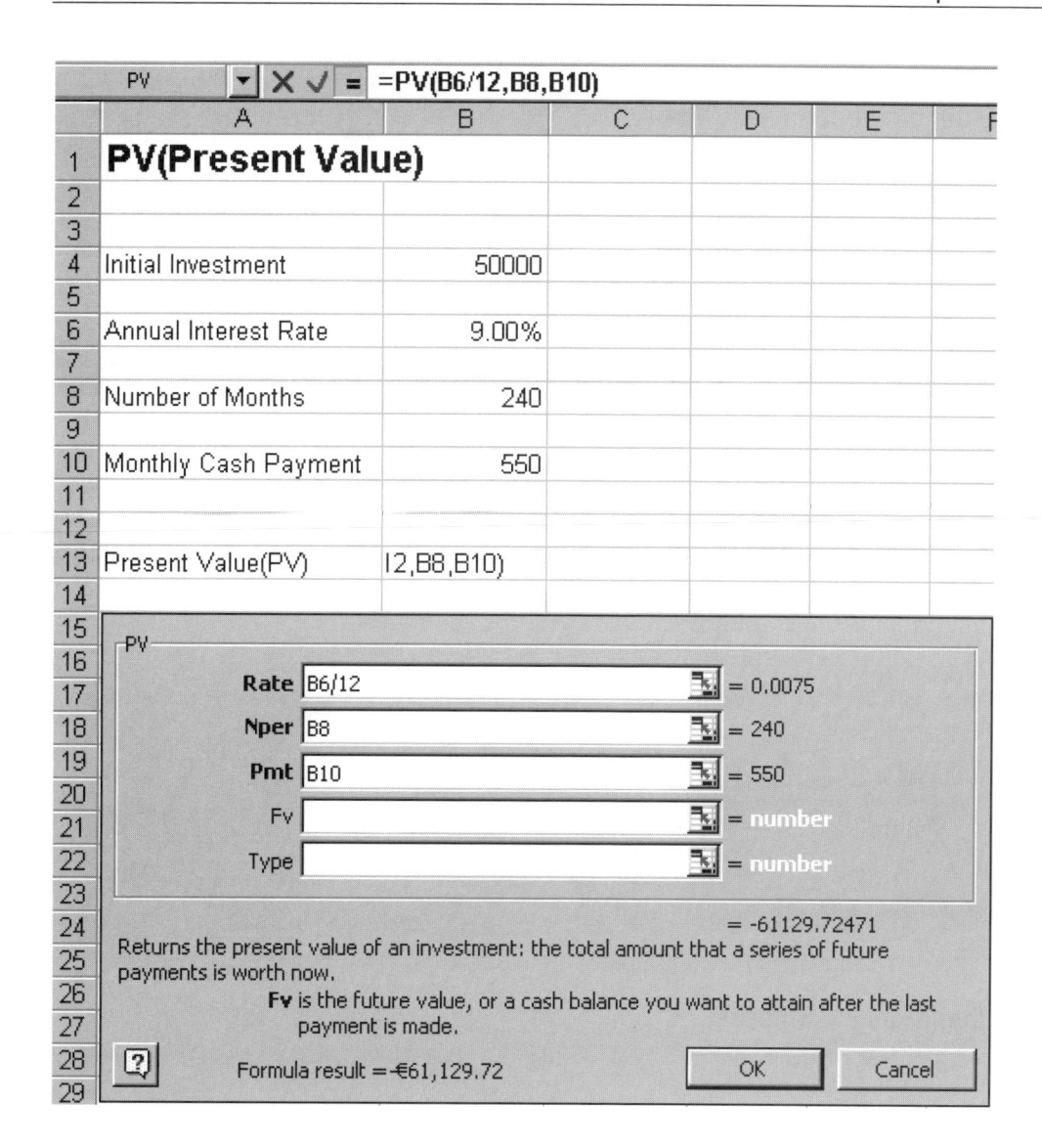

| | A | B | C | D | E | F |
|---|---|---|---|---|---|---|
| | PV | ▼ X ✓ = | =PV(B6/12,B8,B10) | | | |
| 1 | **PV(Present Value)** | | | | | |
| 2 | | | | | | |
| 3 | | | | | | |
| 4 | Initial Investment | 50000 | | | | |
| 5 | | | | | | |
| 6 | Annual Interest Rate | 9.00% | | | | |
| 7 | | | | | | |
| 8 | Number of Months | 240 | | | | |
| 9 | | | | | | |
| 10 | Monthly Cash Payment | 550 | | | | |
| 11 | | | | | | |
| 12 | | | | | | |
| 13 | Present Value(PV) | 12,B8,B10) | | | | |

PV

Rate `B6/12` = 0.0075
Nper `B8` = 240
Pmt `B10` = 550
Fv = number
Type = number

= -61129.72471

Returns the present value of an investment: the total amount that a series of future payments is worth now.

**Fv** is the future value, or a cash balance you want to attain after the last payment is made.

Formula result = -€61,129.72    OK    Cancel

The PV result is given.

- Format the result to two decimal places.

The PV Formula result is **-€61,129.72**

The conclusion is that it is a good investment since the PV is more than you are required to pay (€50000).

Let's look at the following example.
Is the following offer acceptable?

- Select tab **PV2**.

- Place cursor in cell **B13**

- Type **=** followed by **PV** . We are going to enter formula on the **Formula bar**.

Then complete the formula:

- **=PV(B6/12,B8,B10)**

- Click enter on the formula toolbar.

  The **NPV** is given as **-€91565**.

  This is an unacceptable return since it is *less* than the €100,000 you have paid in.

The practice exercises contained in this section relate solely to this manual and do not constitute, or imply, certification by the European Driving Licence Foundation in respect of any ECDL examinations. For details on sitting ECDL examinations in your country please contact the local ECDL/ICDL licensee or visit the European Computer Driving Licence Foundation Ltd web site at http://www.ecdl.com

## Exercise 5D

1   Select tab **PV3**. Using the PV function calculate the PV for each of the following three options. List the three results as 'First', 'Second' and 'No' (unacceptable) by writing in the AutoShapes.

First        No        Second

2   Save the file as **PV Solution**.

## 5.5 RATE

**Syntax: RATE(nper,pmt,pv,fv,type,guess)**

**What it does:** Returns the interest rate per period of a loan or annuity.

**Pmt** – amount of periodic payments- this is fixed.
**Rate** is the interest rate for the period. If payments are made monthly divide it by 12.
**Nper** is the total number of payments made.
**Pv** is the present value.
**Fv** is the future value.
**Type** – 0 or 1, 0 if payment due at end of period, 1 if payment is due at beginning of period.
**Guess** – if guess is omitted it is assumed to be 10%.

- Open file **Rate** and select **Sheet Tab Rate 1**.

- Place cursor in cell **B10**.

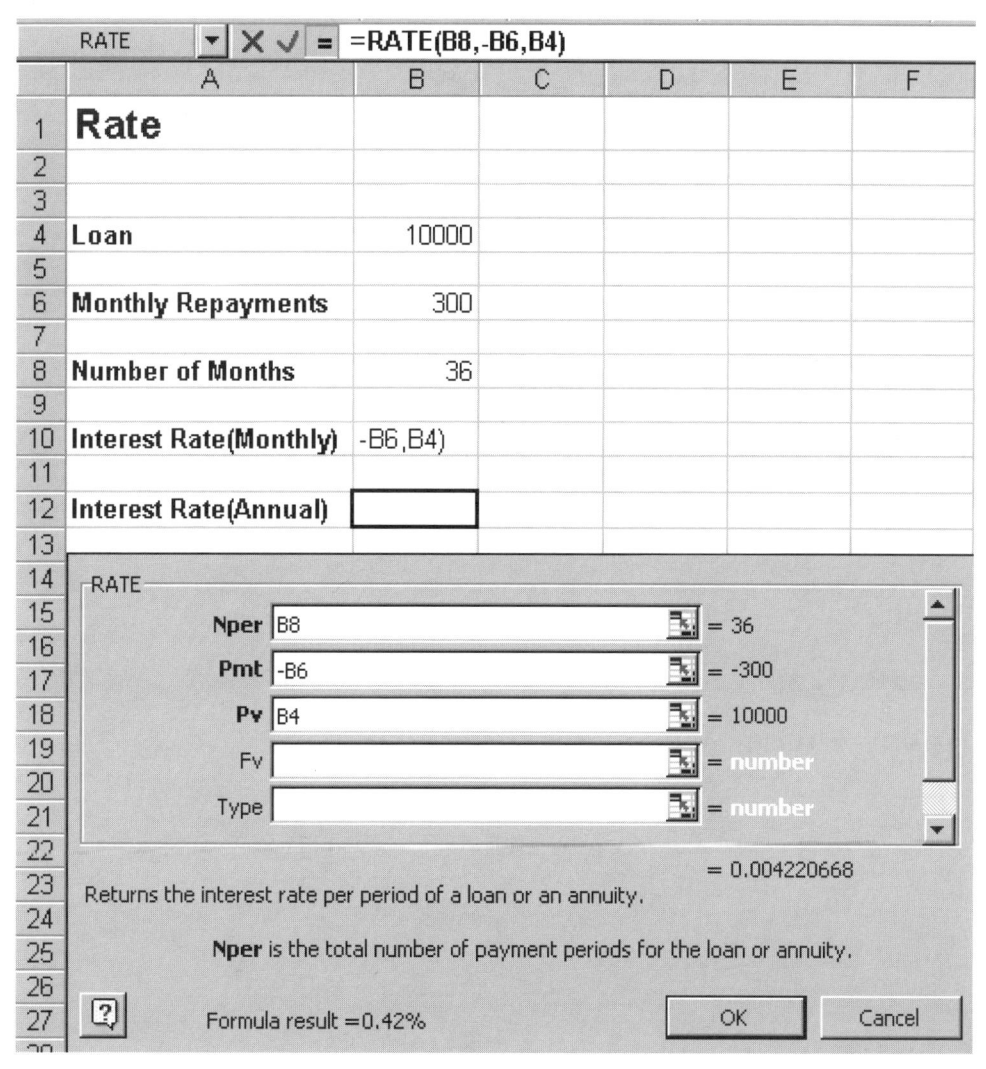

| | A | B |
|---|---|---|
| 1 | **Rate** | |
| 4 | Loan | 10000 |
| 6 | **Monthly Repayments** | 300 |
| 8 | **Number of Months** | 36 |
| 10 | Interest Rate(Monthly) | -B6,B4) |
| 12 | Interest Rate(Annual) | |

Formula bar: `=RATE(B8,-B6,B4)`

RATE dialog:
- Nper: B8 = 36
- Pmt: -B6 = -300
- Pv: B4 = 10000
- Fv: = number
- Type: = number

= 0.004220668

Returns the interest rate per period of a loan or an annuity.

Nper is the total number of payment periods for the loan or annuity.

Formula result =0.42%

Remember to multiply Monthly Interest Rate by 12 to give Annual Interest Rate

- Select **Insert** followed by **Function** or click on Paste function $f_x$ button on standard toolbar.

- Select **Financial** from the Function category and **RATE** as the Function name.

- In the **Nper** box click on cell **B8**. In the **Pmt** box insert a – (minus) sign then click on cell **B8**.

- In the **Pv** box click on cell **B4**.

  Scroll down to Guess. We will omit Guess. It will be assumed to be 10%, by default.

- Click **OK** to return interest rate of **0.42%**.

  We have to multiply this interest rate by **12** to get the annual interest rate.

- Click on the Formula Bar.

- Type in **= B10 * 12**

- Click the ✓ button or press return.

- The Annual Interest Rate is **5.06%**

- Save the file as **Rate**

The practice exercises contained in this section relate solely to this manual and do not constitute, or imply, certification by the European Driving Licence Foundation in respect of any ECDL examinations. For details on sitting ECDL examinations in your country please contact the local ECDL/ICDL licensee or visit the European Computer Driving Licence Foundation Ltd web site at http://www.ecdl.com

## Exercise 5E

1   Click on tab **Rate2** and calculate the interest rates in all three cases.

2   Save the file as **Rate Solution**.

## Section 6  Look Up and Reference Functions (4.3.1.6)

VLOOKUP, HLOOKUP

### 6.1  VLOOKUP

Syntax: VLOOKUP(lookup_value,table_array,row_index_num,range_lookup)

**What it does:** Searches for a value in the leftmost column of a table, and then returns a value in the same row from a column you specify. By default the table must be sorted in **ascending** order.

**NOTE**
The V in VLOOKUP stands for Vertical.

You can compare a VLOOKUP table to a telephone directory. The first column, which is arranged alphabetically, lists the individual names. By referring to a name in this column you can find the telephone number. Also, you can determine address and if it is a business, profession and FAX and Email address. However the main focus of reference is the first column which has to be in **ascending** order otherwise the function will not work properly.

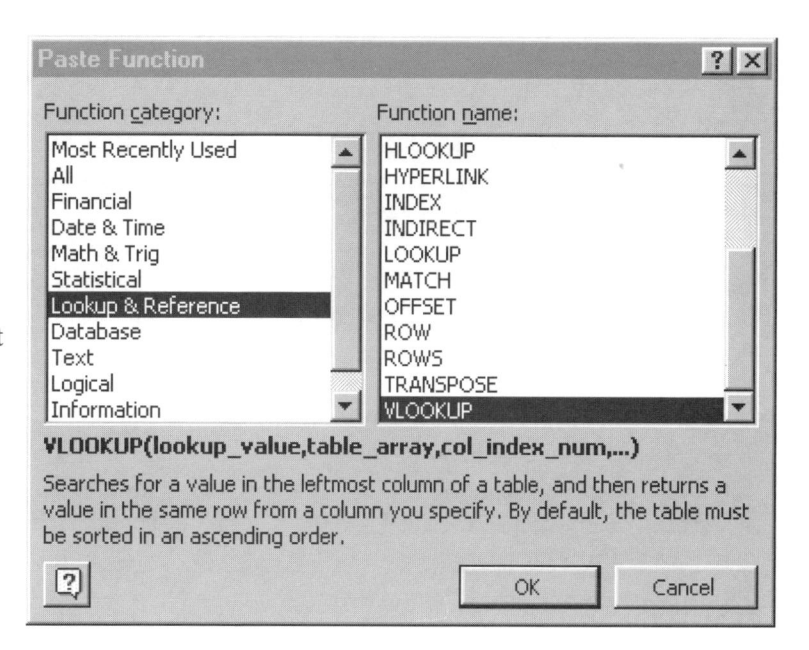

- Open the file **Bookstore**.
- Select **Insert** followed by **Function** or click on **Paste Function** button $f_x$ on the Standard toolbar. Select **Lookup & Reference** from Function category and **VLOOKUP** as function name.

There are five columns, with headings, Number, Book, Author, Price and Location. Notice that in the first column, the numbers are sorted in ascending order, from A5060 – P1060. The Bookstore uses these numbers to obtain further information, such as book name, author, price and location on shelf.
We have been given a reference number for a book, e.g. G1029 and we want to determine the book's name. If the list was short you could check it quickly. You will recognise how useful VLOOKUP is if the list of books was over a thousand.

The file has been set up so that you can answer the questions on the worksheet.

- Select cell **B21**.

# Chapter 3 - Functions

We will insert the references in the VLOOKUP dialog box. The Lookup_value is **G1029**.

- Insert **B20** as the Lookup_value.

The table array is the range of cells we are using, excluding the headings.

- Highlight the range **A4:E18**.

We want to find the **Name** of the book and we can find this in column two.

- Insert **2** as the **col_index_num**.

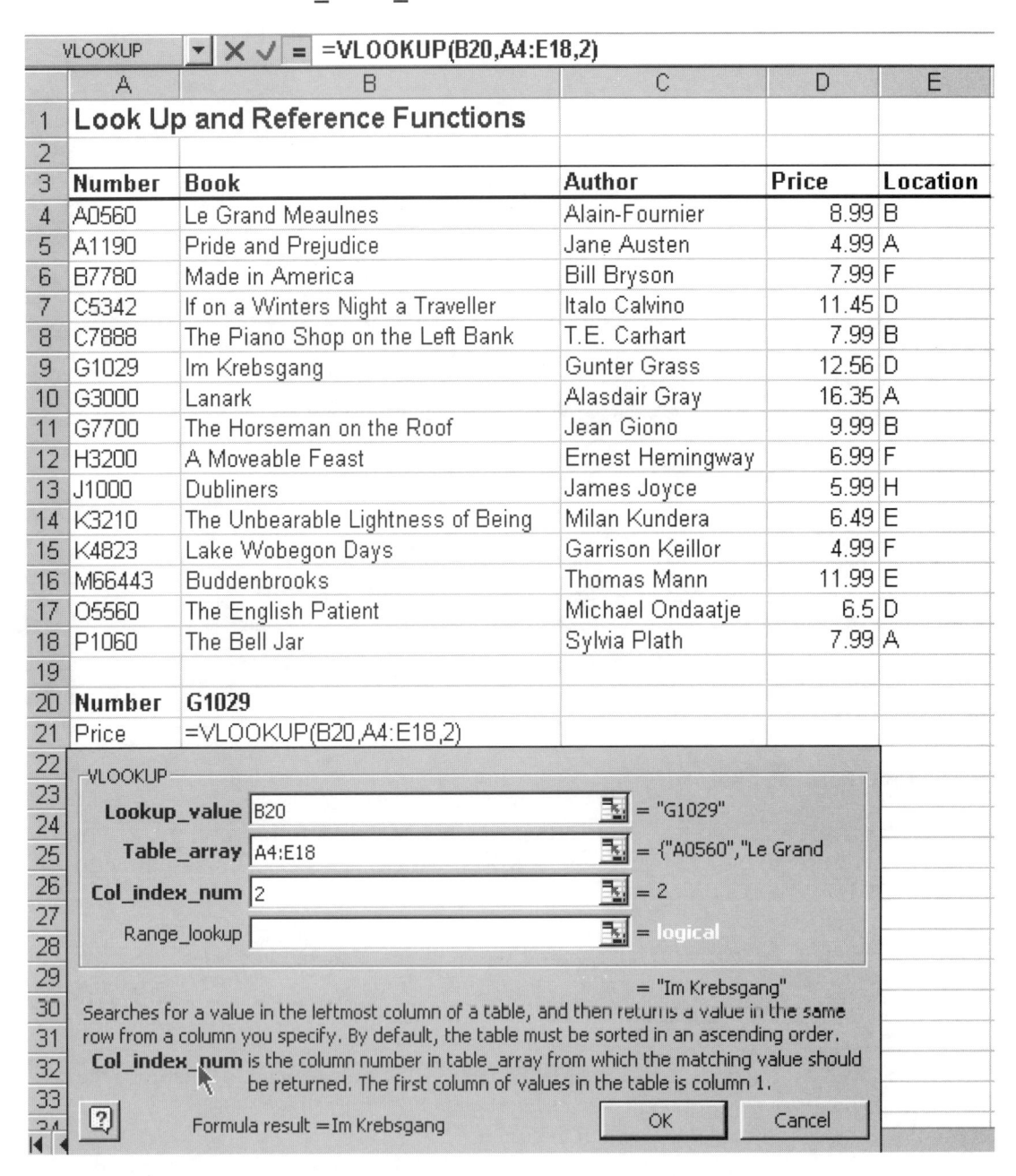

|  | A | B | C | D | E |
|---|---|---|---|---|---|
| 1 | Look Up and Reference Functions | | | | |
| 2 | | | | | |
| 3 | Number | Book | Author | Price | Location |
| 4 | A0560 | Le Grand Meaulnes | Alain-Fournier | 8.99 | B |
| 5 | A1190 | Pride and Prejudice | Jane Austen | 4.99 | A |
| 6 | B7780 | Made in America | Bill Bryson | 7.99 | F |
| 7 | C5342 | If on a Winters Night a Traveller | Italo Calvino | 11.45 | D |
| 8 | C7888 | The Piano Shop on the Left Bank | T.E. Carhart | 7.99 | B |
| 9 | G1029 | Im Krebsgang | Gunter Grass | 12.56 | D |
| 10 | G3000 | Lanark | Alasdair Gray | 16.35 | A |
| 11 | G7700 | The Horseman on the Roof | Jean Giono | 9.99 | B |
| 12 | H3200 | A Moveable Feast | Ernest Hemingway | 6.99 | F |
| 13 | J1000 | Dubliners | James Joyce | 5.99 | H |
| 14 | K3210 | The Unbearable Lightness of Being | Milan Kundera | 6.49 | E |
| 15 | K4823 | Lake Wobegon Days | Garrison Keillor | 4.99 | F |
| 16 | M66443 | Buddenbrooks | Thomas Mann | 11.99 | E |
| 17 | O5560 | The English Patient | Michael Ondaatje | 6.5 | D |
| 18 | P1060 | The Bell Jar | Sylvia Plath | 7.99 | A |
| 19 | | | | | |
| 20 | **Number** | G1029 | | | |
| 21 | Price | =VLOOKUP(B20,A4:E18,2) | | | |

**VLOOKUP dialog box:**
- Lookup_value: B20 = "G1029"
- Table_array: A4:E18 = {"A0560","Le Grand...
- Col_index_num: 2 = 2
- Range_lookup: = logical

= "Im Krebsgang"

Searches for a value in the leftmost column of a table, and then returns a value in the same row from a column you specify. By default, the table must be sorted in an ascending order.

**Col_index_num** is the column number in table_array from which the matching value should be returned. The first column of values in the table is column 1.

Formula result = Im Krebsgang

- Now click **OK**.

The name of the book is "**Im Krebsgang**".

Next we want to find the author of book Number **J1000**.

- Select cell **B25**.

You can if you wish insert the formula by typing and clicking.

- Insert the following formula:

    **=VLOOKUP(B24,A4:E18,3)**

The array is the same, range **A4:E18**, and the column number is **3**. (Author)

This returns that well-known writer "**James Joyce**".

## Error values

We want to look up a book Number **G3500**.

- Select cell **B41**.

- Insert the formula:

    **=VLOOKUP(B40,A4:E18,3,FALSE)**

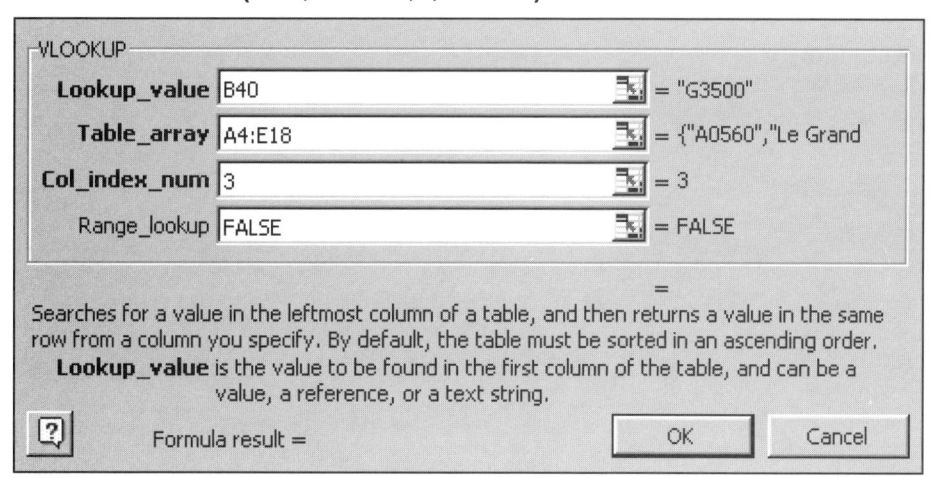

```
VLOOKUP
    Lookup_value  B40           = "G3500"
    Table_array   A4:E18        = {"A0560","Le Grand
    Col_index_num 3             = 3
    Range_lookup  FALSE         = FALSE
                                =
Searches for a value in the leftmost column of a table, and then returns a value in the same
row from a column you specify. By default, the table must be sorted in an ascending order.
    Lookup_value is the value to be found in the first column of the table, and can be a
                        value, a reference, or a text string.

    Formula result =                         OK        Cancel
```

In this case we add **FALSE** to the **Range_lookup**

- Click **OK**

We get the error value **#N/A**.

There is no book **Number G3500**.

We will repeat this with the **Range-lookup TRUE**.

- Select cell **B45**.

- Insert the formula:

    **=VLOOKUP(B40,A4:E18,3,TRUE)**

    This returns the value **"Alasdair Gray"**, which is the closest value in the array.

---

The practice exercises contained in this section relate solely to this manual and do not constitute, or imply, certification by the European Driving Licence Foundation in respect of any ECDL examinations. For details on sitting ECDL examinations in your country please contact the local ECDL/ICDL licensee or visit the European Computer Driving Licence Foundation Ltd web site at http://www.ecdl.com

## Exercise 6A

Using the methods just learned, complete the worksheet.

1. Write a **VLOOKUP** statement to return the name of the **Book** from the book Number G770.

2. Write a **VLOOKUP** statement which returns the shelf **Location** of book Number A0560.

3. Write a **VLOOKUP** statement that returns the **Author** of book Number H3200.

4. Save the file as **Bookstore Solution**.

## 6.2 HLOOKUP

Syntax: **HLOOKUP(lookup_value,table_array,row_index_num,range_lookup)**

**What it does:** Looks for a value in the top row of a table or array of values and returns the value in the same column from the row you specify.

The **HLOOKUP** function operates in the same way as the **VLOOKUP** function.

**NOTE**

The H in HLOOKUP stands for Horizontal.

- Open the file **City Garden**.

The table (range **A1:D5**) shows the unit price of three plants, Begonia, Dahlia and Rose in four towns, Arklow, Dublin, Wexford and Wicklow. We want to find the revenue generated from the plant sales. To do this we have to create the HLOOKUP formula then multiply it by the Unit value. This information is entered in column D.

|    | A       | B       | C       | D       |
|----|---------|---------|---------|---------|
| 1  | TOWN    | BEGONIA | DAHLIA  | ROSES   |
| 2  | Arklow  | 0.91    | 0.33    | 0.45    |
| 3  | Dublin  | 0.85    | 0.36    | 0.54    |
| 4  | Wexford | 0.83    | 0.37    | 0.58    |
| 5  | Wicklow | 0.71    | 0.31    | 0.59    |
| 6  |         |         |         |         |
| 7  | TOWN    | UNITS   | PRODUCT | REVENUE |
| 8  | Arklow  | 3300    | BEGONIA |         |
| 9  | Arklow  | 1800    | DAHLIA  |         |
| 10 | Dublin  | 3100    | ROSES   |         |
| 11 | Dublin  | 1600    | DAHLIA  |         |
| 12 | Wexford | 1400    | BEGONIA |         |
| 13 | Wicklow | 2500    | BEGONIA |         |
| 14 | Wicklow | 1200    | ROSES   |         |

- Click on cell **D8**. Insert the formula:

    **=HLOOKUP(C8,A1:D5,2)*B8**

- Click **Enter** on the Formula Bar.

    This returns the value **3003** (**0.91 * 3300**).

- Select cell **D9**. Insert the formula:

    **=HLOOKUP(C9,A1:D5,2)*B8**

    This returns the value **594** (**0.33 * 1800**)

The practice exercises contained in this section relate solely to this manual and do not constitute, or imply, certification by the European Driving Licence Foundation in respect of any ECDL examinations. For details on sitting ECDL examinations in your country please contact the local ECDL/ICDL licensee or visit the European Computer Driving Licence Foundation Ltd web site at http://www.ecdl.com

## Exercise 6B

1  Complete the table for the next five entries.

2  Add in three more entries of your own choosing.

3  Save the file as **City Garden Solution**.

## Section 7    Logical Functions (4.3.1.7)

**IF, AND, OR, ISERROR**

### 7.1    IF

**Syntax: IF(logical test,value_if_true,value_if_false)**

**What it does:** Returns one value if a condition you specify happens to be TRUE and another value if it evaluates to FALSE.

- Select **Insert** followed by **Function** or click on **Paste Function** button *fx* on the Standard toolbar.

- Select **Logical Functions** from Function category and **IF** as function name.

- Open file **Business Test Results**.

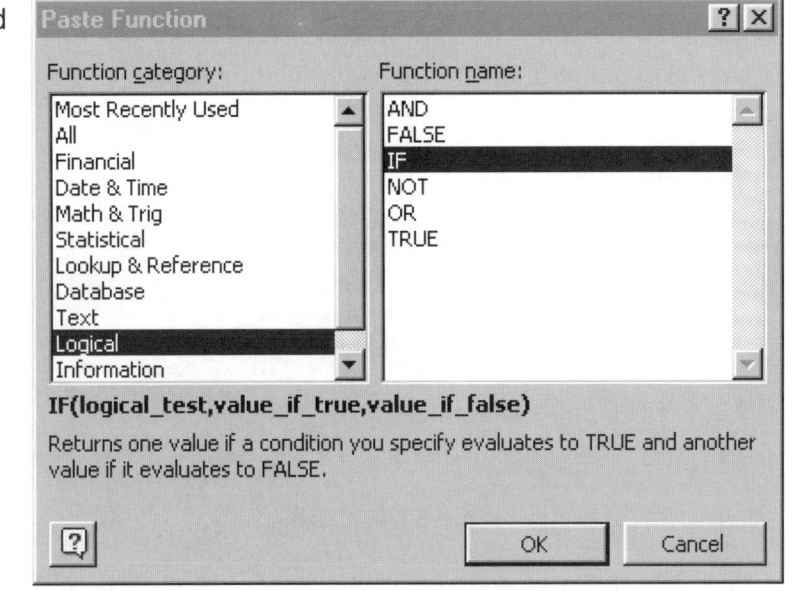

The table gives details of examination results in a college test. The Pass/Fail result is determined by a simple **IF** statement. A student who receives 50 marks or more passes the exam.

- An **IF** statement is created in cell **D6** which reads as follows:

**=IF(C6>=50,"Pass","Fail")**

Note the entries in the **IF** dialog box.

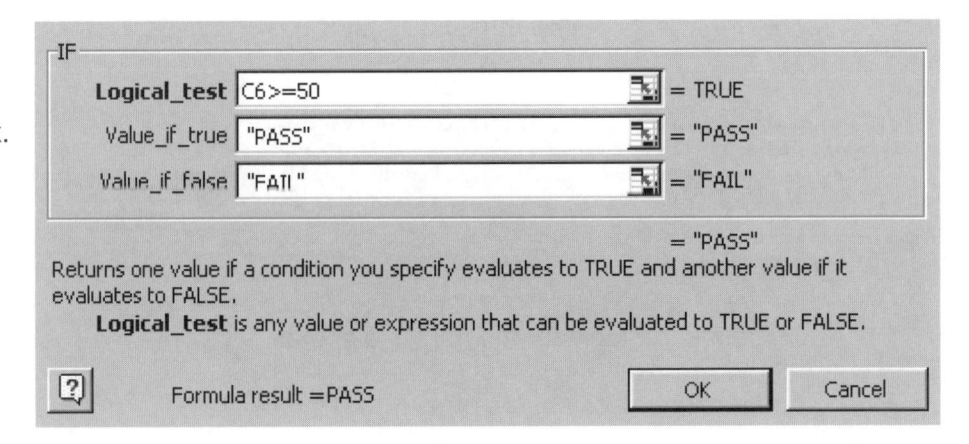

## Chapter 3 - Functions

```
D6         =  =IF(C6>=50, "PASS", "FAIL")
```

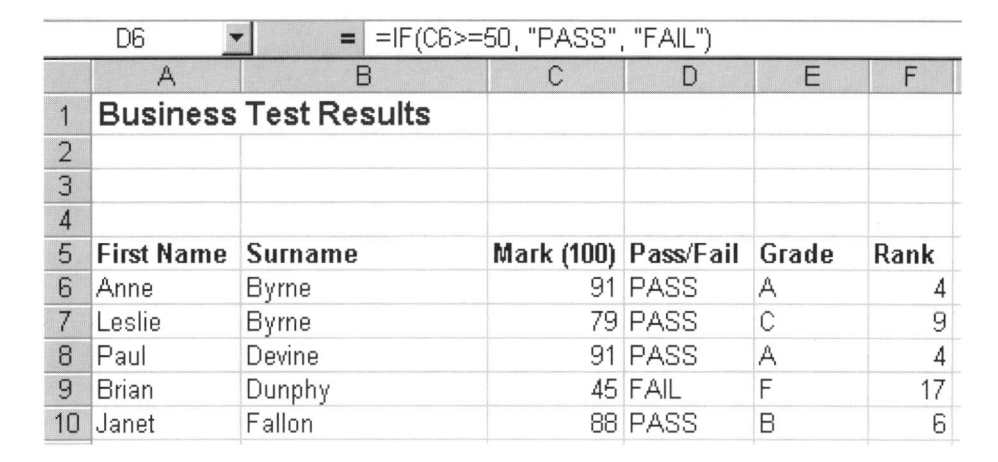

| | A | B | C | D | E | F |
|---|---|---|---|---|---|---|
| 1 | Business Test Results | | | | | |
| 2 | | | | | | |
| 3 | | | | | | |
| 4 | | | | | | |
| 5 | First Name | Surname | Mark (100) | Pass/Fail | Grade | Rank |
| 6 | Anne | Byrne | 91 | PASS | A | 4 |
| 7 | Leslie | Byrne | 79 | PASS | C | 9 |
| 8 | Paul | Devine | 91 | PASS | A | 4 |
| 9 | Brian | Dunphy | 45 | FAIL | F | 17 |
| 10 | Janet | Fallon | 88 | PASS | B | 6 |

A decision has been made to increase the pass mark to 60. We will rewrite the IF statement to reflect this.

- Click on cell **D6**.

- We will make the change on the Formula Bar.

- Delete **50** and replace with **60**.

```
D6         =  =IF(C6>=60, "PASS", "FAIL"
                                Formula Bar  D
```
| | A | B |
|---|---|---|
| 1 | Business Test Results | |

- Click Enter on the Formula Bar.

- Now copy the formula by dragging down from cell **D6:D25**.

- The number of failures increases.

  You can if you wish reduce the pass mark to 40!

- Change the pass mark back to 50.

- Save the file at this stage.

**NOTE**

Click on cell **E6**. It contains a nested IF function which is slightly more complex. We will look at Nested IF statements in Section 9.

---

The practice exercises contained in this section relate solely to this manual and do not constitute, or imply, certification by the European Driving Licence Foundation in respect of any ECDL examinations. For details on sitting ECDL examinations in your country please contact the local ECDL/ICDL licensee or visit the European Computer Driving Licence Foundation Ltd web site at http://www.ecdl.com

## Exercise 7A

It has been decided to give an award to those students who get 90 or more in their examination.

1.  Open the file **Business Test Results**.

2.  Insert the column title **Award** in the cell immediately to the right of **Rank**.

3.  Select cell **G6**.

**4**     Write the **IF** statement as follows.

=IF(C6>=90, "Distinction","Keep Trying")

You can use the above suggestion or devise an alternative.

**5**     Click on **Enter** on the **Formula Bar** and drag down the appropriate range.

**6**     Save the file as **Business Test Results Solution**.

The practice exercises contained in this section relate solely to this manual and do not constitute, or imply, certification by the European Driving Licence Foundation in respect of any ECDL examinations. For details on sitting ECDL examinations in your country please contact the local ECDL/ICDL licensee or visit the European Computer Driving Licence Foundation Ltd web site at http://www.ecdl.com

## Exercise 7B

In this exercise we are going to construct a simple IF statement that will determine whether a bonus will be awarded to a salesperson. In Catering Supplies the sales of tea, coffee and biscuits are added, and if the total is greater than or equal to €15,000 then a bonus is awarded.

**1**     Open the file **Catering Supplies**.

**2**     Select cell **C5**. We are going to insert the formula directly onto the Formula Bar.

**3**     Type in the following IF statement. There are no spaces between characters.

=IF(E5>=15000,"Bonus","No Bonus")

Note that you must *not* include symbol for currency or comma in thousands.

**4**     Click on **Enter** on the **Formula Bar**.

The first sales person receives a bonus.

**5**     Copy the **IF** statement into all the other cells by dragging down the range **A6:A27**.

The completed table should look like the diagram on the next page.

| F5 | | = | =IF(E5>=15000," BONUS","NO BONUS") | | |
|---|---|---|---|---|---|
| | A | B | C | D | E | F |

| | A | B | C | D | E | F |
|---|---|---|---|---|---|---|
| 1 | **CATERING SUPPLIES** | | | | | |
| 2 | | | | | | |
| 3 | | | | | | |
| 4 | SALESPERSON | TEA | COFFEE | BISCUITS | TOTAL | BONUS |
| 5 | Alan | €13,100 | €6,300 | €7,100 | €26,500 | BONUS |
| 6 | Baxter | €7,800 | €4,532 | €568 | €12,900 | NO BONUS |
| 7 | Brown | €8,700 | €11,900 | €400 | €21,000 | BONUS |
| 8 | Connor | €3,000 | €2,340 | €312 | €5,652 | NO BONUS |
| 9 | Davies | €3,467 | €778 | €990 | €5,235 | NO BONUS |
| 10 | Driver | €8,900 | €456 | €1,003 | €10,359 | NO BONUS |
| 11 | Isaacs | €4,480 | €932 | €2,104 | €7,516 | NO BONUS |
| 12 | Johnstone | €7,804 | €775 | €882 | €9,461 | NO BONUS |
| 13 | Joyce | €6,370 | €347 | €775 | €7,492 | NO BONUS |
| 14 | Jupiter | €440 | €7,700 | €554 | €8,694 | NO BONUS |
| 15 | Kline | €10,200 | €2,300 | €2,500 | €15,000 | BONUS |
| 16 | Lepton | €120 | €5,567 | €9,080 | €14,767 | NO BONUS |
| 17 | Neil | €3,490 | €6,670 | €880 | €11,040 | NO BONUS |
| 18 | Pagnol | €10,000 | €2,500 | €2,500 | €15,000 | BONUS |
| 19 | Reid | €2,007 | €128 | €984 | €3,119 | NO BONUS |
| 20 | Reddin | €7,653 | €8,734 | €221 | €16,608 | BONUS |
| 21 | Simplicio | €16,900 | €889 | €256 | €18,045 | BONUS |
| 22 | Twist | €6,700 | €8,900 | €54 | €15,654 | BONUS |
| 23 | Woolworth | €3,420 | €50 | €998 | €4,468 | NO BONUS |
| 24 | Zentill | €1,000 | €4,576 | €7,652 | €13,228 | NO BONUS |

The practice exercises contained in this section relate solely to this manual and do not constitute, or imply, certification by the European Driving Licence Foundation in respect of any ECDL examinations. For details on sitting ECDL examinations in your country please contact the local ECDL/ICDL licensee or visit the European Computer Driving Licence Foundation Ltd web site at http://www.ecdl.com

## Exercise 7C

1   In the column adjacent to **BONUS**, write in the heading **AWARD**.

    Write an IF statement that will return, "AWARD" if the sales total is greater than €15,500, and "Your turn next month?" if the sales is less than or equal to €15,500.

    Remember, you must *not* include symbol for currency or comma in thousands.

2   If the Tea and Biscuits sales combined total is more than €20,000 the sales person gets a trip to Venice, otherwise it's a company picnic at the top of the Sugarloaf Mountain. Write an IF statement to reflect this.

3   Save the file as **Catering Supplies Solution**.

## 7.2 AND

**Syntax: AND(logical1,logical2,…)**

**What it does:** Returns TRUE if all its arguments are true; returns FALSE if any argument is FALSE.

- Select cell **B1** in a blank worksheet and insert the name **DATA**.

- Insert the numbers **40** and **109** in cells **B3** and **B4**.

    In cell **B6** (or any convenient cell) write in the formula:

    =AND(1<B3,B3<80)

    The result is **TRUE** since 40 is between 1 and 80.

- Now write in the formula:

    =AND(1<B3,B3<39)

    This returns **FALSE** because 40 is not between 1 and 39.

## 7.3 OR

**Syntax: OR(logical1,logical2,…)**

**What it does:** Returns TRUE if any argument is true; returns FALSE if all arguments are FALSE.

- Select any cell on worksheet.

- Insert the following formula.

    =OR(TRUE)

    This gives the value as **TRUE** as one argument is true.

- Now insert the following formula:

    =OR(1+1=3,2+2=6)

    We get the value FALSE since all arguments are **FALSE**.

- Finally insert the following formula:

    =OR(TRUE,FALSE,TRUE)

    Since at least one argument is true, it returns **TRUE**.

## 7.4 ISERROR

**Syntax: ISERROR(value)**

**What it does:** Returns TRUE if value is any error value,(#NA ,#Value!, #Ref!, #Div/0!, #Num!, #Name?, or #Null).

- Click on any cell in worksheet but if **A1** is free, use it.

- Insert the following in cell **A1**:

    **#REF!**

    We will use the function **ISERROR** to check if **#REF!** is an error.

- In any cell write the formula:

    **=ISERROR(A1)**

    This returns **TRUE**.

    Repeat this exercise with any of the other error values listed.

The practice exercises contained in this section relate solely to this manual and do not constitute, or imply, certification by the European Driving Licence Foundation in respect of any ECDL examinations. For details on sitting ECDL examinations in your country please contact the local ECDL/ICDL licensee or visit the European Computer Driving Licence Foundation Ltd web site at http://www.ecdl.com

## Exercise 7D

1   Open file **Logic**.

    *Column **A** is dedicated to the **AND** function.*

2   Select cell **A12**.

3   Insert the following formula:

    **=AND(5<A7,A7<A9)**

    This returns the value **TRUE**.

    Since 5 is less than 7, and, 7 is less than 50.

4   Click on cell **C14**.

5   Insert the following formula:

    **=AND(5<A7,A9<A7)**

    This returns the value **FALSE**.

    Since 5 is less than 37, but 50 is not less than 37 the logic function returns **FALSE**.

The practice exercises contained in this section relate solely to this manual and do not constitute, or imply, certification by the European Driving Licence Foundation in respect of any ECDL examinations. For details on sitting ECDL examinations in your country please contact the local ECDL/ICDL licensee or visit the European Computer Driving Licence Foundation Ltd web site at http://www.ecdl.org

## Exercise 7E

*Column **D** is dedicated to the **OR** function.*

Is file Logic still open? If not, open it now.

1   Select cell **D12**.

2   Insert the formula:

   =OR(TRUE)

This returns **TRUE** as one argument is true.

We will construct some **OR** statements using the data in column **D**.

3   Select cell **D14**.

4   Insert the formula:

   =OR(D5+D9=D7,D7+D9=D5)

This returns **FALSE** because all the arguments are false.

5   Click on cell **D16**.

6   Insert the formula:

   =OR(D5+D7=22,D9+D7=16,D5+D7=F5)

7   Before you click enter can you predict whether you will get **TRUE** or **FALSE** as response?

8   Since, at least one argument is true we get **TRUE**.

The practice exercises contained in this section relate solely to this manual and do not constitute, or imply, certification by the European Driving Licence Foundation in respect of any ECDL examinations. For details on sitting ECDL examinations in your country please contact the local ECDL/ICDL licensee or visit the European Computer Driving Licence Foundation Ltd web site at http://www.ecdl.org

## Exercise 7F

*Column **I** is dedicated to the **ISERROR** function.*

1   Select cell **I12**.

2   Insert the formula:

   =ISERROR(I5)

**3** As expected this returned the **TRUE** message.

**4** Select cell **I15**

Insert the formula:

   **=ISERROR(I7)**

Can you predict the result? Is it **TRUE** or **FALSE**?

**5** Click **OK** and the answer is **FALSE**. (It is not an error).

**6** Use **ISERROR** with cells **I17** and **I19** to return **TRUE/FALSE** on cells **I9** and **I11** respectively.

**7** The answer is **FALSE** followed by **TRUE**.

**8** Re-save the file as **Logic Solution**.

## Section 8   Database Functions (4.3.1.8)

DSUM, DMIN, DMAX, DCOUNT

### 8.1   DSUM

**Syntax: DSUM(database,field,criteria)**

**What it does:** Adds the numbers in the field (column) of records in the database that match the conditions you specify.
Database is the range reference in the list, field determines in which column the values will be summed. Criteria is the range reference which identifies the fields and values used to define the selection criteria.

In this example we want to find the total sales from a group of shops, with more than three staff, which are open 24 hours.

|   | A | B | C | D | E |
|---|---|---|---|---|---|
| 1 | Database Functions | | | | |
| 2 | | | | | |
| 3 | | | | | |
| 4 | | Store | Staff | Sales | 24-Hour |
| 5 | | Wide Awake | 4 | 50000 | Yes |
| 6 | | Wide Awake | 5 | 65000 | Yes |
| 7 | | Dream Shopper | 3 | 12000 | Yes |
| 8 | | Dream Shopper | 3 | 10000 | Yes |
| 9 | | Sunshine Discount | 6 | 2000 | Yes |
| 10 | | Sunshine Discount | 8 | 20000 | No |
| 11 | | Wide Awake | 2 | 15000 | Yes |
| 12 | | Dream Shopper | 3 | 5000 | Yes |
| 13 | | Sunshine Discount | 4 | 33500 | No |
| 14 | | Sunshine Discount | 4 | 23000 | No |
| 15 | | | | | |
| 16 | | | | | |
| 17 | | Store | Staff | Sales | 24-Hour |
| 18 | | | >3 | | Yes |

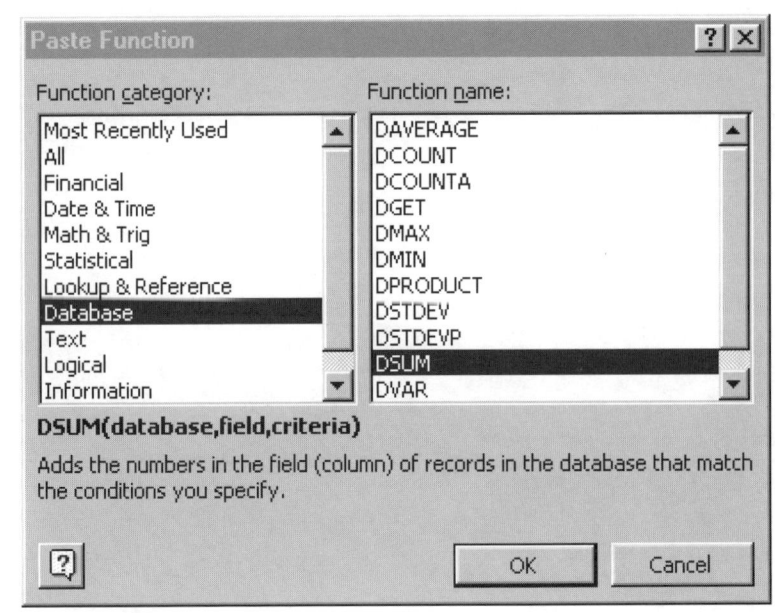

- Open the file **Database**.

  The database range is **B4:E14**. The **field** that interests us is **Sales**. The range reference that identifies the fields and values used to define the selection criteria is **B17:E18**.

- Click on cell **B21**.

- Select **Insert** followed by **Function** or click on **Paste Function** button $f_x$ on the Standard toolbar. Select **Database** from Function category and **DSUM** as function name.

  The DSUM dialog box opens and we add our data.

- In database drag across the range **B4:E14**.

- The field is **Sales** so click on **D4**.

- The criteria is **B17:E18** so enter this in box.

  The total sales amounts to **117000**.

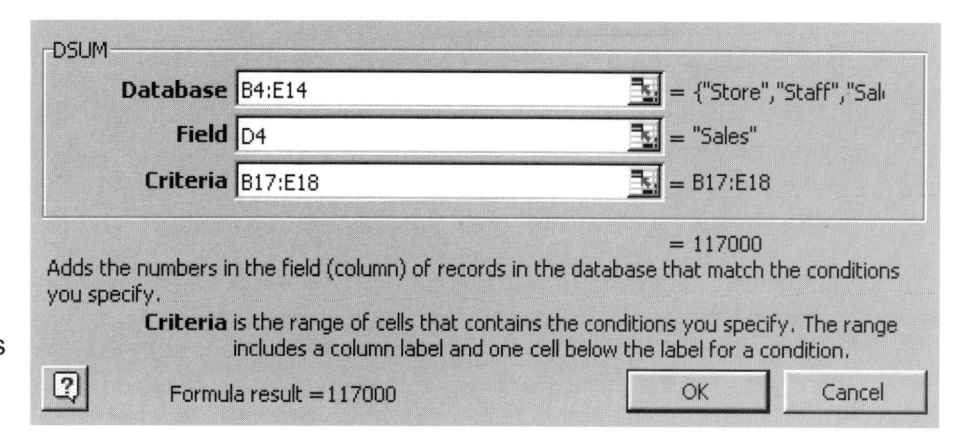

You may wish to calculate the total mentally to identify what sums make up this figure. Do this now.

## 8.2 DMIN

**Syntax: DMIN(database,field,criteria)**

**What it does:** Returns the smallest number in the field (column) of records that match the conditions you specify.
Database is the range reference in the list, field is the column in the database which is examined to find the smallest number. Criteria is the range reference which identifies the fields and values used to define the selection criteria.

We want to find the minimum sales figure from our group of shops subject to the same criteria. The number of staff is more than 3 and the shop is open 24 hours.

- Open the file **Database**.

- Select cell **B23** for the calculation.

- Insert the following formula:

    **=DMIN(B4:E14,D4,B17:E18)**

You will notice that the database range is the same as used in the previous question and includes all fields, the field required here is 'Sales', and the criteria is as defined previously.

- Click the enter button on the Formula toolbar.

  This returns the value **2000**.

  Confirm that this is correct by inspection.

## 8.3 DMAX

**Syntax: DMAX(database,field,criteria)**
**What it does:** Returns the largest number in the field (column) of records in the database that match the conditions you specify.
Database is the range reference in the list, field is the column in the database which is examined to find the largest number. Criteria is the range reference which identifies the fields and values used to define the selection criteria.

We want to find the maximum sales figure from our group of shops subject to the same criteria. The number of staff is more than 3 and the shop is open 24 hours.

- Open the file **Database**

- Select cell **B25** for the calculation.

    Insert the following formula:

    **=DMAX(B4:E14,D4,B17:E18)**

    We get the value as **65000**.

    Confirm that this is correct by inspection.


## 8.4 DCOUNT

**Syntax: DCOUNT(database,field,criteria)**

**What it does:** Counts the cells containing numbers in the field (column) of records in the database that match the conditions you specify.
Database is the range reference in the list. Field is the column in the database which is examined to find the smallest number. Criteria is the range reference which identifies the fields and values used to define the selection criteria.

In this example we are going to count the number of items which meet the criteria.

We want to know the number of 24-hour shops that have more than 3 staff. DCOUNT is the function to check this.

- We will do our count in cell **B27**. Click on it now.

- Insert the formula:

    **=DCOUNT(B4:E14, ,B17:E18)**

    This returns the answer **3**. You can check this manually from the table.

- Save the file as **Database Solution** and close.

*The practice exercises contained in this section relate solely to this manual and do not constitute, or imply, certification by the European Driving Licence Foundation in respect of any ECDL examinations. For details on sitting ECDL examinations in your country please contact the local ECDL/ICDL licensee or visit the European Computer Driving Licence Foundation Ltd web site at http://www.ecdl.com*

## Exercise 8A

In this exercise, we are going to look at the same worksheet but change the criteria in the range **B17:E18**.

1. Open the file **Database**.

2. Select cell **C18** and insert **>2**.

3. Select cell **E18** and insert **NO**.

4. Choose cell **B21**. We will make our calculation here.

    We want to find the sum of the sales in those shops, that are not 24-Hour shops, and have more than 2 staff.

5. Select **Insert** followed by **Function** or click on **Paste Function** button on the Standard toolbar. Select **Database** from Function category and **DSUM** as Function name.

6. In the **DSUM** dialog box, make the following entries:

    **Database: B4:E14**
    **Field: D4**
    **Criteria: B17:E18**

7. Click **OK**.

8. This returns the answer as **76500**.

    Look at the list and total it up mentally to confirm answer.

*The practice exercises contained in this section relate solely to this manual and do not constitute, or imply, certification by the European Driving Licence Foundation in respect of any ECDL examinations. For details on sitting ECDL examinations in your country please contact the local ECDL/ICDL licensee or visit the European Computer Driving Licence Foundation Ltd web site at http://www.ecdl.com*

## Exercise 8B

Using the same criteria (number of staff greater than 2, shop is not open 24 hours), calculate the following:

1. **DMIN**.

2. **DMAX**.

3. **DCOUNT**.

    The answers are **1.** DMIN = 20000, **2.** DMAX = 33500 and **3.** DCOUNT = 3

    - Save the file as **Database Solution**.

## Section 9  Using Nested Functions (4.3.1.9)

**Syntax:** =IF(condition,value_if_true,value_if_false)

**What it does:** Returns one value if a condition you specify happens to be TRUE and another value if it evaluates to FALSE.

The IF function is covered in Section Seven.

Nested functions are particularly useful if there is more than one outcome to a situation.

- Select **Insert** followed by **Function** or click on **Paste Function** button on the Standard toolbar. Select **Logic** from Function category and **IF** as function name.

We want to use the IF statement in our next exercise to calculate the tax on four employees. There are three tax bands, A, B, and C and the Tax Rate is shown. Employees earning 120,000 or more will be taxed at 56%, those earning more than or equal to 50,000 but less than 120,000, will pay tax at the rate of 42%, and those earning more than 30,000 but less than 50,000 will pay tax at the lowest rate, 24%. Those earning less than 30,000 *do not pay* tax.

For the purposes of this exercise we will ignore any tax-free allowances.

|   | A | B | C | D |
|---|---|---|---|---|
| 1 | Using Nested Functions | | | |
| 2 | | | | |
| 3 | | TAX BAND | INCOME | TAX RATE |
| 4 | | A | 120,000 | 56.00% |
| 5 | | B | 50,000 | 42.00% |
| 6 | | C | 30,000 | 24.00% |
| 7 | | | | |
| 8 | | | | |
| 9 | | | | |
| 10 | | | | |
| 11 | | | | |
| 12 | | Employee | Salary | Tax |
| 13 | | Sylvia Lappin | 132,000 | |
| 14 | | Martin Reilly | 32,000 | |
| 15 | | Bill Ireland | 43,500 | |
| 16 | | Jinny Jones | 25,000 | |
| 17 | | | | |

- Open the file **Tax Table**.

- Select cell **D13**. We will construct the nested **IF** statement in this cell.

- Insert the following statement:

   **=IF(C13>=C4,C13*D4,IF(C13>=C5,C13*D5,IF(C13>=C6,C13*D6,"No Tax Due")))**

You may find it useful to attempt to say the IF statement verbally.
Notice that the number of parentheses balance. If one is left out you will be prompted to accept the formula as Excel sees it. Often this is fine, but check before you click **OK**.

- Repeat the procedure for cells **C14:C16**.

   The tax in descending order in the table is **73,920**, **7,680**, **10,440** and **No Tax Due**.

- Save the file as **Tax Table Solution**.

The practice exercises contained in this section relate solely to this manual and do not constitute, or imply, certification by the European Driving Licence Foundation in respect of any ECDL examinations. For details on sitting ECDL examinations in your country please contact the local ECDL/ICDL licensee or visit the European Computer Driving Licence Foundation Ltd web site at http://www.ecdl.com

## Exercise 9A

In this exercise we are going to look at an example of Nested Functions. Then you will be required to create your own.

**1** Open the file **Business Test Results**.

The grades allocated to the students depend on the mark received. These grades are allocated as you have probably checked at this stage, by means of a nested IF function. The statement appears quite complex but once you examine it carefully you will see the pattern in it. If a student gets 90 or more in the exam he/she is awarded an A, if the student gets 80 or more, then he/she gets a B, and so on, until the student with less than 40 gets a No Grade.

| GRADE | MARK |
|---|---|
| A | 90-100 |
| B | 80-89 |
| C | 70-79 |
| D | 60-69 |
| E | 50-59 |
| F | 40-49 |
| No Grade | 0-39 |

**IF Statement**

=IF(C6>=90,"A",IF(C6>=80,"B",IF(C6>=70,"C",IF(C6>=60,"D",IF(C6>=50,"E",IF(C6>=40,"F","No Grade"))))))

| | A | B | C | D | E | F |
|---|---|---|---|---|---|---|
| 1 | Business Test Results | | | | | |
| 2 | | | | | | |
| 3 | | | | | | |
| 4 | | | | | | |
| 5 | First Name | Surname | Mark (100) | Pass/Fail | Grade | Rank |
| 6 | Anne | Byrne | 91 | PASS | A | 4 |
| 7 | Leslie | Byrne | 79 | PASS | C | 9 |
| 8 | Paul | Devine | 91 | PASS | A | 4 |
| 9 | Brian | Dunphy | 45 | FAIL | F | 17 |
| 10 | Janet | Fallon | 88 | PASS | D | 6 |
| 11 | Elenor | Fallon | 75 | PASS | C | 11 |
| 12 | James | Finn | 100 | PASS | A | 1 |

**2** A new grade **G** is introduced for a mark in the range **30-39**. Modify the statement to include this grade.

**3** Save the file as **Business Test Results**.

## Self Check Exercises

1. CONCATENATE is a Logical Function?
   - ☐ True
   - ☐ False

2. Which of the following functions calculates the payments for a loan?
   - ☐ NPV
   - ☐ PMT
   - ☐ HLOOKUP
   - ☐ DCOUNT

3. =IF(A3>100,"Bonus", "No Bonus") is an example of a?
   - ☐ Statistical Function.
   - ☐ Round Function.
   - ☐ Logical Function.
   - ☐ Database Function.

4. What is the correct syntax for calculating the payment on a loan, based on constant payments and constant internal rate?
   - ☐ PMT(rate,nper,pv,fv,type)
   - ☐ FV(rate,nper,pmt,pv,type)
   - ☐ PV(rate,nper,pmt,fv,type)
   - ☐ NPV(value1,value2,…)

5. =ROUND(58.3898,2) will return 58.38 as the result.
   - ☐ True
   - ☐ False

6. What function will return the following, assuming this is the date and time in question. **11/04/2003 14:32**
   - ☐ =DATE()
   - ☐ =TIME()
   - ☐ =DAY()
   - ☐ =NOW()

7. What function searches for a value in the leftmost column of a table and returns a value from a column you specify?
   - ☐ HLOOKUP
   - ☐ DCOUNT
   - ☐ VLOOKUP

8. What function is being used below?

# Chapter 4

Analysis

## Chapter Four: AM 4.4 – Analysis

**AM 4.4.1 Pivot Tables / Dynamic Crosstab**  Page

| | | |
|---|---|---|
| AM4.4.1.1 | Create a Pivot Table or Dynamic Crosstab using defined field names | 193 |
| AM4.4.1.2 | Modify the data source and refresh the Pivot Table or Dynamic Crosstab. | 199 |
| AM4.4.1.3 | Group / Display data in a Pivot Table Or a Dynamic Crosstab by a defined Criterion. | 202 |

**AM 4.4.2 Scenarios / Versions**

| | | |
|---|---|---|
| AM4.4.2.1 | Create named Scenarios / Versions from defined Cell ranges. | 204 |
| AM4.4.2.2 | Create a Scenario summary / Version report | 211 |

**AM 4.4.3 Auditing**

| | | |
|---|---|---|
| AM4.4.3.1 | Trace precedent cells in a worksheet | 216 |
| AM4.4.3.2 | Trace dependent cells in a worksheet | 218 |
| AM4.4.3.3 | Display all formulas or view location of all Formulas in a worksheet | 226 |
| AM4.4.3.4 | Add or remove worksheet comments | 229, 232 |
| AM4.4.3.5 | Edit worksheet comments | 232 |

Chapter 4 - Analysis

# Section 1    Pivot Tables

A Pivot Table is an interactive worksheet table that can summarise and analyse large amounts of data. If changes occur in the original data, this can be reflected in an updated Pivot Table.
You can create a Pivot Table from:

- An Excel List or database.

- An external source such as Access.

- Multiple consolidation ranges.

- A different PivotTable or PivotChart.

**Jumping Beans** is an Excel list that records the sales of health food products. The list is a flat-file database with the following properties:

- Each **column** is a **field**. E.g. Month, Health Product, City and Sales are all fields.

- Each **row** is a **record**. E.g. Row 17 is a record.

- The entire database, field names and records are called a **list**.

|    | Month    | Health Product            | City    | Sales   |
|----|----------|---------------------------|---------|---------|
| 10 | Month    | Health Product            | City    | Sales   |
| 11 | January  | Jumping Vitamin Beans     | Dublin  | € 217   |
| 12 | January  | Irish Bee Pollen          | Dublin  | € 590   |
| 13 | January  | Ten Years Younger         | Dublin  | € 1,200 |
| 14 | January  | Irish Bee Pollen          | Galway  | € 931   |
| 15 | January  | Ten Years Younger         | Galway  | € 839   |
| 16 | January  | Sunshine Energy Tablets   | Dublin  | € 1,118 |
| 17 | January  | Mineral Magic Pack        | Dublin  | € 477   |
| 18 | January  | Irish Bee Pollen          | Galway  | € 717   |
| 19 | January  | Mineral Magic Pack        | Galway  | € 264   |
| 20 | January  | Universal Protein Capsules| Galway  | € 99    |
| 21 | January  | Universal Protein Capsules| Wexford | € 233   |
| 22 | January  | Ten Years Younger         | Wexford | € 89    |
| 23 | January  | Irish Bee Pollen          | Wexford | € 1,099 |
| 24 | January  | Mineral Magic Pack        | Wexford | € 77    |
| 25 | January  | Sunshine Energy Tablets   | Wexford | € 88    |
| 26 | January  | Jumping Vitamin Beans     | Wexford | € 432   |
| 27 | February | Universal Protein Capsules| Wexford | € 493   |

Record — row 17. Field — Health Product column. List — entire table.

**NOTE**
There is a limitation on the size of a list. Details can be found in Chapter 1.

Chapter 4 - Analysis

## 1.1 Creating a Pivot Table using defined field names (4.4.1.1)

**Jumping Beans** of Macroom is an SME (Small to Medium Enterprise) that manufactures a range of Health Food Products. You will be using a **list** that examines the sales of six of its products in Dublin, Galway and Wexford over a six-month period. Your objective is to make as much sense of the product sales by manipulating the data using a very powerful tool, the **PivotTable**.

- Open the file **Jumping Beans**.

There are four field names displayed. These are **Month**, **Health Product**, **City** and **Sales**. The list includes these field names. The list is quite large and you should scroll down through it to familiarise yourself with the content.

- Click on any cell within the **list**. i.e. anywhere in the range **A10:D195**.

- Select **Data** followed by **PivotTable and PivotChart Report...** from the drop-down menu.

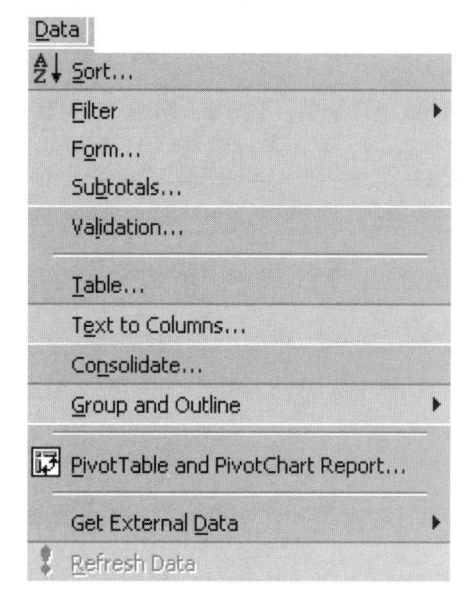

**PivotTable and PivotChart Wizard - Step 1 of 3** opens.
In step 1 you are required to enter the location of the data and the type of report you wish to create.
The data we wish to analyse is a **Microsoft Excel list or database**.

- The **Microsoft Excel list or database** radio button is selected by default – if not select it now.

We wish to create a PivotTable report.

- The **PivotTable** radio button is also selected by default – if not select it now.

Chapter 4 - Analysis

- Select **Next**.

**PivotTable and PivotChart Wizard - Step 2 of 3** opens.
In step 2 we are required to indicate the data that we will use in our PivotTable. As you have already clicked on the list, Excel correctly identifies the range as **Sheet1!$A$10:$D$195**.

- If you have not selected a cell within the list you must enter the range now in the Range box.

- Select **Next**.

**PivotTable and PivotChart Wizard - Step 3 of 3** opens.
In step 3 we are required to specify where we want to put the PivotTable.
The New worksheet radio button is selected by default.

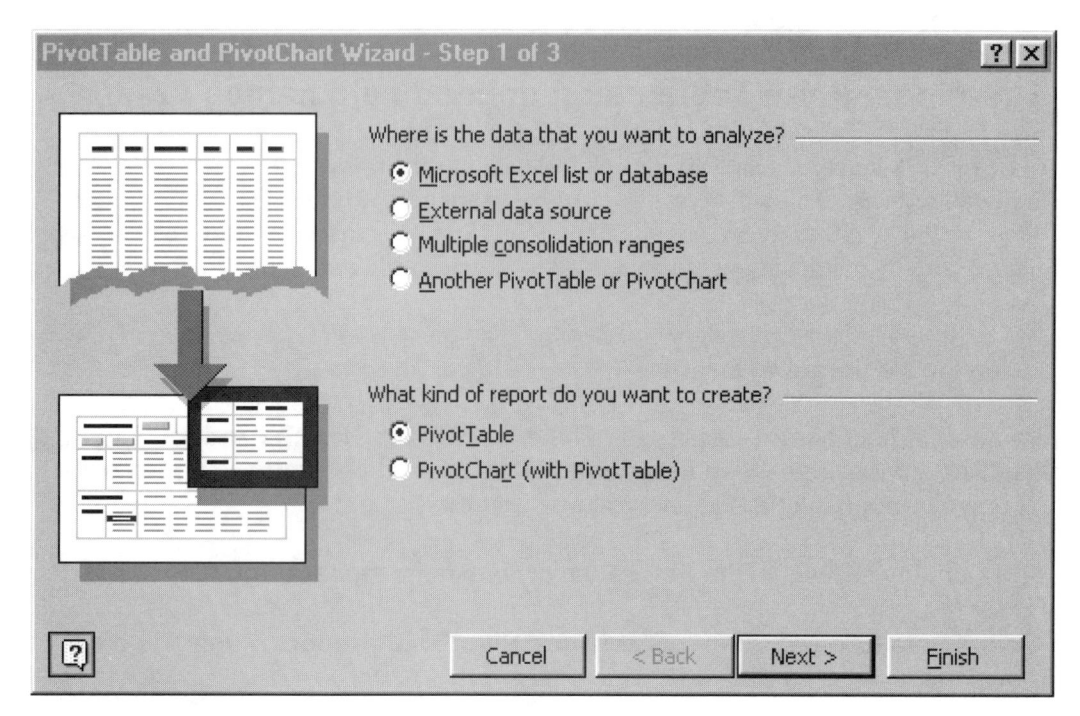

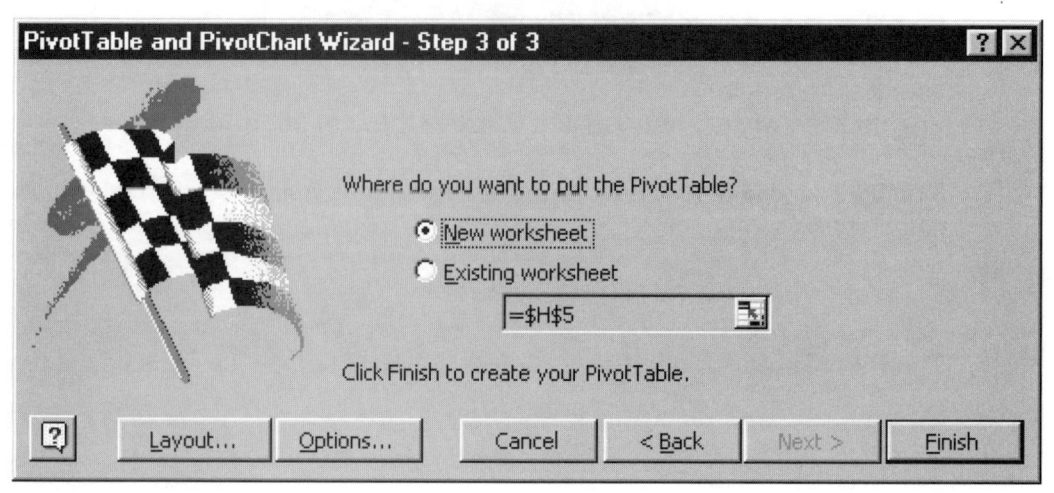

Since we want to save the PivotTable in a **New Worksheet** we accept the default setting.

- Now click on **Finish**.

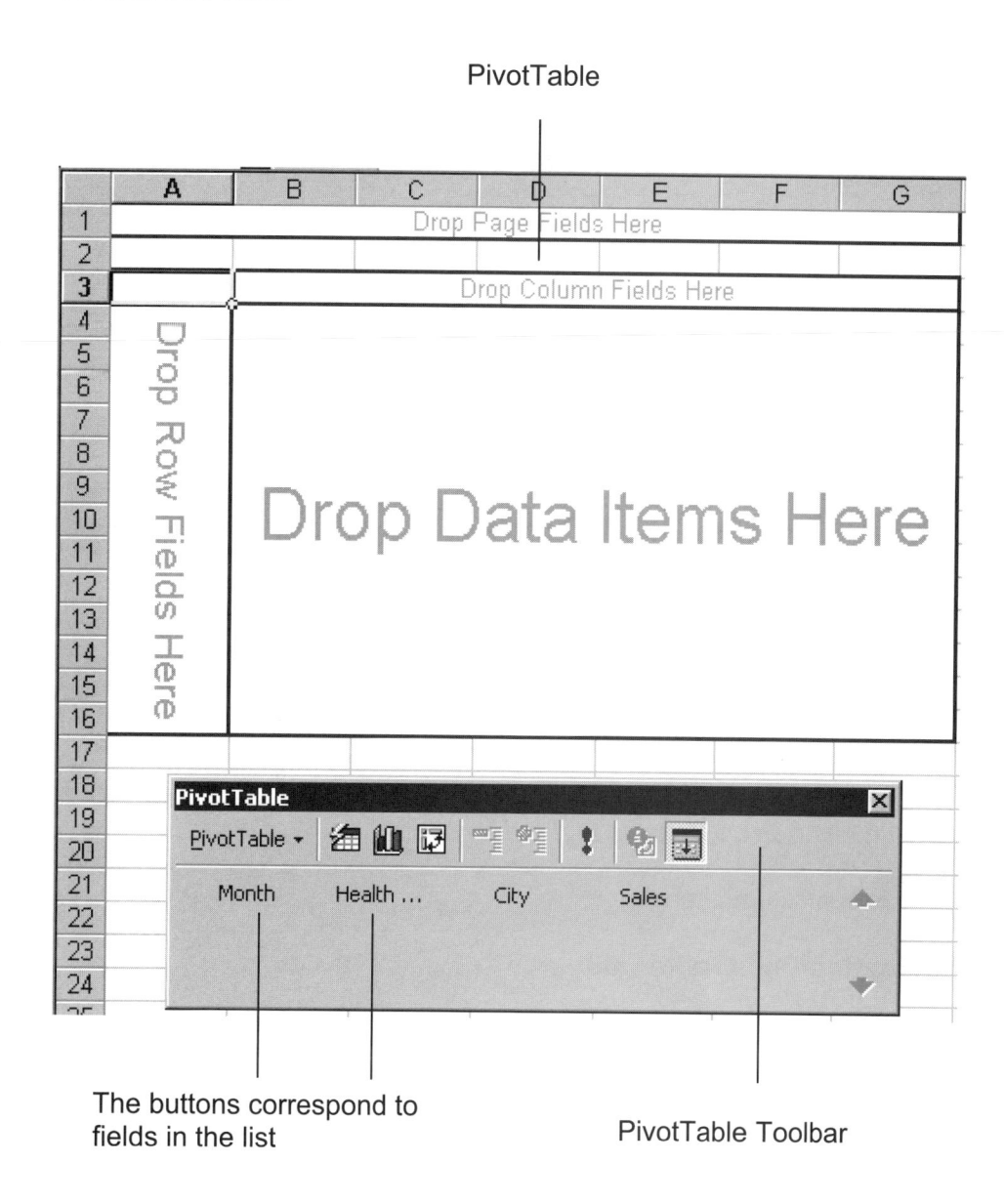

PivotTable

*The buttons correspond to fields in the list*

*PivotTable Toolbar*

The PivotTable opens with PivotTable toolbar. The four field buttons on the PivotTable toolbar correspond to the four fields, Month, Health Product, City and Sales.

The next step is to select and drag buttons from the PivotTable toolbar onto selected locations of the PivotTable.

## 1.2 Selecting Fields for Rows and Columns

Health Product Button

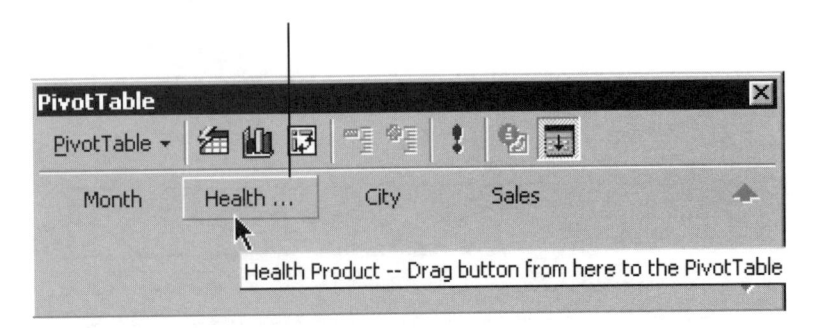

### 1.2.1 Selecting the Row Field

We have to decide which field will be used in the Row. We will select **Health Products**.

- Click on **Health Product button** and drag from the PivotTable toolbar to the PivotTable and release mouse button where it states **Drop Row Fields Here**.

Health Products becomes a Row label.

### 1.2.2 Selecting the Column Field

**City** is going to be our Column Field.

- Drag the button **City** from the PivotTable toolbar to the PivotTable releasing in area marked **Drop Column Fields Here**.

City is our Column Label.

### 1.2.3 Selecting PivotTable Data

We want to tabulate **Sales** revenue.

- Drag the button **Sales** from the PivotTable toolbar to the rectangle labelled **Drop Data Items Here** and release mouse button.

| | A | B | C | D | E |
|---|---|---|---|---|---|
| 1 | | | | | |
| 2 | | | | | |
| 3 | Sum of Sales | City | | | |
| 4 | Health Product | Dublin | Galway | Wexford | Grand Total |
| 5 | Irish Bee Pollen | 8265 | 8416 | 7020 | 23701 |
| 6 | Jumping Vitamin Beans | 4900 | 4671 | 4613 | 14184 |
| 7 | Mineral Magic Pack | 7665 | 6547 | 6311 | 20523 |
| 8 | Sunshine Energy Tablets | 7082 | 7969 | 6237 | 21288 |
| 9 | Ten Years Younger | 6807 | 5684 | 6922 | 19413 |
| 10 | Universal Protein Capsules | 7308 | 6877 | 4679 | 18864 |
| 11 | Grand Total | 42027 | 40164 | 35782 | 117973 |

The completed PivotTable gives a detailed and useful breakdown of the six products in the three cities. A **Grand Total** is also given.

## 1.3 Filtering PivotTable Data

- Click on the **Health Product** drop down menu. You can manipulate the PivotTable by selecting those Health Products whose individual or combined totals that you require.

| Sum of Sales | City | | | |
|---|---|---|---|---|
| Health Product | Dublin | Galway | Wexford | Grand Total |
| ☑ Irish Bee Pollen | 8265 | 8416 | 7020 | 23701 |
| ☑ Jumping Vitamin Beans | 4900 | 4671 | 4613 | 14184 |
| ☑ Mineral Magic Pack | 7665 | 6547 | 6311 | 20523 |
| ☑ Sunshine Energy Tablets | 7082 | 7969 | 6237 | 21288 |
| ☑ Ten Years Younger | 6807 | 5684 | 6922 | 19413 |
| ☑ Universal Protein Capsules | 7308 | 6877 | 4679 | 18864 |
| | 42027 | 40164 | 35782 | 117973 |

- Deselect the following products by clicking on the boxes for Mineral Magic Pack, Sunshine Energy Tablets, Ten Years Younger and Universal Protein Capsules.

- Click on **OK**. Only the **Sales** and **Grand Total** for **Irish Bee Pollen** and **Jumping Vitamin Beans** is given.

- Click on the **Health Product** drop-down menu and select all the products that were deselected and click **OK**.

The practice exercises contained in this section relate solely to this manual and do not constitute, or imply, certification by the European Driving Licence Foundation in respect of any ECDL examinations. For details on sitting ECDL examinations in your country please contact the local ECDL/ICDL licensee or visit the European Computer Driving Licence Foundation Ltd web site at http://www.ecdl.com

## Exercise 1A

1. Click on the **City** drop down menu. Click on the boxes adjacent to cities **Dublin** and **Wexford** to deselect them. Click **OK**.

2. Only the total figures for **Galway** are given.

3. Click on the City drop-down menu again and select **Dublin** and **Wexford**. **Galway** is already selected. Click **OK**. This should return us to our original PivotTable.

## 1.4 Changing the Layout of a PivotTable

One advantage of the PivotTable is that it is fairly easy to manipulate the fields of the list. There is no one way to do this. On this occasion we are going to drag all three buttons back to their original location, the PivotTable Field List.

- Select the **Health Product** button and drag back to its location on the PivotTable toolbar. You will notice the arrow and X once it is dragged off the PivotTable.

- Now drag the **City** button back to its original location. Finally drag the **Sum of Sales** button back to the **Sales** location.

- Select the **City** button and drag it to **Drop Row Fields Here**. Now select the **Health Products** button and drag it to **Drop Column Fields Here**.

  In effect we have swapped the location of the buttons.

- Now drag the **Sales** button into 'Drop Data Items Here'

  The PivotTable should look like this.

| | A | B | C | D |
|---|---|---|---|---|
| 1 | | | | Drop Page Fi |
| 2 | | | | |
| 3 | Sum of Sales | Health Product | | |
| 4 | City | Irish Bee Pollen | Jumping Vitamin Beans | Mineral Magic Pack |
| 5 | Dublin | 8265 | 4900 | 7665 |
| 6 | Galway | 8416 | 4671 | 6547 |
| 7 | Wexford | 7020 | 4613 | 6311 |
| 8 | Grand Total | 23701 | 14184 | 20523 |

Comparing this PivotTable with the original you will realise that they both contain the same data, but present it in different ways. The Grand Total of Sales for Irish Bee Pollen is **23701** in both tables. Check this now and briefly compare other figures.

---

*The practice exercises contained in this section relate solely to this manual and do not constitute, or imply, certification by the European Driving Licence Foundation in respect of any ECDL examinations. For details on sitting ECDL examinations in your country please contact the local ECDL/ICDL licensee or visit the European Computer Driving Licence Foundation Ltd web site at http://www.ecdl.com*

## Exercise 1B

1. Click on the **Health Product** drop down menu. Click on all boxes except **Ten Years Younger** to deselect them. Click **OK**.

2. Only the total figures for the product **Ten Years Younger** is given.

3. Click on **Health Product** drop-down menu again and select all products. Click **OK**. This should return us to our *adjusted* PivotTable.

## 1.5 Modifying the data source and refreshing the Pivot Table
(4.4.1.2)

We have just been informed that the sales figure for Jumping Vitamin Beans for January, cell **D11** of the list is incorrect.

- Click on **Sheet 1**.

- Replace the figure of **€217** with **€1117**, a difference of **€900**.

- Now select the tab that takes you back to the PivotTable. You will note that there have been no changes to the totals in the PivotTable. The PivotTable has to be updated. We must refresh (update) the data.

- Click on the **Refresh Data** button on the PivotTable toolbar.

**The PivotTable Toolbar**

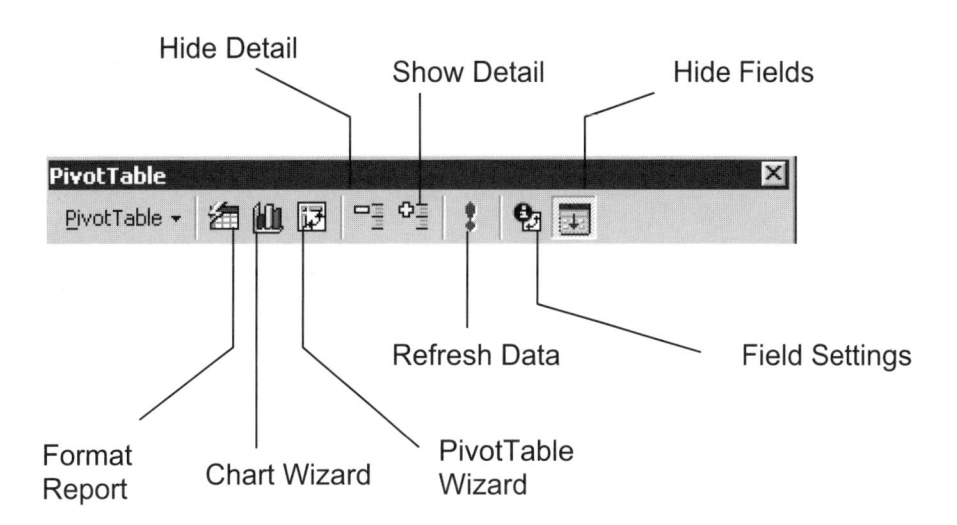

*[Diagram of PivotTable toolbar with labels: Hide Detail, Show Detail, Hide Fields, Refresh Data, Field Settings, Format Report, Chart Wizard, PivotTable Wizard]*

- The figures in the PivotTable are updated. Note that the new total for Jumping Vitamin Beans is **€15084** whereas previously it was **€14184**; a difference of **€900**.

There are a number of ways of **Refreshing** the PivotTable:

- The most common way is by using the **Refresh Data** button on the PivotTable toolbar.

- Also, by clicking on the PivotTable drop down menu and selecting **!Refresh Data**.

- Also, by right-clicking on the PivotTable and selecting **!Refresh** Data from the menu.

- Also, by selecting the PivotTable drop-down menu and choosing **Table Options**. The PivotTable Options opens and by clicking on the Data source options: **Refresh on open**. Every time the PivotTable is opened the data is refreshed (updated).

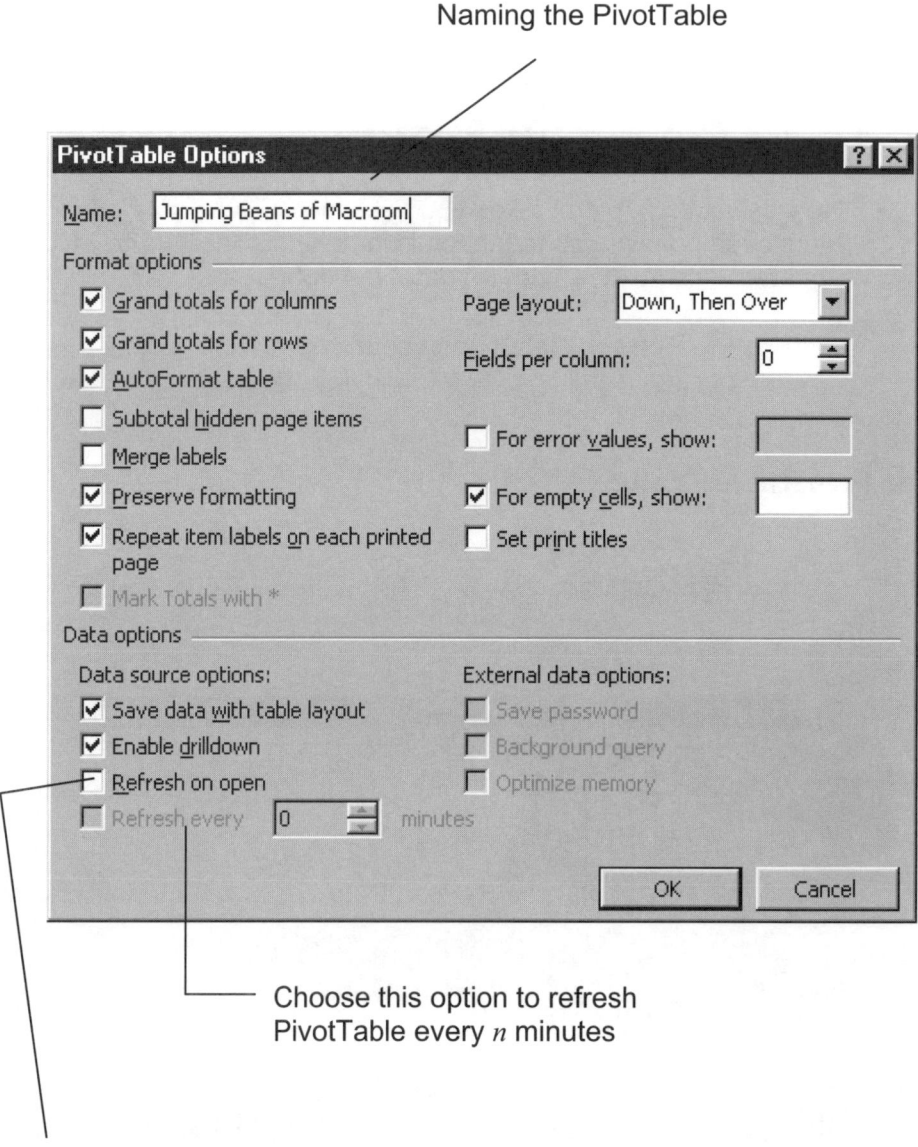

Naming the PivotTable

Choose this option to refresh PivotTable every *n* minutes

When this option is selected the PivotTable is automatically refreshed each time it is opened.

- Open **PivotTable Options** and click on **Refresh every** which is a Data source option. Decide on **10** minutes and click **OK**. The PivotTable will be refreshed every 10 minutes. You decide on refresh time.

- The **Name** box gives you the opportunity to name the PivotTable.

- Click **Cancel** and do not make any changes to the PivotTable options.

The practice exercises contained in this section relate solely to this manual and do not constitute, or imply, certification by the European Driving Licence Foundation in respect of any ECDL examinations. For details on sitting ECDL examinations in your country please contact the local ECDL/ICDL licensee or visit the European Computer Driving Licence Foundation Ltd web site at http://www.ecdl.com

## Exercise 1C

Select the tab that contains the **LIST, Sheet 1**. We are going to make a number of changes to the **Sales** figures in our list, then we will refresh the PivotTable by a number of different methods. You may wish to print a copy of the PivotTable for ease of comparison as the figures are refreshed and updated.

1   Select **Edit** followed by **GoTo** (or use **Ctrl + G**). In the **Go To** dialog box enter the reference **D32**.

2   The Sales figure is **146**. Change this to **946**. Now select appropriate tab for PivotTable. You will notice that the figure for Jumping Vitamin Beans has not been updated. To refresh the PivotTable, click on **Refresh Data** button on PivotTable toolbar.

3   The PivotTable is refreshed and the new sales figure has been added. Return to Sheet 1.

4   Select **Go To** on the **Edit** menu. (or use **Ctrl + G**). In the **Go To** dialog box enter the reference **D48**. You will notice that the previous reference, D32 is stored here. The Go To dialog box stores the last six references which is useful if you want to edit, revise or update a reference.

5   The Sales figure for Mineral Magic Pack is **640**. Change it to **512**. Select the PivotTable tab. There is no change in figures. To refresh the PivotTable and update the figures choose **!Refresh Data** from the PivotTable drop-down menu on the PivotTable toolbar.

6   The PivotTable is refreshed and the new sales figure successfully added.

The practice exercises contained in this section relate solely to this manual and do not constitute, or imply, certification by the European Driving Licence Foundation in respect of any ECDL examinations. For details on sitting ECDL examinations in your country please contact the local ECDL/ICDL licensee or visit the European Computer Driving Licence Foundation Ltd web site at http://www.ecdl.com

## Exercise 1D

1   Select the tab with **LIST, Sheet 1**.

2   The following Corrected Sales figures for the **Irish Bee Pollen** have just been received. Make the changes in the list, but do not refresh PivotTable until all figures have been added.

| Cell Reference | Original Sales Figure | Corrected Sales Figure |
| --- | --- | --- |
| D119 | 960 | 418 |
| D162 | 1105 | 726 |
| D192 | 603 | 240 |

Chapter 4 - Analysis

**3** Right-click anywhere on the PivotTable. Select **!Refresh Data** from the menu.

**4** The PivotTable is refreshed and the new data successfully added.

## 1.6 Grouping or Displaying Data in a Pivot table by a defined criterion (4.4.1.3)

**Irish Bee Pollen** and **Sunshine Energy Tablets** were both launched on the same day. We are interested in grouping together the sales figures for these two products.

- Change the current PivotTable if necessary, to show Health Product as Row Field and City as Column Field.

- Select cell **A5** of the PivotTable. This is the cell labelled Irish Bee Pollen.

- Hold down the **Ctrl** key and select cell **A8**. This cell is labelled Sunshine Energy Tablets.

- Keep the **Ctrl** key depressed and right-click on the PivotTable and from the menu select **Group and Outline** followed by **Group**.

- The PivotTable changes to show Irish Bee Pollen and Sunshine Energy Tablets grouped together as **Group1**.

|   | A | B | C | D | E | F |
|---|---|---|---|---|---|---|
| 1 | | Drop Page Fields Here | | | | |
| 2 | | | | | | |
| 3 | Sum of Sales | | City | | | |
| 4 | Health Product2 | Health Product | Dublin | Galway | Wexford | Grand Total |
| 5 | Group1 | Irish Bee Pollen | 8265 | 8416 | 7020 | 23701 |
| 6 | | Sunshine Energy Tablets | 7082 | 7969 | 6237 | 21288 |
| 7 | Jumping Vitamin Beans | Jumping Vitamin Beans | 6600 | 4671 | 4613 | 15884 |
| 8 | Mineral Magic Pack | Mineral Magic Pack | 7537 | 6547 | 6311 | 20395 |
| 9 | Ten Years Younger | Ten Years Younger | 6807 | 5684 | 6922 | 19413 |
| 10 | Universal Protein Capsules | Universal Protein Capsules | 7308 | 6877 | 4679 | 18864 |
| 11 | Grand Total | | 43599 | 40164 | 35782 | 119545 |

- Click on the **Health Product2** drop down menu.

Chapter 4 - Analysis

| Sum of Sales | | City | | | |
|---|---|---|---|---|---|
| Health Product2 | Health Product | Dublin | Galway | Wexford | Grand Total |
| Group1 | Irish Bee Pollen | 8265 | 8416 | 7020 | 23701 |
| ☑ Jumping Vitamin Beans | Sunshine Energy Tablets | 7082 | 7969 | 6237 | 21288 |
| ☑ Mineral Magic Pack | Jumping Vitamin Beans | 6600 | 4671 | 4613 | 15884 |
| ☑ Ten Years Younger | Mineral Magic Pack | 7537 | 6547 | 6311 | 20395 |
| ☑ Universal Protein Capsules | Ten Years Younger | 6807 | 5684 | 6922 | 19413 |
| | Universal Protein Capsules | 7308 | 6877 | 4679 | 18864 |
| | | 43599 | 40164 | 35782 | 119545 |

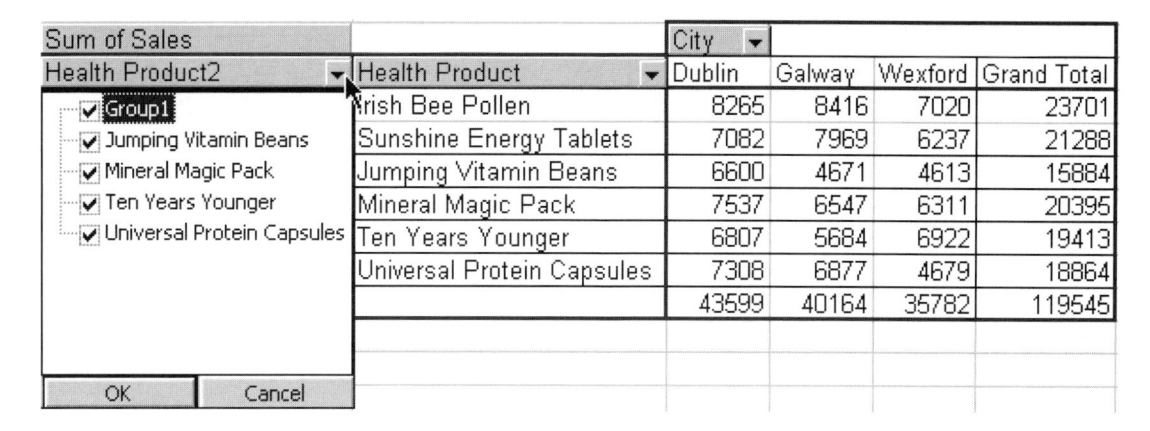

[OK] [Cancel]

You will notice that **Group1** replaces Irish Bee Pollen and Sunshine Energy Tablets.

- Select **Cancel**.

We now want to **Ungroup** the Grouped data.

- Click on PivotTable. Right-click on PivotTable and choose **Group and Outline** from the menu, followed by **Ungroup**.

The PivotTable returns to its original state.

---

The practice exercises contained in this section relate solely to this manual and do not constitute, or imply, certification by the European Driving Licence Foundation in respect of any ECDL examinations. For details on sitting ECDL examinations in your country please contact the local ECDL/ICDL licensee or visit the European Computer Driving Licence Foundation Ltd web site at http://www.ecdl.com

## Exercise 1E

In this exercise we will form a new group that looks at the Health Products, Mineral Magic Pack and Ten Years Younger.

1   Select cell **A7** of the PivotTable. Holding down the **Ctrl** key select cell **A9**.

2   Keeping the **Ctrl** key depressed, right-click on the PivotTable and select and choose **Group and Outline** followed by **Group** from the menu.

3   A new group, **Group** is created, consisting of Mineral Magic Pack and Ten Years Younger.

4   Select and drag the **Health Product2** button off the PivotTable and release anywhere on the worksheet.

5   Save the file **Jumping Beans** with the PivotTable.

## Section 2    Scenarios

Using Scenario Manager you can demonstrate **What-If?** Situations. This is achieved by utilising a **Changing cells** option.

### 2.1 Creating named Scenarios / Versions from defined cell ranges (4.4.2.1)

In this example we are going to use **Scenario Manager** to determine the effect on Total Profit of changes in the Production Cost of three miniature car models, A, B, and C.

- Open the file **Scenario**.

- Familiarise yourself with the information by examining cell contents in the range **C4:C11**.

The Profit per Unit = Sales Price – Production Cost (i.e. **=C6 – C5**).
Total Profit = Number Produced x Profit per Unit (i.e. **=C8 x C7**).
The range, which we will make changes to, is **C5:E5**, the range that refers to **Production Cost**.
The cells **C5**, **D5** and **E5** have been named **Model_A**, **Model_B** and **Model_C** respectively. To view the named cells click on the drop down list on the **Name Box**. Why not click on Model_A, Model_B and Model_C in turn to identify these cells. Remember any changes that we are going to make will be to these three cells. When we are adding values to **Changing cells** it is easier to add values to a named cell.

|   | A | B | C | D | E |
|---|---|---|---|---|---|
| 1 | **Scenario Manager** | | | | |
| 2 | | | | | |
| 3 | | | | | |
| 4 | | | Model A | Model B | Model C |
| 5 | | Production Cost | €12 | €28 | €53 |
| 6 | | Sales Price | €60 | €60 | €72 |
| 7 | | Profit per Unit | €48 | €32 | €19 |
| 8 | | Number Produced | 3000 | 5000 | 2500 |
| 9 | | | | | |
| 10 | | | | | |
| 11 | | Total Profit | €144,000 | €160,000 | €47,500 |

The **Minimum Production Costs** are displayed in the table. Always save the original values before you start. Do this now.

In this scenario we will look at **Minimum Production Cost**, **Expected Production Cost** and **Maximum Production Cost**.

- Highlight the range **C5:E5** as it is in this range that we will be making changes.

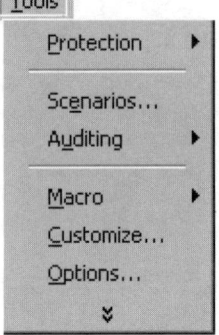

Chapter 4 - Analysis

- Choose the **Scenarios...** command from the **Tools** menu.

    The **Scenario Manager** Dialog box is displayed.

- To add a scenario click on the **Add...** button.

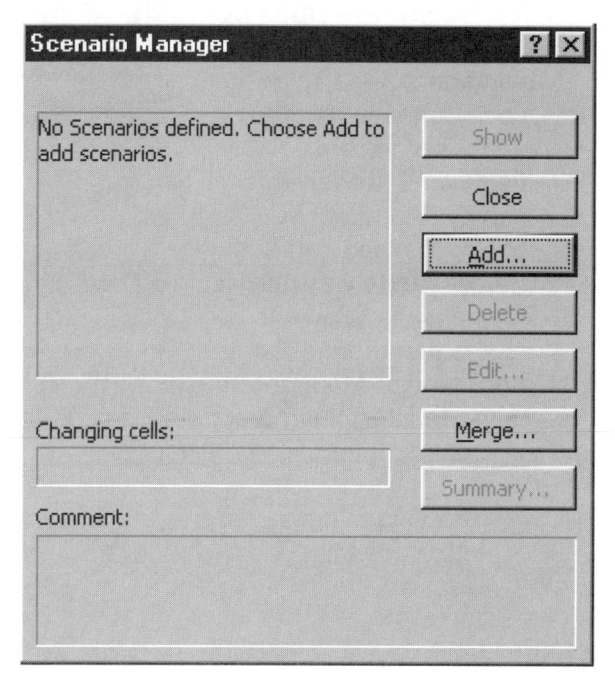

- The **Add Scenario** Dialog box opens.

- In the **Scenario name** box, type **Minimum Production Cost**.

- The **Changing cells** box should have the range **C5:E5** displayed. If not, type in this range now or drag across the range on the worksheet.

- Delete the contents of the **Comment** box and replace with your own name and date. You can always leave it blank.

- Click on **OK**.

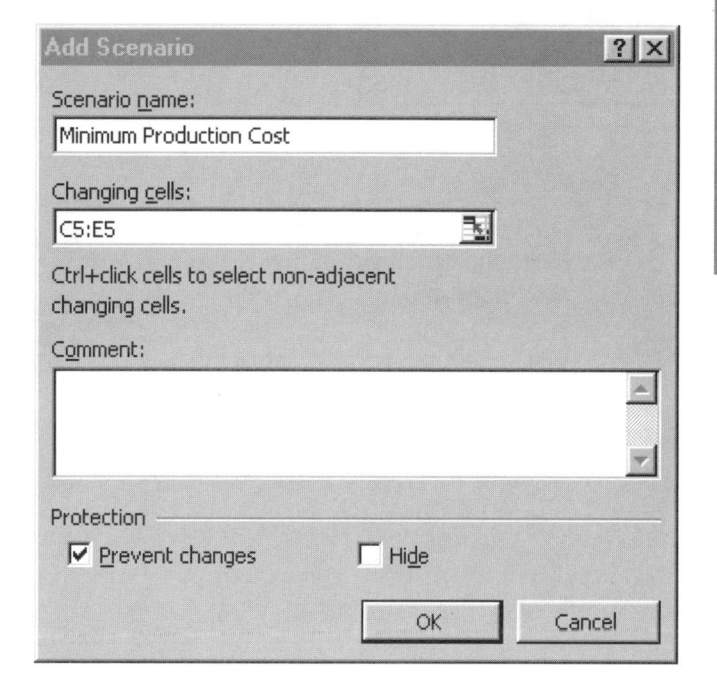

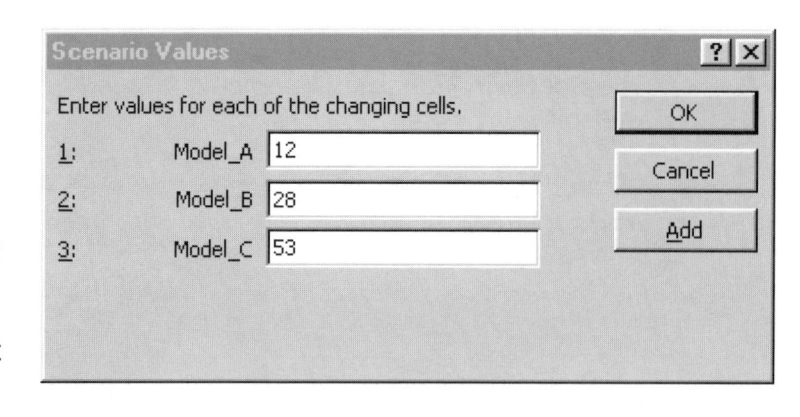

The **Scenario Values** box opens. Figures from the worksheet are displayed. You will notice that the Model names are displayed. **Model_A** is displayed and not **$C$5**. It was mentioned earlier that the cell range was named. It is sensible to do this as it makes the information on the Scenario Manager easier to interpret and certainly makes the Scenario Summary Report which we will be creating later, more meaningful.

The values displayed are the **Minimum Production Cost** so there is **no** need to make any changes to the cells.

- Click **OK**.

The table below shows the figures for all the scenarios.

|         | Minimum Production Cost | Expected Production Cost | Maximum Production Cost |
|---------|-------------------------|--------------------------|-------------------------|
| Model A | 12                      | 15                       | 24                      |
| Model B | 28                      | 35                       | 43                      |
| Model C | 53                      | 60                       | 72                      |

- Now click on **Add** to insert the next scenario.

We will now enter the **Expected Production Cost** figures.

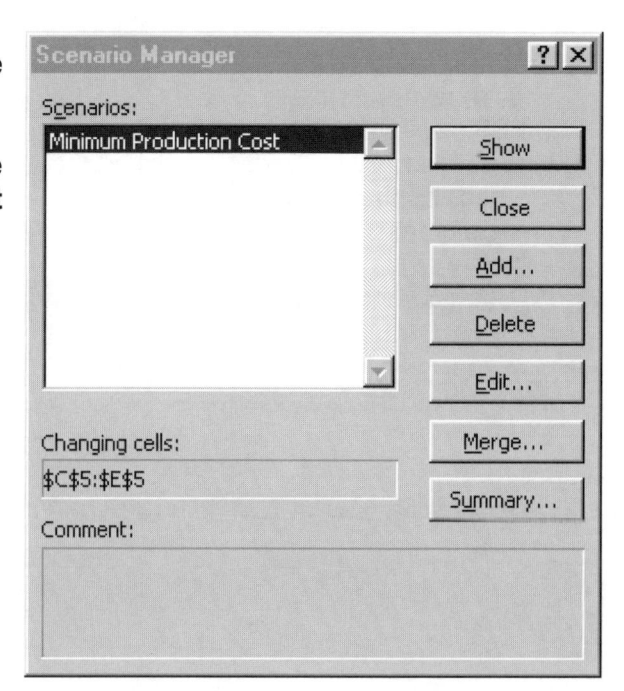

- Type **Expected Production Cost** in the Scenario name box.

- The changing cells should be **C5:E5**. If necessary drag across this range in worksheet.

- Click on **OK**.

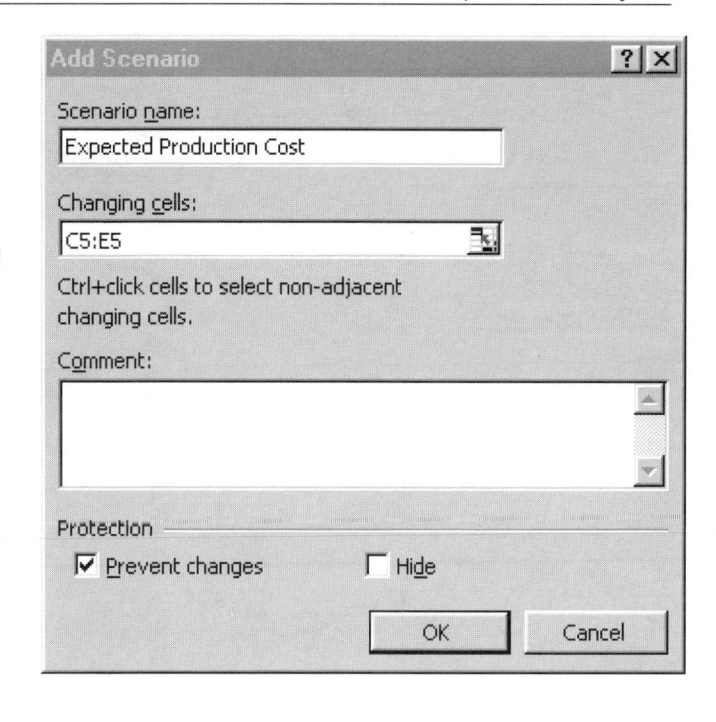

The Scenario Values box opens.

- Add the values for the Expected Production Cost. These are present in the table. Check these are inserted correctly then click on **OK**.

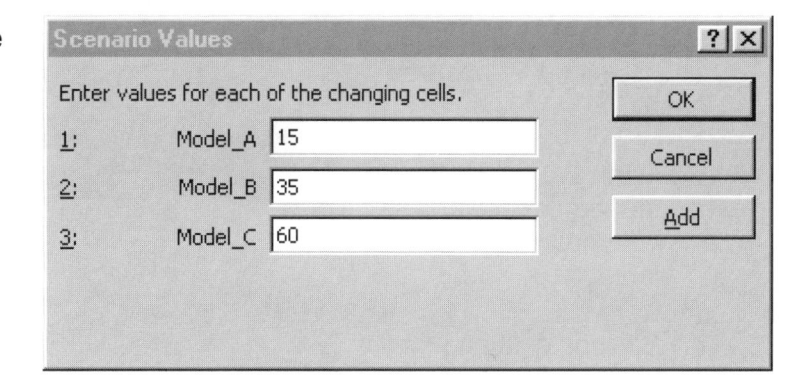

We will now add the final Scenario, **Maximum Production Cost**.

- Select **Add** from the Scenario Manager dialog box.

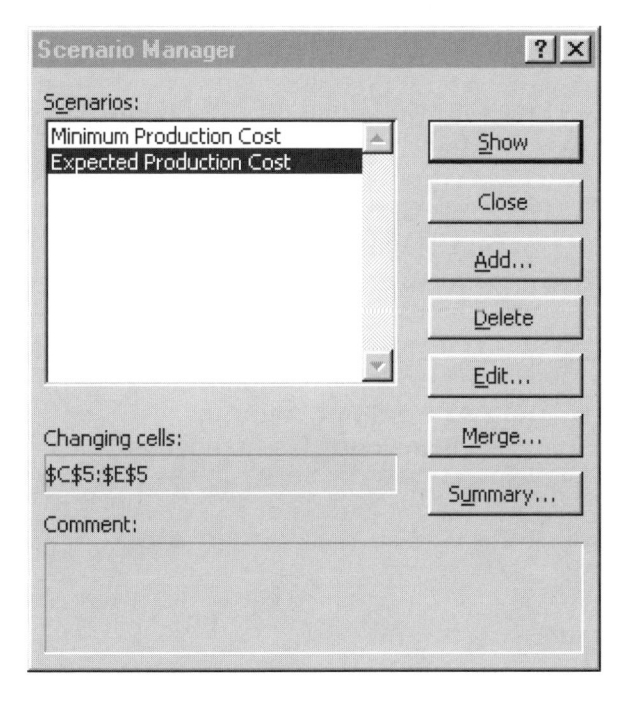

Chapter 4 - Analysis

- Type **Maximum Production Cost** in the Scenario name box.

- Ensure the range in Changing cells box is **C5:E5**.

- Select **OK**.

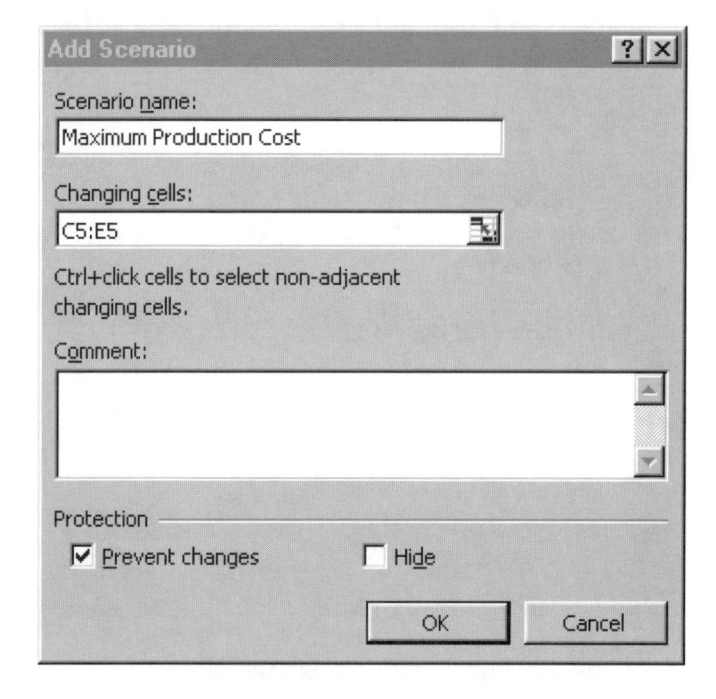

The Scenario Values box opens.

- Insert the values for the three models. The information is in the table.

- Click on **Add** and the Add Scenario dialog box opens. Click on **Cancel** and the Scenario Manager displays the three scenarios.

- Click on **Minimum Production Cost**.

- Click **Close** and save the file at this stage under its original name, **Scenario**.

You have now successfully defined three scenarios. We will use the **Show** button to demonstrate these scenarios.

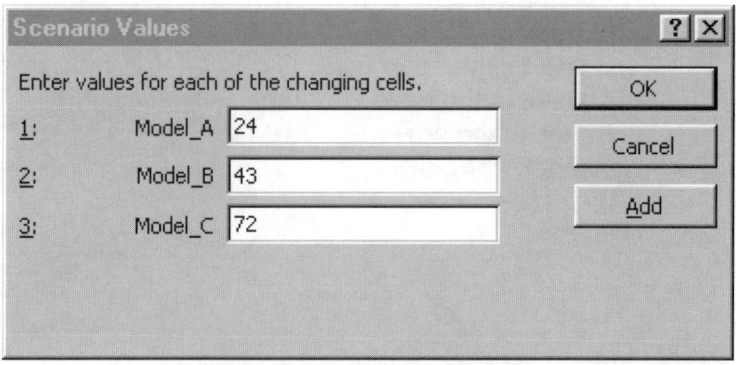

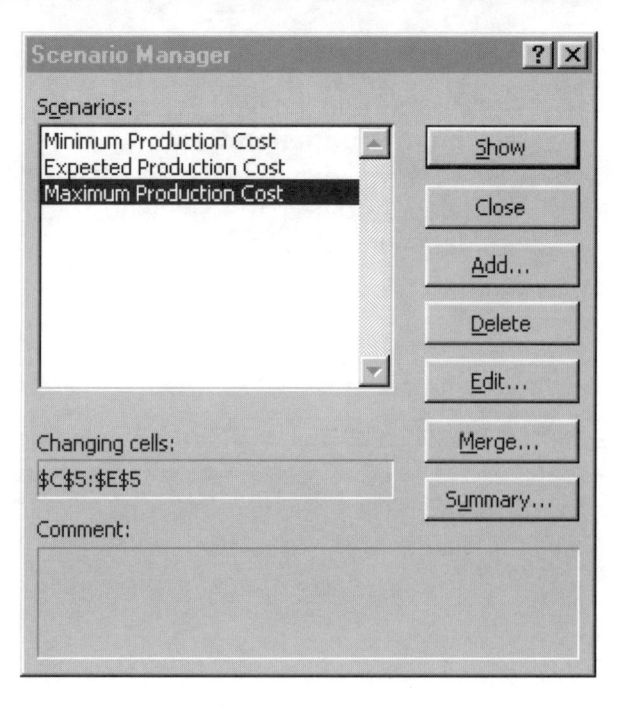

- Select **Tools** followed by **Scenarios**.

- Choose **Minimum Production Cost** and click on **Show**.

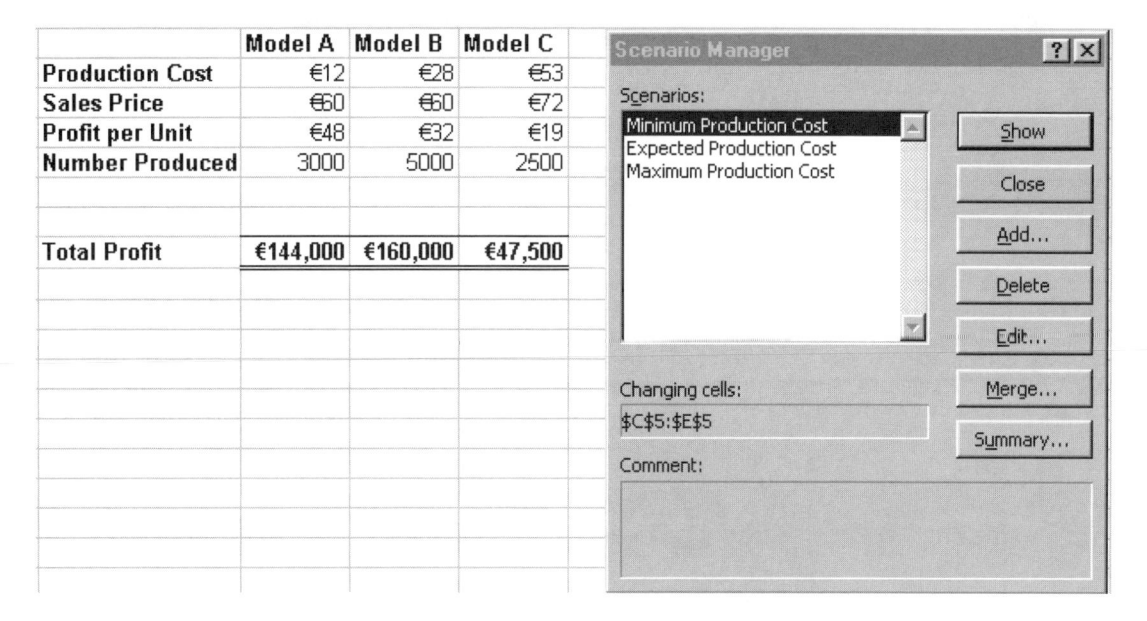

|                  | Model A   | Model B   | Model C  |
|------------------|-----------|-----------|----------|
| Production Cost  | €12       | €28       | €53      |
| Sales Price      | €60       | €60       | €72      |
| Profit per Unit  | €48       | €32       | €19      |
| Number Produced  | 3000      | 5000      | 2500     |
|                  |           |           |          |
| Total Profit     | €144,000  | €160,000  | €47,500  |

The **Minimum Production Cost** values are displayed.

- Choose **Expected Production Cost** and click on **Show** again.

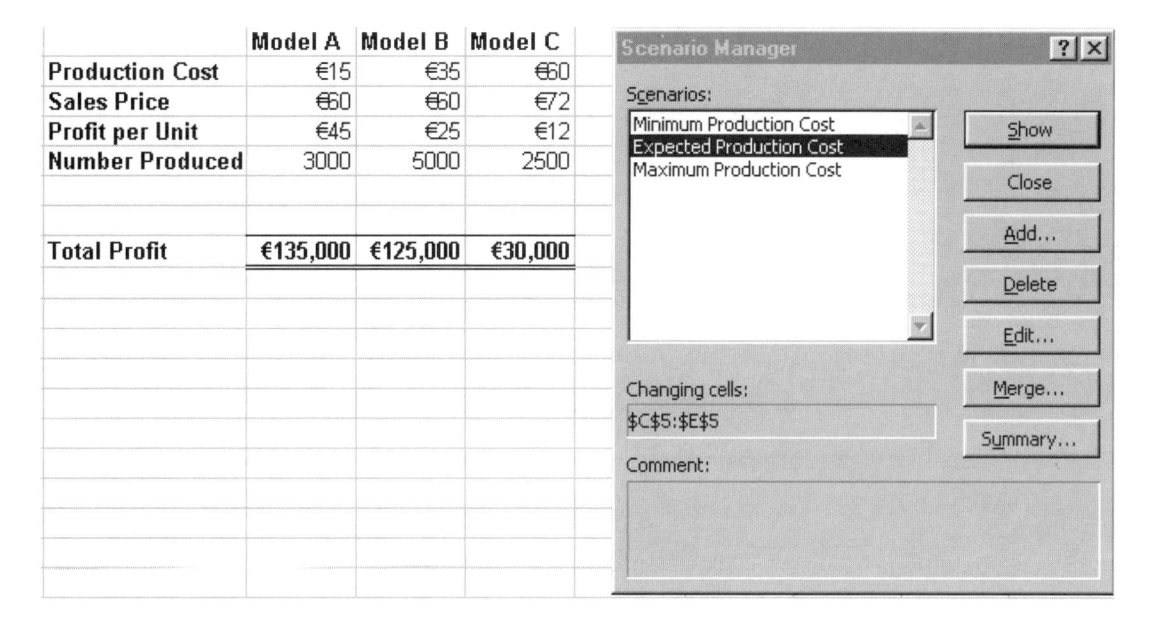

|                  | Model A   | Model B   | Model C  |
|------------------|-----------|-----------|----------|
| Production Cost  | €15       | €35       | €60      |
| Sales Price      | €60       | €60       | €72      |
| Profit per Unit  | €45       | €25       | €12      |
| Number Produced  | 3000      | 5000      | 2500     |
|                  |           |           |          |
| Total Profit     | €135,000  | €125,000  | €30,000  |

The **Expected Production Cost** is displayed.

- Finally select **Maximum Production Cost** and click on **Show**.

|                 | Model A  | Model B | Model C |
|-----------------|----------|---------|---------|
| Production Cost | €24      | €43     | €72     |
| Sales Price     | €60      | €60     | €72     |
| Profit per Unit | €36      | €17     | €0      |
| Number Produced | 3000     | 5000    | 2500    |
|                 |          |         |         |
| Total Profit    | €108,000 | €85,000 | €0      |

**Scenario Manager**

Scenarios:
- Minimum Production Cost
- Expected Production Cost
- **Maximum Production Cost**

Changing cells:
$C$5:$E$5

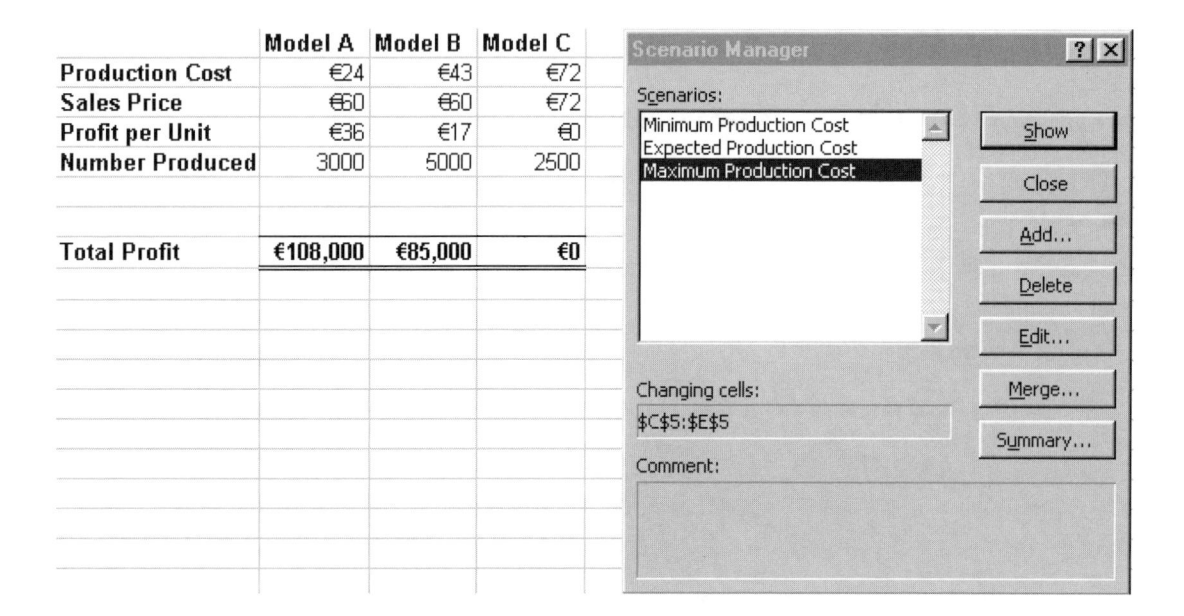

Comment:

Buttons: Show, Close, Add..., Delete, Edit..., Merge..., Summary...

The **Maximum Production Cost** values are displayed on the worksheet.

- Save the file again at this stage but do not close as we are now going to create a **Scenario Summary Report**.

## 2.2 Creating a Scenario Summary Report (4.4.2.2)

The Scenario Manager is useful for demonstrating different scenarios but it is limited in that it can only display one scenario at a time. The Scenario Summary Report is useful for setting out all the scenarios together for comparison purposes.

We are going to create a Scenario summary report that will show the **Production Cost Values** for the three models, A, B and C and the **Total Profit** for each model.

First we will name the cells in the range **C11:E11**. Labelling the cells makes it easier to interpret results in the Scenario Summary Report.

| Cell Address | Cell Name |
|---|---|
| C11 | Total_Profit_Model_A |
| D11 | Total_Profit_Model_B |
| E11 | Total_Profit_Model_C |

- Ensure the file **Scenario** report is still open.

- Label the cells **C11:E11** using the cell names in the table.

- To label cells. Select cell **C11** and choose **Insert** followed by **Name** followed by **Define**. In the **Define Name** option box type in **Total_Profit_Model_A** and select **Add**. Repeat the procedure for cells **D11** and **E11**.

**NOTE**

Clicking on the **Name Box** will indicate all the labelled cells from the drop down menu.

- Select **Tools** followed by **Scenarios**.

- Click on the **Summary...** button.

  The Scenario summary dialog box opens. Our next task is to select the appropriate range.

- Select range **C11:E11** and **Report type**: **Scenario summary**. The latter is selected by default if the mouse is located in the table.

- Click on **OK**.

  The **Scenario Summary Report** opens.

# Chapter 4 - Analysis

|   | A | B | C | D | E | F | G | H |
|---|---|---|---|---|---|---|---|---|
| 1 | | | | | | | | |
| 2 | | Scenario Summary | | | | | | |
| 3 | | | | Current Values: | Minimum Production Cost | Expected Production Cost | Maximum Production Cost | |
| 5 | | Changing Cells: | | | | | | |
| 6 | | | Model_A | €24 | €12 | €15 | €24 | |
| 7 | | | Model_B | €43 | €28 | €35 | €43 | |
| 8 | | | Model_C | €72 | €53 | €60 | €72 | |
| 9 | | Result Cells: | | | | | | |
| 10 | | | Total_Profit_Model_A | €108,000 | €144,000 | €135,000 | €108,000 | |
| 11 | | | Total_Profit_Model_B | €85,000 | €160,000 | €125,000 | €85,000 | |
| 12 | | | Total_Profit_Model_C | €0 | €47,500 | €30,000 | €0 | |
| 13 | | Notes: Current Values column represents values of changing cells at | | | | | | |
| 14 | | time Scenario Summary Report was created. Changing cells for each | | | | | | |
| 15 | | scenario are highlighted in gray. | | | | | | |

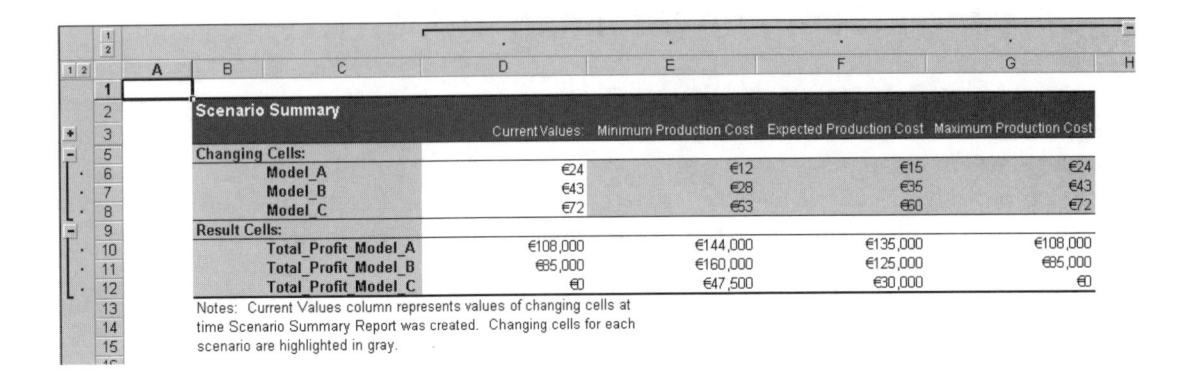

**NOTE**

The + and – symbols indicate outline buttons. Click on these to display or hide areas of the worksheet. To turn off the outline symbols, choose Tools, followed by Options. Click on the View tab and uncheck Outline symbols in the Windows options.

If the Result Cells ($C$11:$E$11) had not been named the Scenario Summary report would not have been as understandable as it is now. It would have made the Report more difficult to explain. It is easier to refer to Total_Profit_Model_A than the value of cell $C$11.

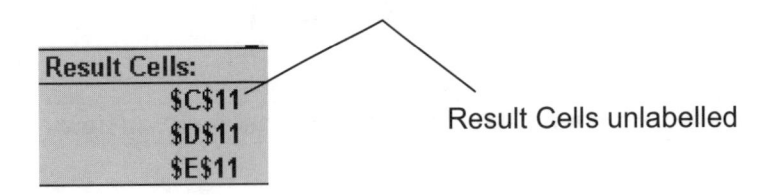

**Result Cells:**
$C$11
$D$11
$E$11

Result Cells unlabelled

- Save the file as **Scenario Summary Report**.

The practice exercises contained in this section relate solely to this manual and do not constitute, or imply, certification by the European Driving Licence Foundation in respect of any ECDL examinations. For details on sitting ECDL examinations in your country please contact the local ECDL/ICDL licensee or visit the European Computer Driving Licence Foundation Ltd web site at http://www.ecdl.com

## Exercise 2A

In this exercise we are going to look at the effect of increasing salaries by 3% and 5% on the Total Expenditure of the company. Finally we will create a Scenario Summary Report to show the effect of these changes on the total company expenditure.

1  Open the file **Alliance**.

2  Check the range **B10:D10**. These cells have been named as **Salaries_Jan**, **Salaries_Feb**, and **Salaries_Mar**.

3  Highlight the range **B10:D10**.

4  Select the command **Scenarios...** from the **Tools** menu. The **Scenario Manager** dialog box is displayed. Click **Add**.

5  The **Add Scenario** dialog box opens. Type **Current Salary** in the **Scenario name** box. Click **OK**. The changing cells should display the **Current Salaries**.

| Month | Current Salary | Salary Increase 3% | Salary Increase 5% |
|---|---|---|---|
| Jan | 80,000 | 82,400 | 84,000 |
| Feb | 80,000 | 82,400 | 84,000 |
| Mar | 84,000 | 86,520 | 88,200 |

6  Click on the **Add** box in **Scenario values** to add the next scenario. In the **Scenario name** box write **Salary Increase 3%**. Check the **Changing cells** range is **B10:D10**. Click **OK** and enter the values for each of the changing cells. These are the values in the middle of the table above. You can tab from one changing cell to the next.

7  Click on **Add**. In the scenario name box type in **Salary Increase 5%** and click on **OK**. Enter the values from the last column of the table above. Click **Add** followed by **Cancel**. Select each of the **Scenarios** in turn and click on **Show** button. If there are any entry errors, use the **Edit** button to make changes. Do not close as we require a **Scenario Summary** report.

8  We will now create a **Scenario Summary** report

   Click on **Summary...** button and the **Scenario Summary** dialog box opens. Highlight the range **B20:D20** (**Result cells**) and ensure **Scenario Summary** box is checked. Click **OK**. The Scenario Summary report opens.

9  Save the file as **Alliance Solution**.

# Section 3 Auditing

## 3.1 Cell Auditing

Excel offers tools which help you track down errors in complex spreadsheets. The auditing commands use tracer arrows to show the relationship between cells and formulas. This makes troubleshooting a spreadsheet easier.

When a worksheet is audited, you can trace the **precedents** or **dependents**.

**Precedents** are cells that are referred to by a formula – these provide data to a specific cell.

**Dependents** are cells which contain formulas referring to other cells – these cells depend on the value in a specific cell.

- Formula tracer arrows are solid blue.

- Error tracer arrows are solid red.

- External reference tracer arrows are shown as a dashed black arrow linked to a worksheet icon.

## The Auditing Toolbar

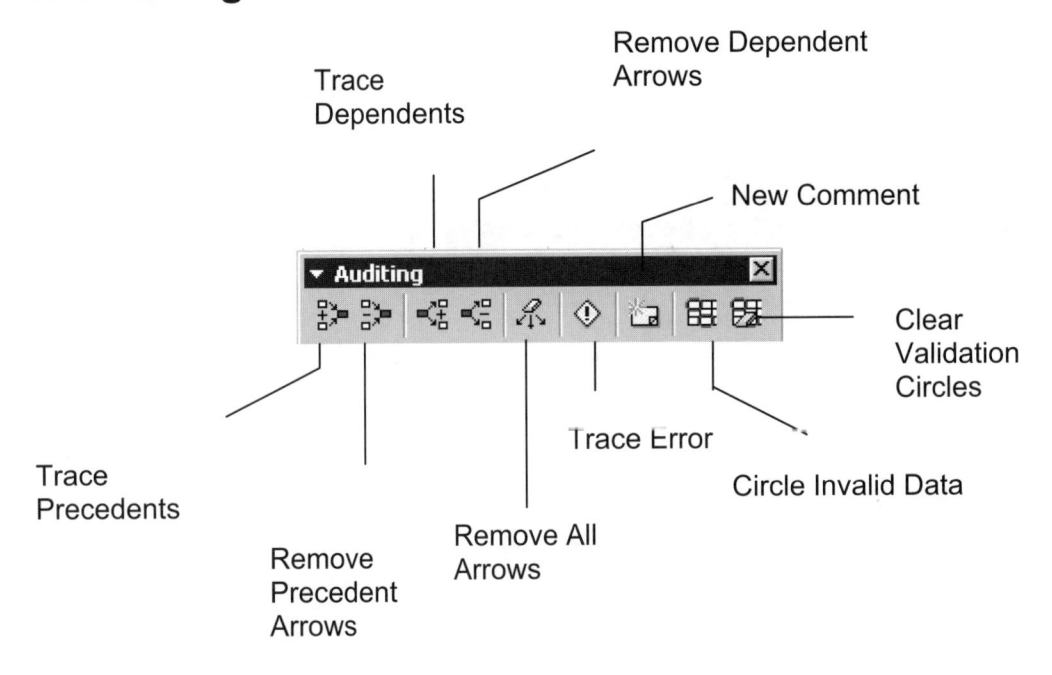

Trace Dependents

Remove Dependent Arrows

New Comment

Clear Validation Circles

Trace Error

Circle Invalid Data

Trace Precedents

Remove Precedent Arrows

Remove All Arrows

**Trace Precedents**: Draws arrows that show the formula cell's precedents. Each successive click on the Trace Precedents button shows further levels of precedents. A border is drawn around the cells used in the formulas.

**Remove Precedent Arrows:** Deletes the tracer precedent arrows from the active worksheet.

**Trace Dependents:** Draws arrows to show a cell's dependents. Each successive click on the Trace Dependents button shows further levels of dependents.

**Remove Dependent Arrows:** Deletes the tracer dependent arrows from the active worksheet.

**Remove All Arrows:** Deletes all precedent and dependent arrows in an active worksheet.

**Trace Error:** Draws an arrow from the cells that contain errors to those cells that may have caused the error.

**New Comment:** Displays the Cell Note dialog box into which comments are added.

**Circle Invalid Data:** Draws a circle around invalid data.

**Clear Validation Circles:** Removes any circles around cells that contain invalid data.

When you right-click a toolbar the **Auditing** toolbar is not listed.

- Right-click any toolbar and choose **Customize**. The Customize window opens.

- Select the **Auditing** option and click **Close**. The **Auditing** toolbar appears.

- Alternatively, select **Auditing** from the **Tools** menu and select **Show Auditing Toolbar**.

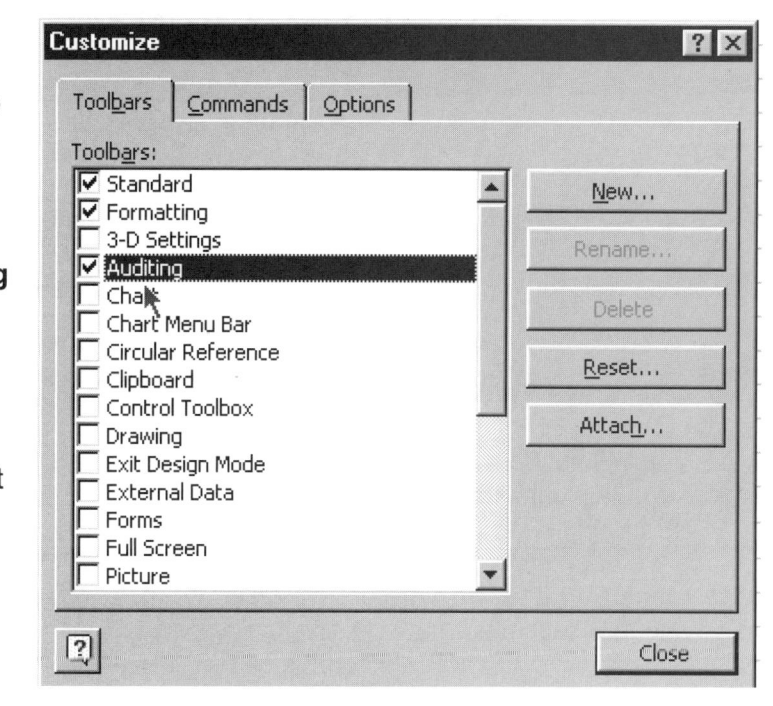

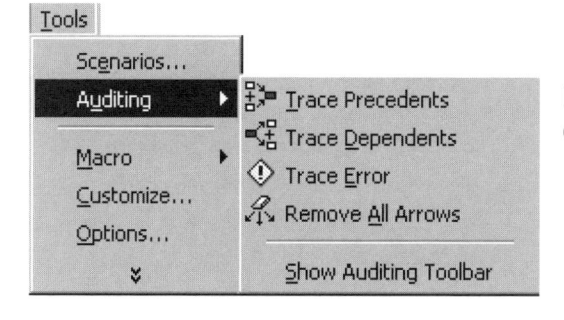

If you wish, double-click on the **title bar** to dock the **Auditing** toolbar.

## 3.2 Tracing Precedent cells in a worksheet (4.4.3.1)

Open file **Audit**. If you receive a message regarding links to another worksheet, select **NO**.

- Make **Auditing Toolbar** visible. Select **Tools**, **Auditing** followed by **Show Auditing Toolbar**.

- Select cell **D20** as the active cell. Cell D20 contains a formula which refers to cells **D14:D18**. Cells **D14:D18** are **Precedent** cells to cell **D20** which is the **Dependent** cell. Let us confirm this using the Audit toolbar.

- Click the **Trace Precedents** button. A solid blue tracer arrow is connected to the active cell. A blue box surrounds the cells that provide data to the formula. These are the precedent cells. Are there more precedent cells?

| Product | Quantity | Price | Value |
|---|---|---|---|
| Cup | 400 | €3.00 | €1,200.00 |
| Saucer | 600 | €2.00 | €1,200.00 |
| Plate | 250 | €4.00 | €1,000.00 |
| Dinner Plate | 250 | €8.00 | €2,000.00 |
| Soup Bowl | 400 | €4.00 | €1,600.00 |
| | | | |
| Total | | | €7,000.00 |

- Click the **Trace Precedents** button again to identify the next level of cells that provide data to the active cell. More solid blue arrows link this new level to the first level.

| Product | Quantity | Price | Value |
|---|---|---|---|
| Cup | 400 | €3.00 | €1,200.00 |
| Saucer | 600 | €2.00 | €1,200.00 |
| Plate | 250 | €4.00 | €1,000.00 |
| Dinner Plate | 250 | €8.00 | €2,000.00 |
| Soup Bowl | 400 | €4.00 | €1,600.00 |
| | | | |
| Total | | | €7,000.00 |

- Click **Trace Precedents** button again to identify a further level of cells that provide data to the active cell. You will not be surprised by this third level of cells. You probably noticed that the formulas in these cells (Price) in the range B5:B9 have been copied to the range C14:C16. Are there any further precedents?

| Product | Price |
|---|---|
| Cup | €3.00 |
| Saucer | €2.00 |
| Tea Plate | €4.00 |
| Dinner Plate | €8.00 |
| Soup Bowl | €4.00 |

2003

| Product | Quantity | Price | Value |
|---|---|---|---|
| Cup | 400 | €3.00 | €1,200.00 |
| Saucer | 600 | €2.00 | €1,200.00 |
| Plate | 250 | €4.00 | €1,000.00 |
| Dinner Plate | 250 | €8.00 | €2,000.00 |
| Soup Bowl | 400 | €4.00 | €1,600.00 |
| | | | |
| Total | | | €7,000.00 |

- Click **Trace Precedents** once more to find out.

This has no effect. You have successfully traced all precedents.

We will now remove the blue tracer arrows.

- Click on **Remove Precedent Arrows**. One set of arrows disappears.

- Repeat twice more to remove remaining arrows.

    You could have selected **Remove all Arrows** button, but we can use that another time.

The practice exercises contained in this section relate solely to this manual and do not constitute, or imply, certification by the European Driving Licence Foundation in respect of any ECDL examinations. For details on sitting ECDL examinations in your country please contact the local ECDL/ICDL licensee or visit the European Computer Driving Licence Foundation Ltd web site at http://www.ecdl.com

## Exercise 3A

1  Ensure file **Audit** is open.

2  Select cell **G18**. Note the formula inside the cell. Can you suggest what the precedents are? Click on **Trace Precedents**. A single blue arrow indicates the precedents. Select **Trace Precedents** again. Cell **B9** is indicated as precedent cell. Are there any further precedents?

3  Click **Trace Precedents** again. There are no further precedents.

   You have successfully traced all precedents.

4  Click on **Remove All Arrows**.

5  Select cell **G22** and observe the formula. Can you deduce what the precedents are to this cell? You may deduce there are quite a number!

6  Choose **Trace Precedents** to show direct level of precedents. Click again to show next level. Click again to show third level. Click again to show fourth level. The pattern may appear complex but when you examine it, you can recognise the pattern in the links.

7  Click **Remove Precedent Arrows** four successive times and note the arrows disappearing until the cursor is left in a single cell, **G18**, the dependent cell.

How do we trace Dependent cells? We will look at this next.

## 3.3 Tracing Dependent cells in a worksheet (4.4.3.2)

- Select cell **C14**.

- Click on **Trace Dependents** button. Solid blue tracer arrows are drawn from the active cell to a cell that refers to the active cell in its formula. Cell **D14** is a dependent of cell **C14**.

| Product | Quantity | Price | Value |
|---|---|---|---|
| Cup | 400 | €3.00 | €1,200.00 |
| Saucer | 600 | €2.00 | €1,200.00 |
| Plate | 250 | €4.00 | €1,000.00 |
| Dinner Plate | 250 | €8.00 | €2,000.00 |
| Soup Bowl | 400 | €4.00 | €1,600.00 |
| Total | | | €7,000.00 |

- Click on **Trace Dependent** button again. Cell **D20** is also a dependent cell.

| Product | Quantity | Price | Value |
|---|---|---|---|
| Cup | 400 | €3.00 | €1,200.00 |
| Saucer | 600 | €2.00 | €1,200.00 |
| Plate | 250 | €4.00 | €1,000.00 |
| Dinner Plate | 250 | €8.00 | €2,000.00 |
| Soup Bowl | 400 | €4.00 | €1,600.00 |
| Total | | | €7,000.00 |

| Product | Quantity | Price | Value | Quantity | Price | Value |
|---|---|---|---|---|---|---|
| Cup | 400 | €3.00 | €1,200.00 | 650 | €3.00 | €1,950.00 |
| Saucer | 600 | €2.00 | €1,200.00 | 800 | €2.00 | €1,600.00 |
| Plate | 250 | €4.00 | €1,000.00 | 550 | €4.00 | €2,200.00 |
| Dinner Plate | 250 | €8.00 | €2,000.00 | 250 | €8.00 | €2,000.00 |
| Soup Bowl | 400 | €4.00 | €1,600.00 | 420 | €4.00 | €1,680.00 |
| Total | | | €7,000.00 | | | €9,430.00 |
| Increase in Sales | | | | | | €2,430.00 |

- Click on **Trace Dependent** button. Cell **G22** is the last dependent cell, and we will now confirm this.

- Click on **Trace Dependent** button again. The tracer arrow links to the **Increase in Sales**.

- Click on the **Trace Dependent** button again.

- This has no effect. You have successfully traced all the dependents.

- Click **Remove All Arrows.**

We will be using this file again but for the moment save it as **Audit**.

The practice exercises contained in this section relate solely to this manual and do not constitute, or imply, certification by the European Driving Licence Foundation in respect of any ECDL examinations. For details on sitting ECDL examinations in your country please contact the local ECDL/ICDL licensee or visit the European Computer Driving Licence Foundation Ltd web site at http://www.ecdl.com

## Exercise 3B

1    Open file **Audit**.

2    Select cell **G14** which contains a formula. We will trace its dependents. Can you predict in advance what they are?

3    Click on **Trace Dependents**. The solid blue arrow points to cell **G20** as a dependent cell. Can you suggest the next dependent cells? There are two.

4    Click **Trace Dependents** and they are revealed, as you predicted, as **G22** and **J22**. The latter cell contains an error and we will look at cell errors later.

Select cells at random and attempt to predict their precedents and dependents before checking with the Audit toolbar.

## 3.4 Using the Go To Special dialog box

We can use the **Go To Special** dialog box to identify cell precedents and dependents.

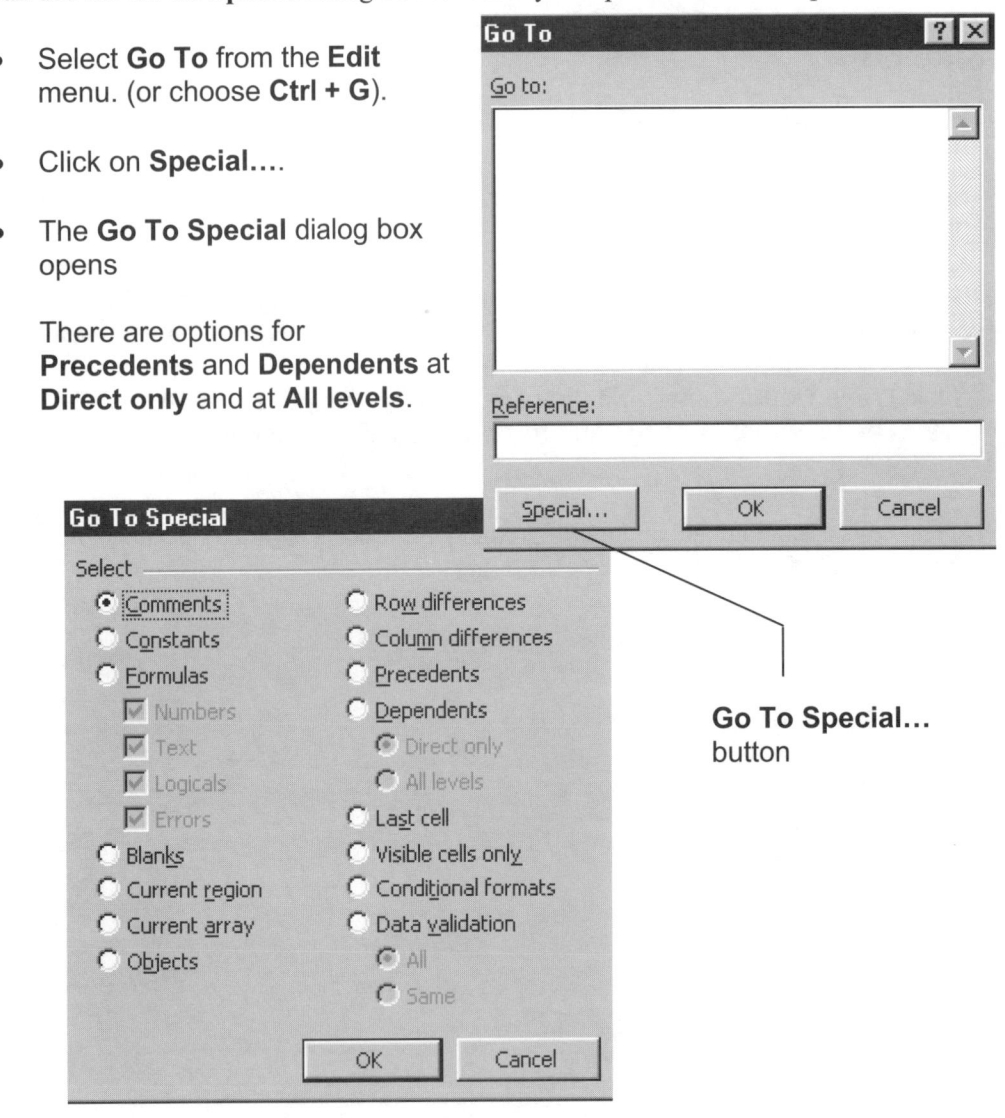

- Select **Go To** from the **Edit** menu. (or choose **Ctrl + G**).

- Click on **Special**....

- The **Go To Special** dialog box opens

    There are options for **Precedents** and **Dependents** at **Direct only** and at **All levels**.

**Go To Special...** button

We will use the Go To Special dialog box in the next exercise.

The practice exercises contained in this section relate solely to this manual and do not constitute, or imply, certification by the European Driving Licence Foundation in respect of any ECDL examinations. For details on sitting ECDL examinations in your country please contact the local ECDL/ICDL licensee or visit the European Computer Driving Licence Foundation Ltd web site at http://www.ecdl.com

## Exercise 3C

1   Open file **Audit**.

2   Select cell **D20**. We have already checked this cell's precedents using the Auditing toolbar. We will confirm the original result using the **Go To Special** dialog box.

3   Select **Go To** from the **Edit** menu (or use **Ctrl + G**) to open the **Go To Special** dialog box. Select **Special** to open the dialog box.

4   Click on **Precedents** and leave the default option as **Direct only**. Select **OK**.

5   The range **D14:D18** is highlighted as you no doubt anticipated.

6   Select cell **D20** again. Choose **Go To** from the **Edit** menu, click on **Special**.... Select **Precedents** and this time select **All levels**. The range **B5:B9** and the range **B14:D18** are highlighted indicating all the precedents.

You may feel that if you are examining a large spreadsheet and want a *quick fix* on precedents of a cell then this is a useful and speedy way to it. Otherwise you may decide to use the Audit toolbar.

The practice exercises contained in this section relate solely to this manual and do not constitute, or imply, certification by the European Driving Licence Foundation in respect of any ECDL examinations. For details on sitting ECDL examinations in your country please contact the local ECDL/ICDL licensee or visit the European Computer Driving Licence Foundation Ltd web site at http://www.ecdl.com

## Exercise 3D

1   Select cell **B14**. Now select **Go To** from the **Edit** menu (or select **Ctrl + G**). and click on **Special...** to open the **Go To** special dialog box. Select **Dependents** and **All levels**, and click **OK**.

2   The Dependent cells are highlighted.

These are the same cells that the blue tracer arrows indicate when the Audit toolbar is used.

3   Repeat the exercise with other cells but first use the Audit toolbar to show all dependent cells with blue arrows. Then use the **Go To Special** dialog box facility to check results.

### NOTE
There are a number of useful options in the Go To Special dialog box, one of these is Cell Formulas and we will examine this on page 226.

## 3.5 Tracing Cells with External References

Is it possible to trace precedents to cells that are in different worksheets but in the same workbook? The answer is yes.

- Select cell **J5**. Note the cell reference **=Sheet2!E9**

- Select **Trace Precedents** button.

    The tracer arrow is displayed as a black dotted line preceded by the worksheet icon.

    Select **Sheet2** tab to check that the source of this information is from the New Stock list, specifically cell **E9,** which gives the price of the Dessert Bowl.

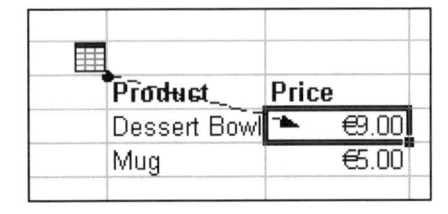

---

The practice exercises contained in this section relate solely to this manual and do not constitute, or imply, certification by the European Driving Licence Foundation in respect of any ECDL examinations. For details on sitting ECDL examinations in your country please contact the local ECDL/ICDL licensee or visit the European Computer Driving Licence Foundation Ltd web site at http://www.ecdl.com

## Exercise 3E

1   You are going to check the precedents of cell **J6**. Before you select the cell can you predict what the reference is? Click it now.

2   Now trace its precedents.

## 3.6 Tracing and Resolving Spreadsheet Errors

When a formula results in an error the **Trace Error** button will help identify the source of the error. The table below gives an indication of the types of error found in spreadsheets and suggests some of the causes.

| Error Type | Possible Cause |
| --- | --- |
| #DIV/0 | Attempt has been made to divide a figure by zero (or empty cell) e.g. 6/0. |
| #NAME? | An undefined name has been used in the formula. This may happen when you forget the colon for a range e.g. =SUM(A1A20). |
| #N/A | The required value is not available to the formula. |
| #NULL! | An intersection is specified in the formula but does not exist. |
| #NUM! | This usually means that one of the numbers that you are trying to add is either too small or too large for the formula in question. This error message may indicate an illegal argument in a function e.g. =SQRT(-7). |
| #REF! | A cell is referenced that is either not on the worksheet or has been deleted. |
| #VALUE! | The wrong type of argument is used for a formula. |
| ####### | The column is not wide enough to display the numeric content |

- Select cell **J22**. An error, (#DIV/0) is displayed in cell. The table above informs you that an attempt has been made to divide by 0 or by an empty cell. In this case, it is obviously the empty cell that has caused the problem. Check the formula. It is **=J20-G20**.

- Click on **Trace Error** button.

## Formula Auditing

| Product | Price |
|---|---|
| Cup | €3.00 |
| Saucer | €2.00 |
| Tea Plate | €4.00 |
| Dinner Plate | €8.00 |
| Soup Bowl | €4.00 |

| Product | Price |
|---|---|
| Dessert Bowl | €9.00 |
| Mug | €5.00 |

|  | 2003 | | | 2004 | | | 2005 | | |
|---|---|---|---|---|---|---|---|---|---|
| Product | Quantity | Price | Value | Quantity | Price | Value | Quantity | Price | Value |
| Cup | 400 | €3.00 | €1,200.00 | 650 | €3.00 | €1,950.00 | 800 | €3.00 | €2,400.00 |
| Saucer | 600 | €2.00 | €1,200.00 | 800 | €2.00 | €1,600.00 | 920 | €2.00 | €1,840.00 |
| Plate | 250 | €4.00 | €1,000.00 | 550 | €4.00 | €2,200.00 | 600 | €4.00 | €2,400.00 |
| Dinner Plate | 250 | €8.00 | €2,000.00 | 250 | €8.00 | €2,000.00 | 350 | €8.00 | €2,800.00 |
| Soup Bowl | 400 | €4.00 | €1,600.00 | 420 | €4.00 | €1,680.00 | 420 | €4.00 | #DIV/0! |
| Total | | | €7,000.00 | | | €9,430.00 | | | #DIV/0! |
| Increase in Sales | | | | | | €2,430.00 | | | #DIV/0! |

- The error tracer arrows are displayed in **red** and the source of the error is clearly traced back to cell **J18** whose formula is incorrect.

You can correct the error by adding the correct formula:

- Double click in cell **J18**. Insert the correct formula.

    **=H18*I18**

- Select **Remove All Arrows** button.

- Resave file with changes but do not close file.

The practice exercises contained in this section relate solely to this manual and do not constitute, or imply, certification by the European Driving Licence Foundation in respect of any ECDL examinations. For details on sitting ECDL examinations in your country please contact the local ECDL/ICDL licensee or visit the European Computer Driving Licence Foundation Ltd web site at http://www.ecdl.com

## Exercise 3F

The file **Audit** is used in this exercise.

1. Select **Sheet3**. Surprised? No? Well we have to hide our errors somewhere! The worksheet is identical to Sheet1 apart from the errors. There are three errors. **#Name?, #Ref!** and **######**.
Eliminate the latter by widening column J. Do this now.
Bad news! A few more errors are exposed. Let us eliminate all of them!

2. Choose cell **D20**. Cell **G22** is a dependent of cell **D20**. By eliminating the error in **D20** we will eliminate the error in cell **G22**. Notice that in cell **D25** there is an **ISERROR** statement relating to **D20**.
Double click on cell **D20**. The cause of the error is the missing colon :.
Insert the colon and click the **Enter** button on the Formula Bar.
The error is eliminated in cell **D20**. The error is also eliminated in cell **G22**. In addition, the **TRUE** statement in cell **D25** changes to **FALSE** which is correct. The cell no longer contains an error.

3. Select cell **I14**. Examine the cell contents. Reference is made to a sheet, **Sheet4**. You may have received a message indicating this when you opened the file Audit. Edit within cell or in Formula bar. Delete **Sheet4**! Now click enter button. The error is corrected.

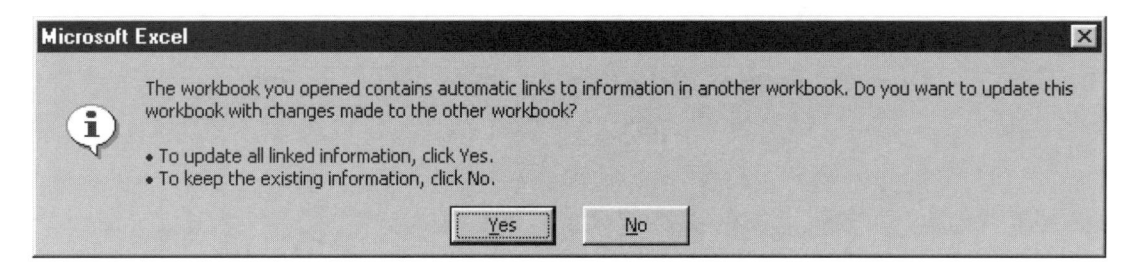

This error is responsible for the message that appears when the file Audit is opened. If there are any other errors in spreadsheet, eliminate them.

This corrects all the errors in the spreadsheet.

4. Resave the file as **Audit Solution**.

**NOTE**

For more information on ISERROR, see Chapter 3.

## 3.7 Displaying all formulas in a worksheet (4.4.3.3)

- Open file **Audit** and click on **Sheet1**.

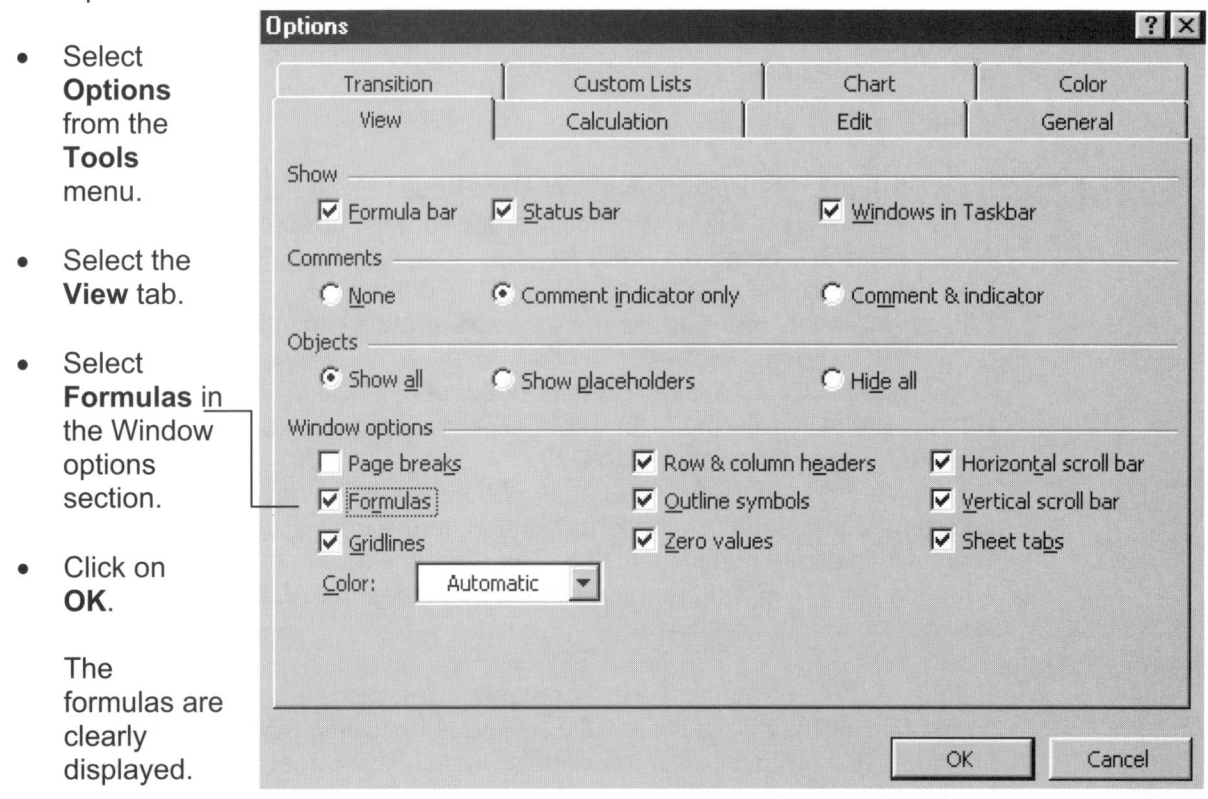

- Select **Options** from the **Tools** menu.

- Select the **View** tab.

- Select **Formulas** in the Window options section.

- Click on **OK**.

  The formulas are clearly displayed.

*With Formulas **not selected** in **Window options**:*

| Product | Quantity | Price | Value | Quantity | Price | Value |
|---|---|---|---|---|---|---|
| Cup | 400 | €3.00 | €1,200.00 | 650 | €3.00 | €1,950.00 |
| Saucer | 600 | €2.00 | €1,200.00 | 800 | €2.00 | €1,600.00 |
| Plate | 250 | €4.00 | €1,000.00 | 550 | €4.00 | €2,200.00 |
| Dinner Plate | 250 | €8.00 | €2,000.00 | 250 | €8.00 | €2,000.00 |
| Soup Bowl | 400 | €4.00 | €1,600.00 | 420 | €4.00 | €1,680.00 |
| Total | | | €7,000.00 | | | €9,430.00 |
| Increase in Sales | | | | | | €2,430.00 |

*With Formulas **selected** in **Window options**:*

| Product | Quantity | Price | Value |
|---|---|---|---|
| Cup | 400 | =B5 | =B14*C14 |
| Saucer | 600 | =B6 | =B15*C15 |
| Plate | 250 | =B7 | =B16*C16 |
| Dinner Plate | 250 | =B8 | =B17*C17 |
| Soup Bowl | 400 | =B9 | =B18*C18 |
| Total | | | =SUM(D14:D18) |

The top screen shows a view of cells without formulas and the lower screen shows a comparable screen shot with the formulas.

- Close the file **Audit** without saving changes.

Is it possible to compare them on the same screen and print out a copy of the worksheet with precise cell locations of formulas?

We will open a new window for the workbook containing the formulas.

- Open the file **Audit**.

- Select **Window** followed by **New Window**.

- Now select **Options** from the **Tools** window and select **View** tab. Click on **Formulas** in **Window options**. Click **OK**.

- Select **Window arrange** and the **Arrange Windows** dialog box opens.

- Click on **Horizontal** (or Vertical) and click on **OK**.

    The two windows appear on the screen.
    You may have to adjust each window to give a close comparison of cell content and cell formula.

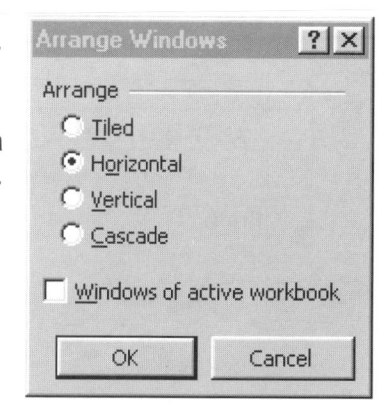

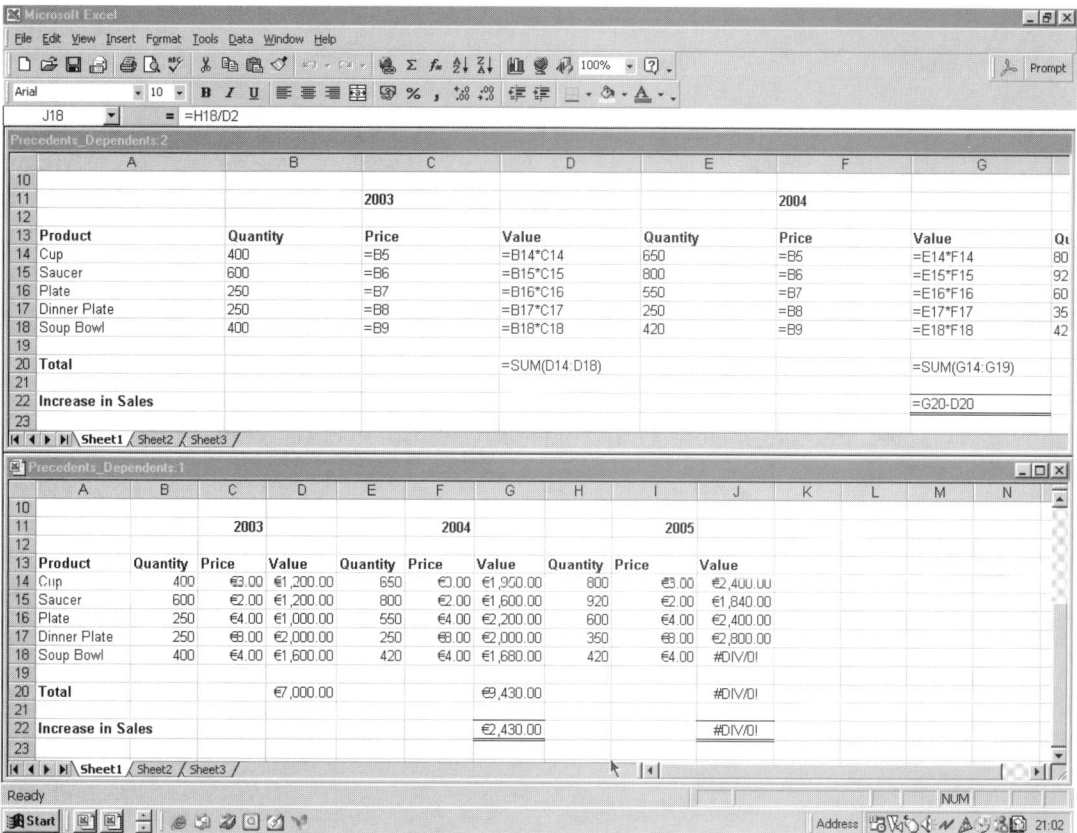

- Change the view so that only one document is viewed.

### 3.7.1 Printing the formulas

- Ensure Audit spreadsheet is open. Select **Options** from the **Tools** menu.

- Select the **View** tab.

- Select **Formulas** in the Window options section and click **OK**.

- Choose **File** followed by **Page Setup**. Choose the **Sheet** tab in the **Page setup** dialog box.

- Click **Row and column headings** in the option box.

- Choose **Print Preview**. The figure below shows the expected print preview.

|    | A | B | C | D |
|----|---|---|---|---|
| 1  | Formula Auditing | | | |
| 2  | | | | |
| 3  | | | | |
| 4  | Product | Price | | |
| 5  | Cup | 3 | | |
| 6  | Saucer | 2 | | |
| 7  | Tea Plate | 4 | | |
| 8  | Dinner Plate | 8 | | |
| 9  | Soup Bowl | 4 | | |
| 10 | | | | |
| 11 | | | 2003 | |
| 12 | | | | |
| 13 | Product | Quantity | Price | Value |
| 14 | Cup | 400 | =B5 | =B14*C14 |
| 15 | Saucer | 600 | =B6 | =B15*C15 |
| 16 | Plate | 250 | =B7 | =B16*C16 |
| 17 | Dinner Plate | 250 | =B8 | =B17*C17 |
| 18 | Soup Bowl | 400 | =B9 | =B18*C18 |
| 19 | | | | |
| 20 | Total | | | =SUM(D14:D18) |
| 21 | | | | |
| 22 | Increase in Sales | | | |

Printing the formulas with their Row and Column Headings can be very useful if you want to know how a spreadsheet was constructed. Or of course if you want to check a spreadsheet of your own construction. What do you think?

## 3.8 Cell Comments

Comments can be added to any cell. These comments (or cell notes) can be of particular use in complex spreadsheets where formula are involved. Comments can give useful supplementary information on cells.

### 3.8.1 Adding a cell comment (4.4.3.4)

- Open file **Comments**.

- Select cell **G19**.

- Choose **Insert** followed by **Comment**.

   A yellow box opens with the name of user (or PC identification or organisation name) in it. You can insert your comment into the box directly at the cursor point.

- Insert the following message:

   **These figures are a significant improvement on those of 2002 (5400) and 2001 (3200).**

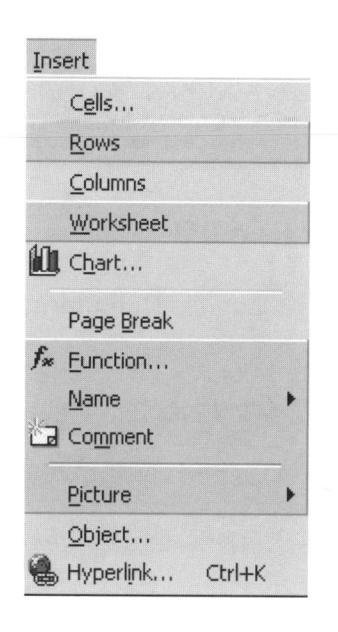

### GREAT OUTDOORS

**Consolidated Income Statement**
**2003**

|  | Wexford | Kilkenny | Kerry | Cork | Galway | TOTAL (€ x 1,000) |
|---|---|---|---|---|---|---|
| SALES | 1200 | 5200 | 7800 | 9600 | 3300 | 27100 |
| COST OF SALES | 500 | 3200 | 2750 | 3500 | 1600 | 11550 |
| GROSS PROFIT | 700 | 2000 | 4090 | 6100 | 1800 | 14690 |
| LESS: |  |  |  |  |  |  |
| OVERHEADS | 230 | 850 | 2200 | 1200 | 800 | 5280 |
| INTEREST | 85 | 175 | 350 | 240 | 340 | 1190 |
| TAXATION | 150 | 350 | 400 | 500 | 125 | 1525 |
| NET PROFIT | 235 | 625 | 1140 | 4160 | 535 | 6695 |

Comment on G19:
**Great Outdoors**
These figures are a significant improvement on those those of 2002 (5400) and 2001 (3200).

- Click on cell **G20** or any empty cell.

   The comment disappears but a small, red, right-angled triangle appears in the top right-hand corner of the cell. The comment is saved in the cell.

### 3.8.2 Viewing Cell Comments

- Place the cursor over cell **G19**. The yellow box with the comment you have just inserted appears. The arrow links the comment box to the cell which contains the comment.

- To view all the comments on a worksheet choose **View** followed by **Comments**.

All of the comments become visible. To hide the comments again simply repeat, **View** followed by **Comments**. This acts as a toggle switching from hiding comments to making them visible.

The practice exercises contained in this section relate solely to this manual and do not constitute, or imply, certification by the European Driving Licence Foundation in respect of any ECDL examinations. For details on sitting ECDL examinations in your country please contact the local ECDL/ICDL licensee or visit the European Computer Driving Licence Foundation Ltd web site at http://www.ecdl.com

## Exercise 3G

1. Open file **Comments** (if it is not already open).

2. Select cell **B7**. Choose **Insert** followed by **Comment** and the yellow box opens with your name in it. Insert the following comment:

   **Opened Spring 2001 with Ciara O'Toole as Manager.**

3. Click on adjacent empty cell on worksheet. The comment should be hidden.

4. Now select **View** followed by **Comments**. Both comments should be visible.

5. Toggle between **View**, **Comments** a number of times.

   Finally, leave the comments hidden.

6. Select cell **H10**. Insert the following comment:

   **Could we have Sales, Cost of Sales and Gross Profit charted using Standard Type –Bar (Clustered Bar)? Thanks.**

   The worksheet should now contain three comments.

7. Finally save the file as **Comments** but do not close.

### 3.8.3 Formatting a Comment

- Open file **Comments**, if it is not already open.

- Ensure all comments are visible. If necessary select **View** followed by **Comments**.

  We are going to format the comment in cell **B7**.

- Click in yellow comment box and highlight the name **Ciara O' Toole**. Select **Comment** from the **Format** options. (or choose **Ctrl + 1**).

- The **Format Options** Dialog box opens.

- Choose Font Style **Bold Italic**, Change the size to **9** and select **Blue** as the colour from the palette. Note that the changes have been correctly made.

- Click **OK**.

- When you save the file the comments are automatically saved.

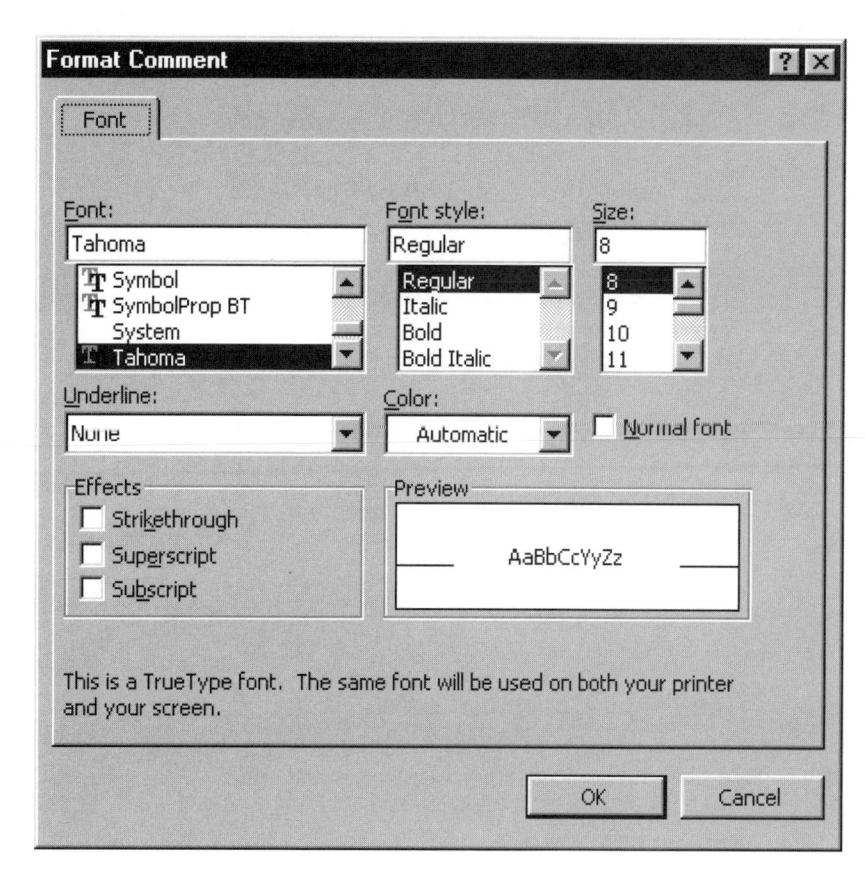

### 3.8.4 Editing Worksheet Comments (4.4.3.5)

We will edit the comment in cell **G19**.

- Is file **Comment** open? If not, open it now.

- Select cell **G19**. Choose **View** followed by **Comments** if necessary.

- Choose **Edit Comment** from the **Insert** menu.

  The correct figure for 2001 is **3375**.

- Replace the original figure of **3200** with **3375**.

- Click on an empty cell.

### 3.8.5 Deleting a Comment (4.4.3.4)

It has been decided not to chart the figures in cell **H10**.

- Select cell **H10**.

- Right-click in this cell and choose **Delete Comment**.

- The comment is deleted.

- Resave the file as **Comments Solution**.

## 3.9 Using the Reviewing Toolbar

If you have a number of comments in a worksheet the Reviewing Toolbar is useful for navigating through them.

- To open the Reviewing Toolbar select **View**, **Toolbars** and click on **Reviewing**.
- Alternatively right mouse click on any currently displayed toolbar and select **Reviewing**.

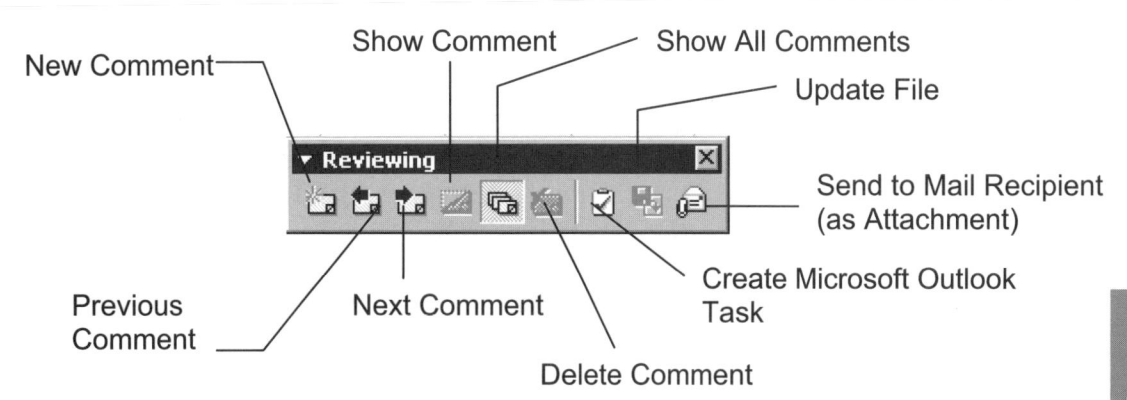

*Reviewing toolbar with labels: New Comment, Previous Comment, Next Comment, Show Comment, Show All Comments, Delete Comment, Update File, Create Microsoft Outlook Task, Send to Mail Recipient (as Attachment).*

- Move from comment to comment in Comments file by clicking on **Next Comment**.

If you get the following message select **OK**.

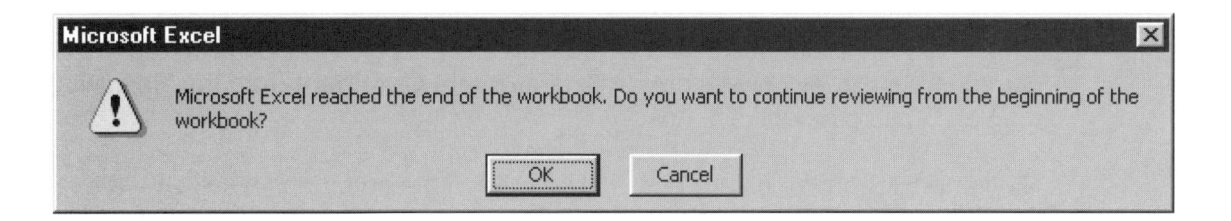

*Microsoft Excel dialog: "Microsoft Excel reached the end of the workbook. Do you want to continue reviewing from the beginning of the workbook?" with OK and Cancel buttons.*

In this next exercise we will carry out a number of operations using the Reviewing Toolbar.

The practice exercises contained in this section relate solely to this manual and do not constitute, or imply, certification by the European Driving Licence Foundation in respect of any ECDL examinations. For details on sitting ECDL examinations in your country please contact the local ECDL/ICDL licensee or visit the European Computer Driving Licence Foundation Ltd web site at http://www.ecdl.com

## Exercise 3H

1   Open file **Express Exports**.

2   Select **View**, **Toolbars** and choose **Reviewing**. (Or **right-click** on the Standard or Formatting Toolbar and choose **Reviewing**)

3   The **Reviewing** Toolbar opens.

4   Select the **Show All Comments** icon. There are five comments in total.

    We are going to edit, delete and add comments. In addition, we will carry out the tasks requested by the Comments.

5   Firstly, we will review the comments. The cursor should be in cell **A20**. Click on the **Next Comment** icon and navigate from comment to comment until you have read them all. When you get the message:

    **Microsoft Excel reached the end of the workbook. Do you want to continue reviewing from the beginning of the workbook?**

    Select **OK** and continue.

6   Return to the Comment in cell **A20** regarding the new employee.

7   Add the information on this new employee directly into the worksheet. To add the Employee Number drag down from cell **A19** and it will return the formula **(A19+1)**, giving the new employee the number **13**.

8   Check that the information is accurately entered. We no longer need the comment so we will now delete it. Select **Delete Comment** from the Reviewing toolbar. The comment is deleted.

9   Navigate through the comments until you reach the comment in cell **D8**. Make the change to the **DOB**. Now select **Edit Comment**. Delete the existing comment (red font) and insert the following message:

    **DOB corrected** – today's date (you put in today's date).

10  Highlight the change you have made and choose **Comment** from the **Format** menu (or choose **Ctrl + 1**). Change the colour to **Sea Green**, **Regular** and **9** point. Adjust the size of the comment box by using the handles, if necessary, to ensure the complete message can be read.

11  Save the file at this stage as **Express Exports Solution**, but do not close as we have a number of operations to carry out in **Exercise 3I**.

The practice exercises contained in this section relate solely to this manual and do not constitute, or imply, certification by the European Driving Licence Foundation in respect of any ECDL examinations. For details on sitting ECDL examinations in your country please contact the local ECDL/ICDL licensee or visit the European Computer Driving Licence Foundation Ltd web site at http://www.ecdl.com

## Exercise 3I

1   Navigate to cell **E9**. Make the necessary Department change on the worksheet. Now select **Delete Comment** from the Reviewing toolbar. The comment is deleted.

2   Navigate to cell **G16** and change Colin Jackson's phone number to **34**. Select **Delete Comment** from the Reviewing menu.

3   Now, navigate to cell **F5** and respond to message. Select any *one* of *three* pictures (Clip Art), reject and delete the other two (by selecting picture and pressing **Delete** on keyboard).

4   Edit the message in **F5** to: **Decision made**: your initials (Insert your initials).

   We can now Email the worksheets with the changes made to it. If you are in a position where you can actually send Email, go ahead and do so. Use your own Email address.

5   Click on icon, **Send to mail recipient as Attachment**. In the **To:** box write your Email address, then click the send button. That is it. You can look forward to receiving the file Express Exports with changes and remaining comments.

6   Select **Hide All Comments** from the **Reviewing** toolbar. Close the reviewing toolbar. Save the file again as **Express Exports Solution**.

# Self Check Exercises

1. What is the correct sequence to display all formulas in a worksheet?
   - ☐ Choose Options from the Tools menu, then select tab View, and ensure Formulas is not selected.
   - ☐ Choose Options from the Tools menu, then select tab View and click on None.
   - ☐ Choose Options from the Tools menu, then select tab View and click on Formulas.

2. What is the most probable cause of this error message?

   **#DIV/0**
   - ☐ The required value is not available to the formula.
   - ☐ The formula is attempting to divide by 0 (or Empty cell).
   - ☐ An undefined name has been used in the formula.
   - ☐ Column is not wide enough to display the numeric content.

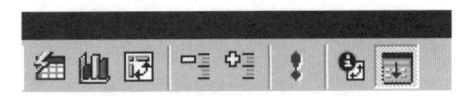

3. The toolbar shown above is the:
   - ☐ PivotTable toolbar
   - ☐ Reviewing toolbar

4. Which of the following statements are true?
   - ☐ Formula tracer arrows are solid blue
   - ☐ Error tracer arrows are solid red
   - ☐ A dashed black arrow linked to a worksheet icon is an external tracer arrow

5. What is the keyboard shortcut to **Go To** a particular cell?
   - ☐ Ctrl + T
   - ☐ Alt + G
   - ☐ Ctrl + G
   - ☐ Alt + T

   A   B   C   D

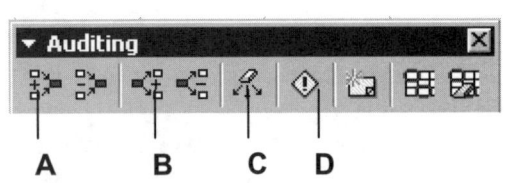

6. Identify buttons A, B, C and D on the Auditing toolbar above?

   Trace Error ( )

   Trace Dependents ( )

   Trace Precedents ( )

   Remove All Arrows ( )

7. What is the name of this button?
   - ☐ Field Settings
   - ☐ Refresh Data
   - ☐ Format Report
   - ☐ Show Detail

8. In which of the following would you utilise **Changing cells**?
   - ☐ PivotTable and PivotChart Report.
   - ☐ Scenario Manager
   - ☐ Editing Cell Comments
   - ☐ Cell Auditing

# Chapter 4 - Analysis

The practice exercises contained in this section relate solely to this manual and do not constitute, or imply, certification by the European Driving Licence Foundation in respect of any ECDL examinations. For details on sitting ECDL examinations in your country please contact the local ECDL/ICDL licensee or visit the European Computer Driving Licence Foundation Ltd web site at http://www.ecdl.com

## Practical Exercises

### Exercise 1

**Pivot Tables**

1. Open the file **Plant Sales**. Click on any cell in list. (Range **A1:E7**). Select **Data** followed by **PivotTable and PivotChart Report…**. When **PivotTable and PivotChart Wizard – Step 1 of 3** opens choose **Microsoft Excel list or database** as option. **Click Next**.

2. The correct range (**A1:E7**) of the list should be highlighted in **PivotTable and PivotChart Wizard Step 2 of 2**. If not, select it now and click on **Next**.

3. In **Step 3 of 3**, select **New worksheet** and click on **Finish**.

4. The PivotTable opens. Select **SALESPERSON** as **Row item** and drag button to where it says **Drop Row Fields Here**. Choose **January** as **Column item**. Drag **January** button to PivotTable where it says, **Drop Column Fields Here**.

5. Finally drag **TOTAL** button to area, **Drop Data Items Here**.

6. The PivotTable is complete.

    We will now make a change to the PivotTable and Refresh the data so that table is updated.

7. Click on **Sheet1**. Aileen's sales for January should be €62000. Make the change on the list. Click on **Sheet4**. **Refresh** the PivotTable by clicking on the **Refresh Data** button on the PivotTable toolbar. You are informed that, *The Refresh Data operation changed the PivotTable report*. Click **OK**. Check the PivotTable to ensure table has been updated.

8. **Aileen** and **Brian** work as a team. Select cell **A5**. Hold down **Ctrl** key and select cell **A6**. Both these cells should be selected. Right-click on the PivotTable menu and select **Group and Outline** followed by **Group…**.
    Aileen and Brian are grouped together as **Group1**.

9. Finally click on **Chart Wizard** button. The chart shows the January sales but links Aileen and Brian together.

10. Save the file as **Plant Sales Solution**.

# CHAPTER 4
## Analysis

# Chapter 5

## Special Tools

**5**

# Syllabus
## Module AM4
## Spreadsheets – Advanced Level

**AM 4.5.1 Macros**   Page

    AM4.5.1.1     Record a simple macro (e.g. page setup changes.)     245

    AM4.5.1.2     Run a macro     248, 249

    AM4.5.1.3     Assign a macro to a custom button on a toolbar     250

## Section 1      Macros

A macro is a set of instructions or commands grouped together to perform one task.
Macros are used to automate a task that is performed repeatedly or on a regular basis. It is a series of commands and actions that can be stored and run whenever you need to perform the task.

Macros can be used to:

Consolidate data in a spreadsheet.
Format pages with respect to page orientation, margins, header and footer and so on.
Enter headings and addresses.
Enter current date and time in spreadsheet.
Carry out complex and time-consuming tasks quickly and without error.

For example you may wish to consolidate the sales data on a weekly basis from four different geographical locations. This would involve a large number of mouse actions. A macro could do this with one click of the mouse button or by using a designated key combination, such as **Ctrl + m** or **Ctrl + Shift + M**.

Macros can be divided into two types-local and global.
A *local macro* is created and used solely in that workbook. The macro is stored in **This Workbook** or **New Workbook** in Excel.
A *global macro* is stored in a **Personal Macro Workbook** and can be used in any workbook file.

In Excel there are two ways of creating a macro:
You can record or build a macro using the **Macro Recorder** or by using **Visual Basic for Applications (VBA)**. We will create a variety of macros using the Macro Recorder.

### 1.1    The Macro Recorder

A macro is created using the Macro Recorder that operates in a similar manner to a tape recorder. When you click on the recorder, it records all the keyboard instructions and mouse actions. When the recorder is switched off, all the instructions are stored in the macro using the name you chose for it before recording.

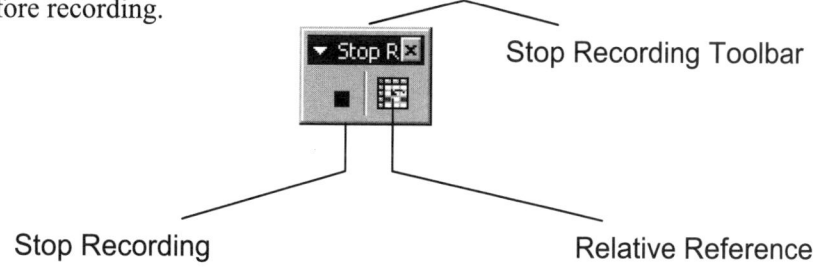

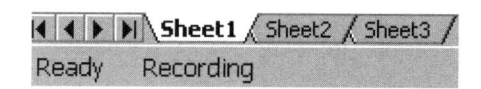

Stop Recording Toolbar

Stop Recording      Relative Reference

When macro is recording you will see **Recording** on the Status bar.

### 1.1.1 Absolute References

When macros are recorded Excel uses absolute reference to cells. If, for example you create a macro which totals sales and bonuses in cells E21 and F21 respectively, when you run this macro it will perform these actions. It does not matter from which cell you run the macro; it recreates exactly the steps in the original macro. If cursor is in cell G40, the active cell, and the macro is run, it will still total the sales and bonuses in cells E21 and F21.
Remember the default is absolute references.

Note: See Exercise 1C for an example involving absolute references.

### 1.1.2 Relative References

Say for example you want to create a macro which creates the name and address of a company formatted to your specifications. You may want such a macro to operate from cell locations in a relative manner. If the macro is run from *any* cell it will list the name and address starting in the active cell. This is useful as the macro is portable throughout the workbook.

Relative Reference button depressed

If you are using relative reference you must click on the relative reference button when you start the macro. Notice that the Relative Reference button on the Stop Recording toolbar above is depressed indicating that relative reference is being used.
It is possible to record a macro using Absolute References then switch to Relative References. Relative References and Absolute References generate different codes and these codes can be examined in the Visual Basic Editor.

Note: See Exercise 1A for an example involving relative references.

## 1.2 Visual Basic for Applications (VBA)

When a macro is created all the commands and instructions are converted into a programming language called Visual Basic for Applications (VBA). A programmer with knowledge of this language can use it to write macros. You are *not* required to understand VBA. However in a later exercise we will edit the code using the **Visual Basic Editor**.
VBA is also used in Word and Access and other programs.

## 1.3 Planning a Macro

What do you want the macro do to? It is important and useful to plan the steps in advance. Perhaps, dare we suggest that you draft the macro first using pencil and paper? Once you have a plan, go through the steps in sequence, as a practice before recording the macro. Remember the macro will record all steps including errors and changes. It is better to be slow and accurate when you create your macro. The speed at which the macro runs does not depend on how long it takes to create it, but on the speed of the processor within the PC.

You may consider the following steps:

- What is it you want the macro to do?

- Are absolute or relative references to be used?

- What macro is appropriate – local or global?
- Relevant name for macro.
- Record macro.
- Save macro

## 1.4 Naming a Macro

The macro name should reflect its function. An appropriate name also helps in its identification. The macro name should have the following characteristics:

- It should begin with a letter. (E.g. PageSettings).
- It can contain numbers (but it cannot start with a number).
- It cannot include spaces or symbols but you can use underscore character (e.g. Consolidate_Returns).
- If you use a macro name that is a cell reference, e.g. A1 then you receive an error message.

In brief, if you choose an inappropriate name you get an error message.

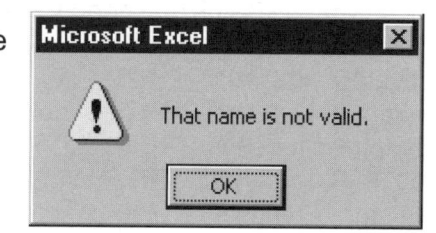

## 1.5 Recording a Simple Macro (4.5.1.1)

We are going to record a simple macro that will make changes to the page setup.

Note: It is good practice to have a backup copy of a file before running a macro. Once the macro is activated its actions *cannot* be undone.

- Open the file **Dublin Film School**. Make sure that you are in worksheet with tab **DFS 2003**.

  First we will look at **Page Setup** to examine the settings.

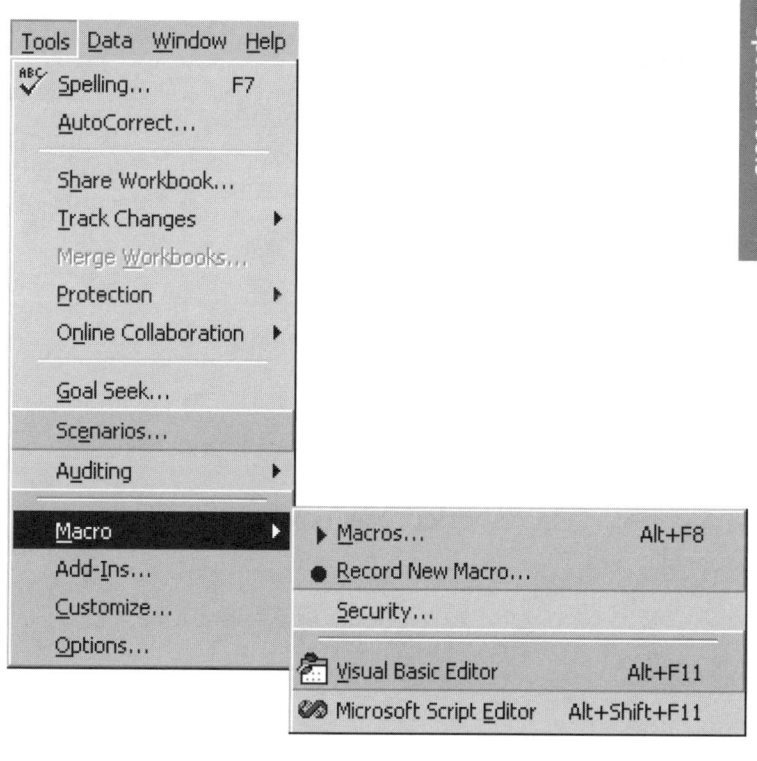

- Select **File** followed by **Page Setup**. Check settings but do not change or add any. The macro you are about to create will do this. Select **Cancel**.

- Select **Macro** in the **Tools** menu.

- Choose **Record New Macro**. The Record macro dialog box is displayed.

  The default name for the macro is **Macro1**. Choose a name that reflects what the macro does. In this case we will call the macro **PageSettings**.

- Insert the name **PageSettings** in the Macro name box.

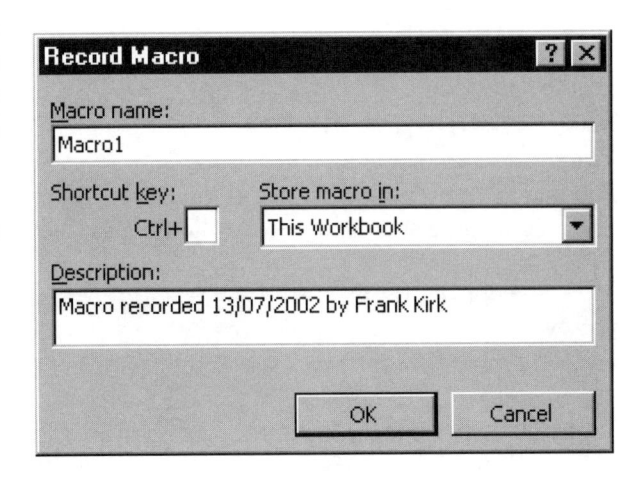

## 1.5.1 Assigning a Shortcut key to a Macro

We will also assign a shortcut key to the macro. The macro can then be activated by using the keyboard. Assign only letters that are not used with other functions. E.g. do not use **Ctrl + C** (copy) or **Ctrl + V** (paste). The table shows a list of common shortcut keys used in Excel.

**Default Excel Shortcut Keys**

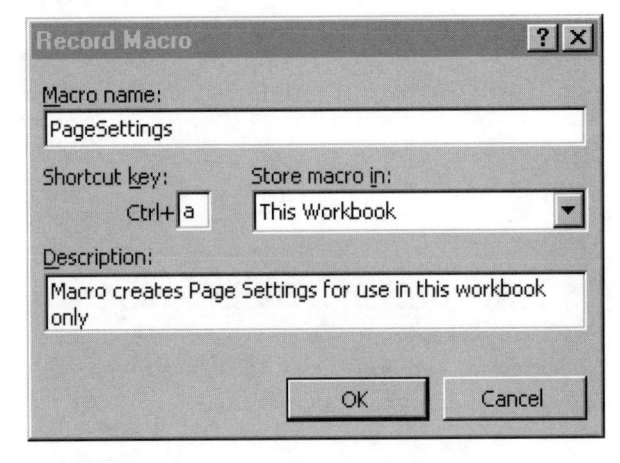

| Ctrl + Y | Repeat New |
|---|---|
| Ctrl + X | Cut |
| Ctrl + C | Copy |
| Ctrl + F | Find |
| Ctrl + H | Replace |
| Ctrl + G | Go To |
| Ctrl + N | New |
| Ctrl + O | Open |
| Ctrl + S | Save |
| Ctrl + P | Print |
| Ctrl + K | Hyperlink |
| Ctrl + D | Down |
| Ctrl + R | Right |

Remember that macro shortcut keys override default Excel shortcut keys

- In the **Shortcut key** box insert the letter **a**.

If capital **A** is used the Shortcut key is **Ctrl + Shift + A**

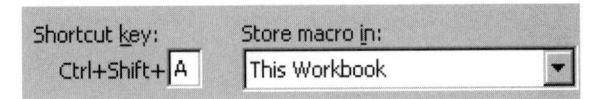

There are three options with regard to storing the macro. It can be stored in **This Workbook**, a **New Workbook** or your **Personal Macro Workbook**. If the macro is saved in the Personal Macro Workbook it is available in *all* workbooks. If it is saved in This Workbook or in New Workbook it is only available for use in that workbook.

- Select the option **This Workbook**.

    Write an appropriate description of what the macro does. Also include the date and your own name.

**NOTE**

If at any stage you receive an error message, select **End** and start again.
See **1.9 Error Messages**.

- Click **OK** and the Macro recorder starts.

- Select **File** followed by **Page Setup**. Choose the **Page tab** first and set the orientation of the page to **Landscape**.

- Now select the **Margins tab** and select both **Horizontally** and **Vertically**.

- Select the **Header/Footer tab** and click on **Custom Header**.

    In the Center Section write: **Dublin Film School** and click **OK**.

- Now choose **Custom Footer**. In the Left section write **Director: Your Name** (insert your own name of course – we are happy to give you the role you have always wanted!) In the **Center** section select the **Page Number** button and finally in the **Right** section choose **Date: Time**. Click **OK**.

- In the last tab, **Sheet**, select **Gridlines** in the **Print** option.

- Click **OK** and **OK** again to exit **Page Setup** menu.

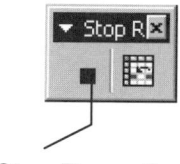

    Stop Recording

- Select the **Stop Recording** button on the Stop Recording toolbar. (Or select **Tools**, **Macro**, **Stop Recording**).

    The macro will have successfully stored the keystrokes and selections made.

- Select **File** followed by **Print Preview** to check that the information has been correctly entered. Your **Print Preview** should look like that on next page.

## 1.6 Running a Named Macro (4.5.1.2)

Now that you have successfully created a macro named **PageSettings**, let us run this macro in another worksheet.

- Click on the adjacent worksheet **DFS 2004**.

    This shows the sales of courses for the Dublin Film School for 2004.

- Select **File** followed by **Page Setup**.

    Check each of the tabs in turn and note the default settings. You will notice that the macro options from your previous exercise are **not** displayed. Select **Close**.

    We will run the macro **PageSettings** in this worksheet and note the result.

- To select the macro select **Tools**, **Macro**, **Macros** (or use **Alt + F8**) to display list of macros.

- Ensure **PageSetup** is highlighted and choose **Run**.

    You may be aware of macro activity as the macro runs.

- To check it has been successful select **File**, **Print Preview** and note that all the instructions have been successfully implemented.

## 1.7 Running a Named Macro using Keyboard Shortcut (4.5.1.2)

We assigned the keyboard shortcut **Ctrl + a** to activate the macro.

- Click on worksheet **DFS 2005**. Check **Page Setup**.

- Run the macro using **Ctrl + a** command.

    Select **Page**, followed by **Print Preview** to check the macro has been successful.

    You will realise how useful the macro is especially if you produce many spreadsheets regularly with the same page settings. Such a macro should be saved in your **Personal Macro Workbook** to be made available to all worksheets (Global Macro)

**NOTE**

Since each worksheet requires page settings to be entered independently you will recognise how useful a macro is with all the required information stored. If you are an accountant producing monthly returns or a teacher or lecturer storing and printing monthly test results the macro you have just created may prove useful.

## 1.8 Deleting a Macro

To delete a macro select **Tools**, **Macro**, **Macros** (or **Alt +F8**) and click on the macro you wish to delete. When the macro is highlighted click **Delete** on Macro dialog box.

You are offered a final option. Once the macro is deleted, this action cannot be undone. If you wish to delete macro, click on **Yes**. If you have changed your mind, or selected the wrong macro for deletion, click on **No**.

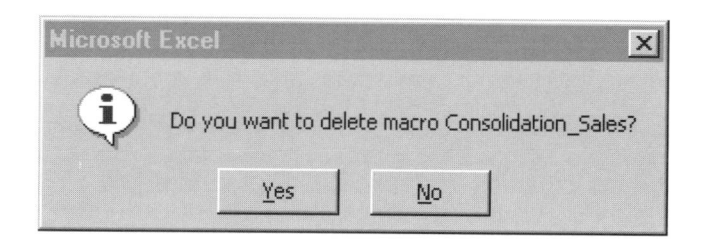

## 1.9 Error Messages

If you get an error message when you attempt to run a macro you are offered three options, **End**, **Debug** and **Help**.

Select **End** and start again

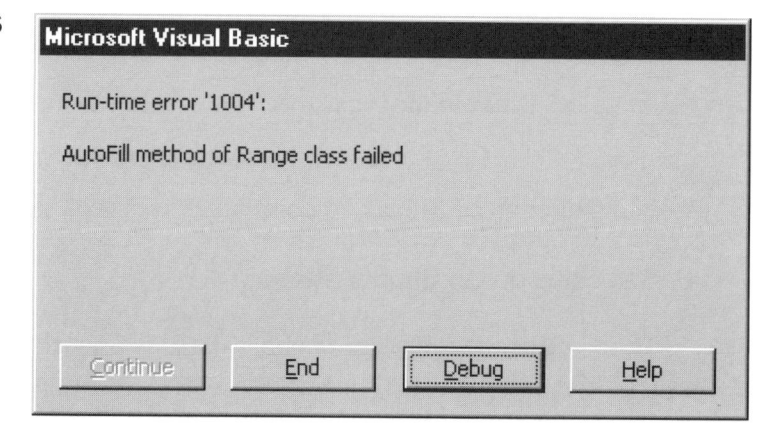

**NOTE**

If you are familiar with **VBA** you can use the **Debug** option or obtain assistance on the error from **Visual Basic Help**. We will not use any of these options.

## 1.10 Assigning a Macro to a Toolbar Button (4.5.1.3)

We have now created and run macros from the Macros dialog box. We have also run a macro using a named keyboard shortcut. However, we can reduce the number of steps taken to execute a macro by assigning the macro to a toolbar button.

- Open file named **Cheeses of Sligo**.

A warning box appears indicating that the file contains macros and that there is a danger of viruses. There are three options.

**Disable Macros** If you select this option the file will open but the macro will not work. However there is no chance of your other files becoming infected if the file does contain a virus.

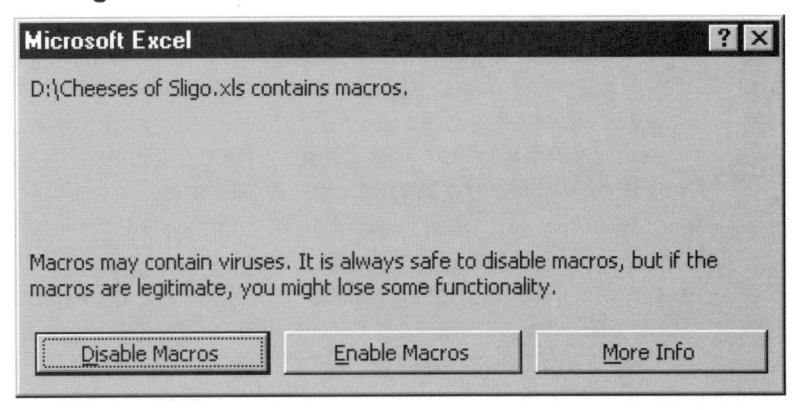

**Enable Macros** If you choose this option, the file opens and the macro will function as normal. If however the file is infected, there is a risk of infecting other files. Choose this if you are certain the file is free of viruses.

**More Info** This gives information on protecting workbooks from viruses, altering the security level for virus protection and virus protection information on the World Wide Web.

**NOTE**

One macro virus you will have heard of is **Melissa**. It affects Word 2000 documents and when launched the virus attempts to start Microsoft Outlook. It will send copies of the infected document to 50 persons listed in Outlook's address book. **Melissa** achieved notoriety in 1999 when Microsoft stopped outgoing and incoming mail to prevent it spreading. Your own PC will no doubt be protected from viruses by the installation of reputable and easily updated anti-virus software such as, **Sophos Anti-Virus**, **PC-cillin**, or **McAfee VirusScan**.

If in doubt select **Disable Macros**.

The file **Cheeses of Sligo** has been checked for viruses, so you can safely open it.

- Select the option **Enable Macros**

    The file Cheeses of Sligo opens. There is one macro present and it is called **Cheese_is_nice**.

- Choose **Tools**, **Macro**, **Macros** (or use **Alt + F8** to display the macro)

- Run the macro **Cheese_is_nice**.

    This macro totals the sales in the period January to June. It also gives a final total and formats the totals in Euro to two decimal places.

Chapter 5 – Special Tools

We are going to assign this macro, **Cheese_is_nice** to a toolbar button. The advantage in this is that we can execute the macro by clicking on this button, which saves numerous keystrokes and valuable time.

The information shows the value of cheese sales at three outlets, A, B, and C.

- Click on cell E15.

- On the **Tools** menu select **Customize**. The Customize dialog box opens.

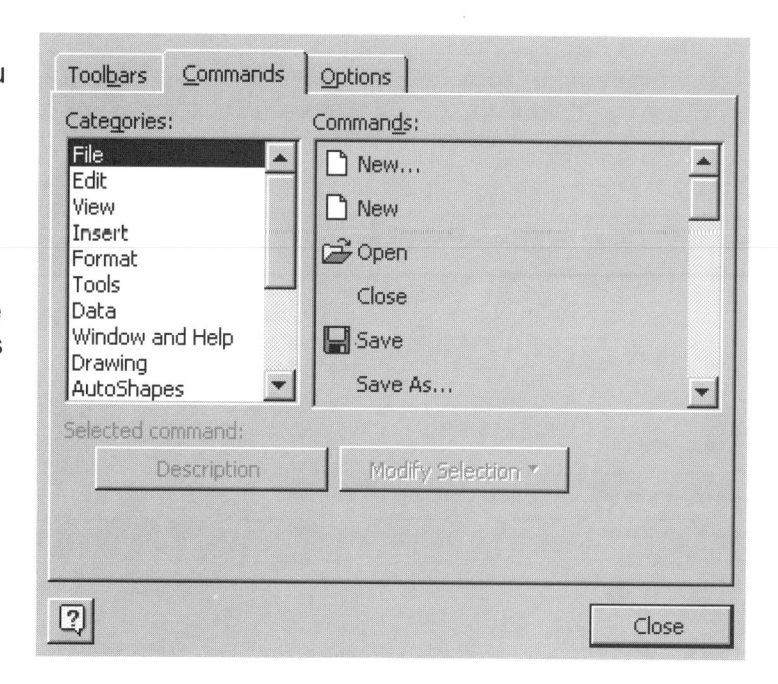

- Select the **Commands** tab and scroll down the **Categories** options to **Macros** and click. **The Custom Button** on the **Commands** list is highlighted. (If not select it now).

- Drag the **Custom Button** to the **Standard** toolbar and locate between the **Chart Wizard** and **Drawing Button**. The black **I** beam indicates where the button will be positioned.

- Release mouse button and the Custom button is now located on the Standard toolbar.

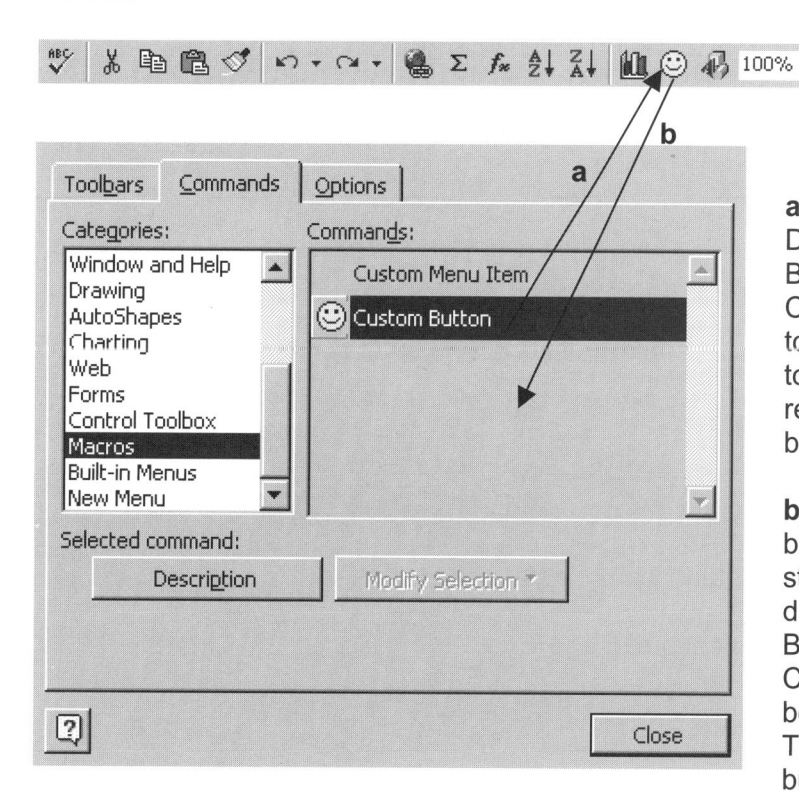

a) To **add** a button: Drag the Custom Button from the Commands section to the standard toolbar. Then release the mouse button.

b) To **remove** a button: From the standard toolbar, drag the Custom Button onto the Customize dialog box.
Then release mouse button.

- Right-click on the button to customize its appearance. In the Name box insert the name: **Cheese_is_nice**. The name is the same name as the macro.

- In order for the macro to execute when the button is clicked, select **Assign Macro**. The **Assign Macro** dialog box opens. Choose the macro name **Cheese_is_nice** from the list. Click OK.

- There are a number of options, including **Change Button Image**, **Edit Button Image** and options that allow you to choose **Text** or **Image** and **Text** on button. Use the default image (Smiley). Click Close when you are finished examining these options.

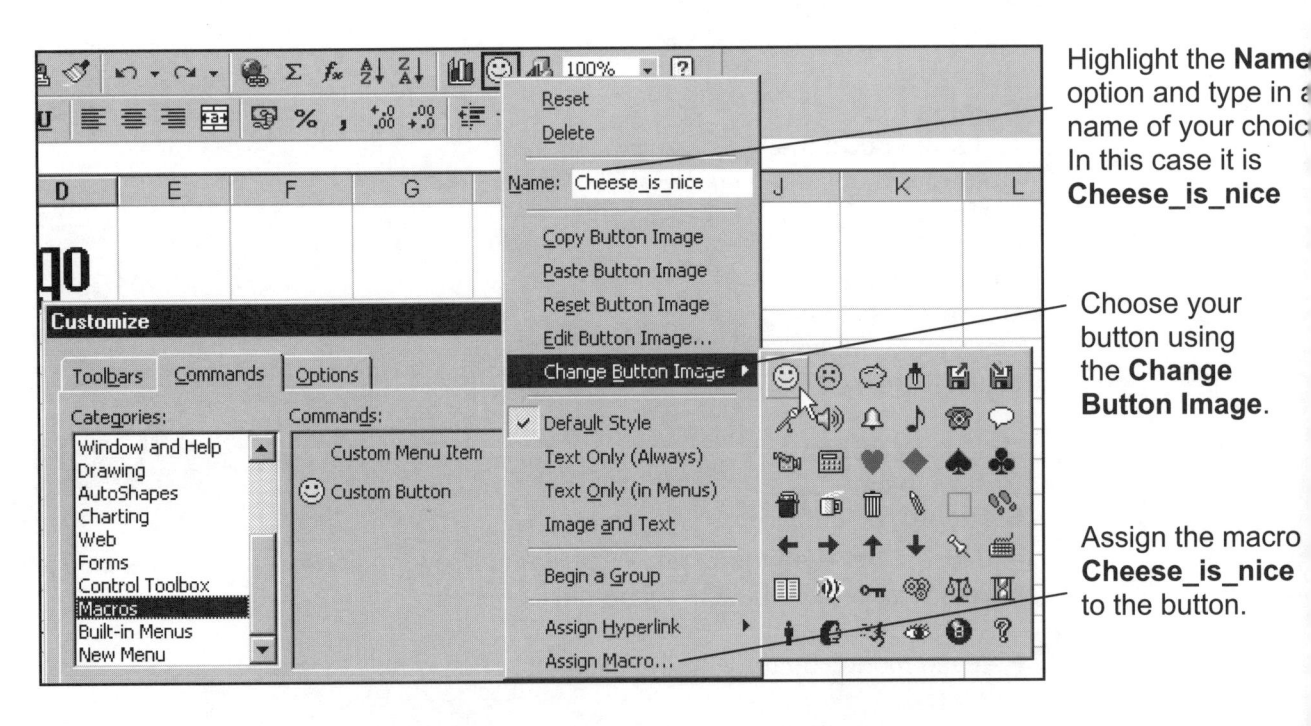

Highlight the **Name** option and type in a name of your choice. In this case it is **Cheese_is_nice**

Choose your button using the **Change Button Image**.

Assign the macro **Cheese_is_nice** to the button.

- Position the cursor over the Button image (without clicking the mouse). The button is identified as **Cheese_is_nice**.

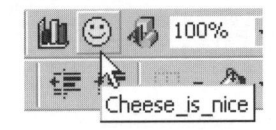

Let's check that the macro will execute when the button is clicked.

- Highlight the range **E12:K12** and choose **Edit**, **Clear**, **Contents Del**.

  This clears the range.

- Now click on the button.

  The macro is executed by this single click.

  Resave the file **Cheeses of Sligo**.

## 1.11 Editing a Macro

It is possible to edit the macro **Cheeses_is_nice** using the **Visual Basic Editor**.

- Open the file **Cheeses of Sligo**.

- Select **Tools**, **Macro**, **Macros** and choose the macro **Cheese_is_nice**.

- Select **Edit** and the **Visual Basic Window** opens.

    Each macro is stored as a **module** by Excel and by examining the code we can make some sense of it.

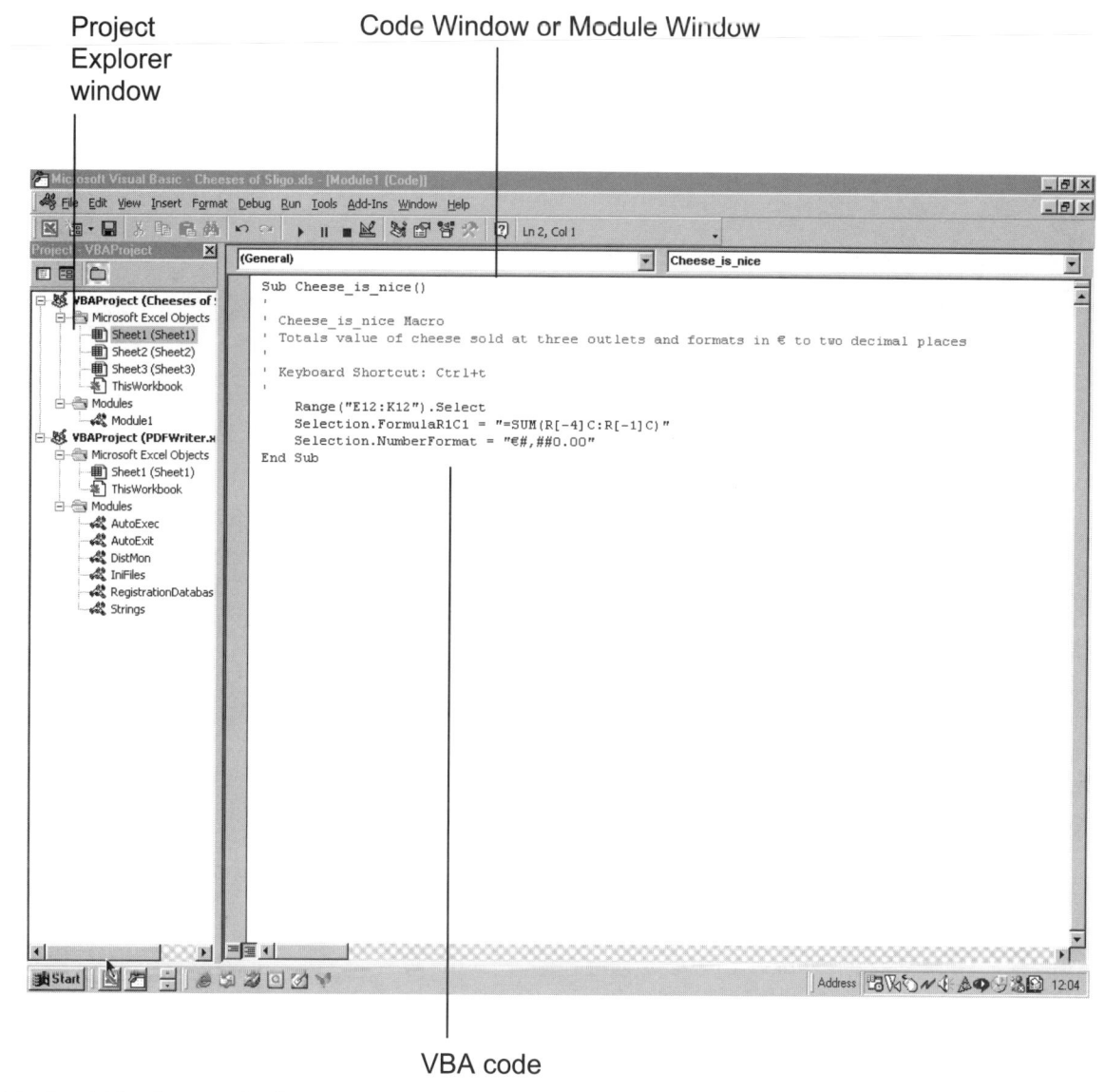

Project Explorer window

Code Window or Module Window

VBA code

**Project Explorer window**

This shows a tree diagram with all the workbooks that are open in Excel. It also shows the workbook, which you are currently using and hidden workbooks. (Use **Ctrl + R** to open).

**Code Window or Module Window**

This shows the VBA code.

# Chapter 5 – Special Tools

- In the code window, go to the line beginning… **Selection.NumberFormat** and place the cursor at last **0** before quotation marks. We are going to change the figures from two decimal places to zero decimal places.

- Delete **0**, **0** and **.** (Full stop)

- Select **Close and Return to Microsoft Excel**. (Or **Alt + Q**)

We will now run the macro again. First clear the range **E12:K12**.

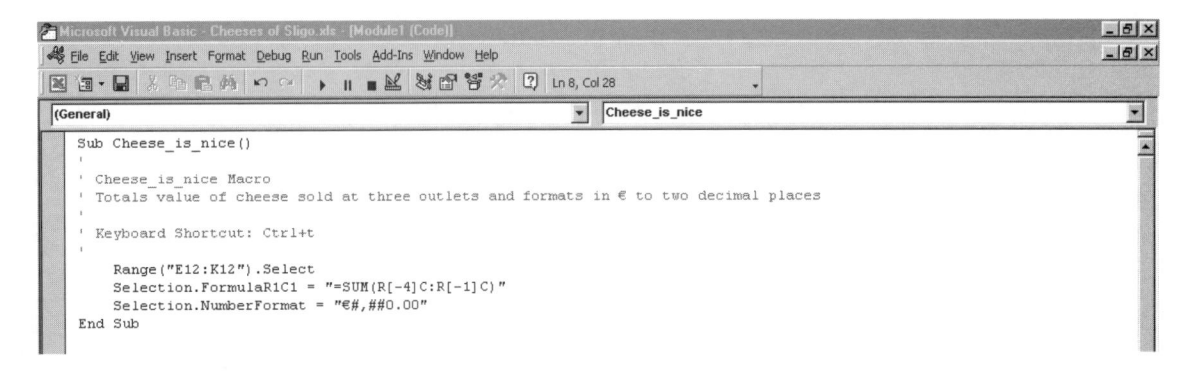

```
Sub Cheese_is_nice()
'
' Cheese_is_nice Macro
' Totals value of cheese sold at three outlets and formats in € to two decimal places
'
' Keyboard Shortcut: Ctrl+t
'
    Range("E12:K12").Select
    Selection.FormulaR1C1 = "=SUM(R[-4]C:R[-1]C)"
    Selection.NumberFormat = "€#,##0.00"
End Sub
```

- Choose **Tools**, **Macro**, **Macros** (or **Alt + F8**) and select the macro, **Cheese_is_nice**.

- Select **Run**.

**Cheeses of Sligo**

|   | Jan | Feb | Mar | Apr | May | Jun | Total |
|---|---|---|---|---|---|---|---|
| A | 1300 | 1100 | 1304 | 1709 | 1642 | 1530 | 8585 |
| B | 2987 | 4539 | 9870 | 8800 | 7324 | 6670 | 40190 |
| C | 4400 | 4650 | 3749 | 2980 | 8754 | 5423 | 29956 |
| Total | €8,687 | €10,289 | €14,923 | €13,489 | €17,720 | €13,623 | €78,731 |

When the macro runs, the figures are changed so that the sales figures are shown to zero decimal places.

- Save the file as **Cheeses of Sligo**.

## 1.12 Using the Button Editor

- Open the file **Cheeses of Sligo**.

We can use the **Button Editor** facility to edit a button or create our own button. The 42(6 X 7) buttons available give you an idea of what can be created in Button Editor.

- **Right click** on the button (Smiley) and choose **Customize** as the option.

- **Right click** on the button again and choose **Change Button Image**.

- Select the coffee mug (Fourth row, second button from left).

- Click on it.

  The coffee mug is now resident on toolbar.

- Right click coffee mug **button** and select **Edit Button Image**.

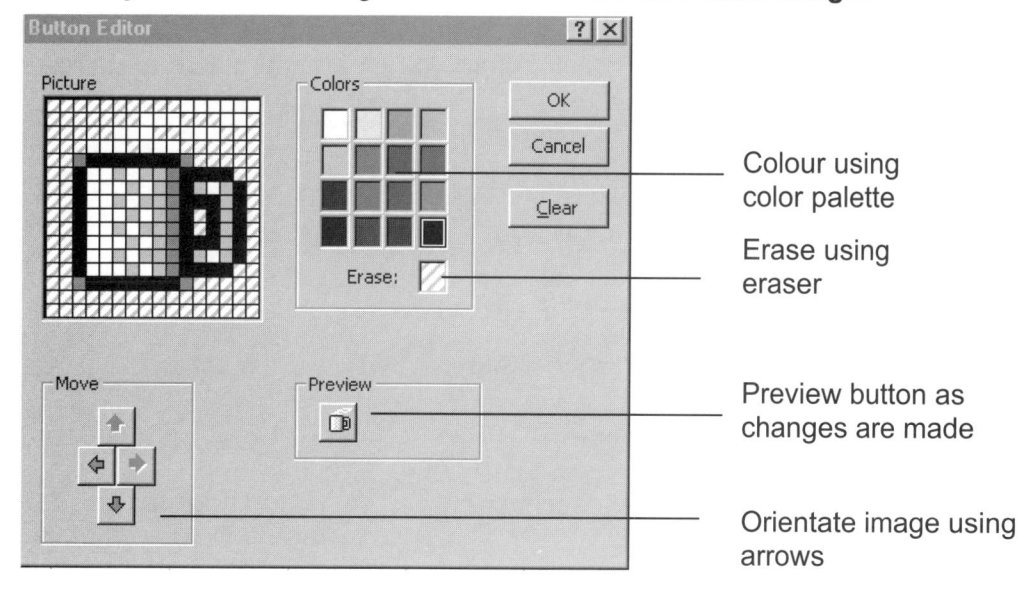

Colour using color palette

Erase using eraser

Preview button as changes are made

Orientate image using arrows

- Using the edit tools available, modify the button to your own taste.

- Add your initial to the mug.

- Click **OK**.

- Save file again as **Cheeses of Sligo**.

Note: You may design your own buttons in company colours or logo. We leave this to your own time and imagination.

## 1.13 Storing Macros

If a macro is stored in a Personal Macro Workbook, all workbooks have access. PERSONAL.XLS is stored in the startup folder. When Excel is started the folder opens making the macros available.

The practice exercises contained in this section relate solely to this manual and do not constitute, or imply, certification by the European Driving Licence Foundation in respect of any ECDL examinations. For details on sitting ECDL examinations in your country please contact the local ECDL/ICDL licensee or visit the European Computer Driving Licence Foundation Ltd web site at http://www.ecdl.com

## Exercise 1A

### Using Relative References

We are going to create a macro that will insert the name and address of the company Blackrock Electronics in the worksheet. The macro will use Relative References. This macro can be run from the active cell. It will produce the name and address of Blackrock Electronics in any cell and any workbook in which it is run. The address specifications are listed.

# Blackrock Electronics, (Arial, Bold, 18 pt, blue).
**3020 Main Street,** (Arial, Bold, 12 pt, blue).
**Blackrock** (Arial, Bold, 12 pt, blue).

A shortcut key **Ctrl + Shift + B** should activate the macro.
Macro name: **Address**

You should practice inserting the information before you create the macro to decide on the order of operations.

1. Open the file **Blackrock Electronics** and place cursor in cell **D2**.

2. Select **Tools, Macro, Record New Macro**.

3. In the **Name macro** box write **Address**.

4. In the Shortcut key box write **B** (**CTRL + Shift + B** will be shortcut).

5. Store Workbook in: **This Workbook**.

6. Insert brief description of macro: **Inserts company name and address**, click **OK**.

7. Click on **Relative Reference** button on the Stop Recording Toolbar.

8. Select cell **D2**. Write **Blackrock Electronics,** (Format Arial, Bold, 18 pt, blue), then press enter. You should now be in cell **D3**. Type first line of address, format and press enter. You should now be in cell **D4**. Enter last line of address, format and press enter.

9. Select **Stop Recording** button to end macro. (Or **Tools, Macro, Stop Recording**).

    To check macro, delete name and address, then run the macro.

    Select **Tools, Macro, Macros,** select **Address** and click **Run**. The macro will operate successfully.

    Also, Click on **any other cell** and run macro: **Address** from here.

10. Finally click on **Sheet2** and run the macro using the Shortcut key **Ctrl + Shift + B**

11. Save file as Blackrock Electronics 1A

The practice exercises contained in this section relate solely to this manual and do not constitute, or imply, certification by the European Driving Licence Foundation in respect of any ECDL examinations. For details on sitting ECDL examinations in your country please contact the local ECDL/ICDL licensee or visit the European Computer Driving Licence Foundation Ltd web site at http://www.ecdl.com

## Exercise 1B

In this exercise we are going to create a macro called **Page** which will insert the Header, Blackrock Electronics, change the top margin to 1.5, set page orientation to Landscape and will switch on gridlines for printing purposes.
You will then assign the macro to a keyboard button that you will locate on the formatting toolbar.

1    Open the file **Blackrock Electronics 1A**.

2    Select **Tools**, **Macro**, **Record New Macro**.

3    Insert the name **Page**, Ignore the Shortcut Key option as you can exercise this option later, **Store macro in This Workbook**, and write your own brief description of macro. Click **OK** to start the macro recording.

4    Select **File**, **Page Setup**. In **Page** tab click **Landscape** in **Page Orientation**; Choose **Margins** tab and set **Top Margin** to **3.0**; choose **Header/Footer** tab select **Custom Header** and type **Blackrock Electronics** in **Center Section**; and finally in **Sheet** tab, select **Print Gridlines**. Click **OK**.

5    Select **Stop Macro** button to stop macro (or **Tools**, **Macro**, **Stop Recording**).

6    Choose **File**, **Print Preview** to ensure macro works. Also select **Sheet2** and run macro from here. Check that it works.

Save the worksheet as **Blackrock Electronics 1B**.

The next step is to allocate the **Page** macro to a Toolbar Button. Select **Tools**, **Customize** and choose **Macros from Categories**. Drag the **Custom Button** to the Formatting toolbar and release the mouse button. Right click the new button and write in **Page** as the button name. The name must be the same as the macro. Select **Change Button Image** and select calculator on third row, second from the left. Select **Close** on the **Customize** option.

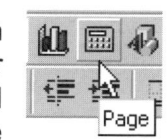

7    Save workbook again as **Blackrock Electronics 1B**.

The practice exercises contained in this section relate solely to this manual and do not constitute, or imply, certification by the European Driving Licence Foundation in respect of any ECDL examinations. For details on sitting ECDL examinations in your country please contact the local ECDL/ICDL licensee or visit the European Computer Driving Licence Foundation Ltd web site at http://www.ecdl.com

## Exercise 1C

**Using Absolute References**

The third macro will calculate the sales and bonuses for workers in Blackrock Electronics and format currency in Euro to zero decimal places.

First we will create the macro.

1   Open the file **Blackrock Electronics 1B**.

2   Select **Tools**, **Macro**, **Record New Macro**.

3   Insert the macro name **Bonus**, ignore Keyboard Shortcut, **Store macro in This workbook** and include a brief description of the macro. Click **OK**.

4   Select cell range **E9:F21** and select **Forma**t, **Cells**, **Number**, **Currency**, **Zero** decimal places, € symbol and click **OK**. In cell **E21** click **AutoSum** on the Standard toolbar and drag formula to cell **F21**. Press **Enter** so that totals for Sales and Bonuses are entered.

5   Stop macro recording.

   Check that macro is fully operational. Delete the totals and run macro **Bonus** again.

6   Save workbook as **Blackrock Electronics 1C**

   Now we will edit macro in **Visual Basic**.

The practice exercises contained in this section relate solely to this manual and do not constitute, or imply, certification by the European Driving Licence Foundation in respect of any ECDL examinations. For details on sitting ECDL examinations in your country please contact the local ECDL/ICDL licensee or visit the European Computer Driving Licence Foundation Ltd web site at http://www.ecdl.com

## Exercise 1D

**Editing a macro using Visual Basic**

Open the file **Blackrock Electronics 1C**.

1   Select **Tools**, **Macro**, **Macros**, ensure **Bonus** is highlighted and select **Edit**. Examine the macro code which appears in the window to the right of the **Visual Basic Editor**. Go to line beginning **Selection:NumberFormat=** and place the cursor between 0 and ". Type in the three characters:**.00 (Full Stop, zero, zero)** To save changes select **File**, **Close and Return to Microsoft Excel** (or use **Alt + Q**) to finish.

2   Run **Bonus** macro again and note that the figures are formatted to two decimal places.

Resave workbook as **Blackrock Electronics 1C**.

The file Blackrock Electronics 1C will now contain all three macros: Address, Page and Bonus.

3   Select **File**, Print **Preview**.

The diagram below shows how it will look.

Macro **Page** made changes to Page Setup – Top Margin, Header and Print Gridlines.

Macro **Address** produced formatted company address.

**Blackrock Electronics,**
3020 Main Street,
Blackrock.

| Name | Sales | Bonus |
|---|---|---|
| Archer | €14,027.00 | €1,052.03 |
| Boland | €17,800.00 | €1,335.00 |
| Devlin | €4,500.00 | €337.50 |
| Donnachie | €6,800.00 | €510.00 |
| Houricane | €22,300.00 | €1,672.50 |
| Kelly | €10,197.00 | €764.78 |
| Mannion | €8,703.00 | €652.73 |
| Molloy | €2,507.00 | €188.03 |
| O'Gorman | €25,619.00 | €1,921.43 |
| O'Hagan | €4,490.00 | €336.75 |
| Rooney | €7,863.00 | €589.73 |
| Smyth | €1,908.00 | €143.10 |
| **Total** | **€126,714.00** | **€9,503.55** |

Macro **Bonus** totals and formats Sales and Bonus columns.

> The macro **Address** uses **Relative References**.
> The macros **Bonus** and **Page** use **Absolute References**.

The practice exercises contained in this section relate solely to this manual and do not constitute, or imply, certification by the European Driving Licence Foundation in respect of any ECDL examinations. For details on sitting ECDL examinations in your country please contact the local ECDL/ICDL licensee or visit the European Computer Driving Licence Foundation Ltd web site at http://www.ecdl.com

## Exercise 1E

Open the file **Lamp Sales**.

*Lighting Up Ireland* has produced a limited range of lamps, which it has sold in Dublin, Barcelona and Milan. The company has projected sales for 2002 and now has the actual sales for that year. In this exercise we will create a macro that will consolidate the projected (project) figures and actual figures.

Information in Dublin, Milan and Barcelona sheets will be consolidated in Consolidation sheet

Select the consolidation tab to check that all data is cleared from this part of spreadsheet.
We are going to copy and paste data from each of the worksheets, **Dublin**, **Milan** and **Barcelona** into the consolidation.

1 Select the Consolidation tab.

| 2 | Select **Tools, Macro, Record New Macro**. Choose **Lamp Sales** as the Macro name and **Ctrl + w** as the keyboard Shortcut. Store Macro in:**This Workbook**. |
|---|---|
| 3 | Select **Dublin** tab and highlight range **B6:C19**. |
| 4 | Select **Edit**, **Copy** from the Standard toolbar. Click on Consolidation tab and select cell **B6**. |
| 5 | Choose **Edit**, **Paste** from the Standard toolbar. The contents are pasted into the worksheet. |
| 6 | Repeat the procedure with **Barcelona** and **Milan**. |

The consolidation should look like this.

|    | A | B | C | D | E | F | G |
|----|---|---|---|---|---|---|---|
| 1  | **Lighting Up Ireland** | | | | | | |
| 2  | | | | | | | |
| 3  | | Dublin | | Milan | | Barcelona | |
| 4  | | | | | | | |
| 5  | Month | Project | Actual | Project | Actual | Project | Actual |
| 6  | Jan | 500 | 630 | 550 | 435 | 560 | 880 |
| 7  | Feb | 480 | 875 | 330 | 525 | 480 | 555 |
| 8  | Mar | 700 | 850 | 600 | 620 | 600 | 630 |
| 9  | Apr | 730 | 720 | 780 | 710 | 730 | 730 |
| 10 | May | 700 | 860 | 500 | 745 | 810 | 945 |
| 11 | Jun | 600 | 550 | 550 | 660 | 630 | 740 |
| 12 | Jul | 830 | 750 | 570 | 860 | 820 | 740 |
| 13 | Aug | 800 | 810 | 845 | 810 | 790 | 920 |
| 14 | Sep | 890 | 990 | 725 | 650 | 770 | 660 |
| 15 | Oct | 600 | 500 | 550 | 670 | 440 | 800 |
| 16 | Nov | 720 | 430 | 540 | 390 | 500 | 420 |
| 17 | Dec | 900 | 880 | 950 | 890 | 450 | 980 |
| 18 | | | | | | | |
| 19 | **TOTAL** | 8450 | 8845 | 7490 | 7965 | 7580 | 9000 |

| 7 | Select **Stop Macro**. |
|---|---|

Let's imagine we have a new set of figures for 2003.
We will delete the figures for 2002 and then run the macro **Lamp_Sales**.

| 8 | Highlight the range **B6:G19**. Now select **Edit, Clear, Contents Del**. |
|---|---|

We will run the macro **Lamp_Sales**. Select **Tools, Macro, Macros** and highlight **Lamp_Sales**. Run the macro. The Projected and Actual figures for Dublin, Milan and Barcelona are consolidated.

You will recognise how useful this macro is. It can be used annually but you must remember to keep a backup copy of the annual figures.

| 9 | Save the file as **Lamp Sales Solution**. |
|---|---|

## Self Check Exercises

1. What is the correct sequence to create a macro?
   - ☐ Open a new workbook, plan macro, record macro, name macro and save macro.
   - ☐ Open new workbook, plan macro, name macro, record macro and save macro.
   - ☐ In existing workbook, name macro, plan macro, record macro and save macro.

2. Where would you save a macro if you wanted it to be available to other workbooks?
   - ☐ This Workbook
   - ☐ Personal Macro Workbook
   - ☐ New Workbook
   - ☐ All of above

3. In the Stop Recording toolbar below, is the macro using absolute or relative references?

   - ☐ Absolute References
   - ☐ Relative References

4. Which of the following programs would you use to edit a macro?
   - ☐ Microsoft Script Editor
   - ☐ Wordpad
   - ☐ Visual Basic Editor
   - ☐ Word

5. Which of the following are suitable as keyboard shortcuts for macros?
   - ☐ Ctrl + X
   - ☐ Ctrl + Z
   - ☐ Ctrl + P
   - ☐ Ctrl + V

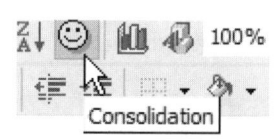

6. A macro *Consolidation* has been allocated to a toolbar button. The advantage in this is that it reduces the number of steps taken to implement the macro?
   - ☐ True
   - ☐ False

7. Which of the following macro names would return the message below?

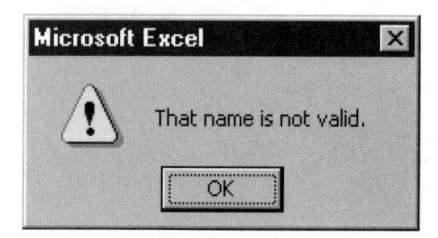

   - ☐ Consol_2004.
   - ☐ InsertLogo.
   - ☐ 2004_Consol.
   - ☐ Chart 2003

8. A macro is stored in a VBA sheet called a
   - ☐ Module
   - ☐ Report
   - ☐ Form
   - ☐ List

The practice exercises contained in this section relate solely to this manual and do not constitute, or imply, certification by the European Driving Licence Foundation in respect of any ECDL examinations. For details on sitting ECDL examinations in your country please contact the local ECDL/ICDL licensee or visit the European Computer Driving Licence Foundation Ltd web site at http://www.ecdl.com

## Practical Exercises

Complete the following exercises as a review of what you have covered in Chapter 5. If you need any help refer back to the relevant section in this chapter.

### Exercise 1

Open the file **Lamp Sales Solution**.

In this exercise we will design a macro that will consolidate the data from the **Dublin**, **Milan** and **Barcelona** worksheets to the range **H6:I19**.

1. Click on cell **H6**. Choose **Tools**, **Macro** followed by **Record New Macro**. When the **Record Macro** dialog box opens choose the following.
   In **Macro name** box insert **Total**.
   Store macro in: **This Workbook**. Ignore **Shortcut key**.
   Click **OK**.

2. Insert the following formula in cell **H6**.

   **= B6 + D6 +F6**

   Click the on Enter button ✓ on the formula bar. Now copy the formula in cell **H6** through the range **H7:H17**.

3. Click on cell **I6** and insert the following formula.

   **= C6 + E6 + G6**

   Click the Enter button ✓ on formula bar. Copy the formula in cell **H6** through the range **I7:I17**.

4. Select cell **H19**. Using **AutoSum**, add the range **H6:H17**. Click Enter. Copy the formula in cell **H19** to **I19**. Select **Stop Recording** on the Stop Recording Toolbar.

5. Resave the file **Lamp Sales Solution**.

## Exercise 2

Is the file **Lamp Sales** open? If not open it now.

In this next exercise we will design a macro that will create a chart of **Projected** and **Actual** sales for Dublin only.

1. Choose **Tools**, **Macro** followed by **Record New Macro**. When the **Record Macro** dialog box opens choose the following.
   In **Macro name** box insert **Chart**.
   Store macro in: **This Workbook**. Ignore **Shortcut key**.
   Click **OK**.

2. Highlight the range **A5:C19**. Click on Chart Wizard button . *Chart Wizard – Step 1 of 4* dialog box opens. **Choose Chart** type **Column** (Default Option).
   Select **Next**. *Chart Wizard – Step 2 of 4 – Chart Source Data* dialog box opens.
   Select **Next**. *Chart Wizard – Step 3 of 4 – Chart Options* dialog box opens.

   Make the following entries:

   Chart title: **Lamp Sales Dublin**
   Category (X) axis: **Month**
   Value (Y) Axis: **Lamp Sales P/A**

   Select **Next**. Chart Wizard –Step 4 of 4 –Chart Location dialog box opens.
   Choose As object in: **Consolidation**. Now click on **Finish** button.

3. Click on **Stop Recording** button on the Stop Recording toolbar.

4. Resave the file as **Lamp Sales.**

## Exercise 3

In this exercise you are to create a simple macro that will return the current date and time in a spreadsheet cell. Running this macro will automatically produce the current date and time.

Open the file **Lighting Up Ireland**.

1. Select cell **A6**. Choose **Tools**, **Macro** followed by **Record New Macro**. When the **Record Macro** dialog box opens choose the following.
   In **Macro name** box insert **Now**.
   Store macro in: **This Workbook**. Ignore **Shortcut key**.
   Click **OK**. The macro starts recording.

2. In cell **A6** insert the following formula:

   **=Now()**

3. Select the **Stop Recording** button on the Stop Recording toolbar.

   If you wish you can attach the macro to any button of your choice but ⌛ may be appropriate.

|    | A | B | C | D | E | F |
|----|---|---|---|---|---|---|
| 1  |   |   |   |   |   |   |
| 2  |   |   | Lighting Up Ireland | | | |
| 3  |   |   |   |   |   |   |
| 4  |   |   | Table of Variable Data | | | |
| 5  |   |   |   |   |   |   |
| 6  | 21/07/02 23:50 | | QTR1 | QTR2 | QTR3 | QTR4 |
| 7  |   |   |   |   |   |   |
| 8  | SALES |   |   |   |   |   |
| 9  |   |   |   |   |   |   |
| 10 | Garden Spot Lights | | £75,000 | £78,000 | £82,500 | £93,200 |
| 11 | Garden Spot Lights Inc/Dec % | | | | | |
| 12 | Outdoor Chinese Lanterns | | £65,000 | £59,800 | £79,300 | £84,500 |
| 13 | Outdoor Chinese Lanterns Inc/Dec % | | | -8.00% | 22.00% | 30.00% |
| 14 | Pagoda Garden Lights | | £32,000 | £29,120 | £31,158 | £40,506 |
| 15 | Pagoda Garden Lights Inc/Dec | | | -9.00% | 7.00% | 30.00% |

4. Finally save the file with/without macro but remove the attachment to button.

# Solutions

## Self Check Exercises

Solutions – Self Check Exercises

## Chapter 1 Self Check Exercises - Solutions

1  If you wanted to calculate the monthly repayments on a mortgage, given a range of rates and varying time periods, -you would use a two-input data table. - True or False?

- ☑ True
- ☐ False

2  What is the correct procedure for naming a range in a worksheet?

- ☑ Choose Insert, Name, Define - and then type name in Define Name dialog box.
- ☐ Choose Insert, Create, Define – and then type name in Define Name dialog box.
- ☐ Choose Format, Insert, Define – and then type name in Define Name dialog box.

3  How do you freeze row and column titles?

- ☐ Select Window and choose Split.
- ☑ Select Window and choose Freeze Panes.
- ☐ Select Window followed by Arrange, and choose Tiled from the available options.

4  When a text file is being imported into Excel, delimiters are used in the procedure. Which of the following are delimiters?

- ☑ Tab, Comma
- ☑ Space, semicolon
- ☐ Windows (ANSI), Fixed width

5  There are 17 possible options when you apply automatic formatting to a cell range. - True or False?

- ☑ True
- ☐ False

6  How will the following custom number format return the value 25000?

Code:  #,###

- ☐ 25000
- ☑ 25,000
- ☐ 2.5,000
- ☐ 2.500

7  In the following formula, what function name does 1 refer to?

=SUBTOTAL(1, B10:B24)

- ☑ AVERAGE
- ☐ COUNTA
- ☐ SUM

8  What cell names would return the message above?

- ☐ Profit.QTR1
- ☐ Profit_QTR1
- ☑ Profit-QTR1
- ☑ D24

## Chapter 2 Self Check Exercises – Solutions

1. Using the Top 10 AutoFilter permits you to filter only the Top 10 Items or Percent in a list.
   - ☐ True
   - ☑ False

2. What is the correct procedure for displaying the AutoFilter menu?
   - ☐ Choose Data, followed by Sort and then select AutoFilter.
   - ☐ Choose AutoFilter icon on the Standard toolbar.
   - ☑ Choose Data, followed by Filter and then select AutoFilter.

3. How do you 'explode' all the segments in a pie chart?
   - ☑ Click on pie chart to select it, click on a segment, choose a handle and drag outwards.
   - ☐ Click on pie chart to select it, double click on segment, select a handle and drag outwards.
   - ☐ Double click on pie chart to select it, choose a handle and drag outwards.

4. To save a workbook as a template you must choose File followed by Save As, type in a name for the template, click the Save as type drop-down arrow and choose Template?
   - ☑ True
   - ☐ False

5. Templates cannot contain formulas - True or False?
   - ☐ True
   - ☑ False

6. Ready-made templates are available from which tabs in the New dialog box?
   - ☑ Spreadsheet Solutions
   - ☐ Business Planner Templates
   - ☑ General
   - ☐ All of the above

7. To consolidate data in adjacent worksheets you could use a:
   - ☐ 2D sum function
   - ☑ 3D sum function
   - ☐ 4D sum function

8. By examining the box above what procedure is being carried out?
   - ☐ A multiple criteria query
   - ☑ A custom sort
   - ☐ A single criteria query
   - ☐ An advanced filter

## Chapter 3 Self Check Exercises – Solutions

1. CONCATENATE is a Logical Function?
   - ☑ True
   - ☐ False

2. Which of the following functions calculates the payments for a loan?
   - ☐ NPV
   - ☑ PMT
   - ☐ HLOOKUP
   - ☐ DCOUNT

3. =IF(A3>100,"Bonus", "No Bonus") is an example of a?
   - ☐ Statistical Function.
   - ☐ Round Function.
   - ☑ Logical Function.
   - ☐ Database Function.

4. What is the correct syntax for calculating the payment on a loan, based on constant payments and constant internal rate?
   - ☑ PMT(rate,nper,pv,fv,type)
   - ☐ FV(rate,nper,pmt,pv,type)
   - ☐ PV(rate,nper,pmt,fv,type)
   - ☐ NPV(value1,value2,…)

5. =ROUND(58.3898,2) will return 58.38 as the result.
   - ☐ True
   - ☑ False

6. What function will return the following, assuming this is the date and time in question. **11/04/2003 14:32**
   - ☐ =DATE()
   - ☐ =TIME()
   - ☐ =DAY()
   - ☑ =NOW()

7. What function searches for a value in the leftmost column of a table and returns a value from a column you specify?
   - ☐ HLOOKUP
   - ☐ DCOUNT
   - ☑ VLOOKUP

8. What function is being used below?
   **Answer: DSUM function**

## Chapter 4 Self Check Exercises – Solutions

1. What is the correct sequence to display all formulas in a worksheet?
   - ☐ Choose Options from the Tools menu, then select tab View, and ensure Formulas is not selected.
   - ☐ Choose Options from the Tools menu, then select tab View and click on None.
   - ☑ Choose Options from the Tools menu, then select tab View and click on Formulas.

2. What is the most probable cause of this error message?

   #DIV/0
   - ☐ The required value is not available to the formula.
   - ☑ The formula is attempting to divide by 0 (or Empty cell).
   - ☐ An undefined name has been used in the formula.
   - ☐ Column is not wide enough to display the numeric content.

3. The toolbar shown above is the:
   - ☑ PivotTable toolbar
   - ☐ Reviewing toolbar

4. Which of the following statements are true?
   - ☑ Formula tracer arrows are solid blue
   - ☑ Error tracer arrows are solid red
   - ☑ A dashed black arrow linked to a worksheet icon is an external tracer arrow

5. What is the keyboard shortcut to **Go To** a particular cell?
   - ☐ Ctrl + T
   - ☐ Alt + G
   - ☑ Ctrl + G
   - ☐ Alt + T

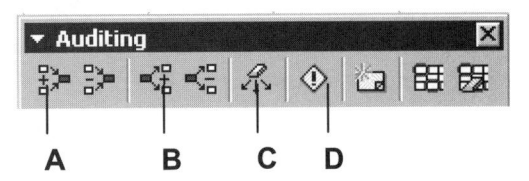

6. Identify buttons A, B, C and D on the Auditing toolbar above?

   Trace Error ( D )

   Trace Dependents ( B )

   Trace Precedents ( A )

   Remove All Arrows ( C )

7. What is the name of this button?
   - ☐ Field Settings
   - ☑ Refresh Data
   - ☐ Format Report
   - ☐ Show Detail

8. In which of the following would you utilise **Changing cells**?
   - ☐ PivotTable and PivotChart Report.
   - ☑ Scenario Manager
   - ☐ Editing Cell Comments
   - ☐ Cell Auditing

## Chapter 5 Self Check Exercises – Solutions

1. What is the correct sequence to create a macro?
   - ☑ Open a new workbook, plan macro, record macro, name macro and save macro.
   - ☐ Open new workbook, plan macro, name macro, record macro and save macro.
   - ☐ In existing workbook, name macro, plan macro, record macro and save macro.

2. Where would you save a macro if you wanted it to be available to other workbooks?
   - ☐ This Workbook
   - ☑ Personal Macro Workbook
   - ☐ New Workbook
   - ☐ All of above

3. In the Stop Recording toolbar below, is the macro using absolute or relative references? 
   - ☐ Absolute References
   - ☑ Relative References

4. Which of the following programs would you use to edit a macro?
   - ☐ Microsoft Script Editor
   - ☐ Wordpad
   - ☑ Visual Basic Editor
   - ☐ Word

5. Which of the following are suitable as keyboard shortcuts for macros?
   - ☐ Ctrl + X
   - ☑ Ctrl + Z
   - ☐ Ctrl + P
   - ☐ Ctrl + V

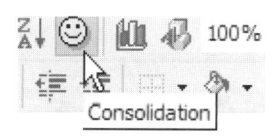

6. A macro *Consolidation* has been allocated to a toolbar button. The advantage in this is that it reduces the number of steps taken to implement the macro?
   - ☑ True
   - ☐ False

7. Which of the following macro names would return the message below? 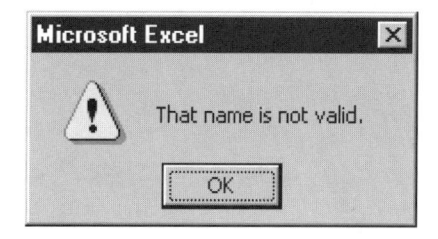
   - ☐ Consol_2004.
   - ☐ InsertLogo.
   - ☑ 2004_Consol.
   - ☑ Chart 2003

8. A macro is stored in a VBA sheet called a
   - ☑ Module
   - ☐ Report
   - ☐ Form
   - ☐ List

# Index

# Index

3D Sum Function

In *Data Handling*: consolidating data in adjacent worksheets using a 3D sum function, 92–93

Advanced Filter

In *Data Handling*: description, 72; using Advanced Filter Options, 81–82

Analysis

In *Analysis*: auditing, 214–233; cell comments, 229–233; pivot tables, 192–203; scenarios, 204–212

AND

In *Functions*: description and syntax, 178

Auditing

In *Analysis*: Auditing Toolbar, 214–215; cell auditing description, 214; displaying all formulas in a worksheet, 226–228; list of spreadsheet errors, 223; printing formulas in a worksheet, 228; tracing and resolving spreadsheet errors, 223–224; tracing cells with external references, 222; tracing dependent cells in a worksheet, 218; tracing precedent cells in a worksheet, 216–217; using the Go To Special dialog box, 220

AutoFilter

In *Data Handling:* activating, 72–73; creating a multiple criteria query, 76; creating a multiple criteria query using the And / Or Filters, 78–79; creating a multiple criteria query with a custom filter, 77–78; custom AutoFilter Operators, 78; description 72; using AutoFilter to find records using a single criteria query, 74; using the Top 10 AutoFilter, 80

Cell Comments

In *Analysis*: adding a cell comment, 229; deleting a comment, 232; editing worksheet comments, 232; formatting a comment, 231; formatting a comment, 231; using the Reviewing Toolbar, 233; viewing cell comments, 230

Cells

In *Editing*: cell comments, 229–233; cell reference, 4; contiguous cells, 4; deleting named cells and ranges, 9; description, 4; guidelines for naming cells and ranges, 4–5; naming cells and ranges, 5–6; non-contiguous cells, 4; tracing dependent cells in a worksheet, 218

Charts

In *Data Handling:* adding a data series to a chart, 110–111; changing the angle of a pie chart slice, 98–99; deleting a data series in a chart, 109–110; 'exploding' segments in a pie chart, 107; formatting chart axes, numbers and text, 100–102; inserting a background image in a 2D chart, 116–119; linking data / chart between spreadsheets, 87–88; linking data / chart between worksheets, 84–86; linking data / chart into a word processing document, 89–90; linking data / chart within a worksheet, 83–84; modifying a chart type for a defined data series, 111–113; re-positioning title, legend or data labels in a chart, 103–106; widening the gap between columns / bars in a 2D chart, 114–115

Columns

In *Editing*: freezing column titles, 31–32; freezing row and column titles together, 33–34; unfreezing column titles, 32; unfreezing row and column titles, 34

CONCATENATE

In *Functions*: description and syntax, 154–155

Consolidating

In *Data Handling:* consolidating data in adjacent worksheets using a 3D sum function, 92–93

COUNT

In *Functions:* description and syntax, 145

COUNTA

In *Functions:* description and syntax, 146

COUNTIF

In *Functions:* description and syntax, 146

Data

In *Editing*: applying automatic formatting to a cell range, 12–13; creating custom number formats, 15–16; importing text files, 25–30; naming cell ranges in a worksheet, 4–10; using conditional formatting options, 18–20; Paste Special options, 22–23

In *Data Handling:* charts and graphs, 98–119; consolidating, 92–93; linking, 83–93; querying / filtering, 72–82; sorting, 66–71; templates, 94–97

Data Tables

In *Editing*: creating a one-input data table, 46–48; creating a two-input data table, 49-50

Database Functions

In *Functions:* DCOUNT, 184; DMAX, 184; DMIN, 183; DSUM, 182–183

DATE

In *Functions:* description and syntax, 131

# Index

Date and Time Functions

In *Functions:* DATE, 131; DAY, 138; MONTH, 138; NOW, 136; TIME, 134; TODAY, 137; WEEKDAY, 138; Windows 1900 date system and Mac OS 1904 date system, 133; YEAR, 138

DAY

In *Functions:* description and syntax, 138

DCOUNT

In *Functions:* description and syntax, 184

Dependents

In *Analysis*: description, 214; tracing dependent cells in a worksheet, 218

Display

In *Editing*: freezing row and / or column titles, 31–34; hiding / unhiding rows or columns, 36–38; hiding / unhiding worksheets, 39; using one-input or two-input data tables, 46–50; using sub-totalling features, 41–44

DMAX

In *Functions:* description and syntax, 184

DMIN

In *Functions:* description and syntax, 183

Document

In *Data Handling:* embedding a chart into a word processing document, 90; linking data / chart into a word processing document, 89–90

DSUM

In *Functions:* description and syntax, 182–183

Editing

In *Editing*: data, 4–30; display, 31–50; protection, 51–54; security 56–59

Embedding

In *Data Handling:* description, 83; embedding a chart into a word processing document, 90

Filtering

In *Data Handling:* activating AutoFilter, 72–73; Advanced Filter, 72; AutoFilter description, 72; creating a multiple criteria query, 76; creating a multiple criteria query using the And / Or Filters, 78–79; creating a multiple criteria query with a custom filter, 77–78; using Advanced Filter Options, 81–82; using AutoFilter to find records using a single criteria query, 74; using the Top 10 AutoFilter, 80

In *Analysis*: filtering pivot table data 197

Financial Functions

In *Functions:* FV, 156–157; NPV, 158–160; PMT, 162–163; PV, 164–166; RATE, 167–168

Formatting

In *Editing*: conditional formatting, 18–20

In *Analysis*: formatting a comment, 231

Formula Palette

In *Functions:* entering a function using the formula palette, 128–129

Freezing

In *Editing*: freezing column titles, 31–32; freezing row and column titles together, 33–34; freezing row titles, 32–33; unfreezing column titles, 32; unfreezing row and column titles, 34; unfreezing row titles, 33

Functions

In *Functions:* arguments description, 126–127; database functions, 182–184; date and time functions, 131–138; description and structure, 126; entering a function by typing and clicking, 129–130; entering a function using the formula palette, 128–129; financial functions, 156–168; logical functions, 174–179; look up and reference functions, 169–173; mathematical functions, 140–144; statistical functions, 145–149; text functions, 150–155; using nested functions, 186

FV

In *Functions:* description and syntax, 156–157

Go To Special

In *Analysis*: using the Go To Special dialog box, 220

Hiding

In *Editing*: hiding a worksheet, 39; hiding columns, 37; hiding rows, 36; hiding rows and columns manually, 38; unhiding a worksheet, 39; unhiding columns, 37; unhiding rows, 36

HLOOKUP

In *Functions:* description and syntax 173

IF

In *Functions:* description and syntax, 174–175; using nested functions, 186

ISERROR

In *Functions:* description and syntax, 179

Labels

In *Editing*: accept labels in formulas, 7

# Index

Linking

In *Data Handling:* description, 83; linking data / chart between spreadsheets, 87–88; linking data / chart between worksheets, 84–86; linking data / chart into a word processing document, 89–90; linking data / chart within a worksheet, 83–84

Lists

In *Data Handling:* limits on list sizes, 66

Logical Functions

In *Functions:* AND, 178; IF, 174–175; ISERROR, 179; OR, 178

Look Up and Reference Functions

In *Functions:* HLOOKUP, 173; VLOOKUP, 169–172

LOWER

In *Functions:* description and syntax, 151–152

Macro Recorder

In *Special Tools:* description, 234–244

Macros

In *Special Tools:* absolute references 244; assigning a macro to a toolbar button 250–252; assigning a shortcut key to a macro 246–248; deleting a macro 249; description 243; editing a macro 253–254; error messages 249; local macros and global macros 243; Macro Recorder 243–244; naming a macro 245; planning a macro 244–245; recording a simple macro 245–246; relative references 244; running a named macro 248; running a named macro using keyboard shortcut 249; storing macros 255; using the Button Editor 255; Visual Basic for Applications 244

Mathematical Functions

In *Functions:* combining the ROUND function with another function or formula, 144; ROUND, 142–144; SUMIF, 140–141

MAX

In *Functions:* description and syntax, 148–149

MEDIAN

In *Functions:* description and syntax, 148–149

MIN

In *Functions:* description and syntax, 148–149

MODE

In *Functions:* description and syntax, 148–149

MONTH

In *Functions:* description and syntax, 138

NOW

In *Functions:* description and syntax, 136

NPV

In *Functions:* description and syntax, 158–160

Number Formats

In *Editing*: creating custom number formats, 15–16; examining the main code sections, 15–16

OR

In *Functions:* description and syntax, 178

Pivot Tables

In *Analysis*: changing the layout of a pivot table, 198; creating a pivot table using defined field names, 193–195; description, 192;

filtering pivot table data, 197; grouping or displaying data in a pivot table by a defined criterion, 202–203; modifying the data source and refreshing the pivot table, 199–200; PivotTable Options, 200; PivotTable Toolbar, 199; PivotTable and PivotChart Wizard, 193–195; selecting fields for rows and columns, 196; selecting pivot table data, 196

PMT

In *Editing*: explanation of PMT function, 48

In *Functions:* description and syntax, 162–163

Precedents

In *Analysis*: description, 214; tracing precedents cells in a worksheet, 216–217

PROPER

In *Functions:* description and syntax, 150

Protecting

In *Editing*: protecting a worksheet, 51–52; protecting designated cells in a worksheet with a password, 53; protecting formula in a cell, 54; unprotecting a worksheet, 52; unprotecting cells, 54

PV

In *Functions:* description and syntax, 164–166

Querying

See Filtering

Ranges

In *Editing*: applying automatic formatting to a cell range, 12; deleting named cells and ranges, 9; guidelines for naming cells, 4–5;

naming a number of ranges simultaneously, 10; naming cells, 5–6; using named ranges in calculations, 8

RANK

In *Functions:* description and syntax, 148–149

RATE

In *Functions:* description and syntax, 167–168

Reviewing Toolbar

In *Analysis*: using the Reviewing Toolbar, 233

ROUND

In *Functions:* combining the ROUND function with another function or formula, 144; description and syntax, 142–144

Rows

In *Editing*: freezing row and column titles together, 33–34; freezing row titles, 32–33; unfreezing row and column titles, 34; unfreezing row titles, 33

Scenarios

In *Analysis*: created named scenarios / versions from defined cell ranges, 204–210; creating a scenario summary report, 211–212; description, 204; Scenario Manager, 205–210

Security

In *Editing*: removing password protection from a worksheet, 58–59; setting a password to open a workbook, 56–57; setting a workbook as recommended read-only, 56; using a password to protect a workbook, 58

Shortcut Keys

In *Special Tools:* assigning a shortcut key to a macro, 246–248; running a named macro using keyboard shortcut, 249

Sorting

In *Data Handling:* creating an original custom sort, 71; performing custom sorts, 69–71; sorting data by a single column, 66–67; sorting data by multiple columns, 67

Spreadsheet

In *Editing*: hiding / unhiding worksheets, 39

In *Data Handling:* linking data / chart between spreadsheets, 87–88

In *Analysis*: list of spreadsheet errors, 223; tracing and resolving spreadsheet errors, 223–224

Statistical Functions

In *Functions:* AVERAGE, 148–149; COUNT, 145, 148–149; COUNTA, 146; COUNTIF, 146; MAX, 148–149; MEDIAN, 148–149; MIN, 148–149; MODE, 148–149; RANK, 148–149; STDEV, 148–149; SUM, 148–149

STDEV

In *Functions:* description and syntax, 148–149

Subtotal

In *Editing*: charting Subtotal, 44; creating Subtotals in a list, 41–42; removing Subtotals, 44; using options in Subtotal, 43;

SUM

In *Functions:* description and syntax, 148–149

SUMIF

In *Functions:* description and syntax, 140–141

Templates

In *Data Handling:* description, 94; editing a template, 96; saving a template, 97; using a template, 94–95

Text Files

In *Editing*: importing a text file and delimiting by space, comma or tab, 25; importing fixed width text files, 28–30; importing using delimiters, 25–27

Text Functions

In *Functions:* CONCATENATE, 154–155; LOWER, 151–152; PROPER, 150; UPPER, 151

Text Import Wizard

In *Editing*: importing fixed width text files, 28–30; importing text files, 25–30; skipping a column, 27

TIME

In *Functions:* description and syntax, 134

TODAY

In *Functions:* description and syntax, 137

Toolbar Buttons

In *Special Tools:* assigning a macro to a toolbar button, 250–252

UPPER

In *Functions:* description and syntax, 151

Versions

See Scenarios

Visual Basic for Applications

In *Special Tools:* writing macros, 244

VLOOKUP

In *Functions:* description and syntax, 169–172

WEEKDAY

In *Functions:* description and syntax, 138

What-If Analysis

In *Editing*: data tables, 46-50

In Functions: PMT, 163

In *Analysis*: scenarios, 204–212

Workbook

In *Editing*: setting a password to open a workbook, 56–57; setting a workbook as recommended read-only, 56; using a password to protect a workbook, 58

Worksheet

In *Editing*: hiding and unhiding a worksheet, 39; protecting a worksheet, 51–52; protecting designated cells in a worksheet with a password, 53; removing password protection from a worksheet, 58–59; unprotecting a worksheet, 52

In *Data Handling:* linking data / chart between worksheets, 84–86; linking data / chart within a worksheet, 83–84

In *Analysis*: displaying all formulas in a worksheet, 226–228; editing worksheet comments, 232; printing formulas in a worksheet, 228; tracing cells with external references, 222; tracing dependent cells in a worksheet, 218; tracing precedents cells in a worksheet, 216–217

YEAR

In *Functions:* description and syntax, 138